Dear Sunn

MW01612846

THE HUMAN DHARMA

THE RIGHT HUMAN WAY OF LIVING THAT HELPS ONE LIVE A GOOD LIFE AND ENRICH THE WHOLE

BY SUSHMA PURI

(Born Sushma Tiwari)

First Edition, March 2014
Printed in the United States of America

Lots of love

Sushma Bua

4/25/2014

Website: www.thehumandharma.org and www.thehumandharma.com (coming up)

The Human Dharma
Copyright © 2012 by Sushma Puri
US Library of Congress
All rights reserved. This book or any part of it may not be reproduced, photocopied or transmitted in any form whatsoever or by any means whatsoever without permission in writing from the author.
For permission to make any copy or photocopy, please email at sushmapurihd13@yahoo.com

ISBN10: 1494277875
ISBN13: 9781494277871

Disclaimer

The tips and Exercises contained in this book "The Human Dharma" are derivations from factual analysis, and are mere recommendations. It is up to the Reader/Practitioner to test and adopt only those tips and Exercises which best suit her/him. The author or the Seller or the Publisher does not assume any responsibility or liability whatsoever for the use/practice of any or all tips and Exercises contained in this book.

—from the author and the Seller of The Human Dharma

PREFACE

I searched the Truth. I found the Truth. Now I want to share it with you all.

I was not able to live. I searched the Right Way of Living. I found the Right Way of Living. Now I want to share it with you all.

The Human Dharma is the product of my own search for Truth and the Right Way of Living.

The Human Dharma is the Human Way of Living, the Right Way of Living, and the Way of Living that helps a human live a good life herself and enrich her Whole.

Sushma Puri
November 15, 2013
California, USA

CONTENTS

PART TWO

THE WAY OF LIVING

CHAPTER 1

INTRODUCTION

Dharma is a Sanskrit word. Its English equivalent word is *religion*. A Religion is a Philosophy of life and a Way of living based on certain Truth(s). A religion answers deep queries of human life, helps a human live a good life herself and enrich her world too. There arose many religions in the history of humanity, like Hinduism, Buddhism, Christianity, Islam, and so on. Each of these has its own central Truth(s), and a derivative philosophy of life and a way of living.

The Human Dharma is a Religion too. It is a particular Philosophy of life and a Way of Living based on certain Truth(s).

The term *Dharma* is derived from the root *dhra*, which means "to wear" or "to adopt." Sages of ancient India used the term *Dharma* to denote an individual's Right and dutiful conduct, which if adopted or practiced by an individual helped her live a good life herself and enrich her world too.

The Human Dharma is my own creation. The term *Human Dharma* means "A Code of Conduct to be adopted by a Human" or "how a human ought to live—a Human's Right Way of living."

There is a Right way to do everything. There is the Right way to stand, the Right way to sit, the Right way to talk, and so on. In fact, you name any task, and it has the Right way of being done—"the" because there is only one Right Way. "The Right way is that way of doing a task that ensures an efficient and fruitful completion of the task. It nourishes the Task and the Doer." (My definition of the Right way.) For example, if you stand the Right way— erect and straight with both knees joined together, with a little space in between your both feet— this keeps your body's inner organs in place, makes your blood flow to all parts of your body, helps you breathe well, and makes you feel alert and healthy. This is a very small example. But the Principle of Right Way can be applied to any task and judged.

When applied to living, *"The Right Way of Living is that way of living that ensures an efficient and fruitful completion of the task of living and nourishes the Liver and the Life itself."*

Every task has its own Right way of being done. In order to derive the Right way of doing a task, you have to study and analyze the entire nature of that task, its purpose, its effects, and so on. In other words, you derive the Right way of doing a task from the task itself. Since the Human Dharma is a human's Right Way of Living, I have derived the Human Dharma from a thorough analysis and definition of a human's being—make, human life, and certain core issues of a human's life—like death, soul, God, and Truth. All of these issues are interrelated too, where one issue leads to the other.

In Part One of this book, titled "Philosophy" (Fact Analysis, Definition, and Derivative Right Way of Living) I have analyzed "What is a human?"; "What is human life?"; "Death"; "Soul"; "God"; and "Truth." As I analyzed each issue, there emerged certain key characteristics or truths about that issue. It was on the basis of those truths that I defined each issue (a separate list of the definitions of these issues is given at the end of this book too), and then derived the Right Way of Living that issue, which means how to look at that issue, and how to incorporate it in our daily lives.

So far these derivatives were scattered— derivative Right Way of Living from each issue.

The Human Dharma is a product of my own deep search for Truth. Amid all the fragility and grossness of life around me, I could sense that there was some Truth(s) which was deep hidden, beautiful, and eternal. And, amid all the confusion and miseries in the blind race of life, I could sense there was a Right Way of Living since there was a Right way to do everything. As described in my chapter on "Truth," I searched. I searched out, and I searched inside me—my Self. The study of sciences gave me certain truths about a human and human life. And, after years of intense Self-search and meditation, one day during my deep meditative moments I heard an inner voice that said, "It is from <u>Me</u> that All emerges, and it is into <u>Me</u> that All comes back." This was such an inner voice coming from my own Self. At that very moment, I had found my Self— my "Ahm"— my "I"— my own origin point, and the Origin Point of All. Now I knew where to start from and where to come back to.

It was after this personal experience, that there emerged "Om"—the Prime Truth, and the Central Truth of The Human Dharma. Om somehow beautifully encompassed all derivatives into it, and came up as one compact Truth containing the gist of all. *Om* is a Sanskrit word made of two letters *Ahm* and *U*. *Ahm* means "I" and *U* means "other than I"— the world outside me. Om has three Sub-truths: First, "Om is The Whole," Second, "Om is The Prime Energy Channel within which the Whole moves," And Third, "Om is The Prime Principle of Living." Each of these is a truth by itself, and is related to each other truth too. Each of these truths has its own derivative Right Way of Living.

Also in my analysis of "What is a Human?" and "What is Human Life?" there emerged Five eternal Human, life-long Values. As long as there is a human on this Earth, these Values will prevail. These are: "Family," "Education," "Work," "Marriage," and "Child." In tracing the history of humanity from the beginning till the present, these Values emerged as five major building blocks of human civilization. And, in tracing a human's life journey from birth till death, these Values came up as the building blocks of a human's life's Edifice, which a human builds during her lifetime, lives in, and leaves to the Whole at her death. These Values support and nourish a human through-out her lifetime. These Values are the milestones through which a human's life journey is assessed. They create the trail of a human's life; and give direction, purpose, and meaning to a human's life on this Earth. These very Values help a human live a good life herself and enrich her Whole—her world too.

It was from the sheer value of these Five Values that I envisioned the Human Dharma Way of Living. *"The Human Dharma Way of Living is a Value-oriented life with short-term goals; and daily objectives of a Rich, Healthy, Happy, and Meaningful Life."*

A human lives a long life of some seventy to ninety years, but she lives it on an everyday basis. Every day is a counting unit of a human's life. Every day is a new day with a lot of potential and possibilities. Also, every day of a human's life is a new brick that she places in building The Edifice of her life in which she lives during her lifetime, rejoices her existence, and which she leaves to the Whole—the world, at her death.

Looking at the sheer importance of every day in a human's life, I summed up the entire Human Dharma—a human's Right Way of Living— into the form of a Daily Prayer, which the Human Dharma Practitioner remembers every day the first thing in the morning, plans her day as per it, and lives the day as planned. After all, Dharma—a religion—The Right Way of Living has to be incorporated in our daily lives and in our daily karmas. Only then do we live the Dharma way—The Right Way. At the end of a well-planned, productive day, at night just before going to sleep, the Human Dharma Practitioner remembers the Prime Truth of "Om" and has a blissful night's sleep.

In Part Two of this book titled "Way of Living", I have explained "Om"—the Prime Truth, and the Central Truth of the Human Dharma; its three Sub-truths; and the Human Dharma Way of Living.

This book has a certain flow about it from beginning till end, where one issue leads to the other, and derivatives of one issue are brought forth and incorporated into another, thus all leading to the final Human Dharma— a human's Right Way of Living. Therefore, the book needs to be read in entirety from beginning till end, and only then will the Reader understand the basic concepts of the Human Dharma, the reasoning behind them, and grasp the Prime Truth of Om and the Human Dharma Way of Living. The Truth of Om has to be understood and lived every day and every moment. "Meditation upon Om" and "Breathe by Om exercises" form an integral part of the Human Dharma. They need to be read, followed, and practiced step by step, and only then will the Practitioner experience the bliss of "Om meditation"; and the sheer finesse and vigor of the "Breathe by Om exercises."

As the Reader will see, the Human Dharma is not a set of my personal opinions but a total derivation —derived from the basic facts of a human's make and human life—Facts brought to light by various sciences, common observations and experiences, and further aided by my own personal experience of Truth.

In my endeavor to derive the Human Dharma—a human's Right Way of Living, the very first topic for our discussion is "What is a human?"—What does it mean to be a human?

PART ONE

_____

PHILOSOPHY

(Fact Analysis, Definition, and Derivative Right Way Of Living)

CHAPTER 2

WHAT IS A HUMAN?

The Human Dharma means a human's Right Way of Living or Right functions of a human. Right functions of an entity are a set of those functions that ensue from the make of that entity, suit it, and help it flourish. In short, Right functions of an entity match its form. Therefore, in order to define the Human Dharma or Right functions of a human, first we need to see "What is a human?" This issue involves the origin of a human, the entire make of a human, and the context in which a human happens or the world around a human—a human's Whole.

A human, first of all, is a living being. Like any other living being, a human is born, lives for a certain number of years, and dies. Like any other living being, a human needs to survive, and rejoice in her survival. These two quests—the quest for survival, and the quest for happiness—are the two prime quests of every human. Every human wants to survive, and every human wants to be happy. Therefore, Right functions or the Right Way of Living for a human must contain those functions too that ensure a human's survival and her happiness.

Before we analyze the make of a human any further, first let us see the origin of a human or where a human has come from? An answer to this question will throw light on the background of a human form, and will help us define the Right functions of such a form—a human.

Human: An Evolved Being

A human being is born as a child from a set of her parents, a female mother and a male father. At the time of copulation, the male father's sperm penetrates and fertilizes an egg in the ovary of the female mother. From this process is formed one single cell, which contains the DNA—the entire genetic make—a blueprint of all genes of the Child. These genes determine the physical appearance, and mental and other attributes of the Child. The Child inherits 50 percent of her genes from her parents and the other 50 percent from the ancestors of each of her parents—her mother's and her father's. ***Thus, a child is a genetic product of her both parents and their ancestors.***

Now, the Child's mother and father, each in turn, is a genetic product of her/his own blood parents and their ancestors. The Child's mother was born from a set of her own parents—a female mother and a male father—each of whom was born from a set of her/his own parents, and so on. Similarly, the Child's father was born from a set of his own parents—mother and father— each of whom was born from a set of her/his own parents, and so on. We can visualize a single human child (in between) born from a set of her parents—mother and father—each of whom has a long line of ancestors behind her and him.

As we keep going back, there is a long line of human ancestors behind each parent of the Child who died but left parts of themselves in the form of their genes inherited by the Child. We can keep track of a few ancestors, but we assume a long line of human ancestors behind each parent. As we go further and further back, some millions of years back, there comes a point when the Child's human ancestors had evolved from and looked like apes and monkeys (as evidenced by the Science of Anthropology). And, as we go further back, the child's monkey ancestors had evolved from other forms of life. (All of these are scientific facts evidenced by the Science of Biology and the Science of Anthropology, verifiable by any standard college textbook on the subjects or by a reputed encyclopedia.)

The fact of human evolution was brought to light by a group of inter-related sciences, mainly the science of Biology and the science of Anthropology. Thousands of scientists through hundreds of years of research have proved beyond any doubt that a human has evolved from other forms of life.

Science of Biology studies the entire phenomenon of Life: its origin, its multitudes of living beings, their interrelatedness, and their interdependence. As per Biology, Life is a vast phenomenon, a Continuum that started on the Earth some 3.8 billion years ago. In the very beginning, there was no life on the Earth. Then by natural process some atoms got together and created different molecules of water, hydrogen, oxygen, and other gases—substances conducive to the creation and sustenance of Life on the Earth.

These molecules formed the atmosphere on and around the Earth, which protected it from the Sun's direct light and created the breathing air. Some of these molecules, hydrogen and oxygen formed water on the Earth—the oceans.

In the presence of these favorable life conditions, some millions of years later, there sprouted a tiny green plant beneath the waters of the oceans— the very first form of Life. Gradually it multiplied, spread up, and gave rise to the vast plant life beneath the oceans.

Plants provided more favorable conditions for the growth of other forms of Life. After further millions of years, again by natural process, various molecules below the waters got together and formed a one-celled living being—an amoeba. The amoeba eventually gave rise to a multi-cellular living being like a fish. From the fish there emerged the amphibian—a form that could live both in waters and on land. Then, after hundreds of thousands of years later, the amphibian gave rise to the reptile, which lived only on land. From reptiles some five hundred million years ago were born mammals. Mammals multiplied and spread into a large variety of mammals including primates—gorillas, orangutans, chimpanzees—the ancestors of the present human. From these ancestors, after million of years, there emerged a human form.

During this entire unfolding of life, we see one form of life changing into another. This is evolution—a gradual process by which one form of Life changes into a more complex, better form.

The Science of Biology explains this dramatic change in the form of living beings with the law of natural selection and the theory of genes. By the law of natural selection, a living being develops certain traits good for its survival. It survives, reproduces, and passes off its traits to its offspring through genes.

The law of natural selection was first introduced by Charles Darwin in his book *On the Origin of Species,* published in 1859. Darwin, after years of research, concluded that individuals of any one species are not identical: they differ in their physical and other traits. For example, he observed a large variety of beaks in one species of bird. Some had pointed beaks, while others had blunt ones. He noted that individuals with certain traits survive better than others and reproduce their own kinds. But Darwin did not know how. This was explained by the scientists—Mendel and Lamarck.

Mendel, after years of extensive research and experiments on peas, introduced his theory of genes— how traits of an individual are passed off to its children in the form of genes. Lamarck, a French naturalist, further explained the process of evolution with his principle of the inheritance of acquired traits or characteristics. As per Lamarck, changes take place in an organism's structure throughout its lifetime by its use or disuse of certain traits. Also, an organism in its quest for survival acquires or develops certain traits good for its survival. These changes are then transmitted to that organism's offspring in the form of genes. For example, an athlete's children will have stronger muscles than average.

Applying these principles in the vast unfolding of Life from beginning till present resolves the mystery of evolution— one Life form changing into another.

Life is an interplay between a living being and its response to the constantly changing environment. A living being, in its quest for survival, and in response to a changed environment, does away with certain traits and adopts certain new traits that help it survive better. With a little use of imagination, we can see how one form of life changed into another. For example, some millions of years back, maybe the waters dried out in certain parts of the oceans or few fishes swam to the shore and found no food in shallow waters of the shore. Some of them ventured forth onto the land part of the beach and found food there. Many of them died in the process, but a few survived. They learned how to forage on the beach, once in a while, to find food. In this process they developed certain traits, like the ability to breathe out of water, and some physical structural changes. Their changed traits were passed off by genes to their offspring who were born

with the ability to survive partially on land. With every forthcoming generation, these changes strengthened, and they eventually gave rise to an altogether new form—an amphibian, like a
frog who could live both in water and on land.

Some of these amphibians spent more time on land and found
that sliding quietly on land was better than hopping to catch prey.
They tried to slide rather than hop, which changed their physical
structures. They passed off these changes to their children. Very
gradually, over millions of years, their forthcoming generations
did away with their feet and took to sliding only. This gave rise to
a totally different form—a reptile, like a snake. Eventually a variety of reptiles blossomed and produced their own kinds.

By the same process, over the next millions of years, there
emerged the bird from the reptile, and then from the bird the
mammal. The mammal survived, and thrived in a variety of
forms, eventually leading to an ape, the ancestor of the modern
human. It was from the ape that we humans and our cousins,
chimpanzees, came forth.

All this happened over millions of years. As we noted earlier,
the present "Life" with its millions of living species, is the outcome of some 3.8 billion years of evolution.

That the present human form has evolved from an ape ancestor, common to both chimpanzees and us, is further proved by the
Science of Anthropology. The science of anthropology is the study
of the humankind. It traces the origin of the present human and
her entire physical and cultural evolution. Anthropology bases
its findings on the fossils of early human skeletons, footprints,
and tools etc. found in many archaeological diggings. As per
Anthropology the present human and chimpanzees evolved from
a common ape ancestor some eight million years ago. In other

words, chimps are our closest cousins. This is proved by striking similarities between humans' and chimps' physical structures, genetic make, and behavior. Chimps' facial features, such as foreheads, eyes, and jaws, strongly resemble ours. Their hands are very much like ours. Though not fully bipedal, they occasionally walk on both feet. Above all, their genes are 97.4 percent identical to ours— a fact attested to by the Science of Genetics.

Also, chimps' behavior strongly resembles ours. Go to any zoo, and observe their behavior for a few minutes: their piercing gazes, their pondering moods, the way they lie down with arms over their heads. A number of anthropologists, after years of living with chimps and observing their behavior, documented close similarities between chimps' and humans' behavior. Chimps' compassionate and social behavior, long-term family and social relationships, highly sensitive natures, and many other traits are identical to ours.

After originating from a common ape ancestor some eight million years ago, chimps and humans started evolving in two different directions. Many fossil findings clearly prove the slow evolution of an ape into the present human: how an ape first became bipedal and thus freed her hands to hold weapons and make tools; how she gradually developed other humanlike features, like a rounder brain and short canine teeth; how her brain gradually increased in size and she became more and more intelligent.

Fossils of footprints at Laetoli in Tanzania, dated some three million years old, show how an early human started to walk on two feet. These footprints, though not fully human, are remarkably similar to modern humans.

Findings from the skeleton of a child found in 1924 in a mining cave in Taung, South Africa show the slow transition of an ape into a human. This skeleton belongs to a transitional form between an ape and a human, who had more humanlike features, like a rounder brain, short canine teeth, and the position of foramen magnum—evidence of bipedal movement.

The Neanderthal findings in 1856 show the early, fully developed human form. The Neanderthal species of humans lived some three hundred and fifty thousand years ago in parts of Asia and Europe. They were our grosser forms, massive and stout in build, though they walked upright and had large brains. They used fire, and buried their dead.

In addition to these, thousands of other fossils clearly evidence the gradual evolution of an ape into the present human.

The Science of Anthropology also traces the entire cultural evolution of humankind from its sheer struggle for survival up to its present comfortable and luxurious living. There are fossils to indicate how a human first scavenged food—that is, ate the food left over by other animals. Then he gradually learned how to make tools and hunt, and finally started growing food on farms. He first covered himself with tree barks and leaves; then learned how to weave cloth; and wore coarse, handspun clothes finally leading to the finest clothes of today. He first protected himself in dark caves, and then learned how to make huts and camps finally leading to the finest houses of today.

It was during the last twelve thousand years, since humans started living sedentary lives on farms that different human societies and cultures flourished and made stupendous progress in all walks of the human life. More and more comforts were accumulated; and different braches of Art, Music, and Literature flourished. The human heart and mind reached the pinnacles of their growth and expression. Along with Art, Music, and Literature there flourished Philosophy and Science. Different societies in different parts of the world made their contributions in developing each of these. There evolved Language and Mathematics. While Art and Religion solaced the human heart and spirit, Philosophy and Science raised questions about human existence. Different branches of Science developed that solved many riddles about humans, human life, and the world we live in. Science has been a true blessing to the human. Science cleared the mist of human ignorance. The field of Medicine provided humans with long and healthy lives. The field of Engineering created skyscrapers, dams, and bridges. The inventions of electricity, the car, and the plane, together with countless other scientific inventions, discoveries, and products, provided us with the most comfortable and luxurious living.

This sums up the physical and cultural evolution of the human from the most rudimentary life-form to the present human. An amazing, hard to believe saga, but true—brought to light and evidenced by the Science of Biology and the Science of Anthropology.

Derivative Right Way of Living

The above peek into the origin of humans brings up the fact of human evolution. From this fact we can infer certain important derivations:

First, a human's make is very deep. We as humans are products of the Whole of Life— the entire flora and fauna. We have evolved from them. Consequently, we are deeply related to the entire flora or plant life and all living beings in our bodies, in our genes, and in our psyches. As we will see later, we all are deeply interdependent too for our survival. Keeping this fact in mind, we humans ought to live in close communion with nature. Living close to nature—near a river, amid mountains, amid flora, and fauna— comforts our psyche and pleases our hearts. It relaxes us and makes us happy. Also, we ought to respect all other forms of life. "Live and let live" should be our attitude toward all living beings. ***Do not kill other forms of Life. Let them live.*** We need them— the Whole of Life needs them. Nurturing nature and respecting other forms of life are The Right way of Living.

The second important derivation from the fact of human evolution is the realization of the disturbing fact that beneath all our human ethics, morality, and civil code there lies inside us a volcano of animal passions and emotions. These animal passions, like fear, greed, anger, and violence, keep lurking beneath our human polish all the time. Though a gift of evolution, and necessary for survival, these animal passions and emotions blind our minds and push us into making wrong and drastic life choices and decisions. For example, when angry you are not capable of thinking, and you may hit someone or even shoot someone without thinking of the consequences. The Right way of Living would be that which incorporates this fact into our living. We as humans ought to understand the presence of animality inside us in the form of raw, wild passions and emotions. We ought not to live as victims of our animal emotions and desires, but be able to think and control them. ***Our all emotions and desires must be seasoned with thoughts.*** The ability to think rationally, and Self-control distinguish a human from an animal, and help her live a good life. Rational thinking and self-control need to be taught right from childhood and practiced throughout one's lifetime.

The fact of human evolution also raises a question: what makes us humans? How are we truly different from animals? This takes us into another aspect of a human's make: her complex, multi-dimensional being. An analysis of the various dimensions of a human's form will show us the sheer depth and height of her make.

Human: A Multi-Dimensional Being

The human, a product of nature's millions of years of labor, is a real marvel of nature. There lies inside her the deep human compassion, a variety of distinct human emotions, a razor-sharp intellect, pearls of human thoughts, an instinctive human sense of right and wrong, and an all-encompassing spirit—a beatific mixture of the highest intellect, a keen sense of right and wrong, and a deep human sensitivity for All.

A human is a highly complex, Multi-Dimensional being. Various dimensions of her being are Physical, Emotional, Intellectual, Moral, and Spiritual.

Figure 1

Human - A Multi-Dimensional Living Being

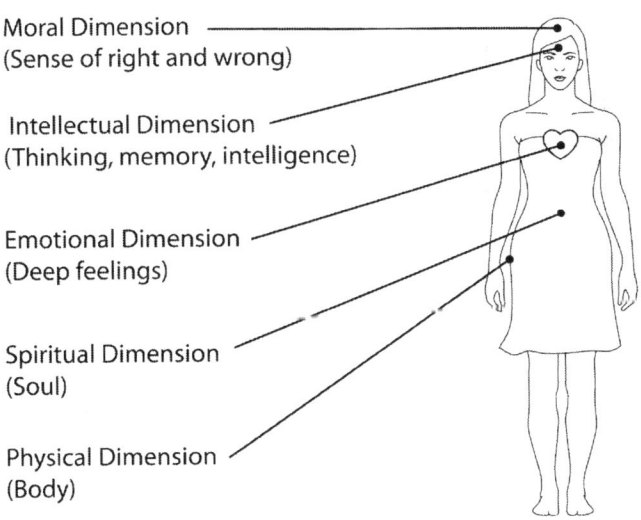

Moral Dimension
(Sense of right and wrong)

Intellectual Dimension
(Thinking, memory, intelligence)

Emotional Dimension
(Deep feelings)

Spiritual Dimension
(Soul)

Physical Dimension
(Body)

Each of these dimensions has its own importance, and one cannot be replaced by the other. Exercising and developing each of these dimensions helps one develop into a wholesome human and live a good life. Next, I will discuss each of these distinct dimensions of a human's being, define them, and take a derivative Right way of Living from each.

Physical Dimension

The physical dimension denotes the body of a human. The human body as the result of millions of years of evolution is a highly complex, autonomous system. What we see with our eyes is the gross, outer body, but inside the human body is made of trillions of extremely fine cells invisible to our eyes. A cell is the basic unit of a human body. It contains one's DNA or complete genetic information and other fine molecules required for life.

A group of cells is organized into a tissue. Tissues are further organized into an organ. A group of different organs are then organized into an organ system: the breathing system, nervous system, digestive system, and reproductive system, and so on. All of these organ systems work together and run the body. They are all interconnected and interdependent. No one system is absolutely independent. Good or bad functioning of one system affects all other organ systems. For example, a human's nervous system is one of the finest systems. It is made of one's brain and millions of teeny-tiny, extremely fine nerves, extending from one's brain down to one's spine and all body organs. Sad and depressing thoughts in one's mind depress and slack all other systems and the whole body, while happy and motivating thoughts exhilarate and activate one's whole body. These different organ systems are housed inside and attached through muscles to one's skeleton system or basic bone structure. Bones protect our tender organs. This is the basic structure of a human body.

A human's body is one whole autonomous system that runs by energy. A human gets this energy from breathing, food, and actions.

Breathing is a function of inhaling oxygen, retaining it, and exhaling carbon dioxide and other toxic gases. Oxygen inside one's body flows through blood, reaches all cells, and energizes cells to metabolize and reproduce. Oxygen is so vital to a human's body that one cannot survive without it for more than two minutes. This fact makes breathing as one of the most vital functions of human body. Right breathing keeps one healthy and active while wrong breathing makes one lazy and causes a number of diseases.

Food after we eat it is digested by our digestive system. Digestion of food is a complex process in which intestines work and grind the food into a fine paste. Then various vitamins, minerals, and carbohydrates are extracted from the food and taken to cells by blood. Cells work further and convert the food into energy. A human needs very limited amount of vitamins, minerals, and carbohydrates to survive and run her body. The rest is converted into fat cells and stored inside one's body.

Our actions energize us. An action is any movement or work by any part of one's body. An action can be purely physical or mental or a combination of both. Some examples of purely physical actions are walking, running, and playing. Some purely mental actions are thinking and memorizing, while writing is a combination of both actions. It requires sitting upright, thinking, and using one's hand.

A purely physical action, like walking, running, swimming, or playing, makes one's heart function faster and speeds up the blood flow to all body organs from tip to toes, while a purely mental action stimulates the blood flow to one's brain.

Our all actions need energy, consume energy, and energize us too.

Definition

The Physical dimension of a human denotes the human body. A human's body, the product of millions of years of evolution, is a highly complex, autonomous system that runs by energy gained by breathing, food, and actions.

Derivative Right Way of Living

A human's body is the prime tool through which a human works and lives in this world. It is the prime source through which we either enjoy or curse our existence. Having a healthy body makes one active, vibrant, and happy. Therefore, maintaining a good, healthy body should be one of the daily goals of living.

A healthy body is a slim, supple body with a lot of energy and vigor.

A human's body is a purely genetic product. We have no control on the kind of body we have. Some of us are healthy and energetic by birth, while others are sick and weak by birth. But as humans we have a lot of control of our actions. One can gain and maintain a healthy body by Right Breathing, Right Diet, and Right Exercise. A human ought to maintain a healthy body, be active, and enjoy her life.

The concepts of Right Breathing, Right Diet, and Right Exercise infer from the analysis of the human body. As we saw in the above analysis, breathing is the most vital body function, through which one inhales oxygen, retains it, and exhales carbon-dioxide and other toxic gases. The importance of breathing cannot be emphasized enough. Our breathing affects our emotions, thoughts, and overall physical and mental health. The quality of one's breathing can cause or prevent a number of diseases, like blood pressure, heart disease, and even cancer. Short, shallow breathing supplies one's body and mind with less oxygen and thus hinders one's ability to think and act calmly. People with short, shallow breathing patterns are anxious, hasty, often make foolish choices, and act without thinking of consequences. While long, deep breathing supplies one's body and mind with ample oxygen and thus helps one to remain calm and energetic. People with long, deep breathing habits are often calm, alert, make well-thought-out choices, and act after thinking of consequences.

Right breathing consists of long, deep inhalation; good retention of breath; and strong, forceful exhalation. Of course it is not possible to breathe Right all the time since different activities affect our breathing patterns. But one should watch one's breathing and regulate it whenever possible during the course of the day.

Learn some good breathing exercises. When tired, do some calming exercises, like exhaling hard and long, and then inhaling anyway. Doing this for five minutes relaxes you after a day's hard work. When feeling low and depressed, do some stimulating exercises like inhaling deeply. Inhaling deeply for five minutes supplies your body with oxygen and vigor. Besides, one should do a good yogic breathing exercise like *Pranayama* every morning to inhale plenty of oxygen and exercise one's overall breathing system. I have included it in Right Exercise.

<u>Right Diet</u>

Right diet is crucial to a healthy body. Right diet means eating the Right type of food, in the Right amount, and the Right way.

As we noted earlier, a human body requires a very limited amount of vitamins, minerals, carbohydrates, and fat. Right diet is that daily diet which supplies one's body with enough vitamins, minerals, carbohydrates, and fat. A human's daily diet should consist of some fruit, milk, yoghurt, salad, vegetables; light meat/fish/lentil; and some bread with a little butter or cheese. Butter, cheese, and oil should be eaten as little as possible.

Divide your daily diet into four meals: breakfast, lunch, supper, and dinner, with four hours' gap in between. There is a wise saying regarding food that is good for all: "Give breakfast to yourself, lunch to your friend, and dinner to your enemy."

A healthy and heavy breakfast will run your body the whole day. Dinner should be as little and as light as possible. The reason is that at night during sleep the body relaxes and rests. All organ systems rest too. If you eat a heavy dinner, your digestive system has to work overtime to digest the food. This interferes with your sleep and does not let your body rest. Moreover, during sleep, when there is no physical or mental movement, cells metabolize, reproduce, and do other work, which is essential for healthy functioning of the body. Your digestive system's working overnight interferes with the cells' work.

Plan your every day's four meals in the morning, and then follow them. Start your day with a good Breakfast consisting of fruit, yoghurt, toast, and a little butter or cheese. Follow it with a

Lunch of some bread; vegetables; and lentil, meat, or fish. Meat should be avoided as much as possible. If one must eat meat then eat very little meat. Then have a Supper or light evening meal in the form of a healthy snack with juice, light tea, or coffee. End your day with a Dinner of only milk or soup or salad. Food temperature should be as per the weather: hot food in winters and cold food in summers. As a principle one should eat only when hungry and only small portions. Food should be eaten slowly and quietly. Conversation should be avoided during eating. Speaking during eating interferes with eating. Every solid food should be chewed well to a paste form before swallowing.

Marinating the Right diet should be a human's everyday goal because that ensures her every day's health and her life-long health too.

Action

As noted in the definition of physical dimension, the human body gains energy by action too. An action is any physical movement like walking or running; a posture like standing straight or sitting upright; or any concentrated mental labor, like reading, memorizing, or solving a puzzle.

A human gains energy from breathing and food, and then indulges in an activity and exhausts his energy; he gets tired, rests, eats again, and regains his energy which he needs to exhaust again. The human body, or for that matter the body of any living being, runs as per nature's rule of energy gain, energy exhaustion, and energy regain. Every living being is bound by this rule, be it a plant, an animal, or a human.

Hence, a human cannot live without any action. It is a principle of nature that if you gain energy, you have to exhaust it too.

If you don't do that, you will grow fat, lazy, sick, and depressed. Moreover, during any activity like walking, running, or reading with concentration, as you spend energy, you need more energy too. You tend to inhale faster and deeper to draw in more oxygen and gain more energy. That is why active people are often energetic too and happier than lazy ones. Thus there is a close connection between action and energy.

From this we infer that leading an active lifestyle, working, and being busy the whole day with ample rest at night make one active, energetic, productive, and happy.

Right Exercise

Exercise means work out. Working out a particular part of the body strengthens that part, and working out the whole body strengthens and invigorates the whole body.

A human's body is a collection of different body organs and muscles. Each organ needs to be strong, and all muscles need to be flexible. Also, the whole body needs to be energetic and active. Though an active lifestyle contributes to this, but a daily set of physical exercise is required to maintain a healthy body.

Right Exercise is a set of some breathing exercise, some organ-cum-stretching exercise, and some aerobic activity. A combination of these three exercises done five days a week keeps one's body slim, supple, and energetic.

Breathing Exercise

Breathing is a crucial body function that runs the whole body. Our breathing is controlled and regulated by our respiratory system. Our respiratory system is a collection of different organs, like the nostrils, the windpipe, the lungs, and the diaphragm.

The diaphragm, located below the stomach, is the central organ of breathing. It contracts during inhalation and expands during exhalation. Right breathing requires a strong diaphragm. One must not be overweight and fat in one's stomach. This lazes the diaphragm.

Breathing exercise strengthens one's diaphragm and other breathing organs. There are many forms of breathing exercises. A good breathing exercise is the one that exercises the whole respiratory system.

Pranayama is a good breathing exercise introduced by the sages of ancient India who understood the importance of Right breathing. *Pranayama* is a Sanskrit word made of two words: *prana* and *ayama*. *Prana* means life force or oxygen, and *ayama* means taking in life force. Thus *pranayama* means taking in life force by controlled breathing. There are many types of *pranayama*. The easiest is the *Anuloma-Viloma* or alternate breathing. This exercise is done by standing straight, closing the left nostril, inhaling through the right nostril; retaining the breath; and then exhaling through the left nostril. Next, repeat the same procedure by closing the right nostril. Another version of the same exercise is doing so by both nostrils—inhale by both nostrils, retain, and then exhale. A breathing exercise should be done early in the morning in open air, amid nature.

Conscious, effortful inhaling, retaining, and exhaling in open air gives one a fresh supply of oxygen, and strengthens one's respiratory organs and diaphragm.

Doing *pranayama* for thirty minutes every day makes you feel energetic and improves your breathing habits.

Organs-cum-Stretching Exercise

Our organs need to be strong, and our muscles need to be supple. This creates a strong, supple body. Right organ exercise is the one that strengthens our different body organs and makes them flexible. It includes an exercise of some important body organs like the eyes, neck, hands, arms, shoulders, legs, and feet.

Exercising each organ in order from top to bottom ensures each organ's exercise. Starting with the eyes, a good eye exercise is moving eyes up and down, sideways, cornerwise, clockwise, and then anticlockwise for a count of ten for each movement. This relaxes one's eyes muscles and makes them flexible. After the eyes comes the neck. Bending one's neck left to right, forward and backward, moving clockwise and anticlockwise for a count of ten for each movement makes one's neck muscles flexible and prevents aches and strains in the neck. Closing both hands into tight fists and then opening them wide is a good hand exercise. Doing so repeatedly for a count of ten strengthens one's paws. Moving arms in a circular way for a count of ten is a good arm exercise. After the arms, comes the feet exercise. Feet exercise is well done by closing and opening one's toes for a count of ten and bending one's foot backward and forward for a count of ten each. After the feet, one can do a leg exercise by bending each leg backward and forward from the knee for a count of ten each. Each exercise should be done very slowly with a lot of care. This whole exercise takes less than ten minutes.

A regular organs exercise, combined with some stretching exercise, like bending sideways, bending down and backward (toe-touching) for a count of ten each, strengthens one's organs, improves their flexibility, and increases blood circulation to one's all organs from tip to toes.

Aerobic Exercise

Breathing exercise improves one's breathing. A regular Organs-cum- Stretching exercise strengthens one's organs and improves body flexibility. And an aerobic exercise speeds up blood circulation to all parts of one's body and energizes it. It does wonders for one's heart and is actually required for good heart functioning.

An aerobic exercise is a running or brisk walking exercise done for a minimum of thirty minutes at a stretch. During running or brisk walking, you tend to breathe faster and thus take in more oxygen. At the same time, your heart has to work harder and pump blood to all parts of your moving body. Its effects are amazing.

Running or brisk walking done for thirty minutes every day in the fresh morning air, amid nature, invigorates and energizes one's body for the day's actions. It must be done amid nature—in a park or by a riverside or a seaside where there is ample oxygen in the air.

Thus, Right exercise is a combination of some Breathing Exercise, Organs-cum-Stretching exercise, and some Aerobic Exercise. A set of these three exercises done every day or at least five days a week keeps one's body slim, supple, and energetic.

Devote an hour every day toward maintaining a healthy body. A healthy body is the prime requirement for an active and happy life. Doing Breathing exercise for thirty minutes,

Organs-cum-Stretching exercise for ten minutes, and brisk walking or running for thirty minutes every day keeps your body healthy and energetic. You can do it in parts or all three at one time.

Right Exercise combined with Right Diet helps one maintain a healthy body.

Maintaining a healthy body should be one's every day goal. Plan your Right Diet and Right Exercise for the whole day, and follow them.

Emotional Dimension

Another dimension of a human's make is her/his Emotional Dimension. Every human has an emotional dimension to her/his person. Emotional dimension of a human consists of a human's feelings and emotions. An emotion is something we feel. But, it is more than a mere feeling. An emotion is much more complex, builds over time, and lasts longer than a mere feeling. For example, we may feel "hot" or "cold." These are just sensational feelings. But we feel "sad" or "angry." These are emotions.

An emotion is an intense inner feeling caused in response to the outside world and its people. We humans, during the course of living, come across and deal with a number of things and people. These things and people affect us in a certain way. Broadly speaking, they are either "for us" or "against us." If something or someone is "for us," conducive to our growth and happiness, we tend to like or love that thing or person. And if something or someone is "against us," hinders our growth and happiness, we tend to dislike or hate that thing or person. For example, I love my house because it offers me safety and comfort; thus—"for me," and I love my parents, because they love me and care for me, thus—"for me." On the other hand, I may hate my jealous colleague who obstructs my work, instigates my boss against me, and thus hinders my growth and happiness—thus "against me."

Emotions are highly complex and hidden in nature and therefore are hard to understand, for example, anger. Anger is a very complex emotion. While angry we often do not know who or what we are angry at. We may be angry at something or someone and take it out on something or someone else. For example, I may be angry at my rude boss and take it out on my family. Also, anger is often a hidden emotion. It keeps lurking inside me unless I face it or express it. I may feel resentment and anger for someone without my being aware of it, but it will keep bothering me unless I face it. Emotional clarity is very important for a good life. From time to time, we should keep asking ourselves how we are feeling so we stay attuned to our emotions. If I am angry, I should try to go back to my thoughts and try to figure out who or what I am angry at and then decide what to do about it.

Our emotions build up over a long time and last long; for example, love. Love is a feeling of deep attachment and care for a thing or person. It builds up after years of association, living together, and positive relationship with that thing or person. For example, I may love my twenty-year-old car that served me well; and I may love my family, with whom I lived, grew up with, and shared many joys and sorrows with for many years. Such love often lasts long, maybe throughout our lives.

An emotion is an overwhelming feeling that affects one's overall being and pushes one to act in a certain way. It is a whole process. As soon as you feel an emotion, depending upon the type, certain chemicals are secreted in your body. Different emotions secrete different chemicals. These chemicals go to your nervous system and motivate you to act in a certain way. For example, when you feel threatened by something or someone, it generates fear inside you. Fear secretes adrenalin which goes to your brain and makes you feel anxious, scream for help, run, or attack. Similarly, love is a very tender, soft emotion. When you feel love for someone, like your child or parent, it bathes your whole inner being, making you feel soft and happy.

Human emotions are very powerful in nature. They play a central role in human behavior and actions. Our deep-seated emotions toward a person or a thing color our perception and motivate us to act in a certain way toward that person or thing. The majority of murders are committed under the grip of jealousy and rage. And many of our acts of charity are the results of guilt, gratitude, and love we feel toward others.

We humans feel a variety and range of emotions. Each of these can be easily placed in any one of two classes, positive or negative. Positive emotions are those that nurture our beings, make us feel happy, and motivate us to be good and do good to others, for example, love, happiness, compassion, and goodwill toward others. Negative emotions are those that agitate us, make us feel miserable, and push us to hurt or harm others, for example, anger, hatred, fear, jealousy. Negative emotions not only disturb our whole beings, but also push us to do things that may ruin our lives.

Definition

In sum, *Our emotions are deep-seated, intense, highly complex feelings toward a person or thing, which color our attitudes and motivate us to behave in a certain way.*

Derivative Right Way of Living

Since emotions are such an integral part of our lives and affect the quality of our beings and lives, why not feel only positive emotions and do away with all negative emotions? Feel only love and kindness, and not feel any anger, hatred, or fear. Is it possible to do this? The answer is No. Our emotions are very natural. Our likes and dislikes of things and people are natural. We often have no control of what we like or dislike. Also, our emotions are our natural responses to the outside world and people. For example, if someone likes me or loves me, I am bound to like or love that person. And if someone dislikes me or hates me, I am bound to dislike or hate that person.

Also, our emotions are our survival tools. Negative emotions have their own value, for example, fear. Fear warns me of potential danger to my safety and well-being. It keeps nagging me until I face it and plan or take some action to protect myself.

We humans ought to listen to our emotions and act upon them with thought.

Season with Thought

One fact about human emotions is that they are savage and irrational. Our emotions are part of the limbic brain which is millions of years old in evolution, while the thinking layer of the brain evolved very recently. That is why our emotions are so powerful and overwhelming. They blind us to reason, and push us to make choices and do things we may regret throughout our lives. Therefore, our emotions must be seasoned with thoughts before we act upon them.

We ought to listen to our emotions, understand them, and then think about what to do. Never act under the grip of a mere emotion. Think before you act or make any choices. For example, if you are angry at someone, think about who you are angry at and for what reason. Then think of a proper action. Don't just yell and attack under anger. There are calmer and more effective ways of handling an angry situation than harming or hurting the other person. Similarly, don't let fear and anxiety run your life. Listen to your fear, think, and then act.

In sum, our all emotions ought to be seasoned with thought and then acted upon.

Practice *Subhava*

We feel and we live. Feeling is an integral part of our daily lives. Since emotions are our deep-seated feelings, they affect the quality of our beings and lives. Negative emotions like anger, hatred, and jealousy hinder our inner growth, and make us suffer and feel miserable. While Positive emotions like love, compassion, and goodwill nourish our beings, and make us feel elated and happy. Whether we suffer or we enjoy our lives has a lot to do with the types of emotions we generally feel.

Subhava is a Sanskrit word. It is made of two words—*su* and *bhava*. *Su* means "beautiful" or "positive," and *bhava* means "emotions." *Subhava* means feeling positive emotions that nourish our beings and lives. Though our emotions are natural, there are certain high, uniquely human emotions that we can practice. These are love, compassion, and goodwill.

Love is a wonderful human emotion. Loving someone and being loved are vital needs of a human. Loving someone means being emotionally attached to that person, caring for her, and wanting to see her happy. Being loved makes you feel cherished, valuable, and happy. Develop and maintain a few loving relationships in your life. Love your family and friends. When we love others, only then do we get it back. You have to give love in order to get it back.

Compassion is a noble, uniquely human emotion. It is higher than love. We love our loved ones, but we feel compassion for all. Compassion means understanding the other person, her situation in life, empathizing with her, and being willing to help if needed. When in the company of the other person, try to understand that person, her nature, her needs and desires, and her situation, and empathize— place yourself in her shoes and try to extend your help and support if needed. Doing so expands your teeny-tiny Self, which is thinking about I, me, and mine all the time. Also, it connects you to others. Compassion is a unique human emotion available to rare, few individuals. We humans are generally driven by our own selfish interests, rivalry, and hostility toward others, not by compassion.

Compassion is a noble human emotion that we ought to practice in our daily lives. It makes us aware of others, enlarges our inner world, and connects us to others.

Having goodwill toward others means you want to see others happy. This is also not natural, but it ought to be practiced. Be concerned about others' well-being and happiness. Smile at them, wish them happiness, and be willing to help. This makes you feel happy and connects you to others.

In sum, the emotional dimension of a human is very important to her well-being and happiness. A human ought to retain her natural human feelings, feel strongly, and listen to her emotions. At the same time, emotions are a savage force that needs to be tamed with thoughts and reason. Season your emotions with thought, and practice *Subhava*—love your family and friends, and have compassion and goodwill for All.

Intellectual Dimension

The intellectual dimension of a human is a higher and uniquely human dimension. The entire progress of humanity can be attributed mainly to this dimension of a human. It is the human's intellectual dimension that has craved for and gathered vast stores of human knowledge; has pondered over and solved many a problems of human existence; and has come up with stupendous inventions and discoveries that have enriched humanity in all fields of human life.

The intellectual dimension of a human consists of a human's mental capacity to acquire and apply knowledge; human intelligence; and an ability to think.

"To know" is to understand a thing, a person, or a subject, and to understand "how to?" or a way of doing something. For example, I may understand the inner functioning of a computer and thus know it. I may understand the nature of my sister and thus know her. Or I may understand the subject of biology by having read it thoroughly and thus know it. Also, I may know how to make coffee or how to drive a car. This makes knowledge of two types: theoretical and practical. Theoretical knowledge is deep understanding of a subject matter, and practical knowledge is "how to do a thing?"

A human child is born with a blank mind. Slowly and gradually she starts knowing the world by feeling and exploring, and later by language. For example, a child explores her surroundings, wants to touch everything, and wants to feel it in order to "know it." This is how a child learns about the world around her. As she grows up, she learns language. Then language becomes her main tool for learning. She listens to others, communicates with them, and reads. Thus she acquires a vast amount of knowledge mainly by reading, communication, and education.

This further divides knowledge into two types: First-hand and Second-hand knowledge. First-hand knowledge is what we know through our personal experience, and Second-hand knowledge is what others tell us. Our First-hand knowledge is very definite, and we tend to rely more on it, while our Second-hand knowledge changes over time.

Gaining knowledge is an endless process. There is always something new to know— a new thing, a new person, a new place, or a new subject or skill. It is a hard but enjoyable process.

A human acts and lives by her knowledge. The more we know or understand the world, the better we deal with it. Also, knowledge gives us mental serenity, confidence, and power over others. Knowledge illumines our dark, ignorant minds and gives us a broad worldview.

Gaining knowledge should be a lifelong process. Starting with Right Education, which gives us vast stores of knowledge about different subjects and the world, we ought to keep acquiring new knowledge throughout our lives. This process makes us more knowledgeable, calm, and confident.

Intelligence is another chief aspect of a human's intellectual dimension. It is hard to define intelligence, but generally it means the capacity to gain knowledge, to understand, to think fast and abstractedly, to detect a problem and find a solution, to be innovative, and to be able to reason and plan.

Humans vary in their intelligence. Some are very intelligent, while others are less so. Also, different people are intelligent in different fields.

Though intelligence is genetic, it can be acquired and sharpened. Right Education is the first step in that direction. Also, practicing an alert and inquisitive mind, gaining knowledge, making independent decisions, and solving problems sharpen our intelligence. An intelligent person is often a cam, confident, and happy person.

Human intelligence also denotes thinking capacity. Thinking is a highly complex, mental process that includes imagining, remembering, planning, and reasoning. There are two main types of thinking: creative thinking and critical thinking.

Creative thinking involves thinking anew, thinking differently, and finding a novel solution to a problem. Most of our scientists, writers, philosophers, and innovators have been creative thinkers.

Critical thinking is different but equally noble. It is the ability to reflect about a subject matter in a logical manner, analyze it, and make a decision or pass a judgment. Critical thinking is an extremely fine, discerning ability of the human mind to separate the true from the false or the worthy from the worthless. Philosophers, lawyers, judges, and some other professionals use critical thinking to judge or decide an issue.

Critical thinking is a great mental faculty to have. It clears the fog of superstitions and myths and brings out the light of truth. Someone who is able to think critically thinks clearly and lives a better and happier life based on lasting truths.

Critical thinking requires knowledge of the principles of logic or the science of reasoning. It must be learned. Right education should include teaching of Logic to students from the beginning. Once learnt, one can apply it in daily life to determine one's belief system or to make choices.

Definition

The intellectual dimension of a human is a human's mental capacity to gain and a store a vast amount of knowledge and apply it, human intelligence, and an ability to think.

Derivative Right Way of Living

Intellectual dimension is the true mark of being a human. If developed, it enables a person to enjoy the sheer bliss of human existence. Knowledge illumines a human's mind and gives her a broad worldview. Practicing intelligence and good thinking ability help a person deal better with and solve life's problems. Also, a person with a strong intellectual dimension is often a calm, wise, and confident person who makes better life choices and lives a happier life.

Every human, by the virtue of being a human, has an intellectual dimension to her being. Though as per Scientific findings three fourths of human intelligence is genetic, it can be exercised and developed by Right Education; and by one's private, consistent everyday efforts like practicing an alert, inquisitive, and thinking mind; learning something new; and reading et cetera.

Moral Dimension

A human has another higher dimension to her being, in fact one of the highest— the moral dimension. It is considered higher because it deals with issues of right and wrong, truth, and justice, and so on. These are very fine issues and can best be determined by a human equipped with a highly intelligent, discerning mind and a compassionate soul.

We humans live by certain do's and don'ts in all realms of life— in our private conduct, in our behavior with others, and in arriving at just decisions in disputes. This is morality: rules of private conduct, rules of social behavior, and rules of resolving disputes. Different people live by different moral codes.

Is morality innate or natural to us? Are we humans born with it? The answer is no for most of us. Though a few of us are born with strong consciences, an inborn sense of recognizing right and wrong, for most of us morality is a learned concept and often hard to practice. We humans are taught morality or the right, virtuous conduct by our family, society, and religion.

A human child, from the very beginning is taught a set of certain do's and don'ts both in terms of private conduct and social behavior. For example, "get up early," "take a bath every day," "brush your teeth at night," "don't be lazy," "don't be greedy," or some other rules of private conduct; and, "respect others," "be polite to others," "don't talk to strangers," "don't lie," "don't cheat," "don't steal," or some other rules in terms of social behavior. A child's whole life is governed by a moral code instilled into and enforced by her family and society. This is a narrowly defined morality: conduct considered right by your family or by your society.

There is another type of morality, which is universal: the conduct considered right by rational people all over the world. This can clash with the narrowly defined morality of a particular family or a society.

Right conduct is also introduced and enforced by a religion. Every religion, be it Hindu, Muslim, Christianity, or any other, is in fact a moral code.

Definition

As we can see from the above, there is no set definition of morality. Rules of right conduct vary from family to family, society to society, and religion to religion. Every family, society, and religion teaches its own moral code. Still, there are certain eternal rules of Right conduct that are good for all humans, for example, practicing discipline, punctuality, self-control, and personal hygiene in private conduct; and not lying, cheating, or stealing and being fair and just in dealing with others in social behavior.

The question is, why be moral? After all, morality is hard to practice. It is easier to let yourself go and enjoy the moment than to be disciplined and punctual, and easier to be lazy and sleep than to study hard or work. Similarly, why not lie and cheat and thus take advantage of the other person; steal rather than do hard, honest labor; and make a fool of others rather than be fair and just? The answer lies in the importance of morality.

Morality or rules of right conduct are important for the growth and prosperity of a human individual, as well as for a human society. We can test this concept with certain eternal rules of morality.

Right private conduct helps one live a good life. For example, practicing discipline, punctuality, and self-control help you live an active, productive, and happy life. They help you grow and prosper as an individual. Discipline means doing certain things at a certain time, no matter what— like getting up early, or studying, or working even if you feel lazy. Punctuality or being on time saves you your own time and shows respect toward others' time. Good time management is important for success. Self-control is one of the highest human virtues. It helps you ward off momentary temptations and stick to your lifelong Values and goals. Self-control helps in all realms of human life.

Right social behavior helps us live in peace and harmony with others. There are certain eternal rules of Right social behavior. Compassion and goodwill are two golden rules. These are inner feelings that motivate you to be good, and do good to others. Compassion means understanding the other person, her situation and empathizing with her. This helps us greatly in dealing with others. Take a moment to understand the other person you are dealing with— her nature, her situation, and her problems. See if the other person is tired, stressed, sad, or angry; try to feel her situation; give her time and space; be a little tolerant; approach accordingly; and help her if you can. Compassion connects us to others and does wonders in dealing with others. Goodwill is wishing others happiness. Both of these are not natural and are very hard to practice, but if practiced they make one feel good, be good, and do good to others.

Respecting others and being polite to them eases social interactions. Being fair and just in our personal and business dealings gives us a firm footing, avoids fights with others, and earns us a good social reputation. Everyone likes to deal with a fair and just person both as a personal contact and in work or business.

Derivative Right Way of Living

In view of the importance of morality, we humans ought to exercise and develop our moral dimension. First, we should try to follow the rules of right conduct as taught by our elders. However hard they are, we should at least test them and see their effects. If we are not convinced by the given moral code, then we should try to develop our own: think about what is right and wrong both in terms of private conduct and in dealing with others. Define the Right rules, test them, and if they work, stick to them. Right is what works for all, is fair to all, and is good for all.

Above all, a human ought to practice certain eternal rules of morality both in her private conduct and her social behavior, like practicing discipline, punctuality, and self-control in private conduct; and practicing compassion and goodwill towards others, respecting others, being polite to them, and being fair and just in personal and business dealings.

Morality works. It helps one live a good life, and helps build a harmonious human society.

Spiritual Dimension

The Spiritual dimension is the highest dimension of a human being. It is considered the highest because it deals with abstract, metaphysical queries that are far above the mere survival quest of a human. These queries relate to the true nature of one's Self; a higher purpose and the meaning of life; death; God; and ultimate Truth.

There is a part of a human that feels life's pains and miseries deeply, not only her own, but others' too— like poverty, sickness, old age, and death. It is deeply perturbed by them and asks questions. It lifts up its head, looks at the vast sky and stars, and wonders about God. It can see through the fragility of life, think, and pose certain questions, such as "Who am I?" "Why am I here?" "What is the true purpose and meaning of my life?" "Is there a God?" "What is the ultimate Truth?" etc. This is the spiritual dimension of a human. It seeks answers to the big issues of life.

Our spiritual dimension is not a body part we can see with our eyes, but a composite of our deepest feelings and highest thinking, and it emanates from a human's deep Self or soul. It has both— the deep sensitivity of the human heart and her highest intelligence.

It is a human's strong spiritual dimension that gives birth to a religion. Once every few thousand years, a human is born with deep sensitivity and highest intelligence, is deeply perturbed by life's miseries, poses deep questions and seeks answers to them, and searches for the ultimate Truth. Such a person searches for answers from various sources, like existing religions and knowledge; wanders around, does not sit with peace; and remains deeply perturbed and anxious till she finds answers to them. It is most of her lifetime's search. Once she finds the ultimate Truth, and answers to these queries of life, she is perfectly calm, serene, and joyous. Her answers to these queries form a Religion—a Thought system based on the ultimate Truth(s) and their Derivative Right Way of living. Gautam Buddha, The Founder of Buddhism; Muhammad, The Founder of Muslim religion; and Jesus Christ, the Founder of Christianity belong to this sect of humans— humans with very strong spiritual dimensions.

All of us have this dimension. It is repressed in most of us but is very strong in a few rare individuals. This part does not raise its head in our daily lives, but when we are faced with life's deeply painful moments, like sights of sheer poverty, human suffering, and death, especially of a loved one, it raises its head and asks questions. Depending upon its strength, it remains deeply perturbed till it finds answers. Many of us already follow a religion that answers these questions and gives us solace and peace, while some of us do not believe in any religion and try to find answers on our own.

Definition

A Human's Spiritual dimension relates to her Spirit or Soul— the deepest Self of a human that feels deeply, and seeks answers to deep issues of life, like the true purpose and meaning of one's life, death, God, and the ultimate Truth.

Importance of the Spiritual Dimension

The Spiritual dimension is unique to a human. It is only a human who is deeply affected by life's miseries and death, and raises abstract, complex spiritual questions.

Each of us has a spiritual dimension. If satisfied, it makes a person calm and happy, gives her a vast worldview, and helps her live a good life. If dissatisfied, it makes one anxious and perturbed. In order to live a good life, a human's spiritual dimension needs to be satisfied.

Derivative Right Way of Living

A human ought to exercise and develop her spiritual dimension. Doing so attunes her to her deepest Self—Soul— and gives her an inner joy and compassion for all. A religion often satisfies our spiritual queries and helps us live good lives. If you do not believe in any religion, then at least test it. It may offer some answers.

Seeking the Truth and knowledge on one's own is another way to satisfy one's spiritual dimension.

Regular prayer and meditation are two major ways to satisfy one's spiritual dimension. Prayer emanates from our faith in God or some Power running the Universe. Different religions have different prayers, but they all have a common theme. Every prayer denotes faith in God, a wide worldview, and love for All. Saying a prayer restores one's faith in God, one's Self, and teaches her a wide worldview and love for All. Thus it satisfies one's Spiritual dimension.

Meditation is another way to access one's deep Self or Soul. Different religions teach different meditation techniques, like chanting a *mantra* or a single word; watching one's breath; or concentrating on a picture or a statue of a deity. All of these aim at silencing the mind and taking one to one's deep Self or Soul, located at the center of one's body. Connecting to one's Soul gives one an inner joy, and compassion for All.

Meditation is the proven technique to calm one's mind and make one joyous.

In order to satisfy one's Spiritual Dimension, a human ought to practice a religion, and either say a prayer or meditate every day. Doing so connects her to her Soul, and makes her calm, serene, and joyous.

Live a Balanced life: Exercise Each Dimension

The above discussion of a human's various dimensions shows the make and importance of each dimension of a human—Physical, Emotional, Intellectual, Moral, and Spiritual. Each of these dimensions is different and has its own unique importance in a human's life. A human ought to exercise and develop each of these dimensions. Doing so helps her develop into a wholesome human, enjoy the sheer bliss of being a human, and live a good and balanced life. There are certain ways to exercise and strengthen each of these dimensions. "Right Diet" and "Right Exercise" help one stay healthy on a physical level. Maintaining a happy family, a set of happy friends, and feeling compassion and goodwill for All nourish one's emotional dimension and make her a joyous person. Getting good formal education; reading; and practicing an alert, thinking mind develop one's intellectual dimension. Education strengthens and enriches her brain, while good thinking ability helps her solve daily life's problems in a calm and logical manner. Practicing honesty, discipline, and punctuality in everyday conduct and being fair and just to others develop one's moral dimension. Having a good character gives one an inner strength and helps her live a good life. And being fair and just to others helps one in one's social dealings.

A human's highest dimension is her spiritual dimension. Practicing a religion, saying a prayer and doing meditation connect a human to the Divine in her and give her a wide worldview and love for All.

Human: A Part of The Whole

A human is not alone on this Earth. There is a vast world around a human in which she is born, lives, and dies. A further analysis of a human and her world reveals that a human is a close and intrinsic part of this world outside her. Not only this, but taking a human as the Center, when we analyze each aspect of the entire world outside a human, there emerges One vast Whole in which a human, and each part of her outside world are interrelated in a way so that they create One Whole. The Whole is a Whole. It contains All inside it. *A human is a part of The Whole.*

Taking a single human as the Center, The Whole can be viewed as made of three Sub-Wholes: *"The Human Whole,"* *"The Whole of Life,"* and *"The Universe."*

Figure 2

HUMAN – A PART OF THE WHOLE

Now, a thorough analysis of a human (in the center), and each of these Sub-Wholes (around a human) will show the emergence of each Sub-Whole as a bigger and bigger group around a human of which she is a close part, and how each

Sub-Whole is related to its bigger Sub-Whole, and thus "The Whole."

A Human—the Center

An individual human is the focus of my study. When we discuss The Whole we need a center point from where we start, and where we come back to. I take it as a human: one single human being, be it a woman or a man. Now I will show in steps how a single human is a close part of each of the Sub-Wholes around her, and how each Sub-Whole is a part of its bigger Sub-Whole, and finally how all of these put together constitute One Whole.

The Human Whole

A human's immediate Sub-Whole is "The Human Whole" of which a human is an integral part. A Human is born, lives, and dies in The Human Whole, not in a jungle.

The Human Whole is our human made world in which we humans live. It is a world made of the humans, by the humans, for the humans. The Human Whole is made of us All—some 7 billion humans—the Humanity, and our—Humanity's Cumulative Achievements in all aspects of the human life.

A human, since birth lives and functions within certain groups of humans: "Family," "Society," "Country," and "Humanity." These are the natural groupings of humans that have evolved over thousands of years of human civilization around a single human to fulfill her/his various survival needs.

We humans live in a human made world, not in a jungle. Everything we need and everything we use has been created by humans. For example, right now I am sitting at my <u>study table</u>, writing with a <u>pen </u>on <u>paper</u>, under the <u>light</u> of an <u>electrical lamp</u>. Each of these—<u>the study table</u>, <u>the pen</u>, <u>the paper</u>, <u>the electric light</u>, and <u>the electrical lamp</u>—was created by some human(s). There is this <u>computer</u> lying in front of me, a <u>clock</u>, and few <u>books </u>on the side. Each of these—<u>the computer, the clock, and the books</u>—was created by some human(s). The <u>house</u> I live in, the<u> air conditioner</u> that keeps my house cool, the <u>electric light</u> that lights my house, the <u>car </u>I drive, the <u>plane</u> I fly in—each of these has been created by human. I live in a well-planned <u>city</u> with well-paved <u>roads</u>, with a beautiful <u>park</u>, a <u>school</u>, and a <u>hospital</u>. Each of these—<u>the city, the roads, the park, the school, the hospital</u> —has been created by humans to fulfill various human needs.

<u>Our Universities, our Libraries, our Museums, our Bridges, our Dams, and our Skyscrapers; the dazzling array of our Achievements in Arts, Science, and Medicine; our Rockets, and our Space Shuttles</u>— all of these sing the glory of the human brain and the human labor that created them.

I call all of these— the things we humans need and use, our Cumulative Achievements. They are Achievements because they have been created and maintained by billions of humans' labor during thousands of years of human history. And, they are Cumulative because all human societies in countries all across the globe have contributed to this Common Pool of Humanity's Achievements.

Our Human Whole is a human Construct built brick by brick, by billions of humans, over thousands of years of humanity's history. As we will see in following pages how each of these human groups— "Family," "Society," "Country," and "Humanity"—arose over time to fulfill certain human needs. And, we will see how each and everything we humans use—starting from our daily need items, like <u>Food, Clothes, Housing to our Cities, Skyscrapers, and Space shuttles and to our Advanced knowledge in Art, Science, and Technology</u>—all of these and each of these was created by some human(s) in the past to fulfill human needs.

Today we humans live in ***The Palace of The Human Whole***, constructed by the humans during thousands of years of humanity's history. This Human Whole is like a palace under construction. We got this palace from our ancestors, we add on our achievements to it, make it better, and leave it to our children. Our children, in turn, will make it more beautiful than they found it and will leave it to their children, who in turn will beautify it more and leave it to their children, and so on.

This was a breezy overview of The Human Whole. In order to understand the sheer depth, vastness, and magnitude of "The Human Whole", we need to analyze it from the beginning, understand each of its components, and record its growth from beginning till present.

When we take a human as the Center, The Human Whole can be viewed as increasing groups of humans around a single human (groups of *Family, Society, Country,* and *Humanity*), and their *Cumulative Achievements* in all aspects of the human life. The following diagram will make it clearer.

Figure 3

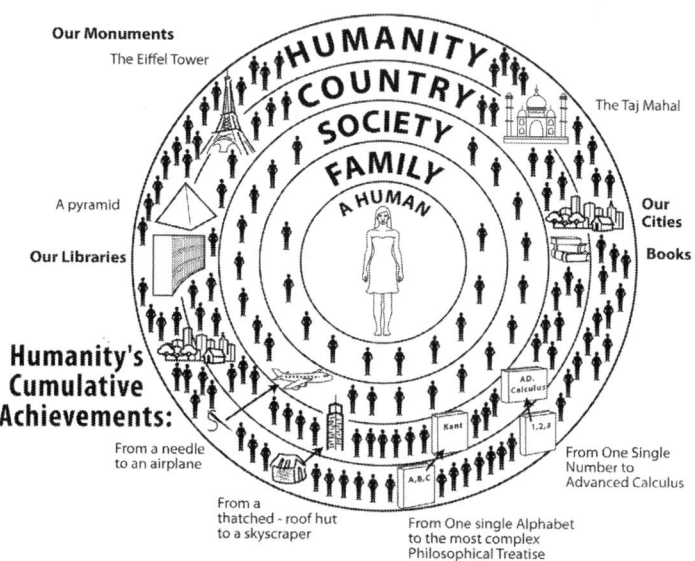

THE HUMAN WHOLE
A network of a human's family, society, country, humanity
and their cumulative achievements in all aspects of the human life

Now we will see the make of each of these groups and how a human individual is part of each of these in her being and by her actions. We will also see how each Sub-Group is related to its bigger Sub-Group, and how all our Achievements are Cumulative—achieved and shared by all countries and their humans—and how they all build up One Human Whole.

A Human in the Center

Once again, as a reminder, I have taken a human individual— be it a woman or a man as The Center of The Whole. I will analyze The Whole from this angle— how an individual human is related to each Sub-Whole, and the part she or he plays in making of each Sub-Whole, and The Whole.

Family

Family is the first natural group of humans around a human. A human, throughout her lifetime goes through two sets of families: First Family— Family by Birth, and Second Family— Family by Marriage. A human is born and reared in her First family— Family by Birth. Sometime during adulthood a human marries, produces children, and creates her Second Family— Family by Marriage.

First Family—Family by Birth

A human is born as the most helpless infant, who requires twenty-four hours' care and attention during the first few years to survive; and constant care and rearing in later years, till (s)he becomes an adult of twenty+ years. It is a Newborn's birth parents (or parents by adoption in rare cases), siblings, and other blood relatives who give her constant care, attention, and guidance till she becomes an adult. This group of humans is a human's First Family or Family by Birth. They are naturally attached to the newborn child because of blood relations, and because of living together.

<u>Definition of First Family</u>

A human's First Family is comprised of her/his Parents (Mother and Father), siblings (sisters and brothers), and other blood relatives, like grandmother, grandfather, aunt(s), uncle(s), and cousin(s).

A human is born and reared in her First Family. It is in the cradle of her First Family where a human first opens her eyes and is cared for and reared. It is in here that she is fed, comforted, and protected for twenty-four hours a day during the first few years after birth. It is in here where she first learns how to walk, talk; study or not study; and work or be lazy. It is in here where she grows up moment by moment, day by day amid the love and care of, and in close company of her parents, siblings, and other relatives. She sleeps with them, eats with them, and plays with them. She is chided and guided by them every moment as to what to do and what not to do. Thus she grows deeply attached to all of her First Family members, especially those who love her and care for her the most. Thus she learns a deep set of her do's and don'ts— her lifelong Values that shape her future life and guide her for the rest of her life.

Consequently, a human's First Family remains a very close part of her deep Self—"my Mother," "my Father," "my Sister," "my Brother," "my Grandma," "my Grandpa," etc. throughout her lifetime. A human derives her First, Prime identity from them. They are her roots in this world. It is amid them that she spends the most formative years of her life—her gradually building being. Attachments she forms (Prime bonds with her parents and siblings); do's and don'ts that she learns every day for every small act of hers; and Values (things and acts valued and taught most by her elders, like 'Family,' 'Study,' 'Profession,' and so on) remain with her throughout her whole lifetime. Thus a human's First Family is the most integral part of her existence and deep Self. This is the prime platform on which she stands, survives, and imbibes her lifelong Values during the first few weakest, most formative years of her life.

Derivative Right Way of Living

A human needs a strong, loving First Family in order to survive, and live well for the first twenty years of her life. This makes Family one of the most valued institutions in a human's life and in a human society. A human ought to marry, build, and maintain a strong family (as we will see later too). Also, a human ought to maintain her ties with her First Family throughout her life. *"Care, Communicate, and Support"* are three key do's to maintain one's family ties. Doing so keeps one connected to her roots, her prime identity, and gives her a deep satisfaction— a satisfaction unmatched by any of her other relationships.

Second Family—Family by Marriage

Sometime during adulthood a human marries, produces children, and acquires a Second Family or Family by Marriage.

Definition of Second Family—Family by Marriage

A human's Second Family—Family by Marriage, consists of a human's spouse (a female wife or a male husband), In-Laws (Spouse's family), and Children—Sons and Daughters.

A Human's Second Family is another group of humans amid whom a human lives and functions from adulthood to the end of her life. A human acquires her Second Family by Marriage. By Marriage she acquires a spouse, a set of In-Laws (Spouse's family), and children. This makes marriage one of the most important institutions in a human society. It is by a Marriage that a human acquires and retains her Second Family.

Since time immemorial, marriage has been one of the most valued institutions in every human society. Marriage is a social, legal, and sacred (as we will see later too), religious bond that unites a woman and a man into the lifelong bond of their mutual Support, Sex (including sexual faithfulness), Companionship, and Child(ren). Marriage creates, maintains and tracks a human's Family. This fact makes Marriage the Founding Stone of a human Family and a human Society.

Marriage unites a woman and a man, and their families. After marriage a woman and a man live together as "Wife" and "Husband" to each other; support each other financially and personally, and in every day's tasks; have sex together; give company to each other; and produce and rear their own children.

After marriage a human acquires a Spouse and a set of In-Laws (Spouse's Family). Sometime after marriage, the married couple (the wife and husband) produces their own children and rears them. They watch their child(ren) twenty-four hours a day, give them a home, and fulfill their all economic and other needs from birth up to her adulthood.

After acquiring a Second Family, a human's roles and responsibilities change. A woman has to fulfill certain duties of being a "Wife" to her husband, of being a "Daughter In-Law" to her husband's family, and of being a "Mother" to her children. Similarly, a man has to fulfill duties of being a "Husband" to his wife, of being a "Son-In-Law" to his wife's family, and of being a "Father" to his children. Every society has its own duties for each role. These are major roles and entail heavy responsibilities, but they have their immense gains too. Thereby a human gets lifelong support, company, and warmth of his Second Family.

Now a human has to be a provider and caretaker for her/his family. She has to assume responsibilities for her spouse and children. She works, earns money, and fulfills the economic needs of her Second Family. At the same time she has to give time, company, and personal care to her spouse, in-laws, and children. Now a human spends most of her time with her Second Family. Consequently she creates and forms an emotional bonding with her spouse and children. She grows emotionally attached to her Second Family. They become a part of her Self— "my husband" (or wife as applicable), "my child(ren)" et cetera. A human grows especially attached to her children. She views and treats them as parts of her own flesh and blood, of her own Self. A parent-child relationship is one of the closest human bonds.

Thus we see how a human remains an integral part of her family throughout her whole lifetime. During the first twenty years, she is emotionally and economically attached to her First Family or Family by Birth. Then, during the later part of her life, she grows emotionally and economically attached to her Second Family— Family by Marriage. Both families are big groups of humans of which a human remains a part throughout her lifetime.

Definition of "Family"

A human's family is a group of humans related to her by blood or by marriage.

Derivative Right Way of Living

Family is one of the most important institutions in human society. A human is born and reared in the cradle of her First Family—Family by Birth. She needs its love and support in order to survive, and grow as a happy and successful human being. Later, she marries and acquires her Second Family—Family by Marriage in which she lives for the rest of her life. She needs the love and support of her Second Family in order to cope successfully with the daily demands of life and feel emotionally secure.

Family is a ship of love and protection in the rough, hostile ocean of life. It gives a human love, support, and warmth of her own people— people who care for her. At the same time, it provides her with a strong foothold from which she operates from birth until death. A human needs a strong and loving family in order to survive, and live as a happy and successful human being throughout her/his lifetime.

Keeping its value in mind, a human ought to view her family as a lifelong Value that she acquires, maintains, and cherishes. As an adult human, she ought to keep in touch with her First Family through "Care, Communicate, and Support." Maintaining emotional ties with her parents, siblings, and other First family relatives keeps her connected to her roots, nourishes her emotionally, and makes her happy.

A human as an Adult ought to marry, produce and rear her own children from marriage and create and maintain her Second Family. A strong and happy marriage and constant spousal support help a human grow and succeed in life. Having one's own child(ren) brings out a human's best, makes her moral, and emotionally tender. Having and rearing her own children gives her direction, purpose, and meaning in life.

Thus we see how family is the very first group of humans of which a human remains an integral part from her birth until death. She needs her family in order to survive and live well. She is affected by the kind of family she has, and she affects her family by what she does for them.

Society

A human, and her family in turn, are parts of a bigger Whole— the Society. A society is a big group of humans amid whom a human lives and functions. A human is deeply tied to her society. She needs it, depends upon it for the fulfillment of her various needs, and cannot live outside it.

Like family, a society is a natural grouping of humans that emerged over time to fulfill a variety of human needs. A human is a very weak living being who needs the company of other humans and a large number of things and services in order to survive and live well. First, she or he needs to live in the company of other humans for safety and human interaction. Then she needs a number of things for her survival and comfort. She needs food, clothes, shelter, and hordes of other products and services to live. She cannot produce them all on her own. She needs to buy them from others. These various needs of a human gave birth to a society.

That is why a human, since the beginning, always lived in a society. A human society starting from the very basic rudimentary form of a "Herd," got bigger and more complex over time, went through other forms of a "Tribe," an "Agricultural Society," an "Industrial society," and finally leading to the "Industrial-cum-Information Age Society" of today.

In the very beginning of humanity's history, some thousands of years back, a human lived in a herd. A herd was a small group of humans who lived together, defended themselves from other animals and calamities together, collected and hunted food together, and distributed food amongst themselves. Each herd member contributed her or his skills and labor toward the fulfillment of these common needs of all herd members. Each did what she or he could and what she or he was good at. Women did the simple job of collecting fruits and berries from a jungle, while men did the harder job of hunting. One built sticks and arrows, while other(s) shot them. One built fire, while other(s) cooked food. Thus all heard members lived together, worked together, and kept the herd together. And, in the process, each member got food, shelter, and company of other humans.

Slowly, over time, humans became more settled and formed a larger group— a "Tribe." While a herd wandered from place to place, a tribe settled down and lived in one place. A tribe was a bigger group of humans, which meant more safety and better resources for all group members. Therefore, a human preferred to live in a tribe. When a large number of humans lived together, there arose disputes among them. Thus arose the need for a Chieftain to resolve their disputes. Therefore, each tribe had a Chieftain to solve its disputes and also to lead the tribe.

As humans became more settled, they started making better weapons to defend themselves, tried to grow food, and tried to domesticate animals for their use. Very slowly and gradually over time, this gave birth to an "Agricultural society." In an agricultural society, a very large number of humans lived in one place, grew their food, and domesticated animals. Now a human was safe and well fed, and had a lot of spare time to do other things. Every human did what she or he could and what she or he was good at. Different fields of Labor arose. Using her precious knowledge, now a human made much better weapons; came up with better farming techniques; introduced writing; and then started developing Art, Music, Literature, and various Sciences. Different fields of labor were introduced by humans, which future generations built upon and improvised.

With time, different societies became stronger and more civilized and cultured. Societies grew and resources were better utilized. This gave birth to an "Industrial society." In an Industrial society, the products and services of humans need were manufactured and sold at massive rates by huge factories and industries. More and more humans, including women got jobs, and the human population grew.

Today we humans live in an "Industrial-cum-Information age Society"— the biggest and most complex, but most well-connected society so far. Different countries are well connected by strong trade ties, and the economy of one country affects those of others. Humans all over the globe are connected by fast means of communication—like radio, TV, newspapers, the postal service, phone, and above all the Internet. Some two billion people all over the world communicate with one another by Internet. This is something like a global society, in which people from all over the world are connected to one another by trade and communication, and affect one another's lives and thinking.

This was a short summary of different types of human societies, which emerged over a long period of humanity's history to fulfill common human needs of living together for safety, interaction, and support.

The term *"society"* literally means company of other humans. A society can be a group of humans living together in the same neighborhood, town, village, or city. But people merely living in the same area do not create a society. A crowd of people living in one place without being connected to each other is just a crowd, not a society. People need to be related or connected to one another in order to form a society. There are certain unseen ties which connect one human to another in a society. They work like strings and create the Canopy of a society. These are the ties of a human's personal and business relationships. These relationships form the basic fabric of a human society. A human needs and forms these relationships in order to survive and live well. We can imagine a human individual in the Center, and strings of her personal and business relationships with other humans. *A society, in fact, is a network of a human's personal and business relationships.*

One's personal relationships are those with family and friends. A human connects to and relates to a large number of other humans through her personal relationships. She has a number of family and friends whom she connects to, or relates to. A human, throughout her lifetime is bonded and connected to both her families— First Family or Family by Birth, and Second Family or Family by Marriage. As we saw earlier, how she is emotionally and economically related to a large number of other humans in her First Family like her parents, siblings, aunts, uncles, and cousins et cetera. And, she is emotionally and economically related to a number of other humans in her Second Family—like spouse, children, and in-laws. Together with family, a human connects to a number of other humans with friendship. Friendship, like any other relationship, is an emotional bond of mutual care and support between two individuals. A human in her course of daily life meets a number of other humans, tends to like some of them, shares common interests, and makes friends with them. She communicates with her friends, spends time with them, and helps them in their need— personally and financially.

A human, besides her personal relationships is related to a large number of other humans through her business relationships. Business relationships are primarily of two types: as a "Buyer" and as a "Seller."

A human needs a variety of products and services in order to survive and live well. Primarily she needs food, clothes, and home, and then she needs an endless number of products and services for her comfort and enjoyment. She cannot produce them all on her own. So she buys them from those who have them— an individual owner, a retail store, or a business firm. This creates the relationship of a "Buyer" and a "Seller." This relationship is solely economic, in which a human buys things from a Seller with money. Through this relationship a human connects to a large number of other humans directly or indirectly.

A human at the same time, also connects to a large number of other humans as a "Seller" of her "work" or profession. One's work may be in the form of a business or a job. A human either operates her own business or works for some one—an employer. A businessperson manufactures or sells a product(s) or a service(s). As a manufacturer she can be a farmer, an owner of a factory or an industry producing goods, a singer, a lawyer, or a doctor running her own practice and selling her services to others.

As a businessperson, a human is connected to all her clients and buyers— those who buy her products and services. For example, I run a law firm. I sell my services to my clients who need them. Through this business relationship I am connected to all my clients—buyers who buy my services.

A human may do a "job" or work for an employer. This is also a business relationship, in which a human provides services to her employer for money. This creates one's workplace relationships, in which a human connects to her employer, her colleagues, other workers, and her firm's clients or buyers.

Thus a human (an individual) is connected to a large number of other humans as a "Buyer" of their products and services; and as a "Seller" of her own "work" or profession. This creates a network of a human's business relationships—another string that ties a human to her society, and a chief building block of a human society. *We can envision a society as a vast canopy tying one human to another by the strings of personal and business relationships.*

A society is also a vast pool of a large number of products and services that fulfill various human needs.

At times within a society, there exist a large number of sub-societies. A sub- society is a small group of humans tied together by a common culture or purpose. It can be a religious, ethnic, professional, or some other group— like a Christian society, Jewish society, Lawyers' society, or a Single-Parent society.

The above analysis brings up certain key components on the basis of which we can define a human society.

Definition of Human Society

A society is a large group of humans living together and tied to one another by their common interests; personal relationships, business relationships; or by some common culture or goal. Some of the building blocks of a society are a family; a group of friends, neighbors, colleagues; and a Sub-society or an organization.

In sum, *A Society is a network of a human's personal and business relationships, and a vast reservoir of various products and services that a human needs for her survival, comfort, and happiness.*

Human: A Part of Society

A human is an integral part of the society in which she lives and which she deals with. A society is a large number of other humans to whom an individual is connected by her living amid them, by her personal and business relationships, by her work or profession, and by her membership in a Sub-society.

A human is a part of her neighborhood, town, or city— people amid whom she lives. She is connected to them by the fact of her living with them, which creates certain interests common to its all members, like their safety and well being. A human's personal and business relationships are the prime strings that tie her to a large number of other humans. Her personal relationships are all her family and friends to whom she is emotionally and economically attached. A human's family and friends provide a big emotional and economic support to her.

A human, at the same time connects to a large number of other humans through her business relationships. She is connected to them both as a "Buyer" and as a "Seller." As a '"Buyer" she is connected to all those "Manufacturers" and "Sellers" whose products and services she buys. For example, I as an individual am connected to all those people who sold me the house I live in, the car I drive, and who produce and sell me the food I eat, the clean water which I drink, the clothes I wear, the electricity I use, the newspaper I read, and each and every thing I use in my daily life. There is a large network of people behind all this who produce and sell these products and services to me. I am connected to all of them as a "Buyer" of their products and services.

At the same time, a human connects to a large number of other humans as a "Seller" to whom she sells her own products and services by her "work" or profession. A human works or indulges in a profession through which she sells products and services to others. For example, a businessperson who sells watches connects to all her buyers through her business relationships as a "Seller." And a lawyer who sells her services connects to all her clients through her business relationships as a "Seller." Also at a workplace— a factory, a store, or an office— a human connects to her boss, supervisors, and colleagues through her business relationships.

"Work" or profession is the chief mode through which a human connects to a large number of people in her society. Through her work she affects many people and their lives. One's work may be in the form of one's business or a job.

Thus a human is a close part of her society. She is deeply connected to a large number of people by the fact of her living amid them, by her personal and business relationships, and by her work or profession.

Since a human is an integral part of her society *she is deeply affected by it, and she affects it too.*

A human is deeply affected by her immediate society— the society in which she lives and deals with. She is affected

66

by the kind of people she lives amid and deals with which includes all her personal relationships with her family, friends, and neighbors; and her business relationships with her colleagues, clients, and customers et cetera. She is affected by their cultures— their beliefs, their Values, and their ways of living, whether they believe in God or not, whether they value family or individuality, whether they value work or laziness, whether they are moral or immoral, whether they are honest or dishonest, the kind of food they eat, and the kind of clothes they wear et cetera. A human grows up and lives, watching them every day and dealing with them at every step. She slowly gets colored in the culture of her immediate society. She develops the same beliefs, the same Values, and adopts the same way of living. She starts thinking and acting the same way.

Besides culture, a human is affected by the economy of her immediate society. A rich and productive society opens many doors for an individual's growth, and offers a variety of products and services; whereas a poor and unproductive society hinders a person's growth, and offers a limited number of products and services for one's use and enjoyment. Thus a human is deeply affected by the culture and economy of her immediate society.

A human affects her society too. However weak an individual may seem in front of her society and its culture, she does play an important part in shaping it the way it is. She affects her society by her own beliefs, Values, and her way of living. An individual by her way of living is a walking example for others. She affects the people around her by the way she thinks and acts. She affects her family, friends, neighbors, clients, and colleagues by her Values, talks, by her actions, and by her behavior. For example, if you are God-fearing and hardworking, you consciously or unconsciously motivate me to be the same; if you are compassionate and helpful in your personal relationships, and honest and punctual in business relationships, you—by your living example will encourage others to behave the same way, and more so if others see some good coming out of it. On the other hand, if you are apathetic and selfish in personal relationships; dishonest and unpunctual in business relationships and "work," you— by your living example will encourage others to behave the same way.

An individual is an important agent of her society and a catalyst too. She, by her own actions deeply affects her society, and makes her contribution toward its growth or downfall.

A human's work or profession is the chief mode through which she affects a large number of people in her society. The type and quality of your work directly affect a large number of people who buy your products and services. Through your work you either enrich your society or harm your society. For example, an industrious and honest businessperson or worker produces the best quality of products and services, which benefit her buyers, while a lazy and dishonest business person or worker sells a poor quality of products and services that harm her buyers.

Derivative Right Way of Living

In view of a human's integral relationship with her society and her influence upon her society, a human ought to enrich her society and make it better than she found it. After all, the kind of society I live in, does affect me and my loved ones. My society's culture may have a number of vices that adversely affect me too. I ought to fight them and work toward correcting them. For example, if I live in an illiterate and superstitious society, I may start projects to educate people and make them more rational. In the process, I may change a few people, who in turn will change others.

A human's personal and business relationships are the very strings that create and hold the canopy of a society. One human's relationships with others, and others' with others— these ties form the fabric of a society. If these ties are smooth and strong, they create and maintain a well-knit and harmonious human society. And, if these ties are discordant and weak, they break the connection of one human to another and weaken the society.

I as a human ought to make my contribution toward this. For example, if I am compassionate, helpful, and honest in my personal and business relationships, I develop smooth and strong relationships with people I deal with. Compassion is the ability to understand the other person's situation and pains; and helping the other person makes her strong, and may alleviate her pains. Compassion truly bonds one human to another.

Also, if I am honest in my business relationships or work, I give a good product or service to others, which satisfies them, and they pay on time. This creates a smooth relationship between the Buyer and Seller, where both want to deal with each other. This helps a society grow economically.

Work or profession is another chief mode through which a human enriches her society. A person's work ought to be the contribution of her best to her society. First, one ought to choose a profession which best matches one's talent, education, and skills. This way she will contribute her best to her society. Second, the quality of one's work directly affects others. If one is true to her work or simply does her job well, then no matter what she works as—a sweeper, a waiter, a teacher, a lawyer, or as the president of a country— she provides excellent services to her clients and thus enriches her society. Similarly, if a person runs her own business, then she ought to give the best quality of products and services to her clients and thus enrich her society.

Country

A human, her family, and her society in turn are parts of a bigger Whole— a Country. A country houses a large number of humans, their families, and their societies within it. All of these may be diverse but are tied together as the residents or citizens of one single country.

A country, as an entity originated, and exists till date to fulfill a human's certain needs. Let us first look into the origin of a country or how a country as a separate entity developed. This will give us insight into the makings of a country, its purpose, and a human's relationship with it.

We saw earlier how a human since beginning lived in a group, which gave rise to different types of societies over a period of time, namely a herd, a tribe, an agricultural society, and finally our modern industrial-cum-information age society. It was a tribe, and later an agricultural society that eventually gave rise to a country. A tribe or an agricultural society was a group of humans who lived together in one place in a certain geographical area marked by its own boundaries. They grew their food there, domesticated animals, and made tools. Once their survival needs were fulfilled, they made progress in other fields like Art, Literature, and Science. As a group lived together in one place for centuries, its people started developing their own culture— a certain philosophy of life and a way of living that helped them survive as a group and live well. It included their total belief system, their God(s), their common Values, and their way of living. It was their common culture that tied them strongly as a group and distinguished them from other groups or societies. To date it is primarily culture that separates one group from the other group.

As a society lived together, there arose the need for a leader— someone who could control the group, keep it united, look after its interests, solve disputes, and defend and increase its territories. Possessing more land meant more resources and more power for the group. The leader arose from the group— someone who was physically strong and mentally competent to control the group, keep it united, and lead it. In a tribe, it was the Chieftain who performed these functions. He controlled the group, and his word was the law. In an agricultural society, it was a King who controlled a large number of people, looked after their interests, solved their disputes, developed his kingdom to offer its people a better living, and increased the borders of his kingdom by conquering other places.

Once a tribe or an agricultural society had all these components—lived in a fixed geographical area for years, had a common culture, and had a strong leader— a chieftain or a king to govern or protect them, it named itself as a country and was recognized so by other countries.

This is how a Country was born and lived. And this is how different countries in different parts of the world were formed. In the great history of humanity, many countries were born at different times. Some perished while others lived on.

Today we have some 196 different countries on our planet Earth. Some are old, with thousands of years of history behind them, like India, China, and Greece; while others are new— formed during the last few hundred years, like the USA, and a few others. Each country has its own territory, its own government, its own history, and its own people.

Thus we see how a country, like a human family and a human society, is a natural grouping of humans tied together by its members' common culture and common needs of safety, identity, and growth. A country needs and acquires power to protect itself and its people.

Definition of a Country

A Country is a political entity located in a specific geographical area within fixed borders; having its own territory, resources, and people controlled and governed by its government; and recognized as an independent political power by other countries in the world.

A country, like a family and like a society, is a product of human need. A country protects its resources, its people, and their cultures; fulfills their prime needs of safety, food, health, and housing; and provides opportunities for its citizens' growth and good living by a strong government and efficient legal system.

Human: A Part of Her Country

A country is the whole of which a human is a part. A country is a vast piece of land, housing millions of its citizens and residents, where each citizen and resident is deeply connected to her/his country and plays a role in shaping her/his country the way it is.

A human is a part of her country either by birth or by living in it or by both. Most humans live and work in countries of their birth, but some of them migrate to other countries, and live and work there. Especially in modern times, with fast means of transportation and communication, many people live and work in countries other than their birth countries.

A human is emotionally attached to her country of birth. One's country of birth is the country where one was born and reared and where her family and forefathers lived for generations. A human traces her roots or ancestry to her country of birth and therefore is very attached to it. Moreover, this is where she first opens her eyes, learns its language and culture, is taught patriotism in school and family, celebrates her country's Independence Day every year, sings patriotic songs in school, watches patriotic movies, and thus is gradually immersed in her country's culture and history to the extent that she views her country as a part of her deep identity and ego—"my Country." For the majority of us, "my Country" is the home country or country of birth.

In fact, a human is more directly tied to the country where she lives and works. She is tied to it economically, through her work, and through other ways. She is directly affected by this country, and she affects it too.

A human, as a resident or citizen is directly a part of the country where she lives. In this capacity, she enjoys all the rights and benefits bestowed by its government to its people. She is affected by its government's economic policies— availability of loan money, amount of taxes, and its overall policies of health, safety and others. She is affected by its constitution and its legal system.

As a resident or citizen she works, pays taxes to the government, and thus contributes to the government's earnings.

Through her work she directly affects the country where she lives and works. If she runs her own business, she comes up with new products and services and creates jobs for others. Thus she enriches her immediate society and country. If she works for someone then through her honest work she gives quality products and services to others and thus enriches her immediate society and country. She is an important part of the country's workforce which runs the country and helps it prosper. No matter what position such a person works in—as a teacher, as a doctor, as a sweeper, or as a farm-worker—she affects her immediate country—where she lives and works. She either enriches it with her hard and honest work or deteriorates it with her poor work.

Every citizen and resident of a country is an individual man or a woman who contributes his/her intelligence, resources, and hard work to that country's growth and prosperity. After all, a country is made of its people.

Derivative Right Way of Living

A human is affected by her country, and she affects it too.

A human is directly affected by the country where she lives. She is affected by the kind of place it is, the kind of people she lives amid, their Values, and their culture. She learns their values and culture. She is affected by the kind of government the country has, its policies, and its administration. If it is liberal and efficient, she benefits from it. If it is orthodox and ineffi-cient, she is harmed by it. She is affected by its legal system. She enjoys all legal rights and benefits of a fair legal system. A rich and strong country helps its citizens grow and prosper, while a poor and weak country hampers their growth.

A human, as a resident or a citizen directly affects her country. She affects it by being the type of individual she is and the type of citizen she is and by her work. If she is educated, industrious, and honest; has a broad worldview; and does good quality work she contributes to her country's growth and prosperity. If she is uneducated, lazy, and dishonest; has a narrow worldview; does not work or does poor quality work; she contributes to her country's downfall and poverty. As a good and law-abiding citizen, she helps her country run smoothly. She reports untoward incidents to authorities, is alert to government's functioning, votes, and helps choose a good and efficient government.

A person's work or profession is the chief mode through which she affects her country. Through her work or labor in a specific field, she enriches her country directly.

Since a human is deeply affected by the kind of country she lives in, she would want it to be a great country—a rich, prosperous, and peaceful country with a strong government and an excellent legal system. And since she plays an important role in shaping her country she ought to enrich her country by being an educated, industrious, honest, and law-abiding resident and citizen.

In sum, every individual plays an important role in shaping her country. Knowing this, a human ought to enrich her country. The old adage is right: "Ask not what your country can do for you; ask what you can do for your country." (John F. Kennedy)

Humanity

Tracing from the beginning, we saw how a human (an individual) since birth is a part of her family; how a human and her family, in turn, are parts of a bigger group, a society; and how a human, her family, and her society, in turn, are parts of a bigger group, a country. A human and her country, in turn, are parts of Humanity—the largest group of humans. Humanity is made of its All seven billion humans living in some two hundred (actual figure 196) different countries all over the Earth.

Humanity, though One in reality, is a Conglomerate of starkly different humans and starkly different countries. I often compare Humanity to the multi-faceted face of a woman mounted on a podium, whose each facet has a different look and expression. As you swing the face, a totally different facet appears. One facet is that of poor and destitute humans living in underdeveloped and overpopulated countries. As you swing it again a little, another facet appears— that of wealthy and joyous humans living in well-developed and sparsely populated coun-tries. You swing it a little again, and you see another facet of illiterate and gross tribal people living in jungles, in their dark world of ignorance and superstitions without any confidence and dreams. You swing it again, and there appears another facet of educated and sophisticated humans living in a free, shining world of knowledge, full of dreams and self-confidence.

This is the face of Humanity— though One, but made of extremely disparate facets of humans and nations, divided by chasms of wealth, education, freedom, and other differences.

Its seven billion humans forming One of humanity are so different. They differ in their colors, races, religions, and nationalities. Some are white, while others are brown and black. Some are Asians, while others are Caucasians, Hispanic, Native Americans, and so on. Humans are divided from one another by their religion too. Some are Hindus, while others are Muslims. Some are Christians, while others are Buddhists, and so on. Humans are further divided by their camps of nationality too.

A person born in England considers herself English and looks at others with hostility and suspicion; a person born in America considers herself an American and views others as aliens; a person born in China views herself as Chinese and others as outsiders, and so on.

But a little peek into the undercurrent of humanity will show us that these differences are surface and superficial. They make no difference to the inner make of a human, deep human sentiments, human potential, and common human aspirations and dreams. Every human is Evolved, Multi-Dimensional, and a Part of the Whole. All of us feel the same deep human sentiments of love, hate, jealousy, and compassion. Every human has the hidden potential of receiving a good education, developing her intellect, working, and doing well in life. All of us want peace and prosperity and healthy and happy lives for us and our children. All of us need a calm and quiet Earth to live and prosper.

Then there are unseen ties that connect one human to another. These are ties of family, ties of society, ties of country, and above all the tie of human compassion. As we saw earlier, a human is deeply connected to her family, her society, and her country. These are sub-groups of humanity that connect one human to others.

Human compassion is the strongest tie that connects one human to another and even to strangers. Compassion is that unique human sentiment by which one human understands and feels the other person's pains and situation and is motivated to help her. It is by compassion that a human aids others, even strangers, in their troubles and crises. Examples of this can be seen in crises like war, famine, flood, and earthquake, where humans living in one part of the world reach out to aid humans living in other parts of the world. A large number of international nonprofit organizations are run by donations given by people to aid strangers.

Moreover, today we humans live in an information age connected by fast means of transportation and communication. Through the thick network of domestic and international flights, a human can travel the length and breadth of her country and even the whole globe within a few hours. This facilitates their business and personal meetings. Mass media and the Internet inform us about one another and help us communicate fast. Some 4.5 billion humans are connected by international TV channels, phone, and the Internet. Media informs us about other people living in distant parts of the world, their cultures, their problems, their pains and crises. All these means of communication tie us together.

Human compassion, together with wonders of air flights, mass media, and the Internet have created a global village where millions of humans exchange information, communicate, connect, and aid one another.

Thus we see how humans, though different on the surface, are all alike in their makes and dreams and are deeply connected.

All these seven billion humans live in 196 different countries— another component of Humanity. These countries differ greatly in their sizes, histories, their peoples, their resources, and their political power. Some countries are big while others are small; some countries have thousands of years of old history while others are new; some countries' average people are educated and industrious while others' are uneducated and lazy; some countries have plenty of natural resources while others have few; some countries are rich and developed while others are poor and underdeveloped; some countries have strong and well-run governments while others are marked by anarchy and unstable governments. Finally, countries differ in their political power and foreign policy. Some are strong and dominating while others are weak and submissive.

But, as with humans, there are strong, unseen ties which connect all 196 different countries and create *One of Humanity*. Countries are tied by ties of neighborhood; culture, knowledge, and other exchanges; pacts, trade, and treaties; and aid to one another in crisis.

Countries located close to one another share common borders, like the USA, Canada, and Mexico in the West, and India and Pakistan in the East and thus they have an easy interflow of people and products among them. Different countries of the world differ greatly in their resources, culture, knowledge, level of development, and strength. They need each other's products, knowledge, and support in crisis. For example, some are rich in oil while others are rich in food and edible crops, or in technology. They need each other's products. Countries differ from one another in their achievements in art, music, and sports. Each country has its own pool of unique achievements in art, science, and technology. They share them with one another by various means. These countries differ in their sizes and strength. Some are small and weak, while others are big and powerful. Weak countries need powerful countries' support and aid in crisis.

Countries sign pacts and trade treaties through which they export and import a large variety of products and services from one another in different areas of human life ranging from daily need items like food, clothing, cars, and planes to electrical appliances, science and technology. Different countries' achievements in art, culture, and science seep in to others. A large number of books, paintings, sculptures, and other art products are exchanged among countries. Music and movies are exchanged amid different countries on a vast scale and very rapidly too. Yoga, meditation, and religion originating in one country are taught in many other countries. International trade shows, cultural shows, and sports are held in which different countries display their own products and achievements. Thus they inform and enrich each other. The Olympics—a world sports event, is a symbol of all countries' unity in one field. In science and technology countries export and import from each other a great deal of knowledge; a large number of electrical appliances, and electronic goods; computer technology, and rocket and space shuttle technology. All this interflow of products, art, culture, and science among different countries inform people of these countries about one another and enrich them. These also affect their own cultures, thinking, and ways of living.

Treaties of trade, and cultural and scientific exchange connect different countries in neutral pacts and relationships.

Countries also sign peace treaties with each other through which they promise to maintain cordial ties and not attack each other.

Countries aid one another in crises and calamities like floods, earthquakes, and wars. They provide each other with food, resources, and military assistance as and when needed.

Thus we see how all 196 countries are interconnected by the same neighborhood; trade and other exchanges; treaties, pacts, and mutual aid.

Today, fast means of transportation and communication and strong trade relations have connected all countries like never before, and have created one global village marked by global culture and global economy. Metros of different countries share a common culture of fast food, music, movies, and other cultural values. International corporations have manufacturing plants in one country and distribution and branch offices in other countries. These, together with strong trade relations, have tied the economies of different countries into one economy whereby stocks' ups and dips in one country affect stocks and the general economy in other countries as well. Economic recession and depression in one country slows down the economies in other countries.

This emergence of a global village with a global economy indicates how different humans and different countries are actually connected by many unseen ties and thus create *One of Humanity.*

We humans all over the world are further connected by our common human needs and aspirations. All of us need clean air, clean water, and a rich vibrant Earth to live on. All of us want to live good lives ourselves and leave a better world to our children. We all breathe the same air. Polluted air flows from one part of the Earth to the other. Our oceans are interconnected. Seawater flows from one ocean to others. Massive amounts of chemicals and pollutants are poured into our rivers and oceans every day, which pollute our waters. Overpopulation, deforestation, and air and water pollution in one country affect other countries and kill many other forms of Life, whom we all need for our own survival.

All of these tie us—we seven billion humans, and our 196 different countries—into *One of Humanity.*

Definition of Humanity

Humanity is the largest group of All—seven billion humans, tied by their common human needs, dreams, and human compassion; living in 196 different countries, which are further tied by their mutual treaties, trade, and other relations, interflow of products and knowledge and thus All creating One of Humanity. **Humanity is One.**

Human: A Part of Humanity

Humanity is the largest group of humans, containing three sub-groups of Family, Society, and Country within it. It is a collection of all 196 countries housing seven billion humans. As we saw earlier, how a human is a close part of her Family, Society, and her Country.

A human is a part of Humanity simply by being a human. After all, humanity is made of its all seven billion humans. Humanity is a vast collection of humans of which every single human is a unit. A human is tied to other humans by information, communication; human compassion; the same human needs and goals; by her work; and by her child(ren).

Today we humans live in a global village, well connected and run by fast modes of communication and transportation. A human living in one part of the world is well connected to and informed about other humans living in other parts of the world. She can communicate and talk to other people living in far-off countries by phone and the Internet. TV, radio, and newspapers inform us about other humans living in distant countries, their living conditions, and their crises.

We see other humans. We are moved by their conditions and are motivated to help them. This is human compassion, through which one human understands another human's pains and helps her. Compassion connects even strangers.

Further, a human is connected to other humans by common human needs and goals. All of us need a clean and green Earth to live on. We need to live, and let other forms of Life live too. We need them for our survival.

A human is tied to other humans by her work too. Through her work she affects not only her own Society and Country but also people of other countries too. A writer's books are read all over the world. A scientist's discovery enriches all of us. A doctor's medicines work for all humans. Work ties one human to other humans on a vast scale.

The Child is another prime mode through which a human connects to and enriches her Humanity. Every single child is one addition to the group of humanity. A human leaves the best of her talents and Values in the form of her child(ren), who will form the future Humanity. At the same time, a human ought to keep the fact in mind that all of us share one Earth Home with limited resources. Through her number of children, a human either contributes to overpopulation or helps keep world population in check.

A human's "work" and "child" are the two most lasting modes through which a human enriches her Humanity.

Derivative Right Way of Living

Humanity is the largest group of All humans tied by their common human needs and aspirations. It is a cumulative total of humans and their actions. Every single human is a part of humanity simply by being a human; is affected by it; and affects it too by her own actions.

I as a human ought to have a concept of humanity and view it as One. I am affected by other humans, their living conditions, their pains and poverty. I am affected by the kind of world I live in— less populated, peaceful, prosperous, and clean or over-populated, war-torn, poor, and dirty. Economies and exchanges of countries are tied up. Conditions in one country affect other countries as well.

I as a human affect the humanity by my own worldview and actions. I either enrich it or harm it. After all, humanity is a group made of its subgroups of family, society and country, and its seven billion humans. Every subgroup affects it, and every single human affects and contributes to humanity the way it is.

In view of a human's close connection to humanity, a human ought to enrich it by her own worldview, actions, work, and child(ren).

I as a human ought to view humanity as One, made of us seven billion humans. I ought to view other humans not on the basis of their color, creed, or nationality but as simple humans, just like me, with the same human needs and dreams; and nurture goodwill towards them, and view the other as—"I am a human" and "you are a human." I ought to view all humans with compassion and goodwill.

I as a human ought to understand the Oneness of Humanity and work towards global peace and prosperity. I contribute my share to it by living in peace and harmony with others and by being an industrious and responsible human.

I as a human share this Earth with seven billion other humans and trillions of other forms of Life. All of us need a clean and green Earth to live on. We humans need to live and thrive, and let other forms of Life live and thrive too. We need them for our survival. Maintaining a safe environment is the key to this.

Our actions affect one another. Air flows the same all over the Earth. Polluted air flows from one part of the world to other parts and pollutes it too. Polluted seawater from one country's seas flows to the seas of other countries and pollutes it too. Massive amounts of pollutants and chemicals are poured into our rivers and oceans every day, which pollute our waters and kill many other forms of life, whom we all need for our survival. They need to survive and thrive in order for "The Whole of Life" to go on. Moreover, overpopulation and deforestation are causing massive extinction of other forms of life.

"I as a human ought to cause less pollution, grow more plants, and have fewer children." This will be my contribution to keeping our Earth clean and green. This is *Svadharma*—doing my share of work.

A human can contribute to causing less pollution by reducing the use of pollution-causing things—like using less plastic; driving smog-free cars, using carpools or public transport; and using less of Air conditioners and other electrical equipments.

All of us share our Earth Home. Our Earth has limited resources, and human population is growing at an alarming rate. Overpopulation is causing grave economic problems, deforestation, and extinction of other forms of life. Every human plays a role in increasing or decreasing human population. A human ought to have fewer children, a maximum of two. This will be her share in controlling the human population.

"Work" and "Child" are the two prime modes through which a human enriches her Human Whole and Humanity. These two give the most lasting meanings to human life. ***I as a human will die one day but will leave behind my work and my child(ren) to The Human Whole.***

My work is the contribution of my best to my Whole. I as a human ought to find the best of my talents, make a profession of it, and enrich the Humanity. As we will see in the following pages, all achievements of humanity are the results of human "work" only. A human ought to choose a work or profession that exhibits the best of her talents, knowledge, and skills.

A "Child" is a symbol of a human's highest Values and dreams that she contributes to her humanity. A human ought to conceive and rear her child with this view.

In sum, Humanity is a vast whole of which a human is a part. A human ought to understand this, have a large worldview, and enrich the Humanity by her actions, "work," and "child." Living motto for a human is, *"Have a concept of the Whole of humanity, her connection to it, develop compassion for others, cause less pollution, have fewer children, and leave behind her best in the form of her 'work' and 'child' who will make the Humanity more beautiful."*

Cumulative Achievements of Humanity

A human, her Family, her Society, her Country, and Humanity— a group of all 196 countries and their All seven billion humans— live in a human made world, a world made of the humans, by the humans, for the humans. This is the Human Whole— the world of humans, their products, their services, and their Achievements.

We humans live in a human made world, not in a jungle. Everything we use and live by has been created and maintained by humans. For example, my safe and comfortable <u>home</u> I live in, <u>the clothes</u> I wear, <u>the food</u> I eat, <u>the things I use</u> every day— my <u>phone,</u> my <u>computer</u>, <u>radio</u>, <u>TV</u>, <u>the car</u> I drive, <u>the plane</u> I fly in— all of these and each and everything we use has been created and maintained by humans. Our well-planned, safe <u>cities</u> with their <u>parks</u>, <u>schools</u>, and <u>hospitals</u>; our <u>monuments,</u> our <u>museums,</u> our <u>libraries,</u> our <u>universities,</u> our <u>hospitals;</u> our huge <u>shopping malls,</u> our <u>skyscrapers</u> and <u>bridges</u>—all of these are the creations of the human mind and the human labor only.

This magnificent Human Whole, our human made world we live in, was not created in a day or two but is the Product of humanity's thousands of years' hard labor. I say Humanity because all our Achievements are exchanged and enter into One Common Pool of Humanity's achievements, where they are shared by all and benefit all.

It took humanity thousands of years to be where it is today. It was especially during the last ten thousand years that humanity made stupendous progress in all walks of human life, ranging from basic human need fulfillment objects to different fields of human knowledge— Science, Art, culture, and major inventions and discoveries that changed human life for ever.

In the very beginning of humanity's history, some 2 million years ago, a human started out rough in a jungle, like any other animal. He lived in dark caves, ate food left by other animals, and dressed in tree bark. Then, slowly and gradually, over a period of time, through many trials and errors, and through the hard, consistent labor of many, he learned how to make tools, how to hunt food, how to make things for his daily use, how to build a house, and how to grow his food. Human's progress had a lot to do with the type of society he lived in.

Since a human was too weak to defend himself alone, he always lived in a group or society. First, he lived in a hunter-gatherer society. This group wandered from place to place in search of food. By this time humans had learnt how to make tools and hunt animals instead of eating meat left over by other animals. He hunted, ate raw meat, and supplemented his diet with wild fruits, nuts, and berries. He lived in temporary camps.

Some two hundred and thirty thousand years ago, the human invented fire, which proved a blessing to human existence. Now he could light his home, keep himself warm, and cook his food. Fire became and still is a prime human need fulfillment item.

Some ten thousand years ago, a group of humans settled down, mostly by a riverside where the land was fertile, and there was good supply of natural food and water. This gave birth to an agricultural society—the foundation of humanity's entire progress. This society learned how to grow food instead of depending solely on hunted and wild food. They grew their own food and domesticated animals like cows, goats, dogs, and horses for their various uses. They started making more permanent types of houses than camps and tents.

Once settled, humans started accumulating knowledge in each and every field of human endeavor and passed it off to the next generation, who made it better and passed it to the next, and so on. It was from this time onward that different branches of human labor were created, for example, housing, food, clothing, transportation, pottery, tools and weapons, and cattle breeding et cetera. Each field of labor was worked in and improvised upon by every new generation of humans, leading humanity to where it is today.

First, humans live in mud huts. Then future generations started making brick and mortar houses. As time advanced, and with further additions of knowledge, humans started building bigger and stronger houses, villas, mansions, and palaces, leading to the skyscrapers of today. They created many awe-inspiring and wondrous monuments in the field of architecture that dot many countries and are their pride till date.

First, the human ate scavenged food— food left over by other animals. Then he learned how to make weapons of hunting, like bows and arrows and spears, and started hunting his food. Now he ate meat and other wild food like fruits, nuts, and berries of his own choice. With the advent of agriculture, he started growing food— like vegetables, fruits, and grains— in plain mud. Then he invented manure and different techniques of farming. With the aid of these, he grew better crops. First, he dug the mud with a stick. Then he invented the plow, ox-driven vehicles, and then tractors. As time progressed, and with every new generation's contribution, farming tools and techniques were perfected. Today we have excellent farming tools and techniques that enable humans to grow a large variety and quantity of crops and other food in small tracts of land.

The earliest human covered himself with tree bark. Then he started growing cotton. Someone started weaving cotton in his spare time and saw a thread taking shape. Others joined him or worked in the same field. Eventually someone came up with the bright idea of weaving fabric out of thread. The future generations working in the same field started making cloth. Each new generation came and contributed to that field, making it better and better. Today we have the entire textile industry with giant machines spinning out a spectacular variety of the softest and the best cloth in cotton, silk, synthetics, and so on, and an equally breathtaking variety of different types of dresses and clothes for all.

The advent of machines and industries in the industrial age around the seventeenth century enabled humans to produce a huge quantity of food and goods in every field.

Like food, clothing, and housing, transportation is also a prime human need. The field of transportation, like any other field of human need developed to its present extent very slowly and gradually. In every age, humans have traveled for different purposes— for trade, curiosity, pleasure, or work. The earliest human walked. He could actually walk for very great distances. Later he started using animals, like the donkey, elephant, or horse, for a ride and to carry goods. After some time, someone built a carriage, someone else a buggy, another a horse wagon, and still another a man-pulled rickshaw. Progress in the same field continued. After thousands of years of work and knowledge in the same field, someone made a car that ran on steam. Others built one that ran on coal. Work in the same field continued, and the first car run on gas (petrol) was invented by Karl Benz the Founder of Mercedes-Benz, in France in 1886. Later, in 1908, Henry Ford, the Founder of Ford Motor Company in the USA, invented the first car in the USA.

Now humans could drive and travel to distant places in less time, with more comfort. Still the human brain continued working in this field. In 1903 the Wright Brothers in the USA invented an airplane. Now humans could fly great distances in no time. These fast modes of transportation increased human connection and trade to its maximum. They connected distant cities and countries of the world, which enriched one another with their knowledge and goods.

Thanks to this continued progress and inventions, today we humans live in a smaller, richer, and far more comfortable world than ever before.

Besides basic human needs, Humanity also started from scratch, and in time made stupendous progress in higher endeavors of the human brain, like Knowledge, Art, Science, and Technology.

Knowledge means to know something or to understand something. Knowledge can be of a subject, a place, a tool, or a technique et cetera. We humans live by our knowledge. Humans, since beginning, acquired and stored knowledge in a variety of fields, passed it off to the next generation, who in turn acquired further knowledge, added onto it, and passed it off to their next generation, and so on. This is how humanity has built up vast stores of knowledge in Languages, Literature, Art, Science, Math, and every other field of human labor.

The earliest human acquired knowledge and taught it to others by showing "how to"— how to crack a nut, how to build fire, and how to hunt et cetera. Then, very slowly, human developed language— a mode of communication between humans. Now she could teach others by language. Language developed very slowly. First, human spoke language. They could not write. Slowly, writing was developed.

In the very beginning, humans wrote on tree barks or tree leaves. Then, sometime in 104 AD, paper was invented in China. Now humans could write on paper. Later, in 1440, printing was introduced. Then it became very easy to print large volumes of knowledge on paper and store them too. Now, books became the prime means to store knowledge. Today we have huge libraries and bookstores storing treasures of knowledge in the form of books.

The earliest human taught his knowledge mainly to his children or family. Later on, as language and different branches of knowledge developed, schools were started as centers of learning and imparting knowledge. Children were sent to schools to learn language, Math, and different subjects. With time, the variety and level of education increased in different parts of the world. Colleges and universities were set up for higher, specialized and professional education. They became the centers that prepared future generations of educated humans, professionals, and scholars in every society and country. To date these temples of learning— schools, colleges, and universities— are the prime gems of a city and a country.

Art is another prime field of humanity's achievements. Art is an abstract and indirect form used by a person to express her thoughts and emotions. It is a mode through which an artist communicates to other people. Art can be in the form of a book of Literature or Philosophy. It can be visual, such as a movie, painting, sculpture, photography. Or it can be musical—dancing, singing, or playing a musical instrument. A piece of art appeals to the deep human sensitivity and emotions. It pleases one's heart and mind and inspires new ideas too.

Since the beginning painting has been an artist's favorite mode of communication. The earliest human painted in caves and on rocks. Evidence of the earliest cave painting has been found in France, which as per some historians is thirty-two thousand years old. There are numerous examples of cave paintings in other parts of the world, including India, China, and Australia. In India some rock paintings of prehistoric times dated 5500 BC have been found. In later times humans started painting on silk and other fabric. With the invention of paper, humans started painting on paper and canvas. In earlier times, mural painting in temples and buildings was also very popular.

Some ancient cultures like that of Egypt, have many of them till date. Until the twentieth century, painting was highly religious and representational. From twentieth century onward painting became more abstract and conceptual.

Sculpting on stone, rocks, buildings, and other modes is another form of Art practiced from the earliest times to now.

With the evolution of language, art in the form of Literature started developing. Literature is of broadly two types, fiction and non-fiction. Fiction contains the work of human imagination, while nonfiction is factual writing. Works of fiction include novels and drama while nonfiction includes descriptive technical writings and philosophy et cetera.

Since the beginning, poetry has been a mode of expressing a human's deepest sentiments and the beauty of her mind. It brings out one's deepest pains and aspirations. Novels and drama are another mark of human imagination. They contain a totally imaginary set of characters and plots, which the penmanship of the writer makes seem real. They are different modes of expressing a writer's deepest feelings and thoughts.

Every language and every country in the world has its own pride selection of literature and philosophy ranging from prehistoric times to date.

Another field of art is Music. Music is an orderly interplay of sound, pitch, and rhythm that pleases the human heart and senses. Music is both— vocal and instrumental. Since the beginning to date, music has been one of the most popular sources of entertainment for a human. Music is closely associated with a culture. It depicts a culture's ways and its people's deep desires and pains. That is why it differs widely from place to place.

Music has been an important part of human life since time immemorial. The ancient human pierced holes in a piece of long bone and blew it with the mouth— the rudimentary form of flute. A number of these have been found in ancient archaeological sites. Every culture and country produced its own distinct songs and instruments. India has the oldest musical tradition. Vedas— the ancient Hindu scriptures created four thousand years ago— contain references to Indian classical music. China had its own tradition of court music some three thousand years back. In ancient Greece, music was widely used for religious ceremonies and entertainment. Every culture retained its musical tradition and treasure with every new generation adding onto it and changing it. Eastern and Western countries developed totally different music. Eastern music is mono and more vocal, and Western is mostly orchestral and uses more instruments. Now, with metropolitan culture emerging in big cities in different countries, fast and fun music has become popular. With the help of technology, music is widely available now in the form of records, cassettes, CDs, and DVDs.

Today we humans live amid a variety of comforts and wonders— all products of Science, and with a clear and reliable knowledge of the world given to us by Science. Science is not only a branch of knowledge, but a whole new way of thinking that has changed the human life forever. Science has been a blessing to human existence.

A scientist studies a natural phenomenon, asks a question, conducts thorough research and a number of experiments, and comes up with an answer—a hypothesis, which after many tests becomes a proven theory. These theories are then applied to different fields of human life. For example, Newton as a young boy saw an apple fall straight to the ground. He asked himself, "Why did this apple fall straight to the ground?" "Why didn't it fall sideways?" Obsessed with the question, he searched, conducted a number of experiments, and after years of extensive research and experiments came up with his answer: the theory of gravitation, which till date is applied in many walks of human life.

The whole field of Science is based on reason and evidence. It is a new method of study that is applied not only to the Scientific subjects of biology, physics, math, chemistry, engineering, and medicine but also Social Sciences like political science, economics, sociology, anthropology. Any subject if credited with the term *science* is seen as highly reliable.

Science, like any other branch of human knowledge and labor, quenched human curiosity and fulfilled a variety of human needs. Again, like any other high human endeavor, it came into being in the agricultural age during the last ten thousand years, was added on to by future generations of humans and rose to its present extent, revolutionizing the whole human world and enriching human life in all its aspects.

Physics—often called the fundamental science, studies the basic make of the universe and how it moves or behaves—in other words matter and its movement. Initially it was intermixed with Philosophy, Chemistry, and other branches of human knowledge. Later, in the nineteenth century, it was made a distinct discipline and called Physics.

The field of Physics started with the ancient Chinese, who noticed some attraction between rocks. They observed, worked on it, and named it magnetism. Around the same time, in its neighboring country, India, Indians were studying stars and planets and named it Astronomy, a branch of physics. In other parts of the globe, in the West, Greeks created electricity by rubbing amber with fur. Also, Archimedes, another Greek, discovered thermodynamics, a theory of physics. Curious minds of future generations worked further in the same field, added on their creations and discoveries, and enriched the field of physics. Atoms, molecules, and gases were discovered. Sometime in the eighteenth century, Newton's theory of gravitation was a major breakthrough in Physics. It explained why an apple or anything thrown from a height falls straight to the ground, and how every material object has a center, pulls other objects to its center, and is pulled to other things. Sometime later this theory was further modified by Einstein's theory of Relativity, which explained how all things are interrelated.

These discoveries, theories, and laws of physics were applied in Engineering and were used to create massive build-ings, dams, bridges, movie, video, TV, and a vast array of other dazzling products that made human life more comfortable. For example, the theory of Mechanics is used to build huge bridges and other structures. The theory of Acoustics is used in building big concert halls. Our TVs, videos, and movies are the products of Electromagnetism.

The blessings of Physics are many, and they continue to enrich our lives in many ways.

Chemistry, a sister of physics studies the chemical composi-tion of matter and its changes and chemical reactions. It began with Arabs and Persians in medieval times, who practiced Alchemy, the science of transforming base matter like lead into gold. Indians in the country of India practiced metallurgy. Work in the field of chemistry continued, and a major breakthrough was achieved in the eighteenth century with the creation of a table of chemicals, and their synthesis in labs. Knowledge of chemistry is used in the fields of physics and biology and in extracting metal, dyeing, medicine, and food. Various factories and industries are run by its principles.

The world is not only made of dead matter and its movement. It also includes us living humans and a vast number of other living beings. There were some human minds who watched us and other living things with great interest and wondered about their origins, their bodies, their inner make, and how they ran. They observed, asked questions, and found answers that explained living beings' origins and the make and running of their bodies. All this knowledge forms Biology, one of the greatest sciences, which has transformed and enriched human life forever. Its Blessings are many. On top of all, they have increased human life and given us a disease-free and pain-free life.

Biology studies living organisms. It has three branches: Botany, Zoology, and Microbiology. Botany is the study of plants, while Zoology studies humans and animals, and Microbiology is the study of micro organisms like bacteria and viruses.

The field of Biology started a few thousand years ago and was revolutionized from 1800 onward with the theory of Evolution by Lamarck, and Darwin; the theory of Genetics by Mendel; the theory of DNA by Watson and Crick in 1953, and many other theories and discoveries.

Biology finds its applications in the field of Medicine—a blessing to human existence. I will count its blessings later.

We humans live. We count things, we see shapes, and we wonder and think about them. Our ancestors did this too, and this gave birth to the whole distinct discipline of Mathematics—one of the most reliable and beautiful sciences. Mathematics has three branches: Arithmetic, Algebra, and Geometry. Arithmetic deals with numbers and their use in counting things and money. Algebra deals with abstract, hypothetical numbers. And Geometry deals with various shapes, like squares and triangles, and their use in measuring land and space.

Mathematics, starting in prehistoric times with very basic calculations like counting tools or pebbles, was worked on, added to by forthcoming generations of interested minds, was divided into three different branches, and rose to its present abstract form.

Archaeological evidence shows us that prehistoric people knew how to count things and how to count abstract things like time, days and years. They started with very basic arithmetic like adding, subtracting, dividing, and multiplying. Some three thousand years ago, Egyptians and Babylonians started developing arithmetic, algebra, and geometry and used them for various purposes, like construction and astronomy. Some four thousand years ago, the people of India in the Indus Valley civilization came up with the concept of zero and the decimal system. Work continued in other parts of the world by other humans, and the Egyptians created written numerals in middle times. In later times, many complex mathematical laws and theorems were created that simplified calculations and are used till date.

Mathematics is heavily used in other scientific fields, like Natural Science, Engineering, Medicine, and Social Studies et cetera. It is used in business all the time; in statistics, socials surveys, and computer studies, programming et cetera.

Though the Sciences began some four thousand years ago, a major breakthrough was achieved in modern times (in the form of Modern Science) that revolutionized sciences and transformed human life for ever.

Modern Science

Modern Science, once started in the sixteenth century, soon became a wave, and caused the scientific revolution of the sixteenth and the seventeenth centuries, lasting till present. A number of the best human brains across the Earth were employed in different scientific fields and produced a highly reliable body of knowledge and a variety of products in different walks of human life.

Scientific knowledge in different Academic fields has given us a whole new worldview of ourselves and the world we live in. Scientific theories and laws reveal universal truths. Charles Darwin's theory of evolution (1859) and Gregor Mendel's theory of Genetics combined with the discovery of DNA by Watson and Crick in 1953, show us with evidence how we humans have evolved from other animals; and that a number of our inborn qualities and flaws are purely genetic—Carry forwards of our parents' and forefathers' qualities and flaws. Similarly, Science shows us that the world we live in was not created in a day or two but is a product of the Whole of Life or the entire process of Life, which started on Earth some 3.8 billion years ago; and the human society and the comforts we live amid were not created by God but were created and sustained by humans. Science of Anthropology, Science of Biology and the combined study of all other Sciences prove these points beyond any dispute.

Science has filled our lives with so many comforts and convenience products that we cannot even dream of living without them. Our well-lit, well-gadgeted houses would be a matter of envy to royalty of the Middle Ages. We humans of today live in brightly lit, air-conditioned houses filled with a variety of products— all inventions of Electrical and Electronic Engineering. Electricity, discovered by Benjamin Franklin, and invention of electric light bulb by Edison, in the mid-1800s, proved a true blessing to human existence and changed our way of living forever. Then a number of bright human brains in the field of Electrical and Electronic Engineering, all across the globe, invented a large number of products that made our daily lives so convenient and comfortable—the fan, the cooler, the air-conditioner to ward off the extremities of weather; the microwave, the fridge, and frozen food to serve us ready-made food at any time; TV, radio, video, and music CDs to relax and entertain our tired minds; computers to store vast amounts of information that no human memory ever could; phones, cell phones, and the Internet to connect us to our distant friends, family, and fellow human beings; cars and planes to cover miles of distance in a few hours.

Similarly, our massive dams to control wild rivers; our highways to connect distant places; our Herculean bridges to connect cities across rivers; our skyscrapers to house thousands of humans; our majestic buildings to house museums, libraries, and vast universities; our fine houses; our well-planned cities with proper water and sewage systems; well-paved roads with traffic lights—all are marvels of the Civil and Architectural Engineering, another branch of Science.

Today an average human in a developed country lives for seventy years. Some two hundred years back, before the advent of modern science, an average human lived for some fifteen to twenty years. This major leap to a long and healthy life span of a human is directly the result of scientific revolution in the field of Medicine. In ancient times disease and death were viewed as acts of demons or witchcraft or the will of God. In tribal societies plants were used for treatment and shamans did the job of healing. The whole field of medicine was revolutionized in the seventeenth century.

Old ideas of infectious diseases were replaced with bacteriology. Bacteria and microorganisms were first observed with a microscope in 1676. They played a major role in causing and spreading infectious diseases. Dr. Ignaz Semmelweis in 1847 started the practice of requiring physicians to wash their hands before attending to a woman in childbirth. This practice drastically reduced the death of new mothers from childbed fever.

Louis Pasteur linked microorganism with disease and invented the process of pasteurization of milk and other products, which is widely used to date.

Florence Nightingale, a nurse in France, started nursing and women's participation in medicine in 1852. In the same year, she started her own hospital. The role of Nursing in Medicine brought down patients' deaths.

This evidence-based scientific medicine of our age prevents and cures a number of diseases and allows humans to live long and healthy lives.

Derivations

In counting our Cumulative Achievements and tracing their history, we see how a human started out rough in a jungle like any other animal, and then, prompted by his survival needs and curiosity, over a long time assembled a treasure house of knowledge and a dazzling array of products and services— our Cumulative Achievements of Humanity. They were achieved brick by brick by billions of humans' labor during thousands of years of humanity's history. This shows that our current smug and comfortable world we live in is not a gift of God but a product of sheer hard human labor.

This also shows how all our knowledge, products, and labor get stored in One Common Pool to be used by current humans as well as by future generations of humans.

All of humanity's Achievements can be categorized into different branches of human labor or profession. For example, starting from a human's basic needs—the entire food industry and Farming, the Clothing and textile industry, Housing and Architecture; Education; the legal system and Medicine to massive constructions like dams, bridges, and skyscrapers in Civil Engineering to a vast array of products in Electrical Engineering. Each of these branches of human labor evolved to fulfill human needs in some field or the other. Consequently, today we humans live in a cozy and comfortable world of ours—all the result of sheer human labor performed by enthusiastic, hard-working humans in the total history of humanity from the very beginning till today.

Also, as we can see from the above, Humanity's all Achievements have been cumulative. Humanity shares a common pool of all these achievements. Humans in every society and country worked in different branches of human labor and invented and discovered new things. Trade and travel since the beginning of human history have been the prime means through which different societies and countries exchanged their goods and knowledge and thereby created a common pool of goods and knowledge that every country could use. Then, in modern times, we have countries signing pacts and treaties and forming alliances whereby they share their achievements in different fields. Thus they benefit each other. Now, with the fastest means of transportation, phones, and the Internet, the vast humanity has shrunk to a global village where all knowledge, products, and information flow freely.

All of humanity's achievements are Cumulative where all 196 countries of the world share their Achievements, learn from each other, and benefit each other.

Definition of Cumulative Achievements of Humanity

Cumulative Achievements of humanity can be defined as *"One Common Pool of All Countries' Achievements in different branches of human labor and knowledge, ranging from basic human need and comfort products to rich treasures of human knowledge—our food; our clothes; our well-lit houses with everything inside them (couches, beds, fridges, air conditioners, phones, TVs, the Internet, music systems); our well-planned cities with their well-paved roads and beautiful parks; our Monuments, our Hospitals, our Libraries, Museums and Universities; our dams, our bridges, and skyscrapers; our cars, planes, and giant ships; our sky-kissing rockets and satellites; our rich languages; Mathematics; our beautiful creations in Arts and Music (our paintings, our sculptures, our cinema, our most enchanting classical and modern music); our treasured books on every Subject from basics to heartrending Literature to our most complex philosophical treatises; and our all inventions and discoveries in the Natural Sciences of Physics, Biology, Chemistry, Anthropology (Electricity, the Theory of Relativity, the theory of Evolution and our blessings of Medicine et cetera)."*

All of these and each and everything we humans possess and use has been created by humans in thousands of years of humanity's history. All our forefathers worked hard and created a Beautiful Palace of humanity's Achievements amid which we humans are born and live; and which we pass off to our children—***a Palace under construction***, made more and more beautiful by every forthcoming human generation.

Human: A Part of Humanity's Achievements

We humans are born and live amid the comforts and convenience of the Palace of Humanity's Achievements. Everything we use, the cities and houses we live in, and the knowledge we gain are all parts of humanity's various Achievements. We need them for our sheer survival and for our enjoyment. These achievements were created and preserved by our forefathers, who left a beautiful world to us. We enjoy the fruits of our forefathers' labor; work hard; and add on to them.

Every Achievement of Humanity is a product of human labor or profession performed in a specific Field—like Farming, Architecture, Art, Science, Law, Religion or any other Field of the numerous fields of human labor.

I as a human am born amid the comforts of these achievements. I use them and enjoy them. I learn and benefit from the treasures of knowledge left to us by our forefathers. I gain education, learn, grow up, and work. It is through my work or profession that I enrich a particular branch of human labor. My work is my contribution to the Palace of Humanity's Achievements. For example, if I work as a farmer, I study and use the previously acquired knowledge, products, and techniques in the field of Farming. I may improvise upon them or make them better. I may invent a new product or technique and leave it behind for future humans' use. Or if I work as a Scientist in a particular branch of Science, say Physics, I learn and use the previously acquired knowledge and enrich it further by my own research findings and maybe a new invention or discovery. Thus, I enrich it and leave it behind for future generations of humans who will benefit from it.

Similarly, every worker in every branch of human labor enriches that field by her own hard and honest work, new knowledge or new invention or discovery.

Thus a human is a part of the humanity's achievements by her need of them, use of them, and the contribution she makes to this Palace by her own "work" or "profession."

Derivative Right Way of Living for a Human

The above shows the sheer value of human profession. Our professions are something which we do for the major parts of our lives, through which we benefit and enrich the lives of others, and it is something we leave behind after our deaths. A human's profession is her major contribution to humanity's Achievements.

Humanity's Cumulative Achievements build the Palace of the Human Whole left to us by our forefathers. We live here, enjoy the fruits of their labor, contribute our share of work, and enrich it. We as humans die one day but leave behind our work and a richer pool of humanity's achievements to our children, who in turn will make it more beautiful.

In the above analysis we saw how a human started out rough in a jungle like any other animal millions of years ago. Then, prompted by her survival needs, she started forming big groups and living in them—groups of family, society, country, and humanity. A family is the smallest group around a human and a part of the bigger group, society, which is the part of a country that houses many societies in it. A country, in turn, is a part of the Humanity— the biggest group of humans. These groups gave a human protection and made her progress.

Also within all these years of human's growth, especially during the last ten thousand years, prompted by her need and curiosity humans started accumulating knowledge and products in different walks of human life. Each new generation of humans came, enjoyed the knowledge and products acquired by its forefathers, worked, bore children, made its contributions, enriched the existing pool of knowledge and products, and departed, leaving the world richer and more beautiful than they found it.

Slowly and gradually, within all these millions of years of human growth, especially during the last ten thousand years, was constructed The Human Whole—our modern, wondrous human world in which we humans are born, live, and die. We as humans are born in our human world, live in it, and enjoy its knowledge and products left to us by our forefathers, make our own lasting contributions in the form of our "Work" and our "Children," and depart.

Definition of "The Human Whole"

Starting from a human (one single Human) as the Center, The Human Whole is the network of a human's Family, Society, Country, Humanity, and their Cumulative Achievements in all aspects of the human life—ranging from a needle to an airplane, a thatch-roof hut to a skyscraper, one single alphabet to the most complex Philosophical Treatise, and one single number to Advanced Calculus; our Cities, our Monuments, our Museums, our Libraries, our Universities—in sum, each and everything we humans have ever produced and live by on the face of this Earth.

Derivative Right Way of Living

The derivative Right Way of living is derived from the clear definition of an entity, seeing its importance and the value in a human's life, and then incorporating it into our living.

The Human Whole exists as a Whole as well as in parts, where its each part or component is very important too. A human's derivative Right Way of Living from The Human Whole has to be derived from its each part as well as the Whole.

In my analysis, I discussed each component of the Human Whole: a Human's Family, Society, Country, Humanity, and their Cumulative Achievements in all aspects of the human life. At the end of each component's analysis, I defined that component, showed how a human is a part of each, and then derived a Human's Right Way of Living from that component.

A human goes through two sets of families during her lifetime: First Family or Family by Birth, and Second Family or Family by Marriage. A human is born and reared in her First Family. A human child needs her First Family for her survival and good rearing. A human spends the weakest and most formative years of her life in the arena of her First Family. Consequently she grows very attached to her parents and siblings and other First Family relatives. A human views her First Family as her prime identity and her root in this world and develops lifelong emotional bonds with them.

Viewing its value in her life, a human ought to maintain ties with her First Family. ***"Care," "Communicate," and "Support" are the three key ways to live one's family.***

Sometime in her youth, a human marries and creates her Second Family— Family by Marriage. A human's Second Family gives her a home, stability, and the love and support of her spouse and children. A human needs her Second Family. Keeping its value in mind, a human ought to marry, have a child, and create and maintain her Second Family. A human ought to be a good spouse and a good parent to her or his children.

A human's family is a natural group of persons related to her by blood or by marriage. *Family is a ship of love and protection in the vast, hostile ocean of life.* A human ought to view it this way, value it, and maintain a close-knit, happy family.

A human and her family are both parts of the society. A society is a big group of people amid whom a human lives and operates. It is a network of a human's personal and business rela-tionships. A human is affected by the kind of society she lives in, and she affects it too by her own actions. A society's Values and way of living directly affect a human. And a human affects her society too by her own Values and way of living. A human indi-vidual is a living example for others. Her behavior infects oth-ers around her. Also, as we saw earlier, Work is the chief mode through which a human enriches her society. Keeping this in mind, a human ought to do her share in enriching her society. She ought to practice compassion and goodwill toward others, and try to live in peace and harmony with others. She ought to behave as she would like others to behave with her. She ought to keep public areas clean, and respect others and their rights. Every human ought to work. Work is the prime mode through which a human directly affects her society and enriches it. Also, work gives one money and, if Right, happiness and the meaning of life. A human ought to choose and practice a profession that best matches her talents, education, and skills.

A human, her family, and her society in turn are parts of a bigger whole— country. A country is made of its citizens. A human is affected by the kind of country she lives in, and she affects it too by the kind of citizen she is. A human ought to enrich her country by being a good citizen which means she ought to be honest to her country, stand for her country, enrich it through her work, be aware of its government and its functioning, vote, and thus make her contribution in shaping her country.

A human, her family, her society, and country are parts of the biggest group of humans—Humanity. Humanity is made of All seven billion humans living in 196 different countries. All of us humans and our countries are tied by unseen but very thick ties of personal and trade relationships, the universal economy, and above all common needs of all humans: maintaining peace; and a pollution-free, clean, green Earth Home for us All and our children.

Every single human is a part of the humanity simply by being a human. She is affected by the kind of humanity she lives amid, and she affects her humanity too by her own actions.

In view of a human's close relationships with the humanity, a human ought to enrich her humanity. She ought to have a large vision of humanity, be a good human, view other humans with compassion and goodwill, cause less pollution, and have fewer children.

The last component of The Human Whole is "The Cumulative Achievements of Humanity"—a common pool of all humans' and their countries' Achievements in all walks of the human life, ranging from basic, daily need products and services to vast treasures of knowledge in every branch of human labor. This is the Cumulative Total of all generations of human labor or work performed in different branches of human labor.

A human is a part of it by her need and use of them, and by her own work— profession. A human ought to respect cumulative achievements, preserve them, and add on to them by her own honest work—profession. Every single human works in a particular branch of labor, may be as a Farmer, as a Scientist, or a Physician et cetera. She ought to contribute her best to her profession and thus enrich it by her simply maintaining it or adding a new product, technique, or discovery to it. Thus she contributes her share in making the Palace of The Human Whole more beautiful than she found it.

Vision of The Human Whole

Thus we see how every human individual (be it a woman or a man) is a part of the vast Human Whole around her, is affected by it, and affects it too by her own actions.

Taking a human as the Center, we can have a vision of The Human Whole as gradually increasing, natural groups of humans around her—those of Family, Society, Country, and Humanity, with their vast pool of Cumulative Achievements of Humanity in the form of an immense array of dazzling products and knowledge.

This is The Human Whole—a network of a human's Family, Society, Country, Humanity and their Cumulative Achievements in all aspects of the human life. This Human Whole is made of the humans, by the humans, and for the humans.

A human is born in The Human Whole, lives in it, enjoys its achievements, works, bears children, makes her contribution to it, and dies one day leaving behind her two most lasting contributions to it—her "work" and her "children."

I as a human ought to have a vision of The Human Whole, understand my close relationship to it and very power in it as an individual, and understand that I am affected by my Human Whole—the kind of human world I live in— and that I affect it too by my own actions.

The Right Way of Living in my Human Whole is to value and enrich my family through "Care, Communicate, and Support"; enrich my society by my work and exemplary behavior; enrich my country by being a good citizen; and enrich my humanity by being a good human.

I as a human will die one day but will leave behind my "Work" and my "Child" to the Human Whole—my foot prints in the Human Whole, my two most lasting contributions to my Human Whole, and the two prime meanings of my life on this Earth.

The Whole of Life

A human and her Human Whole, in turn, are parts of a bigger Whole: The Whole of Life.

The Whole of Life is made of the entire Earth with its aura of atmosphere, its Flora (entire plant life), and its Fauna (all living beings). The Earth and its atmosphere, together with their waters and sunshine, provide life-supporting conditions in which the Earth's entire flora and fauna subsist. We can visualize The Whole of Life as our blue-green, round Earth surrounded by a fine veil of atmosphere, with acres of green flora on its lands, and beneath the oceans; and with its multitudes of fauna in the forms of trillions of flying beings in its airs, trillions of crawling and walking beings on its lands, and trillions of swimming beings in its oceans; where Humanity is just a thin streak of walking beings on its lands amid multitudes of other crawling and walking beings. This is a vast, self-supporting Whole of which the human is just a teeny tiny part. This Whole will go on with or without human.

Life on Earth is a self-supporting system made of different components, all of which are interrelated and help each other and The Whole of Life to go on.

In order to understand how Life is a Whole, we will have to go into the very make of life, its origin, and analyze each of its components and its relationship with others.

Life is a process by which a living being is born, grows up, reproduces its own kinds, gets old, and dies. By this definition, the entire Flora or all plants, and the entire Fauna or all animals, including the human, are living beings. All of them go through this process.

Life is unique to Earth. As per our current scientific knowledge, no other planet harbors life.

Life originated on Earth some 3.8 billion years ago. Today we see a dazzling array of Life in the form of an immense variety of green flora all over the land and in the seas, and a variety of living beings in the forms of trillions of air-dwelling beings, trillions of land-dwelling beings, and trillions of sea-dwelling beings. All of this evolved during the last 3.8 billion years.

Our Earth was born from our Sun some 4.5 billion years ago. Initially it was a ball of fire, which cooled down over millions of years. As it cooled down, its mountains and oceans were formed. Also, gradually there formed a veil of atmosphere around the Earth that protected the Earth from direct sunshine and does so till date. The Earth's atmosphere is formed of many layers of different gases, with nitrogen in maximum at some 78.08 percent, then oxygen at 20.95 percent, and then argon and carbon dioxide at less than 1 percent each. Altogether they form the air that we all living beings breathe and live in.

The Earth and its atmosphere together with the Right sunshine and waters created conditions suitable for Life. It was in the presence of these conditions that Earth's entire Flora and Fauna were formed, sustained, and do so till date. In the protection and warmth of the Earth's atmosphere, and in the presence of oxygen and other Life-supporting gases, there sprouted a teeny tiny green plant somewhere deep under the oceans. Soon the plant replicated and expanded into many of its own kinds. Also, there sprouted the first of green algae, which soon replicated and expanded. The first sprouting of plant and algae, replicated and diversified by life's process, gradually gave rise to acres of bright green colorful flora under the oceans. There sprouted and spread a vast world of plant life with plants and trees of all colors and sizes: a carpet of green algae; green, yellow, and orange plants; and tall green trees swaying in the clear blue waters of the oceans.

On the land, the soil mixed with sunshine and rainwaters brought forth the tiny first plant, which by the process of life gradually replicated, diversified, and expanded into acres of green flora on the face of the Earth. There were born a wide variety of plants and trees of all colors and sizes—flower bearing, fruit bearing, and ones with shade. Also, there came forth other forms of flora, like mosses, shrubs, bushes, vines, and grass. Today we see collectives of flora on different parts of the Earth, in the form of the vast savannas of Africa with their tall grasses and other plants; lush green tropical forests, and valleys of flowers in Asia; expanses of green meadows, hills, and mountains in Europe and other parts; and the thick, bountiful forests of the Americas etc. Their beauty is further amplified by manmade farms, orchards, and gardens. Today there exist some three hundred and fifty thousand species of plants on all over the Earth.

The plants by photosynthesis inhale carbon dioxide and exhale oxygen—life breath for Fauna. As flora thrived in the oceans and on lands, it produced a lot of oxygen and brought forth another form of life—the Fauna. Fauna consists of all living beings on the Earth: the fishes of oceans and rivers, all animals on land, and all birds in the airs.

The first of the Fauna was a single-cell living being—an amoeba inside the oceans. It breathed in oxygen, got food from the flora, and lived on. Soon it replicated and produced many of its kinds. Gradually, over millions of years, from a one-celled being were born multi-celled living beings. They copulated, reproduced, diversified, and expanded into trillions of swimming beings—fishes and others of all varieties and sizes in the waters of the Earth. Today we see a vast array of beautiful, bright-colored, small and big fishes and other marine beings in the oceans of the Earth.

Somewhere, sometime during evolution, from marine beings there came forth an amphibian—a living being who could live both in waters and on land, like a frog. An amphibian survived and eventually gave rise to a reptile, a being that just crawled on land, like a snake. From the reptile, there arose eventually a Mammal, which lived both on land and on trees, like a monkey. From the form of a mammal, after millions of years there evolved a bird who just flew in the airs. Initially there were birds that lived both in waters and on land and flew only a little. Birds copulated, reproduced, and diversified into many types and sizes leading to many huge birds that flew great distances and at great heights.

Each of these—an Amphibian, a Reptile, a Mammal, and a Bird—copulated with its kind, reproduced, diversified, and expanded into trillions of Fauna on land and in air. Today we see millions of crawling and walking beings on the land and millions of flying beings in the air. All of these were produced on the bed of flora. It was the flora that gave them oxygen and food and helped them survive and it is flora till date that provides life and food to all fauna.

Thus, in tracing the origin and evolution of life, we see how one part of life brought forth the other, supported the other, and in turn, was supported by others—how Earth was initially just a barren planet; how it was gradually surrounded by the veil of atmosphere; how the atmosphere together with sunshine and waters gave birth to the flora; and how flora brought forth and supported fauna—and how Life itself is a process that replicates and expands itself.

Besides, there are many complex fundamental ways in which the Earth and its atmosphere, oceans and lands, flora and fauna interact, relate, and support one another, and thus create and maintain The Whole of Life.

Life on Earth is directly supported and protected by the Earth's atmosphere—a fine blend of certain gases that needs to be maintained. Some human activities, like depletion of forests, nuclear blasts, and pollution endanger the Earth's atmosphere.

Oceans form the major part of the Earth—some 71 percent of the Earth's surface. Their depths vary but are abysmal in many places. Due to their abysmal depths, they contain a much larger volume of Life than on land. There is a whole different world inside the oceans—most beautiful and colorful—made of its own share of sunshine, acres of green flora with orange coral reefs, tall swaying green trees; and vast and varied fauna in the form of trillions of beautiful small and big fishes and other swimming beings. This marine life provides food for animals of the oceans and lands including humans. It also provides medicine and other useful material to humans. Living beings in the oceans affect the land and the sunshine and Earth's climate and its atmosphere.

Earth's flora on land provides food to all animals. Also, Plants inhale carbon dioxide, and exhale oxygen that is a life breath for all animals including humans. Thus Flora is the main energy source for animals in the form of both oxygen and food.

Plants are highly beneficial to humans. They not only provide us with oxygen but are also the main source of our food. They provide us with a variety of food in the forms of grains, like wheat, maize, corn, rice, and legumes; nuts, herbs, spices, fruits, vegetables, sugar, coffee, tea, and beer. We need and use plants' wood for buildings, paper, and furniture. Plants also provide us with medicine; and we make a variety of dyes, wax, gums, and fibers from them.

Fauna, in turn, helps Flora to subsist and grow. Butterflies, birds, and insects fly from flower to flower, carry and transfer one flower's pollen to the other, thus helping plants reproduce, diversify, and expand. Grazing animals wander from place to place, eat fruits and berries, and disperse seeds thus helping plants grow and reproduce. Bacteria and fungi affect the fertility of soil. Human made plantations in the forms of acres of farms, orchards, and gardens help flora grow and expand.

Thus we see how the major components of Life, like the Earth, the Earth's atmosphere, and its flora and fauna brought forth each other, helped each other grow and expand, and do so till date. All of them altogether make our "Whole of Life." Each of them is important for The Whole of Life to go on.

Definition of "The Whole of Life"

The Whole of Life is our vast blue-green Earth, surrounded and protected by its fine veil of atmosphere, with vast expanses of green flora on its lands and beneath its oceans, and with a vast array of fauna— trillions of flying beings in its airs, trillions of crawling and walking beings on its lands, and trillions of swimming beings inside its oceans.

Figure 4

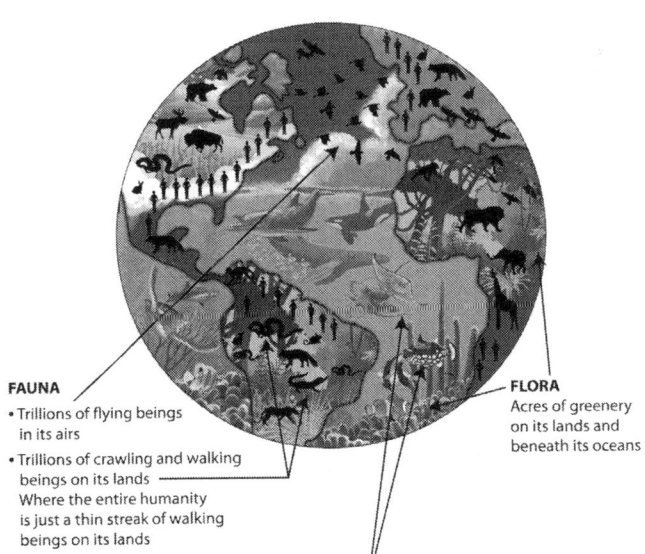

THE WHOLE OF LIFE
The vast Earth with its Flora and Fauna

FAUNA
• Trillions of flying beings
  in its airs
• Trillions of crawling and walking
  beings on its lands
  Where the entire humanity
  is just a thin streak of walking
  beings on its lands
• Trillions of swimming beings
  in its oceans

FLORA
Acres of greenery
on its lands and
beneath its oceans

Human—A Part of The Whole of Life

A human is a product of the Whole of Life. She is born from it. She has evolved within it from other forms of life. (As we saw earlier, the fact of human evolution from other forms of life is brought forth by the Science of Biology, and the Science of Anthropology.) Consequently, a human is deeply connected to The Whole of Life in her inner psyche and emotions. And that is why a human loves nature. She loves its flora, and she loves its fauna. Every human loves the sight of greenery—plants, bushes, trees, and gardens. She loves to be amid it. The sight and company of flora soothe a human's psyche, relax her, and make her happy. Similarly, the human loves fauna. She loves to watch other animals—fishes, land animals, and birds. She likes pets. Keeping pets, nurturing them, and playing with them makes many people happy. We humans are deeply connected to nature—mountains, rivers, jungles, and animals—by our evolution and in our psyches. They touch us deeply.

A human is just a teeny tiny part of the Whole of Life. The Whole of Life is vast. It harbors immensely vast varieties of flora and fauna—some millions of species. A human is just one species of thousands of animal species. And the entire humanity is just a thin streak of living beings on land amid the vast multitudes of living beings on all parts of the Earth. The Whole of Life is vast and self-subsisting. It does not need humans. The Whole of Life will go on with or without a human. A human ought to respect this fact, respect the Whole of Life, and enrich it.

A human depends upon the Whole of Life for her survival and well-being. She needs the Whole of Life to function properly. She needs a perfect atmosphere for the Whole of Life to go on. She needs good climate, fresh air, and good rains, crops, and drinking water. She needs plenty of oxygen to breathe. She needs rich, natural flora—lots of plants and trees et cetera. She needs good fauna, since each animal plays its part in running the Whole of Life. Therefore, in order for a human and the Humanity to survive and thrive, it is imperative that the Whole of Life goes on well.

Derivative Right Way of Living

Since a human through evolution and for her survival is such an integral part of the Whole of Life, she ought to understand this fact and incorporate it in her living.

A human ought to live in the company of nature—near water; amid lots of green trees and plants full of butterflies, birds, and other living beings. If not possible, she ought to at least grow plants at and near her home; and frequently visit places of natural beauty, such as rivers, mountains, beaches, and jungles. Living amidst nature and visiting nature relax a human deeply and make her happy.

Keeping pets, nurturing them, interacting with them, and playing with them are also a highly relaxing and joyous activity. Because of common evolution, we humans are deeply connected to all other animals in our psyches.

A human ought to understand the fact that she depends upon the Whole of Life for her survival and well-being. She needs a perfect atmosphere; timely rains; rich and bountiful flora for oxygen, food, and fulfillment of her other needs; and thriving fauna for their part in running the Whole of Life. Keeping this fact in mind, a human ought to respect nature—its entire flora and fauna. She ought not to destroy plants but use them for her needs and grow more plants. She ought to respect all other forms of life—all animals, birds, and marine beings. "Live and let them live" should be her motto.

Currently humanity poses a great risk to the Whole of Life with its rapidly increasing human population and pollution. At present (year 2012), the humanity constitutes of around seven billion humans, which is expected to increase to nine billion humans in 2042. Such a high population means more and more living space for humans, more and more food for them, and more and more use of raw materials. These requirements of the increasing human population, in turn, are causing the massive destruction of forests to create housing and farms and the rapid depletion of Earth's limited resources.

Forests are cut at an alarming rate to provide housing, fuel, and food for the constantly increasing human population. This is causing the extinction of many animal species. As evidenced by the science of Biology, the Whole of Life is made of and maintained by a variety of flora and fauna and their inter-relationships. There are thousands of animal species who are inter-related and function in ways through which they support and enrich one another and thus help the Whole of Life to go on. Many ways are known to us, and many are unknown to us. All of flora and fauna are required for the Whole of Life to go on. We humans need the Whole of Life for our survival.

Every human ought to understand this fact and make her contribution to the Whole of Life by *having fewer children, growing more plants, and respecting all forms of Life.*

Pollution is another major threat to the Whole of Life. Pollution is causing an impure environment with less oxygen, the depletion of the ozone layer in Earth's atmosphere, global warming, and other serious threats to the Whole of Life.

A human needs a pure environment with plenty of oxygen to breathe. The ozone layer in Earth's atmosphere obstructs ultraviolet rays of the sun, which are very harmful to humans. Global warming is causing less rain and less crops. We need good rain for our crops and drinking water.

A human ought to cause less pollution by using car pools and public transportation like buses and trains, driving smog-free cars, and using less of air conditioners, and keeping our rivers and oceans clean.

In sum, a human ought to understand and **respect the Whole of Life and <u>have fewer children, grow more plants, cause less pollution, and respect all other animals—"live and let them live."</u>** They have as much right to live as we do. A human by following these ought to's makes her/ his contribution to the whole of Life to go on. In short this is Human Dharma—The Right Way of Living for a Human.

The Universe

A human, *The Human Whole*, and *The Whole of Life*, in turn, are parts of the biggest Whole—The Universe.

As we saw earlier, how a human is born and reared in the Human Whole—our human made world on the lands of the Earth, and how our Human Whole flourishes in the lap of the Whole of Life—our Earth with its atmosphere and its flora and fauna.

The Whole of Life is a Construct: a product of nature's 3.8 billion years of labor, created and run by certain conditions suitable to Life and by the law of evolution. It was born on the Earth inside its veil of atmosphere. As per our current scientific knowledge, 'Life' is unique to planet Earth. No other planet is known to harbor life.

Our Earth, in turn, is a part of the bigger Whole—our Solar System. Our Earth moves around the Sun, and gets its own light, heat, and energy— the essence of life from our Sun.

Our Solar System is made of the vast Sun—a star in the center—with eight large planets, five dwarf planets, and millions of small bodies, like meteoroids, comets, and asteroids rotating around it. The Sun is a star. A star is a luminous body made of heat and energy, held together by its own gravity. It shines because of its heat and energy, which are constantly created at its core by its internal thermonuclear fusion. This emitting energy radiates the Sun's surroundings. The Sun attracts planets and other bodies orbiting around it by the law of gravitation. The Law of gravitation is a natural law by which different bodies with mass are attracted to one another. Such bodies remain close, but each of them retains its form by its own gravity. Gravity is the force exerted by a body with mass on all objects within its vicinity or its gravitational field. It is by gravitation that the Earth rotates around the Sun. And it is by gravity that Earth does not merge into our Sun, but retains its separate existence. The Earth moves around our Sun in its own orbit, as do all other planets of the Solar System. Each moves in its own orbit, that is how they don't collide with each other. Moving around the Sun constantly, twenty-four hours a day, the Earth gets its sunshine—all light, heat, and energy—from The Sun. This heat and energy, mellowed by Earth's atmosphere, creates and sustains all Life on the Earth.

There are millions of solar systems in the Universe. Our solar system is just one of them.

Our solar system in turn is a part of the bigger Whole—our Galaxy, the Milky Way. A galaxy is a body that houses billions of stars. All of these stars with their solar systems rotate around the Center of the Galaxy. It is a vast organization of billions of stars and their solar systems. It runs by the same laws of gravitation and gravity. There are some hundred billion galaxies in the universe. They all have different shapes and sizes. Some look like ellipses, others like discs or spirals, and so on. Some are dwarves in sizes, while others are very huge. Our solar system is a part of our Galaxy— the Milky Way, so named because it is long and appears foggy.

Our Galaxy, like other galaxies, is a part of the bigger Whole—a Cluster. The Center of our galaxy moves around the Center of our Cluster. A Cluster houses a number of gravitationally bound galaxies within it. It is a very large group of galaxies. All galaxies within a cluster move around the Center of the Cluster.

A Cluster, in turn, is part of the bigger Whole—a Super-Cluster. The Center of our Cluster moves around the Center of the Super-Cluster. A Super Cluster is one of the largest groups in the universe, containing millions of clusters and galaxies within it, which all move around its center. Super-Clusters are highly organized bodies that look like huge sheets.

Thus in the end all move around one **Center**—the Center of the Universe. Each of these—a solar system, a galaxy, a cluster, a super-cluster—is a scientific fact brought to light by Sciences of Physics and Astronomy. This is the Whole—the Universe

From the above analysis, we can infer certain truths. It is on the basis of these truths that I have defined The Universe. The first truth, as proved by the science of Physics, is that All in the Universe are moving. Things are not the way we see them. We see stationery stars; they are actually moving. We, our Earth, the Sun, and other suns and planets are all moving, each around itself and around the center of the bigger whole. And ultimately all seem to be moving around one single nucleus. It appears there is one Center— Nucleus—a Prime Source of Energy that is moving All. Then there is sheer organization, each body a part of the bigger whole: for example, the Earth is part of the solar system, the solar system is part of the galaxy, the galaxy is part of the cluster, and so on. There is a very strong discipline. Every body moves within its own orbit.

Above all, the universe is organized in a way such that every entity exists for its own survival, and by its very existence and nature it enriches the Whole too. For example, the Sun moves around its own center and emits light and heat, which bathes the Earth and sustains Life on the Earth. The Earth, in turn, moves around its own nucleus, nourishes life on Earth, and gives life and heat to its moon. It is partly from this truth that I have derived "Om"— the Prime Principle of Living. I will discuss it in Part Two, The Way of Living.

Definition of The Universe

The term *universe* literally means one verse, one song. It is so true. *The Universe is a Whole: a very well-organized system containing All within it, made of infinite space, and an infinite number of bodies, like stars, planets, meteors, asteroids, and others—all gravitationally bound—each body moving around its own center and the center of the bigger Whole, each a part of the other, and all bodies organized in the forms of gradually increasing, bigger wholes of a solar system, a galaxy, a cluster, and a super-cluster.*

A human can visualize the Universe as The Whole, starting from herself as a human, then her "Human Whole," her "Whole of Life," her "Earth," her "Solar system," her "Galaxy," her "Cluster," and the "Super-Cluster." This also shows how a human is a part of the Whole—The Universe.

A Human: A Part of the Universe, and the Derivative Right Way of Living

A human is a part of The Universe in two ways. The first way is indirectly: a human is a resident of the Earth, which is part of our solar system; our solar system, in turn, is part of our Galaxy; our Galaxy is part of the Cluster; our Cluster, in turn, is part of the Super-Cluster. The Earth is affected by other material bodies and their motions, and it affects them too. The second way is that a human is a part of The Universe by her/his body. A human exists and lives in the form of a body. A human body, though a product of evolution and thus highly complex, is nonetheless a body—like any other body in the universe, with its own mass and gravity. Thus, it is also subject to universal laws of gravitation and gravity. A human is affected by the Universe, and she affects it too.

Right Meditation balances a human's body and increases its gravity. Therefore, it is advised to practice meditation twice a day—once in the morning and once in the evening.

I view the Universe as a Potter's Wheel, with its own *Center*, which keeps moving and creating new and new creations and throwing them into The Whole, where every creation is created in a way so that through its natural moving and living it enjoys its existence and enriches The Whole. A human, like any other being is a creation of the universe, created in a way such that she exists, enjoys her existence, and enriches her Whole. A creation is just a creation, never perfect, but created in a way so that it somehow fits into The Whole.

It is from the Universe and its functioning that I have derived the prime Human Dharma: *"Live a good life yourself, and enrich your Whole too."* I have discussed it in Part Two: The Way of Living.

Definition of The Whole

The Whole is The Whole. There is nothing which is outside The Whole. *The Whole consists of one single human (a woman or a man) in the center, her Human Whole, her Whole of Life, and The Universe (around her), where each is a part of the other.*

Human—A Part of The Whole

In the above analysis, we saw how a human is not alone and is not an altogether independent entity, but is a part of the vast Whole within which she is born and functions. First, she is part of "The Human Whole"—our humanmade world in which we humans are born and live. Second, she is part of "The Whole of Life"—the Earth with its entire Flora and Fauna amid which a human and her Human Whole are born and live. Third, a human is a part of the Universe—an immensely vast, but a well-organized system within which our Earth, our Sun, and our Galaxy, with trillions of other stars and their planets, move and are subject to its laws; and *"A Potter's Wheel with multitudes of creations"* of which every human is a creation too, created with a purpose, in a way so that she lives, enjoys her life, and enriches her Whole too. A human ought to understand her relationship to The Whole and live in a way so that she lives a good life herself and enriches her Whole too.

After having analyzed different aspects of a human's make, I would like to define a human, and summarize the Derivative Right Way of Living.

Definition of a Human

A thorough analysis of a human's origin and a human's being reveals that *A human is an Evolved, Multi-dimensional, and Part of The Whole living being.*

Derivative Right Way of Living

A human is primarily a living being. Like any living being, a human primarily wants her own survival and happiness. Therefore, a human's Right Way of Living would be that which ensures her own survival and happiness.

As evidenced by the Science of Biology and the Science of Anthropology, a human's form has evolved from other forms of life. A human is a product of Life's millions of years of evolution. This fact shows the relationship between a human and the Whole of Life—the Earth's Flora and Fauna. A human ought to respect this fact, live in the company of nature, feel compassion for other animals, and live and let them live. Doing so deeply nourishes a human's psyche.

Since a human evolved from other animals, there lurks beneath her moral and self-controlled exterior a deep dwelling animality, which, given a little incentive, flares up and makes her act wrong. This deep animality of a human is exhibited by her blind emotions and passions of anger, violence, greed, sadistic traits, and the quest for power. ***A human ought to understand this fact and season her all emotions with thoughts***. A human ought never to act under the spell of mere emotions, but feel, think, and then act.

A human is a Multi-Dimensional living being. The various dimensions of her being are: Physical, Emotional, Intellectual, Moral, and Spiritual. Each of these dimensions has its own need. A human's Right Way of Living is that which nourishes each dimension of her form and thus helps her enjoy the depth, height, and sheer bliss of being a human. This would include Right diet and Right exercise to ensure a human's physical health; Practicing compassion, and having emotionally nourishing relationships like family and friends to enrich her Emotional dimension; receiving a good education, and reading, thinking, and developing logical and other intellectual abilities to fulfill her intellectual dimension; thinking about right and wrong, and trying to do what is right for all to enrich her moral dimension; and practicing some religion, meditation, and having a vast worldview and compassion for All to enrich her spiritual dimension. A human who practices and nourishes each dimension of her being is a happy, balanced human who enjoys the height and bliss of being human.

A human is not alone and independent but a part of the vast Whole—first The Human Whole; then The Whole of Life; and then The Universe. A human in her form and life is deeply related to each of these Sub-Wholes, is a product of each, depends upon it for her own survival, is affected by it, and affects it too by her own actions.

First, a human is part of The Human Whole—our human made world created and maintained by humans, made of us All seven billion humans— the Humanity, and our Cumulative Achievements in all aspects of the human life. A human is born and reared in her Human Whole, not in a jungle.

Our Human Whole is like a Palace under construction in which we humans are born, live, use, and enjoy things and knowledge created and left to us by our forefathers. We live, create our own things and knowledge, add onto it, and leave a better Human Whole for our children, who will do the same for their children, and so on.

It is The Human Whole which gives meaning to a human's life. I as a human will die one day, but will leave behind my work-profession and my child(ren) to The Human Whole. A human ought to enrich her Human Whole by giving her very best in the form of her work and by rearing good children.

I as a human am born into my Human Whole, live in it for certain number of years, make my contribution to it and depart, leaving behind my footprints in the form of my "Work" and my "Child(ren)."

Next, a human and her Human Whole are parts of The Whole of Life. The entire Human Whole flourishes in the lap of The Whole of Life. A human depends upon it for her survival and well-being. The Whole of Life is our Earth with its acres of green Flora on the land and in the seas, and with its trillions of Fauna in its airs, on its lands, and inside its oceans. Our entire Humanity is just a thin streak of walking beings amidst its trillions of fauna on lands, and our Human Whole for its own survival depends on The Whole of Life. We humans need its flora and we need its fauna. We need The Whole of Life to go on. If this goes well, we go well too. A human is affected by The Whole of Life—the way it is—and affects it too by her own actions. Keeping this fact in mind, a human ought to enrich her Whole of Life by growing more plants, causing less pollution, having fewer children, and respecting other forms of life by letting them live too. Doing so will help us maintain a clean and green Earth with its variety of flora and fauna that we humans need for our own survival.

A human, her Human Whole, and her Whole of Life, in turn, are parts of the biggest Whole—The Universe. The Universe is a moving force, much like a Potter's Wheel, which keeps moving and creating new and new, varied and beautiful forms. Our Earth, our Sun, trillions of stars and planets, and humans are all creations of this Whole. It is a vast, highly organized, and extremely intelligent System of which we all are parts.

A human is a creation of The Whole—The Universe—created in a very special way. She ought to understand her own special nature and talent, live per it, choose a profession per it, and enjoy living herself and enrich her Whole too.

I derived the Principle of Om from the working of The Universe. Every entity in The Universe exists and functions in a way so that it enjoys its existence and somehow enriches The Whole too. For example, the Sun enriches the Earth, the Earth enriches the Whole of Life, and so on. The derivative Right Way of Living or the Human Dharma from this is—live by Om—whereby I as a human live a good life myself, and enrich my Whole too. I have discussed it in Part Two: Way of Living.

The above summarizes a human's make and the derivative Right Way of a human's living or The Human Dharma from it.

Next, I will proceed to the second issue of a human's existence—human life. An analysis, definition, and the derivative Right Way of Living constitute the Third chapter of this book: What is Human Life?

CHAPTER 3

WHAT IS HUMAN LIFE?

A human "is" and a human "lives." A human and a human's life are two totally distinct issues.

A human exists as a very definite entity: "an Evolved, Multi-Dimensional, and a Part of The Whole living being."

Next, a human lives. My purpose in this chapter is to analyze a human's life—what is it? What is it made of or its main components? Does it have any meaning, any purpose to it? A thorough analysis of a human's life and its make will churn up certain truths about it which will help us define a human's life. Once we have a clear definition of a human's life, I will derive a human's Right Way of living from it or how a human ought to view her/his life, and how (s)he ought to live it.

Analysis

A human is born, lives for a certain number of years, and dies. We can visualize a human's life as a journey or a pathway enclosed between two doors of Birth and Death.

BIRTH   LIVING   DEATH

..

Birth and death are like two iron doors. There is mystery behind both these doors. All is not clear before birth and after death. We have partial knowledge about both these issues. We don't know for sure if a human's life is "one in many" though we know for sure that the soul exists (as I will prove later), and there has been compelling evidence of rebirths. We are not sure what happens after death, though we know for sure that soul exists, and it is only the body that dies at death but the soul lives on. Many instances of "life after death" have been recorded in which people after going through deathlike experiences return to life and recount their experiences. They indicate that the soul or some part of a human lives on after death. We will leave these two issues where they are, shrouded in partial mystery, and proceed to deal with the open facts of life.

A human is born, lives, and dies. While birth and death are two mere events, living is a long, arduous journey performed over a number of years. Different people live for a different number of years. Some die in their childhoods, while others die in their youths. There are some who make it to late adulthood, like their forties, while many make it to ripe old ages, like their eighties or above. A human's lifetime is composed of her living years. It is during these living years or during one's lifetime that the whole drama of life unfolds. This is where the whole hell breaks loose, this is where the whole warfare takes place, this is where the toughest challenge facing a human is: to survive, to live, and to live well too; to cope with the hostile alien world; to learn; to face life's storms and shocks, and somehow go on living. This is where the whole action is. We live our lives moment to moment, day to day, year to year; and it is very important how we live it, what we make of our lives. While a lot lies in

the outside world, a lot lies in our hands too. It is very important too, because a human's life, however short it is, has a deep
meaning and purpose behind it (as I will show later).

Life is a Given. We have no control of where we are born,
whether we are born rich or poor, ugly or beautiful, healthy or
handicapped, dumb or intelligent. We have no control of our
natures—the way we are. Some of us are gloomy and depressed
by nature, while others are joyous and bright. We have no control of where we are born—in a war-torn, poor country or in a
peaceful and rich country; in a superstitious, backward society
or in an educated, advanced society. The lengths of our lives are
a Given too in many cases. A hale and hearty youth dies of a
sudden heart attack. A highly intelligent and promising child
dies in his childhood. A mature man in the prime of his success
and life dies suddenly, while some very old people cursing every
moment of their existence go on living. We have no control of
our circumstances. Today I run a successful business minting
money and am a great success; tomorrow my business fails, and
I become a pauper and an utter failure. A three year old rich
child loses his both parents in an accident and becomes a poor
orphan in a day. A man has a great career, a loving wife, and two
adorable children, and he loses his whole family in a car crash.

But still, despite its all Givens, life is highly malleable and
elastic too. We as humans can change a number of things in our
lives. We can overcome life's Givens with our faith in life, opti-
mism, and hard work. It is life's job to repress us for a while; it
is our job to fight back and surface as winners. If born poor, one
can work hard, receive a good education, go into a good profession, and earn good money. Even a dumb child may have a talent
and can use her special intelligence. We can increase the lengths
of our lives by living healthy lives. When life's adversities pull
us down and submerge us, we need to endure its impact, wait

for a while, and let time heal its wounds, and then build new goals and dreams and live them.

Life is a distinct entity from me. I and my life are two totally different things. My life is a Given to me that I have to cope with, live, and live well too.

Life moves. There is a certain movement about life, marked by constant changes. Our professions, our relationships, our circumstances, and our activities change moment to moment and day to day. Every moment is a new moment, and every day is a new day. Very often we humans find it hard to accept the change. We tend to stick to our better past and ignore the present. This ruins both—our present and future. We ought to accept the change in life. This makes us calm and wise. We ought to be alert to moving reality, live in the present, and plan a better future.

Four Age Spans in a Human's Life

A human's life is a journey between birth and death. It is a long, hard journey. The duration of this journey differs from person to person. Some die early, while others die in their youths or adulthoods, while many make it to the ripe old age of seventy or above. An average human lives for seventy years or so.

An average human passes through four major age spans during her lifetime.

A human starts out her life as a fresh newborn baby, goes through the phase of childhood and adolescence from birth to the age of seventeen or so—a carefree phase of play and learning; grows and blossoms into a handsome, energetic youth and lives this phase from eighteen to thirty—a phase of dreams and passions; then enters into middle age and lives it from her thirties to sixties—a phase of building and enjoying life's Achievements; and finally enters the phase of old age and lives it from her sixties to death—a phase of further building and enjoying one's lifetime's achievements but at the same time a tough phase of decay and diseases; and then at the end she dies as a withered, spent old person, leaving behind her Achievements to the world.

Each of these age phases has its own characteristics that ought to be incorporated into a human's Right Way of Living.

Childhood

A human is born as the most helpless infant who requires twenty-four hours' care and nourishing in order to survive. She is born raw, though with a peculiar set of genes that determine her basic individual nature. As per scientific research in the field of Biology, a child acquires 50 percent of her genes from her birth parents and the other 50 percent from her both parents' families and their ancestors. These genes determine the basic traits of a child that make her an individual, totally different from others. Some of the genetically determined traits are—physical appearance, health, intelligence, and talent in some specific field of Arts, Sciences, Sports etc. This fact of a child's genetic nature makes marriage a very important event in a human's life. A human ought to choose her spouse very carefully after a fair assessment of one's would-be spouse and her family and forefathers.

A human is born as the most helpless infant, who needs constant care and supervision in order to survive. During the first few months, she needs to be fed, cleaned, held, and soothed very frequently, which requires twenty-four hours' care. Slowly a child learns how to crawl on her knees, how to walk, how to form words and speak, and how to behave with others.

A child, though a genetic product, is a raw human who has to learn everything. She learns by observing others, following them and their teachings. For the first three or four years a child learns everything from her immediate elders and family. She learns not only how to walk, talk, and behave but also general actions and reactions towards her surroundings and others— whether to be compassionate and helpful or apathetic and selfish; whether to fear her surroundings and others or to be bold; whether to be overly dependent or independent. Each of these is a quality and skill that a child learns directly or indirectly from her elders, especially her family in which she is constantly reared. This makes family a very important institution in which a child is born and reared. From this we infer the value of Family in a human's life.

At the age of three or four, a child starts going to school. School is the main center of learning, where a child receives basic education in a variety of fields, ranging from ways of dressing and eating and general social manners and etiquette to gaining knowledge in a variety of mental fields like Languages, Mathematics, Humanities, Arts, and Sciences. Learning languages helps a child understand others, interpret the world around her, and express her feelings and thoughts coherently to others. Learning Math enables a child to handle figures and do abstract mathematical calculations. Learning History informs a child about her own country and other countries' past, and gives her a world perspective. Learning Geography acquaints a child with Earth, mapping, and different countries' locations, their climates and resources etc. Reading stories, poems, and other forms of literature nourishes a child's sensitivity and acquaints her with the sensitive aspect of human life. Learning Biology informs a child about the flora and fauna around her: their origins, their inner functioning, and the facts of evolution and interrelations of all forms of life— plants and animals including humans.

A child learns all this from her teachers through lectures, discussions, drawings, movies, displays, and other theoretical and practical forms of teaching. Receiving education is a hard physical and mental labor that involves long hours of sitting, reading, listening, concentrating, understanding, remembering, thinking, and writing. This labor disciplines and prunes a child's brain and fills it with treasures of knowledge.

From this we infer the Value of School education in a human life.

School is also a social and cultural center where a child meets other children, makes friends, and learns about their cultures. A child is affected by other students' cultures, and she affects them too with her own culture.

A child receives the School education for some twelve years, from the age of four up to the age of seventeen or so.

During the first seventeen years, a child's life revolves around her family and school. Family fulfills the child's emotional and economic needs. A child is loved by her family, and she loves them too. Family provides a child with food, clothes, and home and pays for her education and other expenses. School gives her social interaction and education, which strengthen and enrich her mind. The Family and School each plays its own part in shaping a child's personality.

A child goes through phases of infancy and childhood for the first twelve years of life. From thirteen to seventeen, a child goes through adolescence. Adolescence is the age phase between childhood and youth.

Adolescence is a tough phase in a human's life. In this phase a human is no longer a child and not even a youth or an adult. A number of physical and hormonal changes take place inside the child's body, which disturb her emotionally and mentally. Her sex organs and sexual desire start developing. During this phase a child needs good understanding, guidance, and supervision from her family. She needs a good family mentor who can guide her through this phase.

Around seventeen, after finishing School, a child goes to College, where she spends the next four to six years. A College is a Center for Advanced and Professional education. Based upon her interests and professional goals, a child receives advanced education in a specific field of Arts, Science, or Business etc. Besides, there are different Colleges for professional preparation. Each of these prepares a student for a specific profession: for example, a College of Law prepares a student for the profession of a Lawyer, a College of Medicine for a Doctor, and a Business College for a Business Executive etc.

The average age for finishing college education is twenty-one. This is also the age at which a child is considered an adult. An adult is a fully developed human being who can think rationally and make her own decisions and choices. Education plays a major role in shaping, pruning, strengthening, and enriching a child's brain so that she grows up into a good adult.

From the above we infer the Value of College Education in a human's life.

At twenty-one, a human, having received Right Education, is ready both as an adult and as a young professional.

Youth

At twenty-one, a human enters the phase of youth. This phase lasts for the next ten to twelve years, up to the age of thirty or the early thirties. During this phase a person is full of energy, ideas, dreams, and desires to fulfill her dreams. In fact this is the most beautiful phase of life with unbounded energy to achieve one's dreams. This is also the phase during which one enters a profession, works hard, and succeeds in one's profession be it a specific career or business. Professional or work success gives one a deep satisfaction, good money, and good social identity.

Work or profession is a human's prime identity. It is an application of one's talent, education, or skills in a specific field. Also, it is the prime survival mode for earning money to survive and live well.

During the phase of youth, a human marries, and produces children of her own. Marriage is a social and legal union of a woman and a man into the union of marriage. There is some social celebration, marked by some religious rituals, or presence in a legal court with some witnesses amid which a woman and a man are married and are declared wife and husband.

After marriage a woman and a man, now a "wife" and "husband" to each other, live together in the same home and help each other with money and daily living work like cleaning, cooking, laundry, and in each other's needs. They live in each other's constant company. They have sex together and produce children of their own.

Marriage gives one her own home, the financial and personal support of one's spouse, the spouse's constant companionship, and children of her own.

From this we infer the Value of Marriage in a human's life.

Marriage brings many changes in a person's life. It curtails one's freedom and demands sexual faithfulness from both spouses. Marriage involves living with one's spouse, adjusting to her ways and Values, and somehow creating a common ground in which both can live peacefully. In marriage both spouses have to extend their financial and personal support to each other to make it work. It is very hard to maintain marriage, especially today, when often both woman and man are financially independent, move on their own, and can live on their own. But, marriage has its own advantages. It gives one her own home; the everyday love, support, and companionship of her spouse; and above all one's own children. It also gives one a foothold, a strong and steady base to live from. Consequently, if good, marriage makes one rich, strong, and happy.

From marriage a human produces children of her own. This creates the Prime Human Family: Family of Mother, Father, and Child(ren). A child is a genetic product of her parents— mother's and father's and their families. She inherits qualities and individual traits like physical appearance, intelligence, artistic or spiritual inclination, and hordes of other qualities from her both parents and their families. This makes Family and Marriage very important institutions. The Family bloodline is to be maintained and tracked carefully to avoid incest. And, marriage requires sexual faithfulness of both spouses so that the child is their child only.

Both childbirth and child rearing are very hard and challenging processes. A woman, after going through nine months of pregnancy and its demands, goes through excruciatingly painful long hours of labor and then produces a child.

Child rearing is a long process of good eighteen or more years that starts at childbirth and ends after the child becomes an independent adult. During these eighteen years both parents have to spend an incalculable amount of their time and money in raising their child. They have to feed their child; clean her; watch her; teach her; help her with lessons; and constantly watch, guard, and take care of her. They have to provide her food, clothes, and home; pay her tuition; and fulfill her other demands.

During these long years of child rearing and living together, there builds a deep attachment and an inseparable bond between a parent and her/his child. A child is a deep part of a human. A human views her child as a part of herself and the harbinger of her future dreams too. Most parents rear their child with lot of love and care. Children are the future of humanity and our future too. They need to be raised and educated with lot of love and care so that they grow up to be intelligent, responsible, and compassionate human beings.

These facts make a Child a deep human Value; and the process of child rearing, which actually is highly demanding and challenging, a meaningful process.

A human during this phase of her youth, acquires a profession and a family of her own—a spouse and child(ren).

Middle Age

Between thirty and forty years of age, a human enters the phase of middle age. This phase lasts for the next twenty years, up to the age of fifty-five or sixty. During this phase, one's dreams and ideas start cooling down and one's energy level starts declining. An average person is more or less settled by this age and has a home, a steady job or business, and a family. This may make him slow and lazy. Wrong diet and lack of exercise coupled with laziness and inactivity, cause diseases. These trends go on increasing, and a person has to control her diet, exercise regularly, and remain active despite her body's and mind's unwillingness to do so. Aging is a natural process that slows down one's physical and mental activity and causes quick fatigue.

But this is also the phase during which one enjoys the fruits of one's youth's labor. If lived Right—having received a good education, profession, and family—one can settle down and enjoy one's professional success and the joy of family. Now one has time to travel, read, do some social service, and do other things for pleasure. Often during this phase certain boredom builds. Doing the same things every day becomes monotonous. A person ought to create and pursue new goals to make life more enjoyable and fulfilling. This is also the phase when one starts questioning the meaning of one's life and seeking some higher goal or purpose in life. These are natural human queries that need answers. This is a good time to join some spiritual organization and pursue one's spiritual growth. Also, doing some social/charity work is highly rewarding and satisfying to the human spirit.

Old Age

Around sixty a human enters the phase of old age. A human remains in this phase until death. This phase is the hardest of all life phases marked by a rapid loss of physical and mental health, a loss of income, loneliness, fear of death, and spiritual queries.

Ageing is a natural process that everyone has to cope with. Ageing starts after forty but keeps getting worse after fifty. One's hair turns gray, the skin becomes wrinkled, the eyesight and hearing grow weak, the taste buds and other senses weaken and all of this is coupled with an intense loss of energy. After sixty, you feel tired more often. A little labor tires you. Physical weakness is accompanied by mental weakness too. Old people find it hard to remember things. They cannot think and reason as fast and as well as adults. The ability to make quick decisions fades, like applying brakes to avoid an accident. Old age is also a fertile ground for diseases. Many diseases build up and further weaken one's body and mind. Diabetes, blood pressure, heart disease, and cataracts are common physical ailments of old age. And, Amnesia and Alzheimer's are some dreaded mental diseases.

But old age is also the age of wisdom. By this age one has stored treasures of knowledge and life experiences. An old person is often a wise person. Old people can share their knowledge and professional and personal experiences with others to direct them and enrich their lives.

Sixty is the standard retirement age in many countries. After retirement one faces a loss of income and loss of profession and position. Time hangs heavy after retirement. After retirement one loses a major source of regular income, which can result in poor finances. Losing one's profession and position results in the loss of one's social identity and self-esteem and can cause boredom. Loss of direction, and physical and mental laziness result too.

Old age is also marked by loneliness. By this age, children have left home and get busy with their work and families. They often live in other cities or countries and may visit home occasionally. One may lose spousal support with the death of spouse. Loss of work also causes less social interaction.

It is during this phase that one can see inevitable death approaching. This causes anxiety, fear of death, assessment of one's life and its meaning, and spiritual queries about God, heaven and hell, the soul, and rebirth.

Old age is a fact. Everybody gets old and faces its problems.

The Derivative Right Way of Living for old age is that which enables one to face its challenges, answer its queries, and still live a good life. An old person ought to take extra care of one's health. In this age metabolism slows down, so one should eat a light diet—less carbohydrates and more fruits, soups, and salads; avoid alcohol; and do right physical exercises like stretching and brisk walking. Mental efficiency can be retained and improved by doing some mental labor like studying, taking classes, reading, writing, trying to remember facts, or doing crossword puzzles and doing logic games.

One ought to work as long as one can. One's work keeps one active and gives one money, intellectual satisfaction, happiness, and social identity. One's years of professional experience combined with hard labor will make one's work better. Some countries, like the USA and some European countries, have no retirement age.

Social interaction is very stimulating and fulfilling for a human. One needs it more in old age. Maintaining family ties, having some good friends, and joining some social or spiritual organization can earn one a good set of social contacts.

An old person also ought to look for and join some religious or spiritual organization and follow its practices. It may answer one's spiritual queries and satisfy one's heart and mind.

Old age ends in death. The majority of people die by the natural ageing process. They grow old, wither, and finally die. A person may grow old to the extent that she cannot even get up from the bed, stand or walk on her own. Confinement to bed in the extreme old age is common.

Above gives us a picture of a human's one whole lifetime— how a human is born, passes through four age spans, and then dies. A human ought to have a view of one's whole lifetime with its four distinct age spans and its end in death. Every human is born, passes through four age spans, and dies. Coping with birth's Givens, living each age span the Right Way, and being prepared for death help a human live a good life.

In the above analysis of a human's whole lifetime, there also emerge certain core human life Values such as Family, Education, Work, Marriage, and Child. These are the five eternal Human Values. I will discuss them later in a separate chapter.

Living: A Continuous Process of Feeling, Thinking, Acting, Facing the Consequences of One's Actions; and Coping with The Whole

Living is an Amalgam of a number of things. It is not one single activity. If I observe myself a little, I will find that during any given moment of the day, I am feeling and/or thinking and/or acting, facing the consequences of my past actions, and coping with the Whole. All of these activities go together, affect one another and shape the quality of my life. It would be helpful to distinguish each activity or aspect, analyze it, define it, and then see how to incorporate it into our lives so that it helps us live a good life.

Feeling

Feeling is a very important aspect of human living. We live and we feel. We feel and we live. We feel every moment of the day. We feel our sights and surroundings, every action, every reaction, and the company of others. Each of these and everything else we do evokes a certain feeling or mixture of feelings within us. If I like my sights and surroundings, I'm happy. If I dislike my sights and surroundings, I'm unhappy. During the day I do a number of things, like working, reading, writing, and talking to others, and a number of other actions. I like some of these actions and dislike others. Actions that I like make me happy, and actions that I dislike make me frustrated and angry. During the day I meet a number of people. Each of them evokes a feeling in me. I either like that person or dislike that person. Thus likes and dislikes are two prime reactions to my environment and actions.

A human feels every sight, every smell, every taste, every action, and the company of other persons. A human also feels emotions. While our feelings are temporary and weak, our emotions build over time, last longer, and are very strong. An emotion is a very strong feeling or response that often overpowers one's being and pushes one to act in a certain way. Some of the strong human emotions are love, hate, and anger. All human emotions can be neatly divided into two classes:

positive and negative. Positive emotions are those that nurture our beings, make us happy, and motivate us to be good and do good to others. Some of the positive emotions are love, compassion, and happiness. While negative emotions are those that agitate and disturb our beings, make us feel terrible, and push us to harm others or act in a way we may regret later. Some of our negative emotions are hatred, jealousy, hostility, sadness, and anger.

Our feelings are highly natural and spontaneous. We feel the way we do. We have no control over them. Also, they are irrational. They have nothing to do with thought.

Definition of Feeling

Feeling is a natural inner action or reaction, often irrational, but a very important part of human living.

Derivative Right Way of Living

Since feeling is such an important aspect of life, and we feel all the time, the Derivative Right Way of Living would include doing those actions that make us feel happy. Happiness is a wonderful feeling. It envelops our whole beings in its warmth, nurtures our beings, motivates us to live, and makes others happy too. That being said, trying to feel happy should be one of the objectives of human life.

Feeling is a highly natural and spontaneous process. We have no control of how we feel toward a sight, action, or person. Our feelings are highly irrational too. Therefore, we ought to season our feelings with thoughts. Thinking cools down and rationalizes a feeling or emotion. For example, if I feel angry, I should immediately think about who or what I am feeling angry at, and why, and ask myself how to solve it? Doing so cools down our anger and helps us cope better with a situation.

Also, we can modify our surroundings so that we like them—decorate our homes well and have neat and tidy offices. We should seek the company of those who like us and whom we like but we should always listen to criticism too. It can teach us a number of things about ourselves. Also, we should try to seek happiness by pursuing our hobbies and having happy work, and happy relationships like loving family and friends.

Subhava

We ought to be aware of our feelings and practice *Subhava*— try to feel positive feelings like love and happiness, and view others with compassion and goodwill. View even your enemy with compassion and goodwill. This will help you understand her better and will mellow your heart and ennoble you.

Thinking

Thinking is another important aspect of living. We humans think all the time, sometimes consciously, often unconsciously— without being aware of it. We may feel, think, and act together, or we may just be doing cold, calculated thinking.

Thinking is a highly complex mental activity. To think is to ponder and reflect on something, or reason—think rationally. It may include remembering and imagining, but it is not only remembering and imagining. Thinking is distinct from "RIFing": remembering, imagining, and feeling, which we humans tend to do most of the time.

Thinking evolved at a much later period of human evolution because thinking requires good language. Also, it includes playing with abstract symbols in the mind. Abstract thinking is done in the cerebral complex, the uppermost part and top layer of the human brain, which evolved recently. The ability to think well is the sign of a highly developed human brain.

The Human mind indulges in many types of thinking: creative thinking, problem solving, and critical thinking. Each type has its own purpose.

Creative thinking is done to create a new product or idea. It is a tool of artists. A novelist thinks, creates a plot in her mind, and then writes a novel. Her novel is the product of her creative thinking. A sculptor envisages an image of a statue in her mind and then works with clay to create the statue. A musician creates a symphony in her mind, and then sings or works with instruments to produce it. Many of our daily use products are also the products of creative thinking.

Problem-solving thinking is done to solve some real-life or other problem. It includes identifying a problem and creating and finding a solution to that problem. It requires creative thinking, manipulation, and acquiring new knowledge. It may be as simple as finding a new route while driving or as complex as solving a crime mystery. This type of thinking is required by professionals like lawyers, crime detectives, and high executives. It also helps one cope with daily life problems.

There is another important type of thinking a human mind indulges in called critical thinking. It is one of the finest types of thinking. It involves making a decision about what to do or what to believe in or making choices. This type of thinking requires assessing the whole situation or different choices, weighing their pros and cons, comparing and contrasting, collecting new information or evidence, and then making a decision. This is used by lawyers, philosophers, executives, and even average people in their daily lives who need to make a decision or a choice.

Definition of Thinking

Thinking is a human's highly complex mental activity that includes but is not limited to remembering, imagining, creative thinking, problem solving, and critical thinking.

Derivative Right Way of Living

Thinking is the greatest faculty of the human mind. The majority of humanity's achievements in the fields of Science, Technology, Art, and Administration are products of human thinking. Also, it is required by every human in order to live well.

Thinking, like other human traits, is a genetic trait. Some of us are born thinkers. Others learn and practice thinking. Every human ought to be able to think well and often. This needs to be taught and developed right from childhood. One of the purposes of our education should be to enable students to think independently by teaching them good language and different types of thinking.

Thinking is the mother of ideas and positive changes. We as adults should practice thinking in our daily lives. We should season our feelings with thoughts, and think before acting and behaving.

Suvichara

Our thinking, like our feelings, is often involuntary. Different thought go on in our minds all the times. We as humans ought to be aware of our inner thoughts and practice *Suvichara*—try to think positive thoughts like, love and happiness; think of others; think for All; think high and noble.

Acting, and Facing Consequences of One's Actions

Acting is the most important aspect of human living. To act is to do something. It is synonymous with the Sanskrit word *karma*. The word karma is derived from the root *kri,* which means to do something. Thus, **a *Karma* means an action.**

We humans do a variety of karmas, like standing, walking, running, driving, reading, and writing etc. Though each karma is a concerted effort by both body and mind, some of our karmas are mostly physical, while others are mostly mental. On this basis, all human karmas can be divided into two types, physical or mental.

Physical karmas are those which require mostly physical activity, like standing, walking, running, digging, and cleaning. While mental karmas consist of mostly mental activities, like reading, writing, and thinking.

Every karma is an effort, and is hard. It is an effort by both body and mind to do something. You have to make an effort to stand, to run, to study, to work. Both body and mind have to wake out of slumber and make a conscious effort to do something. Also, every karma requires a certain amount of physical and mental discipline, concentration, training, and knowledge. For example, the simplest karma of standing requires an effort and discipline— to stand straight and in one place. Running requires more effort, discipline, and some amount of concentration so that you don't slip and fall. Reading is a very hard task for the mind: to concentrate one's mind on the written words, understand them, connect them to the context, and grasp the meaning. Studying is one of the hardest karmas—sitting and reading for hours at a stretch, applying maximum amount of prolonged concentration on one subject, the utmost discipline of body and mind, and thinking.

Because of all this, a karma tires us. Every karma causes a certain amount of fatigue. Even the simplest act of standing tires us physically. Walking is more tiring than standing, and running is more tiring than walking. Reading for pleasure is easier than reading for study. The longer you do a karma for, the more amount of effort, discipline, and concentration it requires, and the more tiring it becomes. Of course old people get tired faster than young, but nonetheless doing any karma is tiring to all. Fatigue is the natural effect of a karma.

In short, every karma is an effort that requires physical and mental discipline and concentration, and it tires the Doer. Therefore we humans naturally tend to avoid doing a karma and prefer a lazy state.

But it is the karma that makes one's body and mind active and enables one to taste different aspects of life and achieve money and success in life. When you do a karma, you move your body and mind. This movement makes you awake and active. The body uses up stored energy and strengthens the part of body we use while doing a karma. For example, a physical karma like running strengthens one's legs and physical body; and a mental karma like reading, doing math, or solving a puzzle strengthens one's brain. A karma requires an input and output of energy and therefore fills us with vigor. That is the reason active people are normally healthy. Above all, it is a karma or hard work that leads one to success in education, profession et cetera. These positive effects of karma give all power to karma. And ***these positive effects of karma make fatigue—a natural outcome of karma, actually a shubha— an auspicious omen.***

Fatigue means we did karma. So when you are tired after a day's work and hate fatigue, just think of all the positive effects of your day's karmas. For example, work. Your work gives you money, and if Right, happiness and the very meaning of life too. A human ought not to let fatigue dissuade her from doing karma.

You feel your karma. Every karma evokes a special feeling. This feeling lasts during a karma, and afterward too. For example, running makes you feel active and energetic during running and later too. While eating good food, you enjoy its taste and aroma. You feel fresh and nice while taking a shower, and afterward too. Practicing one's hobby like reading, writing, painting, or singing makes one happy.

You live your karma. Karma is the most important aspect of living. During each day, a human does a variety of karmas. Each karma evokes a special feeling and thought and sheds its own effects. For example, watching a tragic movie makes you feel sad and depressed, and makes you think about the movie and life, and thus affects your mood and mental state. Reading noble thoughts makes you feel good and high, makes you think about ethics, and thus shapes your being.

Every karma sheds its own effects or consequences. It sheds both short-term and long-term effects. Short-term effects last during the karma and for some time after the karma. Long-term effects last during the next few days and maybe throughout one's lifetime. For example, eating wrong food—a highly oily, spicy, or heavy food—makes you feel uncomfortable immediately afterward and causes ill health in the long run. While eating Right food— light and healthy food—makes you feel good immediately afterward, and contributes to your good health in the long run. Studying hard— reading a subject with concentration and understanding it— satisfies you at that time and contributes to your getting good education, and getting a good career that will support you throughout your life. While, not studying, letting your mind wander, makes you feel anxious and uneasy at that time, and contributes to you may be not getting a good education or a good career. Wrong speech, or hurting or hitting someone may jeopardize your relations with that person forever and may put you in jail, which will likely ruin your whole life. Wrong driving may risk your own life and the lives of others and involve you in a lawsuit that will cost you a huge sum of money. A karma done under the heat of some passion, like anger, hatred, or greed, often sheds serious lifelong consequences.

The Power of Karma

We not only feel and live our Karmas, but it is our Karmas that shape our beings and our lives.

Even a feeling or thinking is a karma. Though we feel and think naturally, if we want we can change them. For example, consciously harboring *Subhava*— compassion and goodwill toward others—connects you to others and makes you feel good. While, harboring *Kubhava*— hostility and ill will toward others—disconnects you from others and makes you feel angry and anxious. Similarly, harboring *Suvichara*— high and noble thoughts and calm contemplation—make one a calm and thoughtful person, and make her enjoy the bliss of human existence.

The kind of karmas you do during the day shape you. The best way to know a person is to ask, "What do you do through-out the whole day?" The kind and quality of karmas a person does throughout the day shape her feeling, thinking, and her whole being—personality and quality of life. That is why they say *you should choose a profession carefully because it shapes you.*

Our karmas shape the quality of our lives. From morning till evening, the kind of karmas I do shape my present life and my future too. The kind of food I eat and the amount of exercise I do shape my health. For example, if I eat Right diet and do Right exercise, I feel healthy. But if I eat wrong and heavy food, don't do any exercise, and am inactive, I will feel unhealthy. If I work, have an active profession or busi-ness, and manage my money well, I will be rich. But if I am lazy, do not work—don't have an active profession or busi-ness—and don't take care of my money, then I will end up being poor. Also, Work connects me to others and makes me socially active.

If you want to change your life, change your karmas first.

A karma means every single act you do. It may be cooking, driving, reading, writing, or talking etc. Each karma is distinct, requires concentration, and has its own purpose.

Every karma has its own Right way of being done. The Right way to do a karma is to do it in a way that ensures an efficient and fruitful completion of that karma. Every karma is different, requires some thought and planning and has its own right way of being done. For example, even while doing the simple act of cooking, if you plan it and do it the Right way, it will save you time and help you make tasty food. Of course, you have to learn or figure out the Right way. Preparing a dish the Right way will result in a good and tasty dish. Similarly, while driving, if you plan your trip—know where you are going, know the route, and drive the right way, you will not waste any time, not cause an accident, and reach your destination in time. Reading, like any other karma, requires good concentration and has its own right way. Reading the Right way means doing a quick survey of the entire piece of writing, like an article or a chapter, reading each paragraph, summarizing it after reading, and then summarizing the whole piece of writing. This helps one remember and retain the read material.

Karma Theory

From the above analysis there emerges the Karma Theory or the Law of Karma. As per this theory, Karma is the most important aspect of a human's life. One's Karmas shape her being and her whole life too. If you want to change your life, change your Karmas first. Secondly, every Karma sheds its own effects or consequences. If you do a karma, its consequences will befall you, no matter what. You cannot run away from the consequences of your karmas.

In light of the above Karma Theory, a human ought to choose her each karma very carefully, think of its consequences, and then do it.

Definition of Karma

A karma is any single activity requiring physical and mental effort, discipline, and concentration; shedding its own effects in the form of specific feelings, thoughts, and practical consequences that shape one's being and one's life.

Derivative Right Way of Living

Since our karmas are so important to us—we feel them, we live them, and they shape our beings and our lives—it is imperative that we do Right karmas and do them the Right Way.

A human ought to do Right karmas. ***A Right karma is a Preconceived, Preplanned karma with Positive Effects***. Think before you act, think about its purpose and effects, plan it, and then do it the Right Way.

Doing a karma the Right way means doing it in a way that ensures its efficient and fruitful completion. Every karma has its own Right way of being done. Walking the Right way is different from cooking the Right way. Driving the Right way is different from reading the Right way. One ought to learn and know the Right way of doing a karma and do it the Right way.

A person's present is the product of her past karmas, and her future will be the product of her present karmas. It is my present Karmas which will shape my future life. Therefore our present karmas should be derived from our future goals. Only then will we accomplish our future goals. We as humans ought to be aware of our karma all the time and practice *sukarma*— doing good karmas or doing those actions that shed positive effects for us and for all.

Coping with The Whole

There is this vast Whole—the world around a human of which she is a part. She has no control of it—the kind of place she is born and lives in; the kind of people she lives amid; the situation, circumstances, and calamities that befall her during her life. A human finds it very hard to cope with all this and at times feels very feeble in front of it. But there are ways to help a person deal better with this aspect of life.

We often have no control of the kind of place we are born in and live in. But if it is really a bad place to live in, one can go to some other place and make her home there. It just takes courage and some planning.

Wherever you live there are people around. A human lives amid people and has to deal with people all the time. We often have no control of other people's behavior—how they talk to us or what they do to us.

In dealing with people, our general attitude should be that of compassion and goodwill. Compassion means—observe the other person, try to understand her/his situation in life, and then deal with that person. Compassion is a noble human emotion that makes us aware of the other person and helps us understand her and deal with her better. (Take the other person into account, her/his feelings, situation, desires, and then act.) While dealing with other people, our behavior should not be guided solely by our own selfish interests, but also by understanding the other person's situation, interests, and desires.

Compassion means understanding the other person, empathizing with her, and then acting.

Goodwill should be another guiding factor in our behavior toward other persons. Having goodwill means wanting to see the other person happy. Guided by goodwill, we are more willing to understand the other person, to listen, and to help the other person if needed. Also, in this process we try to smile and be pleasant to the other person, which makes us happy too.

We humans live in a society—in the company of other humans. If each of us is guided by compassion and goodwill towards others, our society will be more supportive, harmonious, and happy.

Both of these emotions—compassion and goodwill—are not natural to us. There are exalted human emotions. But if practiced they enlarge our inner world, connect us to other people, help us understand them better, and make us happy. They do wonders in our interpersonal relationships and in dealing with others.

A human's social dealings—her attitude and behavior toward other people and her interpersonal relationships—are major aspects of living. Their quality affects the quality of one's overall life.

Together with Right attitude—that of compassion and goodwill toward others—Right behavior is another requirement in leading a good life. Right behavior means right gestures, right speech, and right actions toward others. The theory of behavior involves give and take. Our behavior with other people often produces the same behavior from them. For example, if I am rude to the other person, I instigate the other person to be rude to me. Our behavior is often unconscious and emanates from our natures. Since behavior is a very important aspect of our dealings with others, our behavior ought to be conscious. I must know how am I looking at the other person, how am I talking to the other person, and what am I doing to the other person. Secondly, one's behavior ought not to be guided only by one's nature. There are some universal rules of right behavior that ought to be followed. These are RPH: being respectful, polite, and honest to the other person in your all relationships, personal and social. Respect the other person regardless of her/his position in life. Be polite and courteous in your speech and actions toward other persons. Smile at others and give way to them. This will make you happy. Be honest in all your personal and business relationships. Don't lie, don't cheat, and don't steal. Do your job well. Give the best product and service to your clients. These rules of Right behavior make an individual happy and successful, and facilitate social dealings.

All human relationships fall into one of two classes, personal or business relationships. Personal relationships are those with one's family and friends. These are based on emotional attachment and mutual liking. Business relationships are those of the marketplace and workplace. These are based on the exchange of product or service and money.

Each human relationship is distinct. Each has its own title and a derivative set of right do's or duties. These duties emanate from the nature of a relationship. These are the threads a relationship is made of. If you want to maintain a relationship, you have to do its right do's or duties.

The Right way to live a relationship is to live it as per its title. The moment I relate to the other person, the other person has a title. She can be a "stranger," a "neighbor," a "family relationship," a "friend," a "boss," a "colleague," or a "client." Each of these titles has its own set of right do's or duties, which emanate from the nature of that relationship. These are the threads that connect us to the other person. If you want to maintain a relationship, you have to do its right do's or duties. For example, a stranger is a person whom I don't know at all. He could be anyone and could be a good person or a bad person. In dealing with a stranger, the first thing to do is to find out her/his identity by asking her/him and verifying it. Do move with compassion and try to know the person, and then talk and deal with him. Similarly, a neighbor is one who lives in close vicinity to my home or office. One ought to be polite to one's neighbors, get to know them, and help them in need. Behaving so will evoke the same behavior from your neighbors, which is good for you too. A parent is one who produces a child, and loves and rears her child. A parent ought to fulfill her duties to her child. Doing so is deeply satisfying for a person and makes her happy.

A title is the basis of a relationship. I have discussed this aspect of a human relationship in my earlier section on The Human Whole.

Though every human relationship takes two to build and run it, *Svadharma,* if followed, can help build and run a relationship, and may even change the other person and make her do her share of duties too. *Svadharma* is a Sanskrit word, made of two words: *Sva* and *Dharma. Sva* means *"my,"* and *Dharma* means "Right thing to do" or "duties." Doing *Svadharma* means I do my Dharma or my duties well in every relationship and general living, even if others do not. For example, I as a parent—a mother or a father— ought to treat my child with love and patience and provide for her, even if she is unruly, angry, and ungrateful. Doing these duties toward my child, regardless of any returns from her, will deeply satisfy me as a parent and strengthen my relationship with her. Similarly, as a child—a daughter or a son—I ought to treat my parents with respect and care and serve them well in their need. Doing so will satisfy me emotionally and strengthen my relationship with them.

In marketplace dealings, I as a "Seller" ought to provide the best product and service to my client regardless of the nature and dealings of that client. Doing so will spread the good word about my work and help grow my business.

Svadharma means to take an initiative in Right behavior toward others. Practice compassion and goodwill toward all. Respect every individual, and be polite and honest in dealings with others. In a relationship, do your share of duties well.

No doubt, like any other rule, the behavioral rule of *Svadharma* has its own flaws and is open to criticism. Despite that it is a golden rule of behavior, and it works. I will discuss *Svadharma* in detail at the end of this book—a proper ending of Dharma.

Svadharma keeps us calm and is a fixed guide to our behavior. Otherwise, we humans, in our behavior, tend to follow others, behave as others do, and neglect our duties. This makes us uncertain in our behavior, and disturbs our relationships and the harmony of our society too.

Coping with Calamities

A human's life is a long journey of some seventy-plus years. During one's lifetime, every human faces certain exigencies of life. These can be adverse circumstances or calamities totally beyond one's control, like fire, flood, earthquake, war, or the death of a loved one. An adverse circumstance or a calamity may befall anyone anywhere at any time. It shocks us, and depending upon its suddenness and intensity it may even make one lose one's mind or mental balance and make her do something disastrous, like commit suicide etc.

We see them happen to others around us all the time. But we think that they will never happen to us. The truth is that a calamity or an adversity may happen to any of us at any time. A human ought to be prepared for a calamity, face it with courage, remain calm and then act. This will help a human face and overcome life's calamities and get on better with life.

A Human's Life as a Whole

A human's life from birth until death is a Whole—A Whole of some seventy-plus years or the total number of years a human lives for. Some die early, and some die in youth, while others make it to a ripe old age.

We humans live our lives moment to moment, day to day, without any concept of our lives as a whole.

A human's life is an interconnected chain of her past, present, and future. My past affects my present. My present affects my future. I, as a human, cannot uproot myself from my past and start all over. My past memories affect my present. And my present is largely the product of my past karmas. For example, memories of my family will assail me even if I do not keep in touch with them. And, I may regret severely a blunder I committed in my youth.

A human's life is a Whole—one whole chain of a person's life events, circumstances, the kind of place she was born in, the kind of family she had, the kind of schools she went to, the kind of professions she had, the kind of marriage she had. Each of these is a shackle of her life's chain, where one affects the other, and moulds the other, and all of them altogether constitute the Whole of a human's life. For example, a child born into poverty or an abusive family may not go to school and study. But if she goes to school, receives a good education and gets into a good profession, she will earn good money. There is a whole chain here—though born poor, in adverse circumstances, she studied hard and completed her education. Because of her good education, she got a good job. And a good profession, in turn, earned her riches. Though, memories of her abusive childhood will torment her psyche forever.

A human is born, lives, and dies. Throughout her total life-time of some seventy-plus years she does karmas and earns her achievements. It is at death that a person's whole life-time's achievements are assessed—how much money she made; the cars, houses and other property she leaves; how many children and type of children she leaves; the kind of achievements she earned in her profession, like making a great scientific discovery, or writing a great book. All these achievements are counted at the death of a person because they matter, because it is this set of achievements that she leaves behind through which she enriches the world. These achievements acquired and achieved during one's lifetime define her whole life, give it meaning, and make it worth something. Each of these truly countable achievements— amount of wealth she made; types of children she had; and any professional distinction she achieved, was achieved after years and maybe after her whole lifetime's consistent efforts in one direction. For example, if someone is a successful professional or a business person, it is after devoting years of labor in her field. It takes years of time and lots of money and hardships to produce and rear a child. A Scientist labors for years, sacrifices her whole life, and then comes up with a great scientific discovery. A great Writer, troubled by the outside world and her psyche, reads, thinks, ponders, reflects, and after years of hard labor produces a great book. Some great books were written in twenty to thirty years. Each of these shows a person's hard, consistent labor in one direction.

This fact—the final assessment of one's Achievements at death— makes a human's one lifetime a Whole, in which consistent efforts in one direction build her various achievements.

A human ought to view her life as a Whole and live it this way.

Every Day Life

A human lives her life as a whole, but she lives it on an everyday basis. Every day is a unit in which a human's whole life is broken and lived in.

A human's whole life is an Edifice, a Construct that she builds, and retains by her everyday karmas in one direction—be it her profession, family, or any other achievement.

A human gets up in the morning, does her day's tasks, goes to work, attends to her family work, and then goes to sleep at night. The next day she gets up and does the same again. Every day is so important in a human's life. In order for any religion to be lived, any Value to be achieved, any goal to be accomplished, it must be lived and worked toward every day.

Also, every day is a whole new day in a human's life, open to so many possibilities and potentials—a long new day during which one can change one's Karmas, make new choices, and try to live a better life.

A human ought to have a view of her "Whole life," and of "Every Day," in her life.

Definition of Human Life

A human's life is a journey of certain number of years— average seventy years— starting at her birth; lived in four major age spans of Childhood, Youth, Middle age, and Old age; and ending at her death—Life lived as a Whole, as well as everyday and every moment, where living is a continuous Process of feeling, thinking, acting, facing the consequences of one's actions, and coping with The Whole; a Continuous struggle for survival and happiness, but overall a highly meaningful Process by which a human lives a good life herself and enriches her Whole too.

The above is a definition of a human's one lifetime where each component has its own derivative Right Way of Living. I discussed them at the end of each component.

From the analysis of human life there emerge **Five major Life Values: Family, Education, Work, Marriage, and Child.** I have devoted the next chapter to them.

CHAPTER 4

FIVE ETERNAL HUMAN, LIFELONG VALUES

While analyzing "What is human life?" and in tracing the pathway of a human's life from birth to death, there emerged five entities that happen in succession in a human's life; give it direction, purpose, and meaning; and remain with her/him throughout her/his lifetime. These are: ***"Family," "Education," "Work" (profession), "Marriage,"*** *and* ***"Child."*** Also, they are the Five main pivots around which a human's life and human society are constructed. They are footholds that trap a human, and give stability and depth to her life. Since they are so closely interlinked to a human and human existence, they are Eternal Human Values. Till there is a human on this Earth, these five entities will remain as major lifelong Human Values.

These are five major milestones that create the trail of a human's life and through which a human's life journey is assessed. They are Milestones because they are very important events in a human's life, the nature of which shape the quality of a human's whole life.

A human is born as the most helpless infant in the cradle of her <u>First Family</u> or Family by Birth. There she is reared for first twenty years of her life. She receives <u>education</u> from childhood up to youth for the first eighteen to twenty years of her life. As a young adult, she <u>works</u> or engages in a profession through which she enriches her society and earns money. Sometime during adulthood, she <u>marries,</u> produces <u>children</u> of her own, and thus acquires her <u>Second Family</u> or Family by Marriage. From youth until death, she works and lives in her Second Family.

This is the pattern of an average human's life in almost every human society. That is why they are Universal Human Values too. Each of these entities— Family, Education, Work, Marriage, and Child—fulfills a variety of human needs throughout her/his lifetime; therefore they are Lifelong Human Values.

In the next few pages, I will analyze the nature of each of these Values, define it, note its importance in a human's life, and then take the derivative Right Way of Living or see how to incorporate each of these Values in a human's life.

1. FAMILY

A human throughout her/his entire lifetime goes through two sets of families: First Family or Family by Birth, and Second Family or Family by Marriage. I have termed them First and Second family in view of their succession in a human's life.

A human is born and reared in the cradle of her First Family or Family by birth. This is made of a human's parents, siblings, and other first family relatives like grandparents, aunts, uncles, and cousins. A human spends the first and most formative twenty or more years of her life in the arena of her First Family.

Sometime during adulthood a human marries, produces children, and thus creates her Second Family or Family by Marriage. A human's Second Family is made of her/his spouse, in-laws, and children. From youth until death, for the next fifty-plus years, a human lives in the arena of her Second Family.

Both of these families fulfill a human's survival, emotional, and other needs during different phases of her life. A human remains deeply attached to both her families throughout her entire lifetime.

First Family

A human is born as the most helpless infant in the cradle of her First Family. This is where she is born and reared for first twenty years of her life. During this long phase she forms certain prime relationships that last throughout her lifetime. Also, this is the most significant, formative phase during which she is reared and shaped into a certain type of individual. All this happens in the arena of her First Family.

A human's First Family consists of her parents, siblings, grandparents, aunts, uncles and cousins.

A human's parents by birth are a couple of a female mother and a male father who copulate and give birth to their child. Parents deem their child as a part of their own selves and rear her for the first twenty years of her life. From birth, they wash her; feed her; watch her all the time; respond to her every cry; fulfill all her survival needs of food, clothes and safety; give her a loving home; and pay all her expenses. During these long years of close association between parents and child, the child bonds emotionally to her parents and views them as an integral part of her Self and her existence. The Parent-Child relationship is one of the closest human relationships.

A human's siblings are her brothers and sisters born from the same parents. During her childhood and youth phases, a human spends the major part of her time at home with her siblings. They eat together, play together, study, and sleep together. They fight, reconcile, and live together. Each of them differs in appearance, talents, and intelligence. And each of them wants the parents' love and attention. So there does result sibling rivalry and jealousy, but nonetheless, by living together in such close association a deep attachment and emotional bonding forms among siblings, so much so that they view each other as a part of their deep selves. After parents, the sibling relationship is one of the most lasting human relationships. A human remains deeply attached to her parents and siblings throughout her lifetime. Somewhere down in her heart she is deeply concerned about their well-being and cares for them.

A human's grandparents are her both parents' parents: her mother's mother and father, and her father's mother and father. Grandparents often adore their grandchildren, lavish them with love, and view them as parts of their deep selves whom they will leave behind in the world. In nuclear families children live away from their grandparents and meet them once in a while, while in joint families children get the bountiful love of their grandparents. There is always a deep emotional bond between grandparents and grandchildren.

A Human's Aunt is her mother's or father's sister, to whom she/he is either a niece or a nephew. A human's Uncle is her mother's brother, or her father's brother. Being from the same blood family, there is a genetic affinity and natural love between aunts/uncles and their nieces/nephews. In single families children often do not get to communicate with or meet their aunts and uncles often, while in joint families children get the added love and support of their aunts and uncles. In every human heart there is a soft corner for her aunts and uncles or for her nieces and nephews. A human views them as a part of her prime Self or identity.

Cousins are one's aunts' and uncles' children. There is sibling-like love and attachment between cousins, especially if they have grown up together.

A human spends the first twenty years of her life amid the love and support of her First Family relationships. These are the very first relationship a human forms during the first, most tender years of her life. Consequently, she deems them as part of her deep Self and basic identity. She remains attached to them throughout her lifetime.

Rearing

A human is born as the most helpless infant in the cradle of her First Family. Like any other living being, she has survival needs of home, food, safety, proper training and other needs. A human's First Family is her safe home, where all her survival needs are fulfilled and where she learns her lifelong moral and other Values.

A human is born as a very tender, infirm living being who needs to be held, fed, cleaned, washed, and soothed very frequently during the first two years of her life. Often she stays awake throughout the night and cries constantly. It is her parents, especially her mother, who run to her every cry, soothe her, feed and clean her.

From birth until adulthood, a child needs food, clothes, playthings, and living space—a home—and incurs hordes of other expenses, like education and medical needs. All these expenses are paid by the child's parents or/and by other First Family members.

From the age of two, a child starts walking and speaking. She observes others and tries to copy them. That is how she learns everything. She learns how to walk, talk, be lazy or active, and study or not study. She learns her worldview and attitude toward others: whom to like or dislike, whom to trust or mistrust, whom to respect or disrespect. She learns her moral values—whether it is OK to cheat, steal, and lie, or not OK. She learns her overall do's and don'ts, and general behavior patterns by observing her parents, siblings, and other First Family relatives in whose company she lives constantly.

She is rewarded or punished for her every action. Rewards encourage her to repeat the act, and punishments discourage her from repeating the act. If she lies and gets away with it, she lies again. But if she lies, gets caught, and is disapproved of or punished for lying, she tries not to lie next time.

It is in the arena of her First Family that a human imbibes her lifelong Values. If she watches others study and is taught to sit and study, she learns to study. If forced to study every day, to get good grades, and told about the importance of studying all the time, she starts viewing education as a Value. Similarly, if a child grows up in a happy family with parents and siblings and enjoys their love and support, she learns to value Family. The same goes for her other lifelong Values.

Thus a human's First Family is the first and foremost school of her lifelong character and Values.

Definition of First Family

A human's First Family is her Family by Birth—her root in this world. It is a group of her parents, siblings, and other blood relatives. This is her first home, where all her survival needs are fulfilled, all her education and other expenses are paid, where she feels strong and happy amid the love and support of her parents, siblings, and other blood relatives, and where she learns her life-long habits and Values.

Value of First family in a Human's life

A human needs her First Family.

A human is born as the most helpless, weak infant with a variety of survival needs. She needs food, clothes, shelter—a home—medical help, education, and many other things and services. It is her First Family, especially parents, who fulfill all her needs amid their true love and support for their child. They do so right from the child's birth until her adulthood—a phase of some eighteen years. This is also the phase during which a child grows from an infant to a teenager, and then to a young adult. Through all these growing years, a child needs the constant love, support, supervision, and guidance of her parents, siblings, and other First Family relatives who can provide her with a safe, loving home and fulfill all her survival needs. Also, they need to teach good daily habits, and moral and other life-long Values that will help the child live a good life herself and enrich her family and society.

A human passes through two sets of families in her life. Her First Family is the one in which she was born and reared for first most formative twenty years of her life. A human views her First Family as her roots or prime identity from where she came to this world—"my mother," "my father," "my brother," "my sister," "my home." These are parts of her deepest Self. She remains emotionally bonded to her parents, siblings, and other First Family relatives amid whom she spends the first twenty years of her life.

Derivative Right Way of Living

A human's First Family is the one in which she is born and reared for the first twenty years of her life. During these most tender and formative years, she forms deep emotional bonds with her parents, siblings, other First Family relatives, friends, and with her parental home. She also gathers millions of soft, deep memories of childhood. A human carries these bonds and memories with her throughout her lifetime. Later she marries and creates her Second Family, but bonds and memories of her First Family remain with her forever.

Maintaining one's First Family bonds and refreshing her childhood memories make a human very happy. A human ought to remain in touch with her First Family. ***"Care, Communicate, and Support"*** are three key ways to maintain ties with one's family. A human ought to have compassion and care for her parents, siblings, and other First Family relatives. She ought to communicate—talk to them and meet them once in a while. She ought to support them financially and personally in their needs. Doing so nourishes her roots and her emotional bonds and satisfies her deeply. Such a human is a happy human, who through the demands and challenges of daily life can maintain her First Family ties.

Second Family

Sometime during adulthood, a human marries, produces child(ren) of her own, and thus creates her Second Family or Family by Marriage.

A human's Second Family is made of a human's Spouse, In-Laws, and Child(ren). A human spends a good fifty-plus years or the remaining part of her life in the arena of her Second Family. A spouse is a common term used to denote a female wife or a male husband. A woman in the role of wife has some duties toward her husband, and a man in the role of husband has some duties toward his wife. *In-Laws* is another English term used to denote one's spouse's family, where the title remains the same with the added effects of the term *In-Law*, for example mother-in-law, father-in-law, brother-in-law, sister-in-law, and so on. As per this definition and rightly so a human ought to treat her spouse's family like her own family, respect them, and fulfill one's responsibilities toward them as (s)he would have done towards her/his own family. A child is a common term used for a daughter or son. A child is born of a married couple—a female wife and a male husband—or can be adopted.

A human's Second Family is created by marriage. Marriage is a major milestone in a human's life. It brings about dramatic changes in a human's life. Immediately after marriage there is a sudden change in one's roles and responsibilities.

After marriage a woman and a man live together as wife and husband in the same house. In some societies they live in a joint family, where one of the spouses, mostly the wife moves to her husband's house and lives with his family. In many societies, especially modern ones, both the spouses—wife and husband—set up their own home after marriage.

Since a married couple lives together, they both need to understand each other and make major adjustments. They need to understand each other's nature, moods, and temperament and behave in a way so that they both can live together in peace and harmony. A person has to adjust to her spouse's habits, hobbies, and the whole way of living. Both the spouses have to respect each other and learn to tolerate each other's bad habits. Since both are adult individuals from two different families, there may be major differences in their beliefs, Values, and habits, but in order to remain married they have to adjust. In a joint family, a person has to adjust to her spouse's all family members, while in a nuclear family a person has to adjust only to her spouse.

Since a married couple lives together and shares a home, there arise issues of financial responsibility and responsibilities of running the home, with everyday household chores like cooking, cleaning, laundry, and maintaining and buying household supplies.

In earlier societies and in some families till date, there is a clear-cut division of labor in which a husband works and earns money while the wife does the household chores and maintains the home. In modern times, when often both spouses work, there is no such clear-cut division of labor. In modern societies, where both spouses work and earn money, there arises the issue of financial responsibility—who would spend, and how much? Also, both spouses go to work in the morning and return home in the evening, tired from a day's work. Then there arise the issues of household chores and other responsibilities. Who will cook, clean the house, do laundry, and buy home supplies? These may lead to spousal disputes and fights. In some cases the couple fights frequently, and the marriage falls apart, while in other cases, both the spouses behave responsibly, work together, and share the financial responsibility and household chores. Their mutual understanding, love, and support make their marriage last and make everyday life easy for both.

From the above analysis there emerge two prime components of marriage: Support and Companionship. Whatever the society or time maybe, after marriage both the spouses support each other financially and personally and live in each other's constant company.

After marriage both wife and husband have sex together. Regular marital sex fulfills a human's sexual need, is a source of enjoyment for both, and creates offspring(s) of both the spouses. Also, regular marital sex brings together both the spouses, connects them, and keeps them well bonded to each other.

After marriage a human acquires a group of In-Laws— spouse's family— Mother-In-Law, Father-In-Law, Brother-In-Law, Sister-In-Law, and the Spouse's nieces and nephews. The In-Laws are an added family and therefore added obligations and responsibilities, but at the same time, there are an added family bond, support, and joy in sharing family time. Many people maintain good relations with their In-Laws, care for them, and in turn get their care and support.

After marriage both wife and husband produce their own children. A child is another major milestone in a human's life. Arrival of a child brings with it a heavy set of responsibilities for both parents. A child is a major financial responsibility. A huge sum of money goes toward paying her daily survival needs, school and college tuition, and hordes of other expenses. Also, the child needs to be fed, cleaned, watched, and supervised all the time.

This requires time and work from both parents. Which parent, mom or dad fulfills which duty toward the child varies from family to family. In a family where a man is the prime money earner, he bears all expenses of the child; and the mother is responsible for cleaning, feeding, watching the child, and helping her/him with studies. But in a family where both parents work, both pay for their child's expenses, and both devote their time and efforts to clean, feed, watch the child, and help her with studies. Again, major adjustment, coordination, and understanding are required from both parents to rear their child well.

A child is a constant source of joy to both parents, part of their own flesh and blood, dear to both parents. Parents deem their child as a part of their deep Selves.

As years pass by, a human spends a major part of her time in the arena of her Second Family, mainly with her spouse and children. This is where her home is and where her daily needs are met with. There are responsibilities to the spouse and children, but at the same time, there is spousal care and support together with both parents' common love for their children. One feels strong and happy in the warmth of her Second Family. With time there develops an emotional bond between both the spouses and between parents and children. Both the spouses tend to depend on each other more and more. They learn to ignore each other's faults, respect each other's good points, and enjoy the joy of togetherness.

With passing years one enjoys the growing phases of children. Their pranks and their playfulness make one feel young and happy. The hardships of raising your children are marred by the joys of spending time with your children, playing with them, sharing with them, teaching them, and seeing them grow. Once grown, children lend a supporting hand to their parents.

Also, in the Second Family one enjoys the added support and care of one's In-Laws. They are added family who care for you.

Definition of Second Family

A human's Second Family or Family by Marriage is a group of her/ his Spouse, In-Laws, and Children. It is created and maintained by marriage. A human spends a major part of her life—from youth until death—in the arena of her Second Family. It is in here that she has her own home and the love and support of her Spouse, Children, and In-Laws.

Value of Second Family in a Human's Life

A human's life is a long, arduous journey of about seventy-plus years with daily survival needs and hordes of other needs. It requires a lot of labor to earn money and to fulfill the daily needs of home, food, and many other needs. A single human finds it very hard to fulfill all her needs on her own. She requires constant, daily spousal support to fulfill her financial and other needs.

A human needs marriage. The institution of marriage is the most ancient and time-tested human institution. It provides a human with her Spouse's *SSCC: Support,* both financial and personal; *Sex; Companionship;* and one's own *Children.* Also, Marriage provides a human with the added support of a new family of In-Laws.

A child of your own gives you immense joy, deep satisfaction, and added support. Also, you pass off your best to your child. Children carry their parents' genes and symbolize the best of their parents' Life Values. A child marks one of the deepest meanings of a human's life. ***I as a human will die one day but will leave behind my child to the Whole.***

Thus a human needs a Second Family. It provides a human with her own home, the constant care and support of her spouse and children, and the added support of her In-Laws. The spousal bond and bonding with children make one feel strong and happy. After a day's hard work, a human returns to her own home and enjoys the love and warmth of her Second Family.

A human, her/his spouse, and children are the Prime Human Family—the First Founding stone of the human Family and human Society.

Derivative Right Way of Living for the Second Family

The above analysis shows the nature of a human's Second Family and its value in a human's life. Life is a continuous everyday struggle. A human needs the warmth, support, and joy of her Second Family. She needs marriage. Marriage gives one her spouse's *SSCC—Support, Sex, Companionship,* and a *Child* of her own. A child marks the deep meaning in a human's life and is a support in the later years of life.

Sometime during adulthood, a human ought to marry and set up her own home. She ought to view marriage as a lifelong Value and extend her SSCCs of marriage: support her spouse both—financially and personally; be a willing and active sex partner with her spouse; be a good companion; and produce and rear children of her own. She ought to respect her In-Laws and care for them.

Value of Family in a Human's Life

A human, in her lifetime goes through two sets of families— First Family or Family by Birth, and Second Family or Family by Marriage.

A human's First Family is a group of her/his parents (mother and father), siblings (brother and sisters), and other blood relatives. A human's First Family is the Cradle in which she is born and reared from birth till youth. This is her very First Home that fulfills her all survival needs of food, clothes, safety, education, and other needs. This is her First School in where she learns her moral and other lifelong Values.

A human is born as the most helpless infant, who remains weak and helpless during her further years of childhood up to youth. She needs the constant care, support, and guidance of her First Family. A human needs a stable, loving First Home.

Sometime during youth a human marries, produces children of her own, and thus acquires her Second Family. A human's Second Family is a group of her Spouse, In-Laws, and children. It is created and maintained by marriage. After marriage, a human sets up her second home—a base that fulfils her daily survival needs of food, clothes, safety, etc., and in where she enjoys constant care and support of her spouse, the joy of rearing her own children, and the support of her children in her old age. From youth until old age/death, a human lives in the arena of her Second Family.

A human needs marriage. Marriage gives her the SSCC—the financial and personal support of her spouse; regular marital sex; everyday companionship of her spouse; and children of her own. A human needs a child of her own. A child gives meaning to a human's life. A human passes off her good genes and the best of her moral and other life Values in the form of her child(ren). A child is the contribution of a human's best to her whole. Above all, a human needs the everyday support and companionship of one's spouse and a warm and loving home, well-run and maintained by both the spouses' cooperation. A human needs her Second Family.

Family is a ship of love and warmth in the vast, hostile ocean of life—a group of your own people who love and care for you.

The Prime human family is made of a female wife and a male husband tied by the bond of marriage and their children.

A human family is one of the founding stones of human society. We can view a human society as a vast group of humans living together in distinct units of families, where each family marks a distinct group of humans with a distinct home. Each of these groups—each Family is a group of humans related to one another by blood or marriage—is a distinct genetic pool, preserved and maintained by family. It is only by maintaining a Family that distinct genetic pools are maintained and close relatives do not intermarry, which is required for the birth of healthy children.

A strong and stable family loves and supports its children and rears them well. Such a society is a strong and flourishing society whose members have the support of their families and whose children are brought up in loving and stable families.

A family is the Center of morality, which teaches its best moral values to its children and instinctively stops them from doing something wrong.

A human Family is the Treasurer of the human bloodline, traditions, and its ages-old moral and other lifelong Values. It is only by maintaining a family that human society avoids incest and each family's best of traditions, morals and other values are passed off to its children.

Derivative Right Way of Living

A human ought to view her/his family as a lifelong Value, which she ought to acquire and cherish.

A human throughout her lifetime ought to value her both families—First Family or Family by Birth, and Second Family—Family by Marriage.

"Care, Communicate, and Support" are the three key ways to maintain one's family ties. Care means true concern for the well-being and happiness of another person. Deep down we all care for our close family: parents— mother and father, siblings—brothers and sisters, and other family relatives— but we do not realize it in our day-to-day hectic lives. A human ought to live this care by maintaining one's First Family ties— by calling them, meeting them once in a while, and supporting them in need. A human's First Family is her roots—her origin in this world. Maintaining ties with one's First Family nourishes one's roots and gives her a deep satisfaction and true joy.

Sometime during adulthood a human ought to marry, view marriage as a lifelong Value, and live its SSCC—extend her constant financial and personal support to her spouse; be a willing and active sex partner with one's spouse; share happy times and activities with one's spouse; produce children from marriage, and rear them well with lots of love and care. A child gives deep meaning to a human's life.

Care, communicate, and support are again three magic ways to maintain one's Second Family ties. Caring for the well-being and happiness of your spouse and children, talking to them every everyday, spending time and doing fun activities with them, and supporting them in need strengthen and maintain one's Second Family and keep it going.

Maintaining one's family ties makes a person happy. After a day's hard work, returning to one's happy and loving family is one of the greatest human joys.

2. EDUCATION

Education is another Eternal Human, lifelong Value. As a reminder, I have placed Five Values in succession as they appear in a human's life.

A human is born and reared in her First Family. From the age of four or so, a child in a civilized human society starts going to school. She spends a major part of every day in a school, where she receives a formal education. After finishing school she goes to a college, and then to a university—the last step to her formal education. For the first twenty years, an average human lives her life into two major institutions—her First Family and her School or College. Here the developing child is disciplined, pruned, and shaped into an adult human. Both of these institutions—Family and Education—teach their children ages old wisdom, morality, and the treasures of human knowledge accumulated by a human society during the past thousands of years. Every human society carefully preserves every bit of its wisdom, traditions, morals, and other life Values and knowledge and passes them off to its children inside the doors of these two institutions – Family and Education.

Before going any further into the realm of education, let us first analyze the nature and process of education. Then I will define it, and then note its derivative truths and Right Way of Living—see how to incorporate this excellent Value, a blessing to human existence called Education in a human's life.

The term *education* means the whole act or process of educating, where to educate means "train or instruct mentally and morally; provide systematic instruction for" (*Oxford Dictionary*).

Education is a process of teaching and learning that takes place between a teacher and a student. A teacher is an expert in a specific field, who teaches and trains a student or a learner. A teacher teaches by theory—books, lectures, and discussions— and by practice. A student learns by listening to the teacher, by understanding her, by reading prescribed books, taking part in discussions, and by watching the practice and doing the practice herself.

This process is hard for both—the teacher and the student. The teacher has to explain and make the student understand. It is harder for the student, who has to concentrate, listen, read, remember, and practice the lesson. Teaching can be as simple as teaching someone how to drive a car, or it can be as complex as teaching the principles of Calculus, the theories of Physics, or some philosophical concept. But essentially the process is the same, and is hard.

Education can be in any realm of life, ranging from simple language, sports, Arts to Mathematics, Science, Philosophy et cetera.

A little peek into the origin of education will help explain its nature, need, and value in a human's life. Origin of education goes back to the very inception of human civilization. With the beginning of agricultural society some twelve thousand years back, the humans started living in large groups along riversides or near fertile land where they could grow crops to feed themselves and their families. As a large number of people lived together, there arose the need for some strong mode of communication like language. With time different languages developed in different societies.

Also, in an agricultural society, once people's survival needs were met with, they had plenty of free time, in which they could work and develop different products and services to fulfill a wide range of human needs. Some people worked in the field of farming, others worked in housing, and some worked in clothing, while some worked in the field of language. Slowly people learned how to write. This together with other human needs gave rise to different trades and professions.

At the same time, there were some deeply sensitive humans who felt the pains of life or observed around them keenly. They expressed their deeply felt emotions in the form of poetry, paintings, and sculptures etc. This gave rise to the field of Art.

As societies grew more civilized and prosperous, some of the highest human minds started speculating about the origin of the world, the nature of human life and its problems, God, and so on. This gave rise to the field of Philosophy.

At the same time, there were some human minds who interpreted the space in terms of lines and angles. This gave rise to Geometry. Others worked with numbers and developed Arithmetic. Later on, adding the numbers to concepts started Algebra. This is how the great field of Mathematics was started and developed.

With time there arose other fields of human labor and professions like Astronomy, Palmistry, and Religion et cetera. Each of these fulfilled some human need or other.

At the same time, there were some scientific minds that worked with chemicals, or observed nature and worked on its principles. This gave rise to Chemistry and Natural Science, like Biology and Botany in the field of Science.

All this—the stupendous growth of human mind and human heart— happened during the last twelve thousand years.

During all this time different human societies in different countries worked, and preserved their own achievements in different fields of human labor or profession. Every society gained its knowledge and expertise in different fields through the hard labor of its people. And every society preserved very carefully its achievements in each field and passed them off to its future generations in the form of education, first orally and then by books.

As we see, education is deeply linked to human professions— work. During all these years, first, human knowledge was gained at random and then slowly organized in different fields of profession and education. Entire knowledge was structured and organized in different disciplines of Education, namely Language, Sports, Arts, Science, Mathematics, and Philosophy et cetera.

With the invention of writing some five thousand years ago, it became possible to save every bit of knowledge in the form of books.

Also, with time, different schools and colleges were established where knowledge was imparted to students. Educational institutes and their connected libraries till date are temples where human knowledge is taught and preserved in the form of books.

With the passage of time, education became more and more complex and specialized. Today every society sends its children to schools and colleges to learn a wide variety of subjects in different disciplines and to learn its traditions, morals, and other high human Values.

There are two types of education—Formal and Informal. Formal education is imparted in schools, colleges, and universities, and Informal education is gained at home by private means.

Formal Education

In an average civilized human society, a child starts going to school at the age of three or four. First, she goes to school for some ten or twelve years, then to a college for higher or professional education, and then to a university for specialized knowledge. This is the standard pattern of Formal Education.

A human during childhood and youth is a bundle of sheer physical and mental energy, which, if channeled can shape an individual and her life beautifully and give deep meaning to it. And if not channeled, it runs to waste and can destroy that person.

It is Education that channels a human's physical and mental energy during the first, most formative twenty-plus years of her life. The process of education gives purpose to a child, disciplines her body and mind, gives her a good physical and mental exercise, and makes her brain work really hard. This process, though hard, cultivates, strengthens, and enriches a human's brain.

School education is divided into three parts—Elementary, Primary, and High School. It is a process of ten to twelve years, during which a child learns the basic languages, Math, Arts, Science, Sports etc.

A child enters school at a very young and tender age with a highly curious and impressionable mind. The first few years are very hard for a child; where she has to learn discipline and social behavior and get used to studying—listening to and understanding a teacher; reading; writing; memorizing; and speaking.

In an Elementary school, a child is taught the alphabet, numbers, poems, and so on. Various modes of teaching are used to keep the child interested and make her learn. Together with academics, she is also taught social behavior and etiquette, like how to sit, walk, and talk. Slowly a child learns basic words and numbers, and to get along with others and behave properly.

In Primary school, from grade one to eight, a child is introduced to a wide variety of subjects in major disciplines of human knowledge, like Language, Math, Arts, Humanities, Science, and Sports. Now she can construct sentences, read and understand the written language, and write and speak better. She is taught Literature and Grammar in Language. In Math she learns how to do simple calculations. She learns to draw, color, sing, dance, and practice other forms of arts. She is taught History which tells her about her country and the world she lives in. In Geography she learns about the Earth, and different countries and their weather and climates. In Science she learns about plant life in botany, about living beings in Biology, and the basics of Physics and Chemistry. She is taught exercise and Right Diet in Physical Education. She is taught hockey, badminton, basketball, athletics, and many other types of sports.

A child as a student starts her day at school by attending assembly, where all students of the school assemble, listen to a speech or some noble thoughts given by the head or a teacher, pray, and sing their national anthem etc. Different schools conduct their assemblies in different ways, but this is the standard pattern. After morning assembly, during the day the child attends a number of classes. In each class she is taught a different subject. In the middle of the day, children are given a recess time of an hour or so, during which they eat their lunch, chat, and play et cetera. After recess a child attends three or four more classes. During one school day, there are some seven to eight classes. In each class a child sits with other children of the same age and grade in one classroom. She listens to her teacher's lectures, answers questions, reads, writes, and tries to concentrate. So she learns the theory and the practice. She is given home assignments to be completed at home.

At the end of each semester and at the year-end, a child has to take exams. Each exam is a set of theory and practical questions. An exam tests the child's knowledge and abilities. It is a true test to determine how much a child has learned in her class and school. After passing an annual exam, a child is promoted to the next grade.

With each passing year, a child learns more and more. Formal education is structured in such a way that each higher grade is built upon the previous grade's lessons. In each higher grade, a child refreshes and revises her earlier knowledge in a subject and learns more.

School opens a whole new world to a child—a very different world, totally alien from her home and family. This is her school world, where she has to deal with teachers and students, her juniors and seniors. She chats and plays with other students. She learns to interact with other people, deal with them, and handle them.

School education opens a vast mental world of knowledge that illumines a child's mind. The study of language strengthens and develops her language, which helps her learn better, interpret the world better, and communicate with others better. The study of Math and Science gives her a rational interpretation of the world. Knowledge of History and Geography help her understand her world better. Literature rejoices her heart, and sports develop her physique.

Thus we see how all disciplines of Education altogether enrich and strengthen a child's mind, heart, and body.

During study the child has to sit for hours at the study table, practice Math, remember large texts, read, and write. This process of learning is very hard and requires a lot of discipline and concentration from the child. Also, the continuous process of reading, writing, memorizing large texts, and practicing Math harvests and cultivates the student's brain and makes her mentally strong.

Thus education enriches and strengthens a human's brain.

From grades nine to twelve, a child goes to High School. This education builds upon the primary education and is harder and more complex. The subject of Language contains hard grammar and lengthy literature. The study of Math is extended to include harder Arithmetic, complex Geometrical formulas, and abstract Algebra and Calculus. Similarly, Science, and humanities subjects like History, and Geography cover large and complex texts. They strengthen a child's language, and add more to the child's mental world of knowledge.

After eighth grade, a child, depending upon her/his bent of mind, has to choose one of the branches of the study: Science or Arts.

For the next four years, from grades nine to twelve, a student in Science focuses on the study of Math and Science and studies them along with the general study of other Subjects. While a student of Arts focuses on Humanities subjects, like History, Geography, and Civics with the general study of Science Subjects.

Formal education up to twelfth grade or high school, equips a student with good linguistic ability, a general knowledge of all subjects, with deeper knowledge of either Science or Arts. Now she has a good grip on the language with which she can speak, read, and write better. With the knowledge gained during twelve years of education, she can interpret the world historically and rationally, and not rely on myths and superstitions. This gives her self-confidence and ability to cope with the world better.

Education is the prime difference between an ape and a human. An uneducated human's mind is crude, raw, irrational, and dark, filled with vague fears, myths, and superstitions. An uneducated person has limited language with which to speak, understand, and interpret the world. In comparison, an educated person's mind, after years of harvesting and cultivating, learning, and gaining knowledge, becomes fine, strong, rational, and bright with the light of knowledge. An educated person has better language at her disposal with which to speak, think, and understand better; a rational and thinking mind to solve daily life's problems; and a vast reservoir of knowledge which gives her concepts about the world she lives in, together with satisfaction and confidence.

After high school a person goes to College. Colleges are of two types: Academic and Professional. An Academic College provides higher education in different disciplines of human knowledge. And, a professional college provides education and trains a student in a profession or a vocation.

Academic College builds upon and adds to the knowledge gained by a student in high school. For first two years, a student is taught some basic subjects from both Science and Arts (Humanities), including a couple of classes in Philosophy—one of the highest endeavors of the human mind. Together with this, a student also chooses one major, a subject of her choice like History, Physics etc. in which she receives more classes and deeper studies.

After passing the first two years of college, the student studies her major for two more years.

Thus college provides four years of education. After four years of college, the student receives a Bachelor's degree in a particular Subject.

Professional colleges provide special education and training in different professions, like college of Medicine, College of Engineering, College of Law et cetera. They prepare a society's future professionals. Different colleges have different requirements. Normally after passing high school or college, a student can pass the entrance exam for one of the professional colleges and join it. A professional college provides grueling studies in a particular profession. Every college has its own vast library of books, CDs, and DVDs, related to that particular profession. Along with classroom studies, a student studies further in the library. After passing an extensive set of quizzes, tests, and exams during four years of college, a student gets a degree in a particular profession, like a Doctor, an Engineer, a Lawyer, or a Computer Professional etc.

College education is very hard and time-consuming. It requires long hours of studying a subject deeply; extensive reading and writing; memorizing large texts, hard formulas, and principles. At the same time, it is highly interesting if you study a Subject of your interest—intellectually stimulating and an excellent preparation for a profession.

College education further harvests, cultivates, and sharpens a human's brain, strengthens, and enriches it.

After having passed 12 years of high school, and four years of college, a student has a choice to go to a university for higher education. A university is a great center of learning with a great reservoir of human knowledge, well taught in different faculties or departments, and well preserved in the forms of books, CDs, and DVDs in huge university libraries.

A university imparts higher education in a specific subject of Science, Humanities or any other discipline of human knowledge. It can be Physics, Chemistry, Biology et cetera in Science; or it can be History, Civics, Anthropology et cetera in Humanities; or Art or any other subject. A student has the choice to study for two years and get a master's degree in a particular discipline like a Master's of Science or a Master's of Arts. Or a student can go into research in a particular Subject. Research is a hard endeavor taking five or more years. It provides the student with a chance to choose a specific research topic, study and collect all knowledge up to that point, do further research, and come up with a new scientific theory or new findings and knowledge. Research includes field study, prolonged observations, performing tests, getting test results, doing social surveys, getting results, comparing them, and coming up with a new finding or a discovery in a particular field of knowledge.

It is mostly university research that opens new doors of knowledge in a particular subject. It comes up with heavier, all-inclusive concepts in knowledge; new discoveries and inventions; and the finest of medicines etc.

After finishing a successful research, a student is awarded a PhD—a Doctor of Philosophy degree—in a specific field of Science or Humanities.

Receiving university education is an endeavor of a scholarly human brain, one who loves to pursue knowledge.

Thus, formal education is a long road in a human's life, starting from primary education in her childhood to high school and college in her youth and ending in a university.

Formal education is an intense process of learning marked by constant discipline and hard work coupled with the excitement of gaining knowledge and achievements in the forms of intellectual satisfaction, certificates, and degrees. These certificates and degrees are valid throughout one's lifetime and are required for entry into further education or any profession. Once attained, education is good throughout one's lifetime. Formal education of a country is nationally and internationally recognized.

Informal Education

Informal education is another means of gaining education by private study.

Some children never go to school. They study at home or with a private tutor. After long, consistent preparation for a particular exam, they can take the exam, pass it, and get a certificate or a degree. There are few countries which acknowledge this type of education. This is no match for a formal education, which gives a thorough knowledge and training and aims at the overall development of a child.

The process of education does not end with formal education. It is a lifelong process of gaining knowledge in a variety of fields by reading.

Reading is an excellent habit that ought to be developed in childhood and maintained throughout one's lifetime. Everyone ought to read for a minimum of one hour every day. Reading concentrates one's mind, adds onto one's previous knowledge, and gives one a fresh knowledge in a variety of fields. Reading can be for fun or to gain more knowledge of one's profession, or to know more about the world we live in. There are books in every profession that can add onto one's professional knowledge and help one gain more success in her profession and career. Reading is an excellent way to increase one's general knowledge about the world we live in, its make, its history, and its people.

Knowledge gained through the process of education and by reading never goes waste. It is stored in one's mind and comes to her aid in understanding the world and solving life's problems.

Definition of Education

Education is a long and hard process of learning; gaining knowledge, and professional training in different disciplines of human knowledge and professions. Education is of two types— Formal and Informal. Formal education is gained in a school, college, and university, while informal education is gained at home in private. Formal education grants one with universally acknowledged certificates, diplomas, and degrees, which are required for entry into a profession. Informal education adds onto one's knowledge throughout one's lifetime. Education cultivates, strengthens, and enriches a human's mind.

Value of Education

Education is the prime mode through which a society passes off its age's old, carefully preserved knowledge and Values to its children. It is an ever-evolving field getting richer and richer with new discoveries, inventions, and knowledge.

Formal education is a long, arduous process of some sixteen-plus years, which slowly and consistently harvests and cultivates a human's brain, sharpens it, and enriches it with knowledge in a variety of subjects like Language, Math, Humanities, and Sciences. This knowledge equips one with a strong language, and mathematical abilities, and historical and scientific concepts that help one interpret the world and understand it better. It illumines one's mind.

Education is the prime difference between a human and an ape. An educated person has a well-cultivated, calm, and strong mind and good logical, thinking ability. Such a person is not obsessed with vague fears, myths, and superstitions but has a rational understanding of the world. She does not act out of crude passions but thinks and acts. She sorts out life's problems by thinking.

Education is an eternal human, lifelong Value. As long as there are humans, education will be valued because education is the prime mode through which a human society gains and preserves its traditions, values, and achievements in all disciplines of human knowledge and passes them to its future generation of children.

Education is a human's lifelong Value. Education once received, never goes waste. It cultivates and sharpens one's brain and enriches it with languages and a variety of knowledge. Educational certificates, diplomas, and degrees once received are good throughout one's lifetime and are universally recognized. They are required for further education and for entry into a profession. The daily habit of reading for knowledge builds one's reservoir of knowledge and adds onto it, helps one in daily life and in one's profession. Reading for pleasure makes one happy.

Derivative Right Way of Living

Education unfolds the deep, intellectual potential of a human; strengthens and enriches her mind; makes her a calm, thinking person; gives her a wide worldview; and thus helps her live a calm, balanced life. It also prepares one for a profession.

Thus the value of education is immense in a human's life.

A human ought to view education as a lifelong Value. Education once received never goes waste. Formal education taken during the tender and growing years of one's childhood and teens does wonders to the developing brain of a child. It cultivates and prunes her mind and fills it with vast reservoirs of knowledge that help the child understand the world better and live a better life.

Good school education ought to aim at the overall development of the child—her physical, emotional, intellectual, moral, and spiritual development. An overall curriculum of school education should include good physical exercise; the teaching of positive human emotions like compassion and goodwill; the teaching of all basic Sciences, Arts and Humanities; lessons to develop child's logical and critical thinking, and memory; the teaching of ethics and morality; and some spiritual teaching like prayer or meditation.

Every child ought to be sent to a school from early childhood and made to receive a complete education up to graduation. In other words every human ought to receive a complete formal education up through college and be a graduate. There is no match for formal education gained in the strict discipline of a school and college.

Education received in one's profession helps one to become a better professional in her field.

The process of education should never be over in a human's life. After completing formal education, a human ought to keep updating her professional knowledge by private study or by taking classes in that. Reading for general knowledge, reading for pleasure, and reading newspapers should be part of one's everyday living. Reading makes one calm, concentrated, and happy and adds onto to one's knowledge.

3. WORK (PROFESSION)

Just to review the pathway of a human's life, a human is born and reared in her First Family. From the age of four up to twenty-one or so, she receives education. After completing her education, she starts working and works till old age. Thus work is the third major milestone in a human's life, with the prior two being First Family and Education.

I visualize a human's life as a journey between her birth and death, marked by Five major milestones. These are Family, Education, Work, Marriage, and Child. Each of them is a milestone because of its immense value in a human's life. Each is closely related to a human's survival and the kind of life she leads. By calling them milestones, I mean stop, think, and then proceed. A human ought to treat each of them as an extremely important choice in one's life; plan it, and live it well. Before deciding how to view and live work, let us first look into the nature of work: Where has it come from? What is it? And, its Value in a human's life.

Work is an English term, which means "1. Physical or mental effort or activity directed toward the production or accomplishment of something: Labor. 2. Employment: job. 3. The means by which one earns one's livelihood..." (*Webster's II New College Dictionary*). This is a good, concise definition of work, encompassing all aspects of it.

Work is primarily of two classes—one's own business or a job—to work for someone. One's own business means to run one's own enterprise, and to work for someone means to work for a person, or a company, or government et cetera. Further, work is divided into two types a "profession" and a "job."

A profession is an occupation requiring an advanced study—a minimum of a bachelor's degree in a specialized field. A job is work that does not require advanced study in that field. For example, a Doctor, a Lawyer are professions which require advanced study in the field of medicine, and in the field of law respectively; while a taxi driver, a janitor, or an office clerk are just jobs, which do not require advanced study in these fields.

After completing education, sometime in youth, a human starts working. One's prime motivation for working is her need of money. If she does not need to earn money, for example, if she has enough family or personal wealth to support her, then she may choose not to work because working is hard.

But the majority of humans start working in their youth and continues working till old age. Work gives them money to live. Viewed this way, work is the survival mode for a human.

The choice of work depends upon one's family pressure/ motivation and/or one's own liking. Some join their family businesses; while those out of a professional school join their particular professions; while many others just start doing any available jobs.

Money is one's prime motivation to work. Work gives you your own money and often freedom to spend it the way you want. Once a human earns enough to live on her own, she may choose to live alone to enjoy her financial and personal freedom.

Work brings major changes in a person's life. In modern society many people find jobs in other cities or countries. They have to leave their own home cities and move to different cities or countries.

Whether a person engages in a "business," a "profession," or a "job," a person has to devote minimum of eight hours every day to her work. This is the standard work time, common to many human societies. Some people work for more than eight hours to do better than their rivals or because their jobs demand it.

Work timings or shifts differ depending upon the kind of job one has. The majority of people in offices work during the day shift from 9:00 a.m. to 6:00 p.m., while those in hospitals, hotels, and airports may have to work in the evenings and in the nightshift from 10:00 p.m. to 6:00 a.m. Doctors, police, and armed services workers are on call in addition to working their normal work hours.

Whatever the work timings, a person has to work for a minimum of eight hours. The more complex and more responsible the work is, the longer the work hours. For example, a businessperson, or a professional commonly spends more time at work than a person doing a job who has less responsibility. This makes work a very demanding activity in a human's life—you have very little time left to do other things.

Though demanding, work brings discipline to a human's life. Because of its strict timings, a person has to get up on time, get ready, and go to work. Even at work a person has to remain physically and mentally disciplined throughout the work-time. For example, in an office job, she has to sit at her desk for eight long hours, focus, and work. When at work you cannot do what you want. You have to be disciplined and well behaved with your colleagues and clients all the time.

Work is hard. Work requires long, consistent, and concentrated labor in a specific field for eight long hours at a stretch. For example, a businessperson, no matter what she does—runs a factory or a big firm or simply sells clothes in a shop—has to think continuously about her work, make calls, talk to clients/customers, deal with clients and workers, and control various aspects of her business, ranging from production to supply and delivery to accounting, marketing, etc. The bigger the business, the harder the work is.

Similarly, a Professional like a Doctor has to keep studying to keep abreast of new developments in her field. Once at work she has to check her appointments, meet a variety of sick patients throughout the day, advise them on the right medication, solve their health problems, perform surgery requiring extreme concentration, and keep working for eight or more hours despite exhaustion. The same goes for a person doing any job. A bus driver has to drive the bus for eight continuous hours with a short break in between. This factor—doing the same job five or six days a week for eight-plus hours at a stretch— may often make one's work a monotonous or boring routine.

Work of any type (be it one's own business, profession or job) is hard physical and mental labor performed consistently in one direction to produce something or to serve others.

In modern societies there is a large variety of highly specialized fields of labor, such as farming, clothing, housing, food, furniture, textiles, electrical and electronic goods, computers, medicine, and law et cetera. Each of these fields contains a number of businesses, professionals, and jobs under it. And each of these fields of labor serves some human need or other. They are there because humans need them.

A human, in order to live, requires a number of things like food, clothes, house, education, and a large number of other things for her various need fulfillment and enjoyment. She cannot produce them all on her own. She has to buy them from those who have them. This need of humans gave birth to different trades, businesses, professions, and jobs. All of them are there to fulfill some human need or other.

Today we see around us a large variety of different fields of human labor, where each of them is highly organized, developed, and sophisticated. All these fields of labor arose at different times of humanity's history to fulfill a variety of human needs. The majority of them are basics like Food, Clothing, Housing, and Medicine while many came up later, like Electricity and Electronics, Computers, Law, and Engineering.

The origin of "work" can be traced to the advent of the agricultural period in humanity's history. It was some twelve thousand years back, that humans learned how to grow crops, domesticate animals, and live in one place. As a group of humans started living together, their daily needs gave rise to different fields of work or labor. There were some basic human needs like food, clothes, and shelter. A human needed food to eat, clothes to cover his body, and a house to live in. A human also needed utensils, tools, weapons, and hordes of other things for her survival and enjoyment.

Since in an agricultural society a large number of humans lived together, some people worked in farms and some raised animals, while others created fabric to make clothes. Some started building huts and houses, and some made pots and pans. And so it went on. Different types of products were created by different people. Those who needed them bought them from those who had them by exchanging some material goods in return.

In tracing the history of our Human Whole, we saw how each field of labor was born and how each new generation of humans took on each field from where it was left, added her own talent and labor to it, and made it more advanced. This continued, and what we see today is a vast Human Whole with thousands of fields of labor, where each field was invented sometime in the past history of The Human Whole, improved upon by future generations, and made more and more advanced and beautiful by forthcoming generations of humans and their work. Thus, the entire Human Whole is the product of human work or labor, created during the past twelve thousand years of humanity's history. It is a vast pool of entire humanity and its achievements in the form of millions of products, services, inventions, and monuments, and a vast treasure of knowledge.

The Human Whole is like *a Palace under Construction*, where each new generation of humans comes in, works in different fields of human labor, takes it from where it was left by their ancestors, adds onto it, and makes it more advanced, sophisticated, and beautiful. For example, an Electrical Engineer studies all knowledge of engineering acquired by previous generations of humans and stored in the form of books, learns from it, works in the same field, and comes up with new products. Thus he adds onto it. Similarly, a Lawyer learns all previous knowledge gained by previous professionals in the field of Law, fights, and wins new cases. Thus, he leaves new case precedents for others to follow.

Thus, The Human Whole gives a very deep meaning to the human work. Our work does not die with us. Our work is something we leave behind in **the Palace of the Human Whole**. I, as a human will die one day, but I will leave behind my work in the form of some product, some service, some invention, some discovery, or merely by working well in my field of work and making it more beautiful than I found it.

One's work outlives one's life. Examples of an honest cop, a brave firefighter, and a War Martyr leave trails for future youth to follow.

One's work also affects one's immediate society. A human through her work connects to her society and thus affects it.

Depending upon the type of work she does and the quality of work she does, she either enriches her society or harms it. For example, a businessperson in the field of food, who works only to earn more and more profit, mixes harmful ingredients in the food and sells it to people. Unknown people consume it in good faith and ruin their health. Thus, through her work, she harms her society. This is her contribution to her society and to The Human Whole. On the other hand, a doctor who does her job well, cures many people, and saves their lives, benefits her society by her work. This is her contribution to her society and The Human Whole. Similarly, a Cook who prepares pure and delicious food for her customers enriches her society by her work.

A human connects to her society through her work. It is through her work that she meets a variety of people, talks to them, and serves them. Work gives one a social identity.

Work gives you money. Work is an exchange of labor and money between two persons, i.e., a businessperson and her clients; an employer and an employee. A businessperson sells some products and services to customers, and the customer in turn pays money to the businessperson. Similarly, an employer hires an employee, uses her services, and pays her money for her services.

Money is the prime motivation behind one's work. The majority of us work to earn money. But it should not be so. Through our work, we affect our society, our Human Whole, and The Whole of Life. Our work ought to be the contribution of our best to The Whole, and the type through which we enrich others' lives best. Moreover, work is something we do for eight-plus hours every day. It should match our talent and skills. This is Right Work, which makes us happy.

One's talent and aptitude are inborn. Every human is unique in her/his talent and attitude. Talent is that inborn quality of being good at something that gives one an extra edge over others. Also, some people are exceptionally talented in something. For example, a person can be a very good painter, a singer, a magician, a mechanic, or a writer etc. She is naturally good at it without ever learning it. One ought to detect one's talent, practice it, and try to make work/a profession of it. Indulging in one's talent or hobby satisfies a person deeply and makes her happy. Lucky are those who make work of their hobby. For them work brings in a lot of happiness. Also, the products of one's talents are often her exceptional gifts to her society.

Aptitude is one's natural liking for something since birth. Everyone is born with an aptitude. Some people are good in letters, while others are good in numbers, and still others are good in sports et cetera. A person of letters can be a good lawyer, a teacher, or scholar et cetera. A person of numbers will do well in the fields of Math and Accounting. And a person of sports will do well as a sportsperson or athlete. Before choosing one's profession, one ought to detect one's talent and aptitude and choose a profession based on that. Such a person will enjoy her work and will do better than others in her work.

Every human is a unique creation of The Whole. The Whole is the movement of pure conscious energy. The Whole is like a constantly moving *Potter's Wheel*, ever creating new things by its perfect movement. Just as a moving potter's wheel uses clay and by its perfect movement keeps creating a number of beautiful artifacts and throwing them out, similarly the constantly moving Whole keeps moving and creating a number of creations. Everything in The Whole is The Whole's creation—unique and special in its own way—the Sun, the Moon, the Earth—and everything on the Earth—a rose, a thorn, an apple, a whale, an ant, a lion, and a human etc. Further, each of these is unique in its own way. Our Sun is distinct from millions of other suns in the Galaxy; our moon rotating our Earth is different from many other moons; and our Earth, harboring The Whole of Life in its lap, is different from millions of other planets. Look closely, and you will find that one rose is different from other roses, one thorn is different from other thorns, one Apple is different from other apples, one Whale is different from other whales, one Ant is different from other ants, one Lion is different from other lions, and so is one Human different from other humans.

Every individual human is a special creation of The Whole. One human is white, while another is brown or black. One human is quiet and withdrawn by nature, while another is noisy and jubilant. One is deeply intelligent, pursuing a career, while another is ordinary, carefree, taking things as they come. One is a lone Philosopher, deeply perturbed and musing over life and its issues; the other is a highly social Janitor, casual and care-free. One is a Scientist, the other an Artist. This is nature. Each of us is born unique and special in her own way. Each of us is a special creation of The Whole. Each of us plays her part in enriching The Human Whole and running The Whole.

Everything in The Whole is a special creation of The Whole. The Whole has a purpose in making everything the way it is—to enrich the Whole. Each of us enriches The Whole by her own special way and lives best by being herself. A rose gives its beauty and fragrance to The Whole, while a thorn is required to protect it. A rose cannot be a thorn, and a thorn cannot be rose. A philosopher enriches others' lives by her thoughts, and a jani-tor (sweeper) enriches others' lives by keeping their living areas clean. Both are required in The Human Whole. A Philosopher cannot be a Janitor; and a Janitor cannot be a Philosopher. Similarly, a scientist enriches The Human Whole with her new discoveries and inventions; and an artist stimulates our hearts and spirits. A Scientist cannot be an Artist, and an Artist cannot be a Scientist.

A human ought to understand her own basic nature, talent, and aptitude, and choose a profession as per that. You live best when you live as per your nature.

This is Right Work—work according to your nature, your talent, and your aptitude. Right work sheds from your being, from your true nature. Your Right work is the real you. Right work is what you find yourself doing unconsciously, in your own free time, which fills you with immense joy. You are drawn to it. A Painter picks up the brush and paints. She feels relieved and joyous after that. A Composer keeps humming and composing a symphony. Doing so makes her happy. A Philosopher keeps musing and comes up with a great thought. Thinking enlivens her, spurs her, and gives her joy.

A human ought to recognize her talent and aptitude and then choose a profession in the same field. A person of letters should go to Teaching, Law, or another career in the humanities. A person of numbers should go into Math, and a technical person should go into Engineering, Mechanical field. Do what you love to do. By doing so you give your best to The Human Whole, enrich it, and fulfill The Whole's purpose in creating you.

Together with a profession, one ought to practice and cultivate her specific talent or hobby, like singing, dancing, painting, or writing. One ought to practice it for an hour every day and try to make a profession of it at some point.

Work is what you do for eight-plus hours every day. If Right, your work will give you deep satisfaction and joy; and if wrong, your work will fill you with frustration and depression.

Right work is a human's prime Dharma. *Dharma* is a Sanskrit word meaning "adopted Right conduct." A human's Dharma or right conduct is that which emanates from her being; if practiced, it nourishes her being, makes her happy, and makes her enrich her Whole. Right work is that which emanates from the very nature of a person; if indulged in, it nourishes her being, gives her satisfaction and happiness; and is the prime mode through which a human enriches her Human Whole. Through her work she gives a product or service to her society and enriches it. Through your work, you affect the lives of many people.

Therefore, a human ought to view her work as her prime Dharma—a duty to herself and her Whole, choose the Right Work—work as per her talent, hobby, and aptitude—do it very well, and enrich herself and her society.

Your work emanates from your very being. You may lose your relationships, but you never lose your work. Right work gives you money and happiness and is the prime mode through which you enrich your Human Whole

Since work is the prime mode through which you enrich your Whole, it ought to be your best.

I am a human. I will die one day but will leave behind my Work to my Human Whole.

A human's prime contribution to her Human Whole is her work or labor. The entire Human Whole is a product of human's work or labor. We humans work in different fields of labor and leave behind our examples, our legends, our products, our inventions and discoveries to the Human Whole. They enrich the lives of others and are deposited in a common pool of the Human Whole, through which they will enrich the lives of our children, our grandchildren, and all future generations of humans to come.

For example, first of all, any honest, concentrated, and punctual worker is a blessing to her organization and her immediate society. Such a worker, no matter what field of labor she is in, be it a Doctor or a simple data feeding Clerk, will do her job with full concentration—whether perform a surgery or entering data in computer—will ensure her work is done well without any errors, and will be punctual. By working so, she benefits her clients, enriches her society, and leaves behind examples for other workers to follow.

Honesty is the best policy in every walk of life, but it is superb in work because through your work you affect the lives of others. Honest work done to serve others is like God's worship.

An honest policeman, a brave firefighter, and a brave war veteran enrich their immediate society by saving their people from dangerous criminals, fire, and enemies, respectively and they also leave their examples and legends behind for others to follow. Every country and the entire Human Whole remember them and remain indebted to them.

Our Human Whole is made of millions of products, inventions, and discoveries that we humans use every day and cannot do without. The food we eat, the clothes we wear, the houses we live in, electricity, TVs, computers, our lifesaving medicines, planes, our hospitals, our libraries, our museums—each of these and everything we use was created by a human who worked hard in a specific field of labor, created a product, or came up with an invention or discovery, that enriched her immediate society and was deposited into the common pool of The Human Whole to enrich the lives of future humans. This is the meaning and value of one's work.

I am a human. I will die one day but will leave behind my work to the Human Whole. This fact gives deep meaning and purpose to my (a human's life) on this Earth.

Since a human's work emanates from her deep being, her true nature, and since through her work she enriches the Human Whole and the purpose of The Whole, a human's work ought to be the contribution of her best to The Whole.

A human's work ought to reflect the best of her talent, knowledge, and skills. *Find your best and choose a profession in that so that you give your best to The Whole.*

Definition of Work

Work is a human's physical and mental labor in the form of a business, a profession, or a job, performed in a specific field throughout one's lifetime—from adulthood until old age, for eight plus hours every day, and thus a major realm of a human's life. Work is a human's prime survival mode (gives her money to live); if Right, it is a prime source of happiness and the prime mode through which she enriches her whole. Therefore it ought to be Right—work as per one's nature, talent, and aptitude—and it ought to be the contribution of her best to her Human Whole.

The Value of Work in a Human's life

Value of work infers from the above fact analysis and definition of work.

A human ought to view her work as part of her prime Dharma—a duty to herself and to The Whole. She ought to view herself as a special creation of The Whole. The immensely intelligent and perfect Whole had a purpose in making her the way she is. If she lives and works as per her true nature, she fulfills the Whole's purpose, rejoices in her existence, and enriches her Human Whole in a special way that no one else can. A human does her Dharma by doing the Right work—work as per the best of her talent, education, and skills.

Work is an eternal human lifelong Value. Till there is a human, there will be work. Work is born to fulfill human needs. Work is the prime thread of a human society. It connects one human to other humans. Human work affects the lives of many others; therefore it ought to be honest—done to enrich others' lives.

An average human starts working in youth, works till old age, and works every day for some eight-plus hours. This makes work a major realm of one's life, and a Lifelong Value.

Work gives one money—money to survive, money to enjoy life, and money to help others. One's Work gives her a social identity, and if Right a deep satisfaction, joy, and the very meaning of life.

All of the above make Work a human's prime Dharma and an eternal human, lifelong Value.

Derivative Right Way of Living

A human ought to view her work the way it is—her prime Dharma—her duty to herself, to the Creator, and to the Whole. Therefore, one's work ought to be Right. Right work is that through which she enjoys her existence and enriches her Whole. And it ought to be the contribution of one's best to one's Whole.

I am a human. I am a part of the Whole, and a special creation of the Whole. I have a unique nature, talent, and aptitude which no one else has. It is as if The Whole had a purpose in making me the way I am—to enrich the Whole through my special way. I as a human ought to understand my true nature, talent, and aptitude and choose a profession as per them. If I am a person of letters, I can go to Law or Teaching; if I am a person of numbers, I can go into Math or Computers; if I am a person of technology, I can go into Engineering, and so on. Along with my profession, I ought to retain my hobby, which may be singing, dancing, or painting etc; practice it for an hour every day; and try to make a profession of it when I can.

I as a human ought to view and remember my work as my prime lifelong Value, Value—because it gives me money and happiness and is the prime mode through which I enrich my Human Whole. My work emanates from my own being and gives me independence. And it is lifelong because I work throughout my lifetime, from adulthood till old age.

Thus I as a human value my Work or Profession as my prime Dharma and my lifelong Value and choose a right profession—profession that best matches my nature, talent, and aptitude. Along with my Work, I ought to detect and cultivate my hobby, practice it for an hour every day, and try to make a profession of it when I can.

Also, I as a human ought to practice honesty, punctuality, and discipline in my work. These are the three pearls of work that add onto one's Right profession and make it more beautiful.

4. MARRIAGE

A human's life is a long journey from her birth unto her death. A human is born as the most helpless infant, blossoms to youth, reaches the peak of her life at middle age, then gets old, decays, and dies. Viewed this way, life is like a long, hard climb up to a mountain peak or middle age and then traveling downhill until one's death. It is a hard, hard journey throughout. A human cannot live alone on her own. (S)he needs support—support in order to survive, support in order to grow, and support in order to be happy and enjoy life.

A human is born as the most helpless infant in her First Family, family of parents and siblings; receives education, and grows up to youth—all amid the love and support of her First Family. Then a human starts working. Work gives her money; and, if Right, happiness, and the meaning of life.

Sometime during adulthood, a human marries, produces children of her own, and thus starts her Second Family—Family of her spouse and children. From youth until death, a human lives in the realm of her Second Family or Family by Marriage. This is where she gets the everyday support of her spouse and children up to her old age or death.

It is with Marriage that a human starts her Second Family. And it is Marriage which is the mother of the Prime Human Family—Family of husband, wife and child(ren). ***Thus Marriage is the Founding Stone of a human Family. A human Family starts with Marriage and runs by Marriage.***

Before going any further into this great institution called marriage, let us go back and look into the origin of marriage in human society—when and why it started. That will help us understand its prime purpose in a human's life and human society.

The origin of marriage goes back to the very inception of the human society. The human society started with marriage.

A human since beginning always lived in a group. In the very beginning, there was no human society. A group of humans lived together and moved from place to place in search of food. As a group of humans lived together in one place, men and women had free sex, or women were raped. Consequently, women bore children often of unknown or untraceable fathers. Even if the father of the child was known, there was no way to keep track of him for long.

Since there was no way to keep track of a child's parentage, often children of the same parents, or siblings and cousins, had sex together and produced their own children. Soon, after a couple of generations, a group of humans living together realized the faults of incest. Children born of siblings, cousins or close family relatives were physically and mentally weak. There had to be a way to track the parentage of a child and maintain it over generations in order to avoid incest. This need of humans gave birth to the institution of marriage and the resultant family. This was the prime purpose of marriage—to track and maintain a child's parentage—and it remains so till date.

Marriage in all human societies was a social ceremony in which a woman and a man, in presence of their family and friends, performed some rituals in front of God, a priest, or a legal authority. After certain ceremonies and vows the married woman and man were declared "wife" and "husband" to each other. In all human societies, marriage was performed in front of God to stamp marriage as a sacred tie between a woman and a man. The purpose of this was to express the somber nature of marriage, its value in life, and the mutual promise of the couple to retain its purity by never committing adultery.

Thus, marriage was a social, religious, and legal tie between a woman and a man that created an interpersonal and legal relationship between both— woman and the man. Also, by this tie was created a "union" of a woman and a man. The union of marriage combined the personal and financial resources of the married woman and man and their families.

After marriage a woman and a man, now "wife" and "husband" to each other, lived together, worked together, and helped and supported each other in day-to-day tasks, personally and financially, and thus pooled their labor and money. Doing so supported and strengthened both of them personally and financially. Also, after marriage, both the wife and the husband had to control their sexual behavior—have sex only with each other and never outside marriage. This behavior of theirs ensured that children were born out of marital sex only. In this way marriage became the only mode through which a child's parentage could be traced and maintained.

Slowly and gradually, as a human society developed and strengthened, the institution of marriage became stronger, distinct families were established, family names were created (mostly after their professions), and they were maintained over generations. Now it was possible to identify a human by her /his parentage and family. One family could be distinguished from other families by its name.

The form of marriage differed from society to society. Most human societies practiced monogamy in which one person had only one spouse. While some societies practiced polygamy, in which one person, usually a man, kept two or more wives. The form of marriage depended upon the economic needs of the society.

The institution of marriage lived and thrived through all types of human societies, in different ages and times, and does so till date. Soon after its beginning, it emerged as an excellent support system for both—a woman and a man. It regulated the sexual behavior of humans in a society. It established and maintained a family. And, above all, it created a Cradle in which a child was born and reared.

The Institute of marriage changed a group of humans living together to a human society. Since marriage and the resultant family regulated the sexual behavior of men and women, it created a safe and moral society. The resultant family by marriage supported all its members, provided a home and long-term support to its children, and became a Center of morality and other Values. Thus marriage and family brought lot of order and stability to human lives and became the prime institutes and founding stones around which a human society was built and organized.

After marriage, a woman and a man, now a "wife" and "husband" to each other lived together in one house. Usually the woman moved to her husband's home. They lived together and worked together. In a hunting and gathering society, a man hunted and brought food home, while the woman collected nuts, berries, fruits, and other edibles, and brought them home. Since they were nomads and moved from place to place, they made a temporary home. A woman cleaned the house, cooked, and bore and reared children. Because of a woman's weak physique and frequent pregnancies and childbirths, an automatic labor division was created which worked for both—the man and the woman. A man, after a day's hard work, returned to his home, rested, enjoyed hot food prepared by his wife, and relaxed in the company of his caring wife and his own children. This made a woman's life easy too. She did not have to depend on collected food. She got a share out of her husband's hunted food too. Once married, she had the protection of her husband and the legal system of society. Cooking and cleaning were comparatively easier tasks. Now she had to move about less and could keep her children close to her and look after them. Thus marriage created a Family—a group of genetically and emotionally related humans—a husband, wife, and their children, who all lived together in one home, depended on each other, and cared for and supported each other. They felt physically and emotionally secure in the warmth of each other's company.

The institute of marriage continued, and served the same human needs in an agricultural society. In an agricultural society, a group of humans lived in one place, grew food, domesticated animals, and thus fulfilled their survival needs. Now a human built and lived in one permanent home. The mode of survival was hard field work with rearing and using domesticated animals. Man grew grains, vegetables, and fruits in fields. He domesticated wild animals and used them for a variety of purposes—a dog for protection, a goat or cow for milk, a horse for transportation et cetera. Digging, plowing, watering, cutting, and collecting the crops in the open, under the blazing-hot sun or in the bone-chilling winters were very hard tasks, befitted a man's physique better and were automatically done by a man (the husband). While the tasks of feeding, cleaning, and looking after domestic animals were done by the woman (the wife) at home. Together with these, a woman cleaned the home, cooked, and bore and reared children. A man, after a day's hard, bone-breaking field work returned to his well-kept, clean home, enjoyed hot food and loving company of his wife and children.

Again, labor division was automatic. Both—the wife and husband performed those tasks that suited each of them. Also, they helped each other with the other day-to-day tasks.

The advent of the modern Industrial-cum-Information age society opened out-of-home career doors for women. Now a woman could work outside her home in any field of labor. Slowly women proved their worth, and more and more women started joining different fields of labor and earning their own money.

In modern times, in a family where both wife and husband work, many things have remained the same, while a few have changed. After marriage, both wife and husband set up their own home, produce and rear their own children. Both of them go to work for some eight-plus hours every day and return home tired. Now the question arises as to who will cook, clean, do the laundry and shopping, and other household chores? Who will look after and teach the children? The labor division is not so clear. Some couples are calm, responsible, care for each other, and value their marriages. They share the household, child-rearing, and other tasks and make their marriages work. While other couples are disturbed, irresponsible, and don't care for each other or for their marriages. They fight every day over every issue, make their marriages a living hell, and may resort to divorce.

The Institution of marriage is weakening in modern societies. Now a working woman does not need a husband as much for financial and personal support. She works and earns her own money. And she can live alone or with her own parents and siblings.

Whatever the society or time, there are some common features shared by all types of marriages. After marriage, a wife and husband live together; setup and share a home; either a man works, earns money and runs the home; or the wife works, earns money and runs the home; or both—husband and wife work, earn money, pool in their money and labor, and run their home. Since they live together, they need to adjust their times, habits, and hobbies et cetera as per each other's convenience. Who manages the home finances and how is also an issue. The attitude and relationship with each other's family and friends, though required to be respectful, is generally that of natural dislike. Since the wife and husband live together all the time, many habits of one's spouse are intolerable to the other, like burping or sneezing loudly or not doing enough work etc. Since both— wife and husband need to agree on almost everything before making any decision or choice, there arise inevitable arguments, conflicts, and often fights. It is true that after marriage one loses one's independence. The spouse's approval is required for almost everything. Since one spouse's decisions and choices affect the other spouse, both need to agree. Again, calm, responsible spouses who care for each other and their marriages, learn to adjust well, avoid arguments and conflicts, and live with mutual love and respect. While anxious, disturbed, irresponsible spouses who do not care for each other and their marriages fight continuously and make their marriages and homes a living hell.

But many couples after a few years of marriage learn to adjust well to each other, listen to and understand each other, and tend to agree on common choices. They also grow very interdependent and attached to each other. If lived right, marriage can be a beautiful lifelong relationship.

From the above analysis of the origin, history, and general nature of marriage through all human societies till date, there emerge four prime functions of marriage that make marriage a lifelong human Value. These are also four legs on which the Institute of Marriage stands and functions. ***These are SSCC— Support, Sex, Companionship, and Child(ren).***

The first S stands for Support—both financial and personal. Marriage gives financial support to a person. In some cases only one of the spouses may work and the other spouse—usually the wife—may not work, do household work only, and take care of the children. She gets financial support from her husband. In modern times, in many cases, both the spouses work and pool their money. Their combined income means more money, a better home, better comforts, and better savings for both. Marriage makes one rich and helps one save more money.

After marriage, a woman and a man live together and support each other with running the home, and with every day tasks at every step, every day, and throughout their lives. Human existence is very demanding. We humans need a number of things, and need to do a number of tasks every day in order to survive and live well. A human needs a well-stocked, well-furnished, running, clean home to live in. A well-kept, beautiful home is our paradise where we return after a day's hard work to rest and enjoy our existence. Both the spouses—wife and husband—lend helping hands to each other in creating and running their home. They both pool their money and labor and make their home. The husband helps mostly with the tougher tasks of moving the heavy stuff and doing fixtures et cetera, while the wife may do lighter tasks, like keeping things in place and decorating the home et cetera. Their home is a product of their love and dreams of living a good life together. Both—wife and husband—help each other in cleaning, cooking, laundry, buying home supplies, groceries, and child rearing et cetera. Besides, there are numerous other day-to-day tasks that both of them manage together. Doing so makes life easy for both the spouses and is the prime function of marriage.

After marriage both the spouses—wife and husband—take care of each other during a sickness, a long illness, or even during a handicapped phase. All these are parts of a human's life. Marriage gives you your spouse's support during these phases.

Thus marriage can be viewed as a lifelong journey of a wife and husband, walking hand in hand through the trail of life.

Sex is a common human need, very frequent and strong during youth, less in middle age, and lesser in old age. Sex is a need as well as a source of great enjoyment. Marriage gives you safe and regular sex with your spouse. Sex is an important leg of marriage. Marital sex between a woman and a man creates their children. Regular marital sex connects both the spouses physically and emotionally, makes them happy, and thus strengthens their marriage.

The Third important function—leg of marriage—is Companionship. A human by nature cannot live alone. She needs the company of other humans with whom she can talk, share, and enjoy life. After marriage a wife and husband live in close company of each other all the time. Talking and sharing their experiences and other activities together connect them and bring them closer. Also, they can enjoy a number of activities together, like traveling, listening to music, watching TV together, and enjoying quality wine and dine et cetera. Companionship is an important leg of marriage, which is strengthened by regular spousal communication and spending time together.

Having a child of your own is like having a part of you, distinct from you, whom you love the most, rear best, and leave to the world after you are gone. Marriage gives you your own child. Child is the fourth most important leg of marriage. A child of marriage is loved by both spouses—mother and father. A child is a common asset for both the spouses, whom they both love and give their best. Thus a child connects both the spouses and strengthens their marriage.

Marriage is a Cradle in which a child is born and reared. Both wife and husband build and maintain this cradle—a stable, loving home—in which they produce their own child(ren) and rear her with the best of their love, care, and guidance. A human child is born as the most helpless infant, who during the first 18 years of life needs a stable, safe home, and constant care and guidance of her both parents in order to grow into a good human being. This is given by a stable marriage, where both the spouses create and maintain a home in which they produce and rear their child(ren) with the best of their love and guidance.

Thus SSCC—Support, Sex, Companionship, and Children— are the Givens of marriage. Marriage gives you your spouse's Support—both financial and personal, Sex, Companionship, and Children. These are required by a human throughout her lifetime, and therefore they make marriage a lifelong Value.

Also, SSCC—Support, Sex, Companionship, and Children— are the very threads the marriage is made of. These are the pillars of marriage, the very legs on which the great, Human Institute of Marriage stands and functions.

A human ought to view and live her marriage as a deep, lifelong Value—that is what it is, and contribute her share of

SSCC—support her spouse financially and personally, be a willing and active partner in sex with her spouse, talk and share activities with her spouse, and produce and rear their children. I will discuss this issue in detail in Derivative Right Way of Living.

Derivations

The above Fact analysis brings out certain characteristics of marriage that will help us define marriage.

As we saw earlier, the prime purpose of marriage was, and is to produce a child and track her/his parentage. This makes marriage a sacred bond between a woman and a man marked by both the spouses' sexual faithfulness to each other.

Marriage is a cradle in which a child is born and reared. After marriage, both woman and man, now a wife and husband to each other produce their own child(ren) and rear her for the next twenty years or so. This requirement of marriage makes marriage a long-lasting and lifelong relationship.

Marriage is the mother of Prime Human Family—the Family of Mother, Father and Child(ren). Marriage creates a family, runs a family, and distinguishes one family from the other. Therefore, again, marriage ought to be a lifelong human Value.

After marriage, a woman and a man, now a wife and husband to each other, live together, support each other financially and personally, have sex only with each other, have each other's company, and produce and rear their own children. Thus SSCC are the products of marriage and make marriage a lifelong Value. These are the very threads a marriage is made of; and are the four legs on which the noble, human institute of marriage stands and functions.

Marriage in all human societies till date has been recognized by the prevalent legal system.

Definition of Marriage

Marriage is a sacred and legal bond between a woman and a man, created and maintained by threads of sexual faithfulness of both the spouses and their mutual SSCC— Support, Sex, Companionship, and Children. These are the very threads the relationship of marriages is made of. They connect both spouses—wife and husband to each other. Also, SSCC are the four legs on which the Noble Institute of Marriage stands and functions. Marriage is a Cradle in which a child is born and reared, and is the Foundation of the human Family and human Society.

Value of Marriage in a Human's Life

A human needs marriage. Marriage gives an individual—a woman or a man SSCC: Support—both financial and personal, regular Sex, Companionship, and Children from her/his spouse. A human's life is a long, arduous journey of some seventy-plus years marked by daily survival and other needs. Marriage gives one the financial and personal support of one's spouse at every step, in everyday tasks of running the home; rearing children; and in sickness, long illness, and during other weak phases of one's life. Marriage gives one safe and regular sex with one's spouse, which fulfills their sexual needs, is enjoyed by both, and strengthens their marital bond.

A human by nature does not like to live alone. She needs company. Marriage gives one constant companionship of one's spouse all twenty-four hours a day, at every step, in sharing the day's activities and experiences, joys and sorrows; in caring; and in enjoying certain activities together like listening to music, watching TV together, or going out together et cetera.

A child is the most lasting lifelong Value in a human's life. *I as a human will die one day but will leave behind my child(ren) to the Human Whole.* A child is a part of one's deepest Self. Having your own child makes you responsible, caring, and moral. Marriage gives you your own child, loved and cared for by both—you and your spouse.

Marriage gives a human her own Second Family—the Family of spouse and children. A human enjoys its warmth and support till old age.

Marriage with its SSCC makes an individual rich, strong, sexually satisfied, happy, caring, responsible, and moral.

Marriage regulates a human's sexual behavior and makes her moral. A human society with its strong marriages is a moral society.

Marriage creates a family, maintains a family, and distinguishes one family from another. And therein lies its prime social value. A family is a group of individuals tied together by common identity, deep emotional bonds, and mutual care and support. Family is a very important unit of a human society—a ground of support to all its members, and a Treasurer of its ages-old wisdom and morality. A strong family supports its all members, nurtures them with its best, and helps them grow and succeed. A human society with strong families is a strong, happy, and moral society.

It is a human family that creates and retains the pure, beautiful relationships of Parent–Child, Brother–Sister, Sister–Sister, Grandparents–Grandchildren, Aunts/Uncles to their Nieces and Nephews, Cousins, and so on. Each of these relationships has its own purity and fragrance by which each cares for the other and supports the other.

Constant maintenance of family is the only way to avoid incest in human society. Through family we maintain the family bloodline and linage of ancestry and avoid marriage and sex between close family relatives.

Again, it is Marriage which creates, and maintains a family.

Marriage ought to be a lifelong relationship between a woman and a man. A human—a woman or a man needs marriage. (S)he needs its SSSC—Support— both financial and personal, Sex, Companionship, and Children in everyday of her/his life and throughout her/his life.

Marriage is the Cradle in which a child is born and reared. A child needs a stable, happy home, and love of her both parents for first twenty years of her life and later too for her survival, emotional support, and maintenance of her worldly roots.

Marriage is the founding stone of a human family. It creates and maintains a family. The Dissolution of marriage creates great turbulence in an individual's life, leaves lifelong scars; destroys the Cradle in which a child is born and reared and breeds anxiety and insecurity in a child's tender psyche; destroys a family, a family bloodline and thus weakens the bonds of a human society. This is what one single Divorce does.

Therefore, marriage ought to be a lifelong relationship between a woman and a man, marked by their sexual faithfulness and mutual love and support of both—wife and husband to each other with which they create and maintain a happy stable home for themselves and their children, which in turn, leads to their own growth and prosperity, and to the happy growth and success of their children, and to a strong, safe, and moral human society.

All of the above make marriage an Eternal Human, Lifelong Value. Till there is a human, there will be marriage.

Derivative Right Way of Living

After having analyzed the nature of marriage and its value in a human's life, let us see how to incorporate marriage in a human's life—how a human ought to view marriage and live it Right.

Marriage is an independent entity that stands all by itself. Its prime nature and value in a human's life since the beginning has been the same and will remain the same.

Since the prime purpose of marriage is to produce a child and keep track of the child's parentage, marriage is possible only between a woman and a man.

Marriage is the only mode through which a child's parentage can be traced and retained. Marriage establishes a family, runs the family, and distinguishes one family from the other family. This fact makes marriage a sacred bond between a wife and husband—a bond marked by both the spouses' extreme sexual faithfulness to each other. Sex is permitted only between a wife and a husband. After marriage a wife ought to have sex only with her husband, and a husband ought to have sex only with his wife. The very Nature of marriage demands it.

A violation of this rule results in wrong parentage of the child and is an example of the worst cheating a wife could do to her husband. If a wife has sex with a man other than her husband, bears his child, and does not disclose this to her husband, then the child's parentage will still be tracked by marriage and will be wrong. Also, the husband will treat the child as his own and rear him with the same feelings and attachment as to his own child. This will disturb the wife constantly and will hurt her if she has the slightest sense of honesty and conscience in herself. Also, if the husband ever comes to know of this, their marriage will be ruined, and the child may be disowned by the cheated husband.

Similarly, if a man has sex with a married woman and impregnates her, his own child will be known as someone else's child and will be reared by someone else—in this case the ignorant husband of the cheating wife.

But, what if measures are taken to prevent pregnancy? Then, is sex outside marriage allowed? The answer is still No. The reason is that sex between a woman and a man is very deep and intimate. It breeds emotional attachment between the two, especially for the woman. Attachment to a person outside marriage makes one withdraw from her spouse, constantly think of and try to meet her/his lover, and may eventually destroy one's marriage. A human by nature wants sexual faithfulness from her/his spouse. A single instance of extramarital sex can often destroy a marriage.

Therefore, sex outside marriage or adultery is forbidden for both—the woman and the man—by the very nature (and law) of marriage.

The bond of marriage ties a woman and a man and creates a Union. Marriage combines a woman and a man, their financial and personal resources, and their families into one. This strengthens an individual and the human society too. Both the wife and husband ought to preserve their Union of marriage. After marriage both wife and husband ought to view each other's family (In-Laws) as her/his own family, care for them, and support them as (s)he would have done to her/his own family.

Marriage is the Union as well as an interpersonal relationship between a woman and a man made of their mutual SSCC—Support, Sex, Companionship, and Children. These four are the threads which connect a wife and husband, and also are the four legs on which the institution of marriage stands.

SSCC infer from marriage. They are the blood and bone of marriage. Marriage is made of them and nurtured and strengthened by them. Marriage gives you your spouse's Support—both financial and personal, Sex, Companionship, and Children.

The Right Way of Living marriage is that which makes a person do her share of SSCC toward her spouse—extend her support—both financial and personal to her spouse, be an active and interested sex partner with her spouse, be a caring and happy companion at every step of life, and produce and rear child(ren) with her spouse. This will encourage the same behavior from the spouse and will strengthen their marriage.

Marriage is a pool of both—the wife's and husband's money and labor. It demands them from both. Often there are fights over money matters and who does what, like household tasks, rearing a child et cetera. Both wife and husband ought to work, earn money, and extend equal share toward common household and other expenses. Both of them ought to share the daily household and other tasks and the tough task of rearing a child equally. One spouse should not be overwhelmed with most of the work. Having love and compassion for each other does wonders for marriage. Understanding your spouse's feelings and situation and behaving with her accordingly strengthens the bond of marriage. If one is tired, the other can do the work. Contributing one's equal share of money and labor supports the other spouse, reduces marital disputes, and helps a marriage run smoothly.

Sex is an important component of marriage. Active, good marital sex fulfills sexual needs of both spouses, connects them physically and emotionally, and breeds intimacy. It strengthens a marital bond and marriage. Each spouse ought to remain interested in sex, be sexually attractive, and be good in bed with her/his spouse. A happy marriage helps maintain good marital sex while an unhappy marriage filled with constant strife and conflicts, reduces or even kills sexual interest of the spouses for each other. ***Therefore, a marriage ought to be happy.***

Companionship is another important aspect of marriage. After marriage, wife and husband live together. They are together most of the time, often twenty-four hours a day. They ought to be there for each other, have open communication, and share their joys and sorrows and other fun activities together.

Marriage should be a happy companionship. Both spouses ought to chat for at least thirty minutes every day. They should share their day's experiences, crack jokes, and laugh together. They should spend some quality time together, like wine and dine, going out, watching a good movie, going on a trip etc. This makes them open to each other, understand each other better, and enjoy their time together. Open, good communication between spouses and their spending quality time and other time together strengthen marriage.

Child is the Fourth leg, rather the center of a marriage. The prime purpose of marriage is to produce and rear a child. A child is a common and a dear asset to both partners. Both mother and father love their child and want to rear her well. A child brings together both parents and strengthens the marriage.

A married couple ought to produce and rear their own child well. The husband ought to give complete support to the wife during pregnancy and childbirth. After the child is born, both parents ought to spend time with the child together, play with her, teach her, and fulfill all her needs. Doing so strengthens the marital bond of the couple and glues the family together. Seeing a happy and caring set of parents together comforts and soothes a child's psyche and makes her feel emotionally secure and happy. This also instills the value of family in a child's mind.

Thus doing one's share of SSCC—supporting her/his spouse financially and personally; having regular sex with one's spouse; providing a happy companionship to one's spouse; and having and rearing a child by marriage build, strengthen, and maintain a marriage.

Marriage is a Cradle in which a child is born and reared for the first most tender and formative years of life. It is a cradle built and maintained by both —wife and husband. I view marriage as a warm, soft cradle being rocked by both parents. A

Child needs the lullaby of a happy and harmonious marriage of both her parents. A Child needs both parents' love and support in order to grow into an emotionally secure, happy, and successful youth.

Marriage creates and maintains a family. Prime Human Family of mother, father, and child(ren); and Extended Family of siblings, their spouses, and grandchildren are all created and held together by the pillar of marriage. When a marriage breaks, there breaks a family and with that goes away the Cradle of the child, the Treasurer of morality, and the Prime unit of human society through which a human's parentage is tracked and maintained. This creates anxious, emotionally insecure, ill-reared, and immoral children and youth—and incest (sex and marriage between close relatives) resulting in physically and mentally feeble children. **Therefore, a human ought to view and live her marriage as a lifelong Value to maintain the cradle for her children; to maintain a stable, warm, and happy family; and to maintain the purity of her family bloodline.**

Further, marriage gives a human SSCC—Support— both financial and personal, Sex, Companionship, and Children. A human needs them at every step of her life, every day of her life, and throughout her life. Marriage with these attributes makes you rich, strong, and happy. Therefore, **marriage ought to be a Lifelong Human Value.**

A human ought to marry once and maintain the same marriage throughout her lifetime.

A human lives in marriage throughout her lifetime, and also twenty-four hours a day. Marriage is one of the prime arenas in which a human spends the major part of her day.

Having a happy and caring spouse makes one's day, creates a happy home, and nurtures the marriage. Seeing the bright and happy face of one's spouse and enjoying his care add charm to one's everyday life. A happy marriage creates a happy family and a happy home—the home where you return after a day's hard work, to relax, rest, and enjoy the care and cheerfulness of your spouse and children. The home is the place in which you grow and prosper and nurture and rear your children. A happy marriage makes the home a paradise, while an unhappy marriage makes the home a living hell. Therefore marriage ought to be happy.

If married, and till married, a human ought to make her marriage a happy marriage. A human ought to look good, greet her spouse with a smile, respect him and his family, care for and support one's spouse, do her share of SSCC, understand her spouse well, talk, avoid arguments, enjoy good time, and share fun activities that both of them enjoy. In sum **a human ought to live and view marriage as a lifelong relationship of mutual love and support.**

A human ought to view and live her marriage as a life-long sacred bond of mutual love and support with her spouse. This bond is made of their mutual SSCC—Support, Sex, Companionship, and Child(ren)—of both spouses, where each spouse ought to do her/his Dharma—duty by contributing her /his share of Support, Sex, Companionship, and Child(ren) to maintain and strengthen the marriage. Doing your marriage Dharma means extending your share of financial and personal support to your spouse; being an attractive and active sex partner with your spouse; offering your loving company to your spouse to chat and enjoy other activities; and helping your spouse in producing and rearing your own children.

5. CHILD

In tracing the trail of a human's life, Child emerges as the Fifth major milestone in a human's life. It is a milestone because it brings major changes in a human's life—her Values, her perception, and her way of living. Also, it gives a whole new direction, purpose, and meaning to a human's life.

A human is born as the most helpless infant in her First Family or Family by Birth. It is in the realm of her First Family that (s)he receives education, and grows up to be a youth. Sometime during youth a human starts working. Then (s)he marries, and produces her own children. Thus she starts her Second Family or Family by Marriage. It is in the realm of her second family or family of spouse and child(ren) that a human spends the rest of her life, from youth until death. Thus a child forms the major realm of a human's life.

A human produces her child and rears her child with lot of love and care for a good eighteen to twenty years. A human views her child as a part of herself, grows very attached to her, and remains very attached to her in the latter part of her life too. This makes child a Lifelong Human Value.

A human's love for her child is the purest and the best. A human views her child as a part of her deep Self, leaves no stone unturned in his rearing, gives her best, and teaches him the best of her Life Values. A human dies but leaves behind her Child—a part of her deep Self, and the symbol of her purest and the best to the world. Thus Child emerges as another prime mode through which a human enriches her Human Whole. This fact makes child an entity that forms a human's lifetime Achievement and gives meaning to a human's life on this Earth.

Each of the above is a fact that came up earlier in the analysis of human life. Before going any further, let us first analyze the "Child," define it, and then take the derivative Right Way of Living or how a human ought to view and rear her child.

As we saw earlier in our discussion of marriage—how in the very beginning, before the inception of human society and civilization, humans lived in groups and had free sex or women were raped. Consequently, the children of an unknown or untracked parentage (from father's side) were born. Since there was no marriage and family, there was no way to track a child's parentage or distinguish siblings and cousins. This gave rise to incest and also to the issues of who will be responsible for the child and who will rear the child. Very soon humans realized the dangers of incest for the human race, and the issues of child responsibility and rearing. To solve these issues, humans came up with the institution of marriage. Very soon marriage proved to be an effective way to track a child's parentage, and the Founding Stone of a human's Family. Now it was possible to distinguish one family of parents, siblings, and cousins from another family, where members of one family did not have sex with each other. This prevented incest. Also, very soon marriage proved to be the Cradle into which a child was born and reared by her actual parents with their natural love and care. The institution of Marriage continued, and so did that of the Family in all civilized human societies.

Over time it created a pattern in a human's life that continues till date. Sometime during youth a human marries, produces her own children, and thus starts her Second Family or Family by Marriage.

After marriage, a woman and a man—now wife and husband to each other— copulate and produce their own child. Since a child is a natural product of sex between a woman and a man, a child can be a planned or unplanned child. But the facts of child-birth and child-rearing and the value of a child in a human's life remain the same.

A child is a genetic product of sex between a woman and a man. Sometime during sex a man's sperm enters a woman's egg and may fertilize it. If fertilized, from the egg, there forms one single cell that in its nucleus contains the DNA of the child. The DNA is the spiral genetic code that contains the entire blueprint or genetic information about the future child's physical appearance, intelligence, and other mental and personality traits. A child borrows 50 percent of her genes from her both parents and the other 50 percent from the family and ancestors of her both parents—mother and father; hence, the striking similarities between parents and children and their families. There are trillions of genes, and there is no set pattern according to which the genes assemble and form the DNA. Therefore, there also appear a wide variety and differences even among children of the same parents. Nature decides the child's gender—whether it will be a boy or a girl.

Since a child is a pure genetic product of both mother and father, great care should be taken in marriage—in selecting a spouse.

Once conceived, the single cell inside the mother's womb starts multiplying into a number of different cells as per the DNA. The child's different organs and organ systems form, with the palpitating heart. Sometime around the third month of pregnancy, the child starts sensing and feeling, and later starts moving and kicking. It takes a full nine months for the single cell to develop into a fully formed child.

During all the time of nine months, right from conceiving up to the child's birth, the mother carries the child within her, inside her womb. This is where the single cell develops into a fully formed child. The child gets all the nutrients from her mother's diet and is constantly affected by her mother's feelings, thoughts, and physical movements. A well-fed and well-nourished mother produces a healthy child. Though the child's physical appearance, sensitivity, and intelligence are purely genetic, studies have proved that the mother's environment, feelings, and thoughts affect the child's appearance, feelings, and thoughts. Certainly, a child being part of the mother's flesh and blood is constantly affected by the mother's feelings and thoughts. The mother's fears, anger, and jealousy or sense of safety, calmness, and love are all imbibed by the child's psyche constantly and help shape the child's overall persona. The Child feels anxious and contracts with the mother's fears and danger. This affects and retards her development. And the child feels smug and happy with the mother's sense of security, comfort, and happiness. This boosts the child's growth.

In view of this fact, the pregnant mother ought to have a well nourishing, healthy diet and exercise regularly. This ensures the developing child's good health and growth. Also, she ought to live in a positive environment and nurture positive emotions and thoughts within her. Watching beautiful sights, taking a healthy diet, and nurturing love and noble thoughts (within her) by pregnant mother help in producing a healthy and happy child. The child's father and other family members ought to help the pregnant mother in feeling and living this way.

After eight to nine months of pregnancy, the mother gives birth to the child. Childbirth is a phase of deep, excruciating labor pains and equally painful delivery for the mother. But, the pleasure of both—mother and father of the child and their families is immense. They see the child as a deep part of their selves, part of their own flesh and blood, and an extension of their families, which the child actually is.

A human child is born as the most helpless infant who will take the next eighteen years to gradually shape up, develop, and grow into a blossoming youth. These are the most crucial years, during which the child receives her overall body and brain development and her life-lasting self-esteem, Values, and lessons of morality. All of these are determined by the child's rearing, which is mostly done by the parents and family of the child.

Child rearing is one of the most crucial phases in the parents' lives. The arrival of a child brings major changes in a human's life. It changes her whole lifestyle. A human has to devote an immense amount of time, money, and energy toward rearing her child.

A human child is born as the most tender, softest, infirm little baby who needs to be handled very carefully. She needs to be fed, cleaned, and watched all twenty-four hours a day. It is both parents, especially the mother of the child, who during the day and at odd hours of night keeps the baby close, feeds her, cleans her, and soothes her to sleep.

As the child grows up, she starts crawling and then walking. Slowly she starts learning how to speak; how to read; and how to write. Parents hold the child's finger and teach her how to walk; talk; read; and write. They have to spend a lot of time with the child. During play and other times, a child may often fall and hurt herself. Also, she may often fall sick. Parents tend to the child every moment, taking care of her, and rushing her to the doctor when needed. They spend a lot of time, money, and energy in doing so.

This initial phase of child rearing is very hard. A child demands attention twenty-four hours a day. It is harder if both parents are working. Their work gets affected. They may get less sleep at night. They get less time for themselves and other activities.

From the age of three or four a child starts going to school. She needs to be bathed, dressed, and fed in the early morning hours. She needs to be dropped at school and picked up from the school. She needs help with lessons at home. Her school fee, uniform, and other school-related expenses need to be paid. They add up to the other costs of child, like food, clothes, toys, and doctors' bills et cetera. The parents bear all costs of rearing the child. Child rearing is expensive throughout.

As the child grows up, she needs help with lessons at home, and her expenses increase too. The parents have to give time to the child. They help her with lessons, pay her all expenses, and are responsible for her throughout. This adds to the parents' responsibilities and expenses of rearing the child.

Some parents may not be able to cope with the responsibility and expenses of raising the child. They may ill treat the child, beat her, abuse her, or even disown her, which is rare. All this is very sad and wreaks havoc with the child's tender psyche and proper development. A human ought to think well, be aware of the responsibility of child rearing, and then produce a child. A human ought to bring up her child with a lot of love and care. This nourishes the child emotionally, leads to her good growth, and also builds an emotional bond between child and parents.

As a child grows up, she learns everything. She learns how to walk, talk, think, and act. She learns by observing and copying others, especially her parents, elders, and other people in her home and at school. She learns from her family's and her teachers' constant teachings, do's and don'ts, and from her school lessons et cetera. The child's tender psyche and growing brain are gradually molded and shaped by her parents', family's, and teachers' teachings and education.

The growing child's life is divided into two major arenas: family and school. Where family is a ship of love and comfort, school is the challenge. The child has to study hard in school, learn, and cope with her teachers and other students. Some children enjoy going to school, while others don't. Since school is a major realm in a child's life and affects her whole growth and life, parents ought to take an active interest in their child's schooling. They ought to select a good school for their child, which most parents try to do. They ought to have open communication with the child and ask her about school, studies, and teachers etc. They ought to watch the child's progress in school, and inculcate good study habits at home that will help the child always.

Discipline, self-control, self hygiene, honesty, punctuality, and good study habits need to be taught to the child right from the beginning. They help her live a good life.

Adolescence is the teen years of a child's life, which starts at the age of thirteen and lasts until eighteen. This is the most challenging phase of a child's growth, during which a child goes through major physical and emotional changes. Both—girls' and boys' sex organs grow. Girls develop breasts and start their menstrual cycles, while boys start getting hair on their faces and chests. Along with the growth of sex organs, the child feels sexual urges and attraction to the opposite sex. The child needs to be educated about sex at school and at home. Also, parents ought to watch their child's activities, and teach, and discipline her constantly.

The Parents' teachings and control play a major part in a child's growth.

From nineteen to twenty-four, the child—now a fully grown human—goes through the youth phase. This is the age of dreams and passions and trying new things. This is also the time when the child, after having finished formal education, enters a profession.

The child requires the parents' support and guidance throughout, especially in the realm of education. Parents ought to take an active interest in the child's education throughout, be aware of their child's interests and talent, and help her select a suitable profession.

After finishing school at the age of sixteen or seventeen, the child goes to a college or a university. College education is very expensive. Some of the students work and pay their fees, but in the majority of cases, it is the parents who pay for their children's college education.

Overall, raising a child is very expensive. But it is too deep a relationship and too high a Value in a human's life to be assessed in terms of money only.

After finishing college, a child, now an adult of twenty-one years or more, starts working, and prefers to live more or less her own way. This brings up a good point in the discussion.

A human is born as the most helpless infant who is reared and handled by her parents anyway they want. A child's all movements are controlled by her parents. During childhood, the child is too weak to resist her parents and the wrong behavior or ill treatment. But once the child grows up, especially from adolescence on, the child resists too much controlling and wants more freedom. The key is not to overly control the child but to control enough, and give enough freedom to let her enjoy the things she likes or do what she wants.

Discipline mixed with a lot of love does wonders in child rearing.

The above analysis brings up certain key truths about the human child and child rearing, on the basis of which we can define a human child as follows:

Definition of a Child

A human child is a product of her both parents— mother and father—a product of their genes, and product of their love and rearing; part of their deep selves, reflecting their deepest life Values; a true extension of her parents in the world; and finally a contribution of their best and the purest to the Human Whole.

These facts make child the deepest human Value—the prime mode through which a human enriches her Human Whole. ***I am a human. I will die one day, but I will leave behind my "Work" and my "Child" to the Human Whole.***

Value of a Child in a Human's Life

Parents often view their child as a part of their deep selves and as their own extension in the world. They are quite right in thinking so. The child is truly a part of her parents, made of their own flesh and blood and their and their ancestors' genes. Parents in rearing their child give their best to the child and teach her the very best of their life Values, morality, and habits. No love is purer than that of parents' for their child. In this way a child is truly an extension of her parents in this world, an extension of their genes, and an extension of their life Values, morality, and character. Parents depart one day but leave behind their child—a symbol of their best and the purest—to the world.

A Child is the prime mode through which a human enriches her Human Whole. This fact makes a child an entity that gives meaning to the human life. A human's life, after all, is assessed in terms of what (s)he gives to the world.

There is no joy greater than the joy of seeing your baby for the first time, holding her, and spending time with her. Some of the happiest moments in a human's life are the moments spent with her/his child, holding her close, playing with her, and teaching her the right things etc.

A child makes a human social and moral. You have to interact with a number of people because of your child—her friends, her teachers, and so on. When you have your own child, you think about right and wrong, and try to teach your child the right thing.

A child gives your life a direction, purpose, and meaning. When you have a child, you are responsible for her, and you have to take care of her. You have to fulfill all her needs, pay her bills, watch her and make sure that she is safe and happy. Having your own baby and rearing her gives depth and meaning to your life. There is a pure joy in doing this. A child is an eternal Human, Lifelong Value. Till there is a human, a child will form one of the prime human Values. A child's value in a human life derives from the very basic human nature. A human by nature loves her/his child the most, wants to give her the best of everything, and values her as an asset—to be protected, cherished, and furthered. She does further her child to the world.

A human dies but leaves behind her Child to The Human Whole.

A human gives birth to the child and rears her for the first eighteen to twenty years. She does so because she loves her child, cares for her, and feels responsible for her. During these long years of rearing, there forms a deep attachment and bond between parents and children, which lasts throughout one's lifetime. This makes a child a lifelong Human Value.

Derivative Right Way of Living

While living, the most important thing is one's attitude or view toward a thing because it is one's attitude which shapes one's behavior. The attitude toward one's child ought to be derived from the facts of a "Child."

As we saw earlier, a human is a part of The Human Whole. The Human Whole, or our human world in which we live today, is a product of millions of human generations and their labor. Each of these human generations was born of its parent generation, enjoyed the world left to them, worked hard, contributed their own children and labor to it, and made it more beautiful than they found it. This is how The Human Whole was built, and this is how it will go on—*a Palace under construction* made more and more beautiful by every forthcoming human generation. A human is temporary, but the Human Whole is permanent. A human dies one day, but The Human Whole goes on.

For example, I am a human. I am born and live in my Human Whole—the world left to us by our human ancestors and their cumulative labor. I enjoy the fruits of my ancestors' labor. I work in some field of labor and enrich The Human Whole. I marry, have children, and rear them. I am a human, I will die one day, but I will leave behind my "Work" and my "child(ren)" to our Human Whole. My child will be a member of the future human generation, who will inherit The Human Whole we leave to them. Our children will enjoy the world left to them by us, work, marry, and contribute their own "Work" and "Children" to The Human Whole. And so it will go on. This is what a child is—a human's most lasting contribution to The Human Whole—a member of the future human generation who will shape the world. *And this is how a child ought to be viewed by a human—my contribution to my Human Whole—my footprints in the world.*

This fact makes a child an entity that gives depth and meaning to a human's life. It is a deep meaning that ought to be remembered by a human every day, *"I am a human. I will die one day but will leave behind my work and my "Child" to my Human Whole."*

A child is not a product of some casual sex between a woman and a man but a product of their genes, part of their own flesh and blood, their extension into the world, their most lasting contribution to The Human Whole—a member of the future human generation, who will help shape The Human Whole.

A child is a genetic product of both her parents and their families. A child takes 50 percent of her genes from her both parents—mother and father—and the other 50 percent from both parents'—mother's and father's families. She is a true extension of her parents and their families. Great care should be taken in selecting a spouse—a wife or a husband—what type of person she/he is—good-looking, healthy, sensitive, intelligent, educated, and from a long line of family with strong Values; or ugly, sick, insensitive, foolish, uneducated, without any distinct family background. Your child will inherit 50 percent of her genes from your spouse and 50 percent from you.

Another great consideration before marriage is a spouse's family. A family is a long line of human generations related to each other by blood, something like a chain strung together by shackles where each shackle is a generation. A family is also the Treasurer of all its generations' ages-old wisdom, morality, and other life Values. The type of family your would-be spouse belongs to is of great importance—her parents, siblings, aunts, uncles, grandparents, and great-grandparents and their physical appearances, health, diseases, intelligence, education, and moral and other Values. Your child will inherit 50 percent of her genes from your spouse's family and your family. Her appearance, her intelligence, her Values and her worldview will be greatly affected by them.

As noted earlier, a pregnant mother's health, diet, emotions, and thoughts greatly affect the forming child. She ought to eat a nutritious diet and exercise to remain healthy, feel positive emotions like love and joy, and nurture high and noble thoughts inside her. Doing so will help her produce a healthy, happy, and mentally strong child.

Though child is a "Given"—you do not have much control of the genetic make of a child you will have, but a child is also a formation throughout right from the moment of conception inside the mother's womb, to birth, and during the next eighteen years of growing up from a baby to a youth. During all these years the child is constantly being formed and shaped.

A human child at birth, though a genetic product, is at the rudimentary stage of development, with an infirm body and an infirm, empty brain. It is her rearing during the next eighteen years that will shape her into the type of individual (s)he becomes. These are the most formative years, during which a child goes through her own set of experiences; observes her surroundings and others, especially parents, siblings, teachers, etc; tries to copy them; follows their do's and don'ts; and receives education and knowledge. Slowly and gradually her tender heart and developing brain by every day's experiences and teachings are molded into a certain set that will make her the type of person (s)he becomes. Her character traits are built, and so are her worldview and basic life Values, which will last throughout her lifetime.

A newborn child is a world of immense, open possibilities. If raised with thought and care, the child will grow up to be a good and successful human being. It matters very much what type of child we raise. Your child when grown up will be a part of you forever, will affect you and your family, and will be a member of society and future humanity. Your child through her being and her actions will affect you and others and will help shape the world around us.

When we hold a Child in our hands, we also hold the future of the human race and the humanity. This is what a Child is.

This raises the issue of what type of human we would like our child to be—strong, independent, confident, honest, compassionate, disciplined, punctual, educated, intelligent, productive, and moral? Certainly these are excellent character traits that if taught to the child will help her live a good life and be a good member of society and humanity.

Also, a human is a Multi-Dimensional living being. Various dimensions of her being are Physical, Emotional, Intellectual, Moral, and Spiritual. Each of these dimensions is different and plays an important part in shaping the overall being of human and in helping her live a good life. Care should be taken in rearing a child in such a way so that the child's each dimension is nourished and developed. Since childhood years are the most formative years in a human's life, some physical impairment; scarred psyche; undeveloped, ignorant brain; no sense of right and wrong; and a narrow, prejudiced worldview will follow the child throughout her life and damage her being and her future life. While, a careful nurturing of the child's each dimension will shape her whole being into a wholesome, healthy, happy, compassionate, and moral individual.

Since family, especially parents and school, are two prime teaching agents of the child, they should take steps in teaching the child good character traits and in developing her/his each dimension.

Parents ought to view their child as an eternal human, life-long Value and rear her that way. They ought not to rear her any way they want or spoil her. They ought to understand the fact that the kind of child they raise will affect their own lives, society, and ultimately the humanity. And their rearing will shape the child and the kind of life she leads.

Though the child has certain genetic qualities, and she learns by observing and copying her family, friends, and others, careful implanting and instilling of certain character traits and habits can be done with Right Teaching.

First of all, parents and family should love and cherish their child. This boosts the child's self-esteem and confidence and nourishes her emotional dimension. No matter what your child looks like, no matter whether she is dumb or intelligent, even if impaired, love your child and make her feel cherished and valued. Secondly, implant certain character traits that will help her live a good life. Love mixed with discipline does wonders in child rearing.

Teach her courage—not fearlessness, but prudent courage. Make the child strong and independent. Encourage her to make decisions and do things on her own—under your guidance. Teach her compassion toward others—an ability to feel another person's situation and pains. Encourage her to nurture goodwill for all. This will expand the child's worldview and help her deal better with the world. Teach your child a positive worldview.

Care should be taken and school curriculum should be drafted in a way to help the child develop her/his each dimension. Personal hygiene, Right diet and Right exercise should be part of the child's everyday activities. This will nurture her Physical dimension. The child should be taught compassion and goodwill toward others, not hostility and competition. Help her feel positive emotions, like love and happiness. This will nurture her Emotional dimension. Teach your child the value of education from the very beginning, how it increases one's knowledge and strengthens and enriches one's mind. In a child's life, the top priority should be Education. Inculcate good study habits in your child from the very beginning. Assign a separate, quiet place, preferably a room with a proper study table and a chair for your child. Encourage her to sit and study for long with concentration. Make her complete all her home assignments on time. Answer her questions and encourage her curiosity about the world. Teach and encourage the child to think well, critically, and to make her own sound decisions. This will nourish her Intellectual dimension.

Give your child a big worldview. Teach her about the vast Earth and its different countries, people, and their cultures. Teach her respect for all living beings. Teach her about the vast Universe. This will enlarge the child's mental world.

Teach the child the difference between right and wrong from the very beginning, and train her to stick to Right. Teach her discipline and self-control. Teach her respect for elders. This will develop her moral dimension.

Together with all this, the Child's Spiritual dimension needs to be nurtured too. Teach her compassion for all living beings. This will connect her to others. Teach her some religion and some faith in God—not to depend on God but to pray to God first thing in the morning, and request the God to keep her on the right track and make her be good and do good to others. Every religion or God gives a human a vast worldview and love for others.

The Child should be reared well and carefully during different phases of growing. Each phase requires different type of care. Both—family teaching and school teaching should aim to implant excellent character traits in the child and to nurture each dimension of her being. The traits and values implanted early in life will last forever with the child. They are hard to erase in the later years of life. Teaching the child activities that nurture her each dimension will help her live well and will be adopted and followed by her for ever.

The traits, habits, Values, and worldview taught in childhood grow and strengthen with time. They prepare the soil upon which the Child stands and from which she lives her life. ***It is the duty of the parents and teachers to give their purest and their best to our Children—the torchbearers and the vanguards of us all, our society, and our humanity.***

CHAPTER 5

DEATH

A human is born, lives, and dies. Death is the end of a human's one lifetime. Analysis of a human's life cannot be complete without the analysis of death. Death is a major issue in a human life. It is the flip side of life and an event of such a strong impact that it may rob life of its whole meaning. Hence it demands a thorough analysis, a proper definition, and the derivative Right Way of Living—which means how we humans ought to view death and incorporate it into our lives.

While living we do not think about death. We are so lost in our day-to-day lives and in our future planning that we never think about death. For example, once in a while, while driving, I pass by a mortuary. I read the sign mortuary and notice its grey silence. Or I pass by a cemetery, where I see rows of graves. These sights do catch my attention, but I pass by without thinking much about them. Then one day I happened to pass by an accident in which I saw a person thrown on the road, lying on the ground, in the pool of her own blood. I watched the sight and passed by. But the sight hit me hard, so hard that I could not forget about it. It kept coming back to me off and on. It made me think about my mortality, "I drive to work every day. What if I die so suddenly?" It worried me sick about my loved ones—what if it happened to any of them? But after a few days, I forgot all about it.

I go on living, and I do not think about death. I attend others' funerals, get affected for a day or two, and then forget all about it. If I see it in my neighborhood, I get more affected, maybe because of the closeness of death, and also if I have known the person for long. I still remember the day when one of my neighbors simply went for a walk, was hit by a car, and died on the spot. It was so sudden, without any pre warning. Only last evening we had met and talked for a while. Also, we were friends and used to meet often. Losing her so suddenly and for ever was such a shock that it took me days to recover. The First day it hit me like a bombshell. The Second day as I went to work, met and talked to other people, it hurt me less, and still less the third day. After ten or fifteen days, I forgot all about it.

Death, often, is sudden and hits you hard, with an impact that is hardest on the day it happens, lesser the next day, and gradually wears off with time.

Death hits you the hardest when you lose one of your loved ones to death. That is the time when reality of death strikes you. If it is sudden, it may even make a person lose her mental balance. I remember the incident when a girl in my neighborhood was so shocked at her mother's death that she threw herself off a cliff and died; and another—when a woman, having lost her husband and only son in a plane crash, went crazy. There are many such instances of people losing their minds upon the deaths of their loved ones.

Losing your loved one by sudden death is one of the greatest shocks that a human can endure. Also, losing one of your loved one to death is one of the deepest pains a human can endure.

Death viewed from a distance, and to others, does not seem so real. But it hits you in its bare reality, when viewed close, and when it happens to one of your loved ones.

You see death face-to-face when you sit close to a dead person. There is this stony silence and stillness about that person. The dead person lies so still, with her eyes closed. You can move her anyway and can do anything to her without any response from her. It is an eerie feeling, and heart wrenching too, if the dead person happens to be your close friend or family. A person who was so alive until the last moment—walking, talking, laughing, lies there dead; so still, and so without any response. She will never walk again or talk again and will never laugh again. She is gone forever. No wonder death's suddenness and its stark opposition to life can drive a sane person out of her mind.

It is the death of a loved one that is the hardest to bear. First of all, it comes as a shock, because somehow you do not expect your loved ones to die. We go on living our day-to-day lives never expecting death to our family or us until it knocks at our door. And when it happens, you are just not ready for it. That is why it shocks you. It dazes you, disables your thinking. Even if you expected it to happen to one of your family or friends, for example if the person was sick or very old, the pain of losing your loved one forever is very intense.

Watching the death of your loved one and post-death experiences are simply heart wrenching. The closer the relationship, the harder the pain, for example, if your loved one happens to be your family—mother, father, sister, brother, spouse, or child. In a close family relationship, having lived with that person for years, you grow so attached to that person that (s)he becomes a part of your deep self. At times you are so attached that you cannot even distinguish your separate self from that person. It is hard to bear the pain of losing such a loved one to death.

The sight of your loved one lying dead there is unbearable. Some people don't even accept the death, try to wake that person, soothe and rub her as if the person is sleeping. I remember my aunt when her young son of twenty-two went swimming and was brought back home as a dead body. There he was, lying on the ground with a crowd of people around him. His mother was so shocked, unable to understand anything. She sat close to him and tried to wake him up while applying cream to his dry lips. She thought he would wake up. He was the star of her eyes, her rainbow, her sole meaning in life. She never became normal and eventually died.

Even if you accept the death of your loved one, the sight of your loved one lying dead, and finally being taken away for cremation tears you apart from within. The sight of cremation or burial is so cruel—a final goodbye to that person you love so much, grew up with, and lived with for years. That person will never talk to you again, will never laugh with you, and will never be with you ever again. You have lost her forever.

For some people a relationship can be the sole meaning of their lives. It gives them so much—love, support, joy, and so many other things—that they live only for that relationship. For that person losing that relationship amounts to losing the meaning of her/his life, its purpose, and the very reason for living.

Death, whether certain or slow, is an event. It happens and it is over, though its effects last for some time. The impact of death is strongest at the time it happens but gradually wears off with time.

Death is not only a heart-wrenching event; it also raises a number of queries: what is death? What happens to the person after death? Does a part of a person remain after death?

Death is a fact of life. Every living being is born, lives for a certain time span, and dies. This is the prime principle of life. Every living being—be it a plant, an animal, or a human—is subject to this principle. What is born will die one day. Thus death is the certainty of life.

What dies at death? The Body certainly dies. We see the body of a plant dying—withering, falling to the ground, being eaten by insects, and getting mixed with earth. We see the body of an animal dying, lying still, being eaten by other animals or being buried. Similarly, we see the body of a human dying, lying still, starting to decompose, and being cremated. The body certainly dies. For whatever you do with the body, it poses no response.

Together with the body there dies the individual too. An individual plant— my favorite rose plant for instance, an individual animal—my dog for instance, and an individual human— my friend for instance. Each individual was unique in her way, part of the world, enriching the world in her own special way. Her death leaves a gap that can never be fulfilled by any other individual. No other individual will be quite like that. In death you lose that individual forever.

What dies at death? On a human's death, you lose a person, a person who moved, talked, laughed, and cried. That person is gone forever.

Life and death walk hand-in-hand. Where there is life, there will be death too. They are so together all the time. Any living being can die anywhere and at any time. One wrong cut, one wrong fall, a disease, or an accident can cause one's death anytime, and anywhere. Death follows us like a shadow. It is with us all the time.

Death is the flip side of life. It stands in sharp contrast to life. Where life is movement, death is stillness. Where life is bright and cheery, death is still and gloomy. Where life means hope, dreams, potential, death is the end of all hopes, all dreams, and all potential.

Death is the natural end of life. Life ends in death. Every living being is born afresh, blossoms to lovely youth, and then withers, decays, and dies. This principle applies to all living beings—a plant, an animal, and a human. A human is born as the new, soft, tender baby; blossoms to dreamy, energetic youth; and then grays, decays, and dies as an old person.

This fact establishes death as a fact of human life. While living, a human ought to keep death in view—the death of herself and the deaths of her loved ones. Any of us may die any day, any time, and any how. Viewed this way, death should not shock us. We ought to be prepared for death—death of ourselves and death of our loved ones—any day, any time, and any how.

Death is the endpoint of a human's life. A human is born, lives for a certain time span, and dies.

Birth..Death

Life

What happens to a person after death, we do not know much about. How does she feel? What does she do? But we the onlookers do feel the loss of that person and remember that person in term of what she gave to us and others.

Death is the point at which a person's lifetime's Karmas and Achievements are assessed. A human dies but leaves behind an Edifice of his lifetime's Karmas and Achievements—a Cumulative Total of his deeds in the world—something like a Construct that he created over his whole lifetime through his every day's consistent karmas in certain realms of life, like money, work, and family etc. Some people amass a lot of wealth and leave it behind in the forms of their house(s), properties, bank balances etc.; while others live mainly family-oriented lives and leave behind their spouses and well-raised children; and others live mainly work-oriented lives and leave behind their products, discoveries and other contributions in some field of labor. But majority of humans work in each realm of life and leave behind an Edifice containing the pearls of their Achievements in each realm of life—money, family, work etc. For example, one may leave behind a lot of money he earned and saved during his entire lifetime by his every day's hard labor; a loving spouse and well-raised children whom he achieved after some fifty plus years of marriage where he gave part of his every day to maintaining his marriage and rearing his children; and his work (profession)—some product(s), discovery(s), or service in a specific field of labor. Maybe he was a great writer and leaves behind some good books he worked on for years; or he was a Civil Engineer who leaves behind some famous dams and bridges that he created through his years of every day's labor in his profession; or he was a Scientist who leaves behind some important scientific discovery that he came up with after years of hard research in one field; or he was a simple Clerk who leaves behind examples of his good service that he achieved during his years of every day's hard labor in some field of human profession.

This is the Edifice reflecting a Human's Lifetime's Achievements earned by his years of every day's consistent karmas in certain realms of life, like money, family, work etc.

This again brings up two eternal human Values of "Family" and "Work."

This is the Edifice of a human's lifetime's Achievements, as well as his foot prints in the world. A human dies but leaves behind this edifice—his foot prints in the form of his "Work" and "Children," which remind us of that human, long after he is gone. And, that continue to enrich The Human Whole long after he is gone.

It is at death that we assess a human's lifetimes Karmas and Achievements. It is death that makes us take note of a human's foot prints in the world—type of person (s)he was, and what (s) he gave to the world. Thus it is death that gives meaning to a human's life.

Death is a mystery. A human's life is like a passage between two doors of birth and death. She enters through the door of birth, lives a certain life span, and passes through the door of death. These two doors are closed to us. We don't know what happens behind these two doors—before birth and after death. But it is not a complete mystery. There have been instances of after- death experiences in which a person declared medically dead later revives and comes back to life. Many such instances and experiences have been recorded by curious psychologists and writers. There are numerous books and write-ups on them which describe accurately and with evidence "after- death" experience of these people. These people once revived narrated their after death experiences. The things they said were later verified by people present at that time and by further search, and were found true. This gave birth to a whole new branch of Psychology called Parapsychology, which deals with this issue in a scientific manner.

Almost all of these people narrate how they sort of got out of their bodies, flew up, floated, and saw their own bodies lying down there, and other people down there; flew out of the room, and saw their loved ones crying. They flew up and saw things that only a person above could have seen, like dust on top of the ceiling fan and things on rooftops. Then they flew out in the distance. After some time, once revived, they woke up and remembered everything and narrated it to others. These people are living today. If you go, ask them, they will recount the same experiences to you. Or read any good book on Parapsychology or near-death or after death-experiences that list these people's experiences with concrete evidence.

What was it that got out of the dead person's body, flew up, watched others, moved, and was so lightweight that it could fly? Almost all Religions, Sages, Mystics, and now Parapsychologists tell us there is an entity called the Soul. Countless instances have been recorded in which a person remembered her previous life—where she lived, her family, and other things dear to her. All of these things were later verified and were found true. They evidence the existence of an entity called the Soul within a person that remembers her past life.

I personally know there is a soul. I have seen souls (ghosts) very closely and have seen them do things which only a soul or a ghost could do. I deal with this topic in my next chapter, "Soul."

"Soul is one's deepest Self—a light-like, conscious entity that resides in the center of a human's body (every living being) a little below her navel, containing her deepest memories, attachments, and desires of all her previous lives and this life too." This is my definition of soul arrived at by my own personal experiences, by my insight, and further verified by major religions of the world, Parapsychology, and peoples' after-death experiences and true instances of rebirth.

It is a soul that enters a mother's womb right after conception, acquires a physical body (made of DNA and cells), lives inside a person's body as her deep Self—"Ahm" or "I"—throughout her lifetime, pushes her to act in a certain way, and leaves her body at death.

At death a person's body dies, but her soul lives on. The soul leaves a person's body at death, watches the dead body and others, hovers over its loved ones and loved things for a while, flies away, comes back and finally after a certain time period departs for good. Every religion has provisions for certain rituals during this phase of forty-plus days or a year, which if performed by the dead person's close relatives satisfy the dead person's soul.

This is a transition phase for the soul— a temporary time period of a few months or years starting at the death of a person and ending at her rebirth—something like a dark, mysterious tunnel through which the soul passes, goes through a number of experiences, and then takes a rebirth.

We don't know much about this phase. But we do have some knowledge accumulated from various religions, people's after-death experiences, and the experiences of loved ones of the dead person. As per them nothing changes for the soul after death. It does not even realize that it is dead. If it was in the middle of a task, it tries to finish it. There is an example recorded in a newspaper of a man in India. This man, while on his way to buy medicines for his dying wife, met with an accident. He was brought to the hospital and declared dead. Later, his daughter saw some movement in his toe and reported to the doctor. The man was revived and brought back to life. Once he was revived, he remembered his after-death experiences in which he never realized that he was dead. He was still moving, hurrying up, trying to reach the medical store. He was flying, running. He reached the medical store and asked the clerk for medicines. He was surprised that the clerk did not see him or hear him. Nothing changed for him after death except that he did not have a body.

Also, there are recorded instances of how the soul remembers its loved ones and loved things and tries to reach them. It hovers over and near its loved ones. It wants their company but soon realizes that they cannot feel its presence. They cannot see it or talk to it as they did before. The soul is pained and tormented by the fact. But slowly and gradually, after a certain time the soul wanders away and takes rebirth.

The soul takes rebirth—a curious but well-evidenced fact. Since the soul is a person's consciousness containing her lifetime's memories, attachments, and desires, it takes a new birth on the basis of them. A person's new birth is affected by her previous lifetime's experiences, Karmas, and desires. A person's rebirth is also the new birth in which the person apparently does not at all remember her previous lives. But as evidenced by the existence of soul, all her memories and desires of previous lives lie buried inside her soul and motivate her to act and live in a certain way.

From the above analysis there emerge certain truths on the basis of which we can define death.

Definition of Death

Death is the end of one lifetime and the transit phase into another (life).

Death is the end point of a human's one lifetime. A human is born, lives..., and dies. Death is the point where her entire lifetime's Karmas and Achievements are assessed.

At death one's body dies, but her Soul lives on.

After death the Soul goes into the transit phase of a certain time period, during which it hovers near her dear ones and dear possessions. After a certain time period, the Soul then wanders away and takes rebirth. This whole After-death experiences is like *landing at an airport after having taken a long flight (one lifetime); and then passing through a long, dark, tunnel-like walkway (transit phase); and then stepping out into a big, well-lit hall (Rebirth).* At this point one starts a new life. The beauty is that one does not remember anything of her past life at all. But actually it is the Soul that takes rebirth; and the Soul carries with it all one's previous lives' memories, attachments, and desires and pushes one to live in a certain way.

Derivative Right Way of Living

Though we encounter death often in our daily lives—in an accident, in our neighborhood, on TV, or read about it—but we pass by without giving it a second thought. It is only the deaths of our dear ones that shock us and perturb us. Death shocks us because we are not prepared for it, and it perturbs us because we feel as if a part of our deep selves has gone. The closer the relationship, the deeper the pain of separation is. The thought of our own death never crosses our minds. We feel as if we are eternal; we will never die.

Death is a fact of life that is bound to happen to our loved ones and ourselves one day; when, no one can tell. Uncertainty is a friend of death. Somehow we need to accept this fact, expect it to happen anytime, and be prepared for it.

Death walks hand-in-hand with life—like a shadow looming behind us all the time. Each of us walks with this dark shadow of death, which can overtake one's life anytime. Anybody may die at any time. Does it mean we live in constant fear of death? Obsessed by it all the time? Not form any loving, meaningful relationship; not do anything productive; not work; in short, not do anything that nourishes life because, we may die any day and lose them all? For example, I may love a man deeply, marry him, start a new life with him, and may lose him to death suddenly. I may produce and rear my son with a lot of love like a treasure. And he may die in an accident. I may work hard in my profession, and just when success is about to happen, I may die. This uncertainty and nature of death coupled together raises fears and makes us question the worth of our worldly achievements.

The answer is "NO." Though, death is uncertain, but not so uncertain and ill-timed for all of us. With the advancement of our medical science today, the majority of humans without any disease or accident do live a full life span up to ripe old ages. And accidents and catastrophes do not happen every day to everyone. Our loving relationships give as joy, support, and meaning to our lives. Our work gives us money and happiness, and through it we enrich the lives of others. We do die one day, but we leave behind our contributions to The Human Whole, which continue to enrich The Human Whole long after we are gone.

Life is totally distinct from death. Life has its own joys, meaning, and purpose, which must never be marred by the fear of death. A human ought to live life fully, enjoy it, raise a good family, be good in her work (profession), live a life of achievements, and contribute her best to the Human Whole in the form of her "Work" and "Child."

Life and death are two sides of the same coin—both totally distinct, never to be mixed up with each other. Life is the bright side, and death is the flip side.

Death is the flipside of life—dark and disillusioning. It is so sad and cruel that it can strip life of its all happiness and meaning. But we ought to view it the way it is—the end of one lifetime—the point where life ends, again not to be mixed up with one's life. Life has its own joys, meaning, and purpose that are lived, enjoyed, and left behind to The Human Whole.

Nonetheless, death is a Fact that can happen to any of us and our loved ones at any time. A human ought to be prepared for it.

Coping with the Deaths of our Loved Ones

Living amid the hush and rush of life, we often don't get time to talk to our loved ones or spend time with them. But meeting our loved ones and spending time with them is a blessing that we can enjoy only while they and we are alive. Knowing this we ought to spare some time every day for our loved ones, talk to them, and meet them once in a while. This will give us joy during our lifetime and will avoid regrets after our loved ones' death. I have often seen people crying bitterly that their brother or parent died and they had not met him or talked to him for years.

Remember that your loved ones may die any day. So be prepared for it. Let not death shock you. Love your relationships, and help them—your loved ones—live good lives. But be prepared for their deaths.

Endure the deaths of your loved ones with calmness and wisdom. Remember, death is an event of instantaneous impact that hits you the hardest when it happens but will fade with time. Face the moment with strength and this knowledge. Give it time. Let the days roll by. Value your "Work" and other relationships, live them well; go out; travel for change; and meet other people. Try to replace your lost relationship with the new one. As you live on, you find new interests, and build new relationships and new meanings, which help you live a good life and enrich your Whole too.

Deaths of loved ones often invoke memories and regrets. Your Self demands answers. You don't have to ignore them and repress them, but think wisely. Think about what the person did for you and how she affected your life and others' lives. Think about the bright side as well as the flip side of your relationship. This will give you an overall view. Sum up your relationship. But don't ever regret in your life. If you feel you did something wrong, you did not know it was wrong at that time. We do what we do guided by our limited knowledge and motives at that time. At the time of doing you knew only that much and could do only that much. One ought to have no regrets.

If you truly loved that person, then do what would make that person happy. Fulfill her/his desires. That person is dead, but her soul lives on. Do what will make that person happy if you can do it. If you cannot, then let your reasons console you.

Losing your loved ones to death is the worst catastrophe a person faces in her life. But that is the way life is. Accept death as a fact of life.

Human relationships breed deep attachment, especially family ones. At times this attachment becomes so thick and strong that we lose the sense of our distinct selves and identify ourselves only with our most loved ones—"my mother," "my brother," "my son," and so on. No doubt such relationships do give a lot of joy, meaning, and purpose to our lives, but if we were to lose such a loved one to death, our lives suddenly become deserted of their all joys, meaning, and purpose. Therefore, don't make a relationship the sole meaning of your life. A relationship is just a relationship, it is not you. If you truly love a person, help her live a happy life, but don't make her your own identity and the sole meaning of your life. Every human has her own unique identity and derives the meaning of life from her own distinct, individual being, her work, and her deeds.

In sum, be prepared for the deaths of your loved ones at any time. And when they happen, endure the moment calmly, give it time, and remember it is just a phase that will pass. Keep living your "Work," your other relationships, and other pursuits of life. Also, have a wide worldview. Look around. There are so many other people who lose their loved ones in worse circumstances. Some old parents lose their only son—a blossoming youth, full of great potential, their only support in life. A newlywed young girl loses her husband in a car crash. A mother loses her newborn, beautiful Son. Compassion connects us to others and reduces our own pains and sorrows in front of others' worse pains and sorrows.

Coping with One's Own Death

A human ought to remember the fact that she may die any day, and at any time. Knowing this she ought to be prepared for her own death.

Keeping a card with one always that states her name, address, phone number, and names and phone numbers of persons to be contacted at her death is a good idea so in case she dies while driving or while alone her family can be informed of her death.

A human's death will affect her dependents: her spouse, children, and others, most. Knowing this one ought to provide for her dependents—write a Will, create a Trust, arrange some godparents for her children. And, above all, teach independence and courage to her dependents and children.

A human's death like others' death will be an event which will affect her loved ones—family and friends deeply, and also those to whom she gave something while she was alive. Initially it will shock them, but gradually they will learn to live with it. With time her memory will fade, and after some time, they may not remember her anymore.

My death like others' deaths will be an end of my lifetime on this Earth. It will be the point when my whole lifetimes Karmas and Achievements will be assessed by others and maybe by me too. They say that when a person dies her whole life's experiences are replayed in her mind—how she started out, how she married, how she reared her children, and her work etc. Mine will play too. I guess it gives one an overall feeling of the kind of life she lived. Derivative from this is that, I as a human ought to live a good life myself and enrich others' lives too.

At my death my body will perish, but my soul will live on. My soul, like other souls, will hover over my loved ones and my dear possessions. I will be tormented by the pain of my loved ones and by my separation from them. I would want to be at my home in the company of my dear ones and my dear possessions. It will be hard for me to leave so suddenly all my loved ones and my loved things behind—for example, my spouse of fifty-plus years of marriage; my children—my own flesh and blood; my home, my favorite car, jewelry, and other possessions. This will be the transit phase for my soul—the most painful and testing phase, during which I will have to leave behind my all dear ones, and my dear possessions and move on to a new life. Some souls have a short transit phases, while others have long ones— depending upon how attached they were to their worldly relations and things and whether they left some unfulfilled tasks in between.

After a certain time period, my soul will wander here and there and then take rebirth.

From this Fact we infer the theory of detachment, which I will discuss later.

So far I have listed the derivative Right Way of Living from the viewpoint of those whom death affects the most. Now, a few derivatives from the general definition of death: "Death is the end of one lifetime and a transit phase into another (life)."

Death—The End of One Lifetime

Birth..Death

Living

Death is the endpoint of a person's one lifetime. It is the point when a person, after having lived a certain number of years, passes through the door of death. It is the point when a person's one whole lifetime can be seen stretching behind her—her birth, the kind of life she lived, and what she gave to others. Death is the point at which a person's entire lifetimes Karmas and Achievements are assessed by others. She is remembered by others as the kind of person she was, how she affected the lives of those around her, and whether she was good to others or bad to others. Her attitude, her words, and her deeds toward others are remembered by those who knew her. The kind of life she lived and what she gave to others are summarized at one's death only. Thus death sums up a person's life.

Whether my death is mourned or rejoiced and by how many sums up my life on this Earth. My kind words and deeds are remembered and so are my harsh words and deeds. Whether I enriched others' lives or hurt and harassed them is remembered at the time of my death. Death is the only time that marks what I gave to others and to how many.

A human dies but leaves the residue of her Karmas behind. The Karmas of my lifetime are assessed only at the time of my death. The numbers of genuine tears that are shed at my death go to show that I truly gave something to them.

A human is born, lives a certain lifetime, and accumulates certain achievements in different realms of human life, like money, family, and work et cetera. Some people amass a lot of wealth and leave it behind in the form of their house(s), car(s), and other property, and bank balance. Others live mainly a work-oriented life, and after years of, often a lifetime's sheer hard work leave behind their contributions in specific fields of labor, for example, a Scientist who leaves behind some important, groundbreaking theory(s) or discovery(s); or a Philosopher who, often after a lifetime's search leaves behind the pearls of her thoughts in the form of book(s); or an Engineer who envisaged and built massive dams and bridges et cetera. There are many others who live mainly a family oriented life—get married, produce children, raise them well, and leave behind their children— future members of humanity.

But the majority of humans throughout their lives work in each of these realms and at their deaths leave behind Edifices of their achievements in each of these realms—money in the form of house(s), car(s), bank balance; family—a loving spouse of some fifty-plus years of marriage and well raised children; and their work—contribution in some field of labor.

This is an Edifice of a human's lifetimes Achievements— something like a Construct, a Building, which she erected brick by brick with her every day's consistent Karma in certain realms of life like money, family, and work et cetera.

This is an Edifice of a human's achievements as well as her footprints in the world. It is at death that we assess this Edifice. It is at death that we trace a human's footprints in the world. A human dies but leaves behind this Edifice, her foot prints that continue to enrich the Human Whole long after she's gone.

From this we infer the derivative Right Way of Living for a human. A human ought to live a Value-oriented life—acquire and maintain each of the Five Eternal Human Values of **Family, Education, Work, Marriage,** and **Child**—and give her best to each of them.

<u>Transit Phase</u>

At death a human's body dies, but her soul lives on. The soul is one's deepest Self—a nonmaterial and eternal entity that resides in the center of one's body, a little below her navel, containing one's deepest memories, attachments, and desires of one's all previous lives and this life too. The soul is one's core, conscious Self—"Ahm" or "I"— that feels, thinks, and motivates one to act in a certain way.

Nothing changes at death. One just does not have a body, but exists as a soul. After death, one's soul hovers over her own dead body and near her dear ones and her possessions. It is very hard for the soul to leave them behind and move on. The soul is tormented by the pain of her loved ones and her separation from them. It also finds it hard to leave behind her dear worldly possessions that she enjoyed for a long time and got attached to, for example, her home, her favorite car, and jewelry et cetera.

The soul is further tormented by its manifold desires for worldly things. It wants to drink, smoke, enjoy good food, and have sex et cetera. It tries to fulfill them though without much success because it does not have a body. There is recorded evidence of this stored in a number of books on Parapsychology and others on 'After death', 'Soul' et cetera. I also know this from my own personal experience, which I will narrate later in my chapter on "Soul."

The soul lives in this phase for a certain time span. This is the transit phase, lasting from a few days to a few months or years depending upon how attached the soul was to her loved ones and loved things.

From these facts we derive the theory of detachment. A human ought not to get overly attached to her loved ones and her dear personal possessions like home, and jewelry et cetera.

Death demands detachment, not only my own death but those of my loved ones' too. A human ought not to have excessive desires either. Excessive attachments and desires perturb a soul after death.

Now a little peek into the nature of attachment and desires: how they build up? Is it possible to be detached from my loved ones and my loved things? And not to have any desires?

Attachment is a natural emotion of every living being including a human. It is a feeling of deep love for a person or thing marked by a strong desire to seek its well-being and its constant company.

Desire is a craving for the company of my loved ones and loved things. In a way desire is a part of attachment.

Attachment builds all by itself over a period of time. It creeps in by utility and the close companionship of certain people and things in a human's life. I am a human, but a *jiva*—a living being after all, who needs certain relationships and certain things in order to survive and enjoy life. As a child I need my First Family of parents and siblings with whom I spend the first twenty years of my life. As an adult I need my Second Family of spouse and children with whom I spend next fifty-plus—remaining years of my life. I need and love my home which offers me safety and comfort. I need and love my car, favorite dresses, jewelry, books, and many other personal possessions etc. Living in the close company of my dear ones and dear possessions for a long time, breeds strong attachment for them. The longer the companionship, the stronger the attachment is.

This attachment gradually seeps into my Self—I, whereby I tend to deem my loved ones and loved things as solely mine—"my mother," "my husband," "my son," "my home," "my car" et cetera—and be overly possessive of them. This "my" keeps seeping into my self or soul for years, so much so that after a certain time, I may forget my individual existence and individuality of other person too and make that person or thing a part of my deep Self to the extent that I cannot live without that person or thing for long.

Excessive attachment (*aasakti* in Sanskrit) to a person or thing is bad in this life as well as in Afterlife. In this life it makes us overly possessive and emotionally dependent on that person or thing. Being overly possessive about a relationship harms both me and the other person. After all, that person exists as an individual and is open to other relationships too. Being emotionally dependent on a person means staking my whole life and happiness on that person's life and happiness. If he lives, I live. If he dies, I die too. If he is happy, I am happy. And if he is sad, I am sad too. It is never worth to do it even in the closest relationship. After all, that person exists and acts as an individual, does his own karmas, and by his own karmas is either happy or sad. If I love that person, I will motivate him and help him to do those Karmas that will make him live a good life. I cannot do more than this. That person will ultimately act as per his own nature and will choose his own karmas which will shape his life. I must not stake my whole life and happiness on another person's life and happiness. My (every human's) life on this Earth has got its own value, which is derived solely from my own being, my own nature, and my own Karmas.

Similarly, excessive attachment and desires cause deep pain and torment to the soul after death. After years of companionship, my Self—soul gets so deeply attached to my loved ones that I cannot tolerate their separation for long. I want their constant company even after death. I have no idea of my individual existence both as a human and as a soul. At times some souls in case of excessive attachment to a loved one do not leave that person for long. They hover around that person for years, causing pain and frustration to themselves, because there is nothing much they can do after death.

While living a human ought to remember the fact of death and not be overly attached to her loved ones and loved things. A human ought to live every relationship by the Principle of "Om"—"I" and "you," and "the relationship," where both I and you exist as two individuals and there exists the relationship between both of us with its certain duties. If I love you, I teach you to do those things that will make you live a good life. But after all you will live by your own nature and your own Karmas which will either make you live a good life or a bad life. Every human exists as an individual human and an individual Soul. (S)he ought not to let a relationship usurp her entire identity and individuality.

A human ought to exercise certain detachment toward her loved things too. A human ought to remember that she will die one day and will leave behind all her dear worldly possessions, like her house, car, favorite jewelry, and dresses et cetera behind. Therefore (s)he ought not be overly attached to them.

A human ought to remember the fact of death while living.

Desire is a part of attachment. It breeds from attachment. After death the soul desires the company of her loved ones and loved things. Also, desire is a deep wish to do something. It can be as simple as wanting a drink, a smoke, or a favorite dish or as deep as desiring the company of your loved one. Exercising self-control to control one's desires is good in this life as well as in Afterlife. Detachment also kills desires.

Into Another(life)—Rebirth

During the transit phase, the soul hovers over her loved ones and loved possessions for a certain time and then wanders away. It wanders here and there unless it enters the womb of her would-be mother. A soul carries her past lives' memories, attachments, and desires with her, and takes a new life on the basis of them—to fulfill an unfinished task, to seek the company of her loved ones et cetera.

This is a fact evidenced by my personal experiences of soul, many recorded instances of rebirth, and major religions of the world.

Every soul has a certain make or character that is shaped by a person's lifetime's predominant feelings, thoughts, and Karmas (actions). They shape one's deep Self or soul as either vast, generous, and joyous or narrow, selfish, and perturbed.

Soul is a fact and rebirth is a fact. Knowing this a human ought to practice *Subhava, Suvichara, and Sukarma* through which she rejoices in her being— her deep Self—during her life-time and in the afterlife too. They shape a human's deepest self or soul into a beautiful and noble mode.

Subhava is a Sanskrit word made of two letters: *Su* and *Bhava*. *Su* means "beautiful," and *bhava* means "emotions." Practicing *Subhava* means harboring beautiful emotions inside one's deep

Self, like love, joy etc., and viewing others with compassion and goodwill. These are high, uniquely human emotions, which if practiced make an individual's Self—Soul—vast, noble, and joyous. Thus she enjoys her inner being all the time.

Suvichara is another Sanskrit word made of two letters: *Su* and *Vichara*. *Su* means "beautiful" and *Vichara* means "thoughts." Practicing *Suvichara* means thinking high and noble thoughts. This is a higher, uniquely human faculty available to very few, rare individuals. But it can be practiced by having a vast worldview, thinking of others and their lives, wishing them well, gaining knowledge, and reading noble thoughts. If practiced it enlarges one's worldview and makes her inner Self noble.

Sukarma—a composite of *Su* and *Karma*—means doing good actions—actions that help one live a good life and enrich others' lives too. Since our karmas (actions) are so powerful—they shape our lives and our beings— practicing *Sukarma* helps us live good lives and shapes our inner beings—our Selves— our Souls as good and noble.

The constant practice of these three—*Subhava, Suvichara,* and *Sukarma*— makes a human's deep Self—Soul vast, joyous, and noble. Thus she enjoys her being, her present life, and afterlife too. Above all, she enjoys her own being—her Self, her Soul, be it here or in the afterlife. Because her Self—Soul will always remain with her. You can run from the world, but not from your own Self—Soul, which is always with you. Your soul is your constant companion, so make your soul beautiful.

While living a human ought to remember the fact of death always—like the back of her hand, a shadow looming behind her all the time, which can happen to her and her loved ones any day, any time. Doing so helps us value our lives, our loved ones; live a more meaningful life; and makes our Selves beautiful.

Death balances life—life's greed, selfishness, excessive attachments, and desires. It cools the tide of life and reminds us that this is not all, this is not the only life we are living; there are many more to come, shaped by this life's karmas. It reminds us of our Souls—our deep Selves and our constant companions—and urges us to make them beautiful and noble. Thus it motivates us to do good karmas and make our souls more beautiful and noble.

CHAPTER 6

SOUL

A human is born, lives, and dies. "Death is the end of one lifetime and the transit phase into another (life)" (my definition of death). At death a human's body dies, but her Soul lives on. It is the Soul that goes into transit phase and takes re-birth. What is soul? How do we know there is soul?

Soul is a core issue in a human's life. It comes into picture at the time of one's death, where some people experience its presence at the death of a loved one or in their own near-death experiences. What is soul?

All major religions refer to soul as a conscious entity—an eternal Truth— and stress its importance during living, as well as after death. Some religions make Soul as their Central Truth, and derive their major philosophy of life and way of living from it. For example, Buddhists' *Nirvana*, or Hindus' ascetic way of living in search of one's Soul.

What is Soul? Though widely acknowledged and believed in, soul is a highly mysterious entity, not so readily visible to our eyes and open to our everyday experience. Nonetheless it exists, and has been seen and experienced by some people at some odd moments of their lives. Since time immemorial, people from all races and cultures have experienced soul in some form or other. Their experiences are very similar and indicate to an entity that does not die at the death of a human, but lives on. This entity is called soul.

Soul is a fact as evidenced by people's experiences, major religions, and my own personal experiences. *I know there is soul. I have seen and experienced soul.*

People's Experiences

The very first reference to soul comes from people's mouths. There is recorded evidence that since ancient times to present, people from all societies and cultures have experienced some aspect of the soul. Some people report having seen or talked to ghosts, while others narrate their own near-death experiences, and very few remember and talk about their previous lives. These experiences have been recorded by curious writers in literature, Parapsychology, and other books with convincing details, accuracy, and evidence.

All of these experiences strung together clearly indicate that a part of a person does not die at death, leaves the body, lives on, and takes rebirth.

The very first and most common of these experiences is a ghost sighting. Often in the case of a sudden or tragic death by accident, murder, or suicide, the loved ones of the dead person report seeing the dead person, feeling her/his presence, and being talked to by the dead person. Often at a cemetery or in a haunted house, people report having seen a person all clad in white appear out of nowhere and vanish in the dark of the night. There is a striking similarity in the descriptions of all these people. Almost all of them regardless of their age, society, or culture have reported that they saw the dead person as she/he was, though pale, with the same body contours, all clad in white. In the case of a loved one's sighting or experience, the dead person came to her loved one, talked to her, and in some extreme cases touched her and behaved as if she was alive. My best friend's husband died in a car accident. He came to her at night, tried to hug her, and kept saying, "It was not my fault."

In the case of a haunted house sighting, people saw the dead person moving around the house, moving things, making some noise, running the tap and so on.

There are countless such experiences recorded in numerous books. Go to any library or bookstore, browse through and read books on "soul," "near death," "after-death" topics, and you will know. Listen to the people who narrate their experiences, and you will know.

There have been instances where a dead person after being dead for a while came back to life and narrated her after-death experiences. I addressed them in detail in my last chapter on Death. In all of these recorded experiences, these people narrate their flying-like experiences after death—how they felt as if they got out of their dead bodies, flew up to the ceiling, saw their own dead bodies and the doctors below them, and saw their loved ones crying. The majority of these descriptions were found true when later verified.

These "after-death" experiences of people indicate at, and evidence that at death a part of the person does not die and lives on. This part is called the soul.

Besides, there have been recorded "Rebirth" instances in which a person remembered her previous life. Though rare, but enough to evidence the existence of the soul, these instances have happened either during the early childhood years of one's life (when the mind is not yet filled with the current life's experiences) or during a hypnotic state in which the mind goes blank. There is a famous example of Shanti Devi, an Indian lady, who in her early childhood years started talking about her previous life, like where she lived, her husband, and her son. She remembered her husband's name and how she had died a few days after giving birth to her son. First her parents and teachers took it as a child's blabbering, but after her repeated, confident narrations, they took her to her old house. There, to their utter amazement, they found everything true. Her descriptions matched her house, her husband, and her son. Her husband, upon being asked, said yes, he had a wife who had died ten days after giving birth to their son. Often such cases are printed in newspapers and recorded in books on rebirth.

In another famous case, recorded in a newspaper and often quoted in "Rebirth" books, a woman under hypnosis, suddenly started speaking English in a British accent. Now this woman was an Indian, had never spoken English before, and did not know English at all. Not only this, she also started narrating some experiences that clearly did not match her current life. The psychologist later said that the only explanation he could find was that she remembered her previous life.

There are countless such experiences about ghosts, the afterlife, and rebirth that indicate that at death a part of a person does not die, lives on, goes through a transit phase, and takes rebirth. This part is called soul, acknowledged and believed in by many people all across the world, in all times.

Major Religions

People's belief in soul is further strengthened and given credence by religions. All major religions in humanity's history so far, namely—Hinduism, Muslim, and Christianity, refer to the soul as an integral but distinct part of a human's being that lives on even after the body dies. All of them believe in soul as an eternal Truth and stress its importance in this life and the afterlife too.

A religion starts with its Founder's quest for eternal Truth. All religion founders—some unnamed sages, and others wellknown, like Lord Krishna of Hinduism, Mohammad of Muslim, and Jesus Christ of Christianity—and others sought eternal Truth. They searched outside, and they searched within themselves. Each of them, after a lifetime's genuine and persistent search, ultimately experienced the eternal Truth within his Self. They called it Soul. Some of them experienced its extraordinary power and called it God.

A Religion Founder is a deeply sensitive and highly intelligent person, who, perturbed by life's fragility and sufferings, poses certain questions, seeks answers to them, and seeks eternal Truth. Each founder's quest is intense and genuine, so much so that it keeps him perturbed all the time. He does not sit with peace until he finds answers to his questions and the Eternal Truth. He is a loner who is willing to make any sacrifices to find the Truth. He wants only Truth and nothing else. So much for the credibility of what a religion Founder teaches; and when he says Soul is an eternal truth, that means he has experienced Soul, and knows that Soul is an Eternal Truth.

The *Upanishads* and the *Gita*—two prime religious texts and sacred books of Hinduism—refer to soul more or less the same way. The *Upanishads* is a series of philosophical books on the metaphysical reality, written by unnamed sages who did not leave their names—so beyond any ego or desire for fame. The *Upanishads* propagate two theories about soul, and the origin of All—God. These are: *"Adwaita"* and *"Dwaita."* *Adwaita* is a Sanskrit word, which means "One without any division." As per *Adwaita* every being's soul at all times remains a part of the One—uncreated—Supreme Soul—the origin of All, named Brahma. Hence the saying *"Ahm Brahmasmi"* which means "I am Brahma"—I—in my deepest *Self/soul* am a part of the *Brahma the One—The Uncreated—Origin of All—the Supreme Soul (The God)*.

As per *Dwaita* theory, a being's or a human's soul originates from "The One," The Uncreated Supreme Soul—Brahma; leaves it, takes up a body, transmigrates from one body to another in a cycle of many births—from lower to higher life forms—and ultimately gets liberation or *moksha*, and merges back into the Supreme Soul. A being's soul is a *jivatman*, and the supreme Soul is the *Parmatman*. *Atman* is a Sanskrit word meaning one's deepest self or soul. *Jiva* is a living being, and Supreme Soul is God. Thus a *jivatman* is a living being's soul and *Parmatman* is the Supreme Soul or Self of All, or God.

The Gita (a sacred Hindu religious book) refers to the soul as *purusha* and a human's or a living being's body as *prakrati*. *Purusha* means a conscious, feeling, thinking entity, and *prakrati* means nature or innate matter. It is *purusha*—the soul—that enters the *prakrati* or material body (of a human or living being), infuses it with life, feels, thinks, and motivates a living being to live in a certain way. Further, one's soul is called *"Satchidananda"* or made of three components: *Sat,* meaning "truth"; *chida,* meaning "consciousness"; and *Ananda,* meaning "bliss." Thus one's soul is a conscious, feeling, thinking entity containing pure truth and sheer bliss within it.

The Koran—the holy book of the Islamic religion—refers to soul as an entity distinct from one's body, which enters one's body forty days after fertilization of the egg inside the mother's womb, inhabits the body throughout her lifetime, and leaves the body at death. After death the soul goes into a short transit phase and then goes to heaven or hell as per its lifetime actions.

The Christian religion also refers to soul in more or less the same way. As per Christianity the soul is an entity distinct from one's body, enters one's body at birth, lives inside it throughout one's lifetime, and leaves it at death. After death one's soul goes to heaven if the person during her lifetime believed in God and Jesus Christ and confessed and repented her sins—or to hell if she did not do so.

Every religion talks its Truth and teaches Truth—Truth as perceived by its Founder. All religions describe Soul as the eternal Truth—an entity that was, is, and will always be there, and the First Truth—an entity too fine to be captured by one's mere senses.

This was a short summary of People's experiences and Religions' references to soul, enough to make one believe in soul, but still portraying soul as the truth experienced by others.

My Personal Experiences

How do you really know something? How do you take something to be true? The most credible test for truth is one's personal experience. Once you have personally seen something, heard it, touched it, or felt its presence, then that thing is true for you. You know it exists, no matter what others tell you.

I personally know there is soul. I have seen souls, have been touched by souls, and have felt a soul's continued presence near me in the same room.

I have seen souls as clear as I see my hand, this pen, this lamp, or any other object in front of me right now. I have seen a soul's inner perturbations and her actions inspired by her inner feelings, jealousy, and other deep desires. I talk about soul from my own personal experiences—my clear and vivid experiences that proved to me beyond any doubt that soul exists. A human dies but her soul lives on and carries with it its deepest memories, attachments, and desires of its all previous lives and this life too.

My first experience of soul happened years ago, during my young years of twenties. I was visiting my aunt's home during summer holidays. One afternoon I went to sleep and slept on till evening. At the time of dusk I was still fast asleep in my room. Suddenly I felt as if someone was shaking my shoulders very vigorously from my back. I woke up, startled, and looked up and back. There was a tall man all clad in white standing behind me. There were two or three similar forms standing next to him, all clad in white. I got frightened and screamed. Then I looked to the other side of the room. There I saw someone lying on the bed covered in a white sheet, rubbing his feet together, turning over as if in great pain or agony. I thought they were my cousins, playing some prank on me. But I was very scared. I got out of bed, wide awake, and called out my cousins' names. There was no response. Then I turned on the lights. There was no one—not a single person or form was there inside the whole room. All had simply vanished. I again called my cousins' names loudly, thinking that maybe they had run away. I came out of the room, calling my cousins' names. There was no one outside the room. It was semi dark—dusk time. I crossed the hallway and other rooms, and went running to the kitchen. There I saw my aunt working. I asked her where everyone was. She said that no one was at home. I was still all shaken up. Then I told her my whole experience. She simply shrugged and said that such incidents were common in that house. She and each of her family members had had some experience of ghosts in that house. It was a haunted house.

After a few days, I went back to my house and forgot all about it. It became just a ghost story for me, though it was a very real experience that I did not know what to do with.

My next experience of soul was that of my mother's after her death. It was at a point of my life when I had made a drastic choice of going to a foreign country and living there on my own, all alone. I was all packed up. Just one night before leaving, I lay in bed, ready to go to sleep. At that very moment I looked up from across the window up to the roof railing. There I saw my mother standing, all clad in white. She was my mother— the same body contour and the same face. Her face was hazy, though; I could not see it clearly. But her body was exactly the same. I got scared out of my wits. My mother had been dead for two years. I screamed and screamed. It was late at night. My elder brother came running to me from the other side of the house. He held my hand and consoled me. The next day I left my house. Somehow I never went back to my home after that. My going to a foreign land did not prove to be a good choice. It did not go well. I don't know why my mother came there that night—to say a final good-bye to me or to caution me against going to a foreign land. That was the only time I ever saw my mother after her death.

My next experience of soul was more clear and direct. In it I witnessed deep desires and attachments of a soul carried on after death. I witnessed its envy, its jealousy, and its actions.

It was sometime in my youth. I was working and living alone. I started dating this guy named Richie. He lived just a block away from my home. One day after spending the evening together, he walked with me to my house. It was late at night. As we stood there and talked, a dog in the neighborhood started howling. We did not pay any attention to it and kept talking. After some time he said good-bye to me and went back to his house. I came in.

I spent the next day as usual. When I met Richie in the evening, he told me about the previous night's incident. He told me how after leaving me, while on his way to his home, he could still hear the dog howling. Then he walked back to my house to the howling dog. He stood there for a while and then went back to his house. The dog stopped howling after that. I asked him why he did that. He replied that he did so to release his girlfriend. Upon further asking he told me about his girlfriend who had died in a car accident a few years back. He loved her deeply and was planning to marry her. Since her death he had not dated anyone. I was the first girl he met after that. And he told me how he still remembered her every day, kept her pictures in his wallet, and had not been able to forget her even for a moment. And also, how he still remembered her every night, how she came to him every night, lay close to him, and how they still made love. And he told me how she came to him every night when he was sick or feeling low, sat with him, nursed him, and talked to him. Both of them still loved each other deeply.

I listened to him and thought maybe he was dreaming about her. I did not pay much attention to it. I was working full time and was too busy to think about anything else. I still liked him a lot, and we met every day.

One day Richie called me and told me that he had had an accident and had broken his wrist. He could not move his hands. He was staying at a friend's place and had to stay there till he recovered. He asked me to go to his house and bring some of his clothes and daily use things to him. After work I went to his place and started packing his things. As I fumbled through his pile of clothes in his closet to take out what I needed, I found small packs of red *bindi* everywhere—many of them. (A *bindi* is a brightly colored round piece of plastic worn by an Indian woman on the center of her forehead to enhance her beauty). They were all over the closet—tens of them. I was surprised. What was a woman's *bindi* doing in his closet? Then I went to the toilet to pack his toiletries. There I saw a red *bindi* on the mirror. There was another one on his shaving brush. I was very surprised. He lived alone in his house. Whose *bindis* were they? There was no possibility of his seeing another woman. We were too involved. I kept packing anyway. I packed his clothes and his toiletries and went to see him. Then I told him about the red *bindis,* how they were everywhere in his house. He said, "Oh! That was nothing. Their presence was common in his house. He saw them all the time—in his closet, in his room, and on his shaving brush etc." Then he told me that his girlfriend had always put a red *bindi* on her forehead. So he simply accepted them as a mark of her presence in his house. Now I was a little scared.

We kept meeting. There came this New Year's Eve. Richie and I went to a party to celebrate. There a friend of his took our picture together. It was a beautiful photograph—just the two of us. I put this picture on my study table in my apartment. The next day I went to work as usual. I returned in the evening. As

I entered the apartment and turned on the lights, my feet froze. There in front of me I saw this big, round, red *bindi* on our picture, right in the middle of Richie's and my faces. I stood there shocked and scared out of my wits. I lived alone in my apartment. My apartment was locked throughout the day, and only I had my apartment keys. There was no possibility of anyone entering my apartment in my absence, and why would someone stick a *bindi* on our picture like this? I knew beyond any doubt it had been placed by Sofia—long-dead girlfriend of my boyfriend. I was very scared. Richie—my boyfriend visited me in the evening, and I showed him that picture with the *bindi*. He had nothing to say. We shared this fact together.

The next day I removed that *bindi* and got on with my life as usual. But later other things started happening. I lived alone in my apartment. Sometimes I had an eerie feeling, as if someone was there in my apartment. I could not see it but felt its presence. At times I saw a hazy form or so. I felt as if dead Sofia was there in my apartment all the time. I felt her presence when I was alone, and especially when I was with Richie. I was scared in my own apartment, scared to go to the next room, to go out in the dark, even to go to sleep. I felt so clearly that someone was there. I had never felt this way before. I was scared all the time and was so pent up. I could not go on living this way. One evening as I felt this presence again, I got very angry, angry at my own fear and angry at this dead person. And at that very moment of blind rage, I challenged this presence—this person—this dead girlfriend of my boyfriend—this Sofia—this—whoever it was to come out in the open, in front of me, face to face. I was shaking with anger. I stood there and waited. Nothing happened. No one came out. But after that moment of blind rage, I never felt Sofia's presence again in any form near me. She was gone. And I never felt scared of her again. I lived fearlessly in my apartment and kept meeting

Richie—my boyfriend. We were madly in love, met every day, and could not do without each other. Later Richie told me how one day as he dozed a little during noon, he saw Sofia come and say good-bye to him. After that he stopped seeing her altogether in his dreams or otherwise, and he never felt her presence near him. She was gone from his life.

I knew Richie told me all of the truth about Sofia. He did not dream about Sofia, but Sofia actually came to him every night. He felt her presence, he touched her, and he talked to her. I by my own personal experience know it was true. I saw the evidence of Sofia's presence in the form of red *bindis* everywhere and on our picture. And I felt her presence in my apartment when I was alone, and especially when I was with Richie.

Sofia, long after her death, still loved Richie, remembered him, desired to be with him all the time, and felt jealous of other girls in his life. These derivations infer clearly from this personal experience of mine.

Eventually I got on with life, got married, and forgot all about this experience. A few years after marriage, I had another experience of the form and finesse of soul, and how it enters a mother's womb at the very point of conception. One day during the early morning hours around dawn, my husband and I were enjoying the bliss of our physical union. At that very moment, while he was inside me, I saw an extremely fine, almost silvery ray enter the open window of our bedroom and come to us. My view was partially blocked by my husband on top of me. I could not see any farther. After a few days I came to know I was pregnant. Also, there was a drastic change in my moods and temper (as happens with every pregnancy). I was blissfully happy all the time, woke up in the early morning hours, and loved to listen to temple bells.

Some religions say that the soul enters a woman's womb at the point of conception and takes up a body. I know it is true. This experience of mine proved to me beyond any doubt that a soul enters a mother's womb at the point of conception and acquires a physical body.

The above was a summary of my own personal experience of the soul. They happened at different times of my life in unguarded moments. They scared me and took me by surprise. They also ignited my curiosity about the soul. Later I studied a number of books on "after-death," "ghosts," "soul," and "Parapsychology." I studied major religions for their references to the soul. As I read each book, I realized that my own personal experiences of soul were so similar to other people's experiences of soul, and to major religions' references to soul. Not only this, but today when I put together all my different experiences of soul, I realize that each experience of mine acquainted me with a different aspect of the soul.

Today I know beyond any doubt that "a soul exists and moves in an extremely fine, conscious, energy-like form; enters a mother's womb at the point of conception; acquires a physical body as per its own nature and desires; lives through a lifetime; leaves the body at death; carries with it its lifetime's memories, attachments, and desires; goes into a transit phase; and takes a new birth."

It is on the basis of my own personal experiences attested to and evidenced by other people's experiences and major religions of the world that I define the Soul as follows:

Definition of Soul

A soul is a human's (every living being's) deepest, eternal Self located in the center of one's body, a little below the navel containing one's deepest memories, attachments, and desires of her all previous lives and this life too. It enters a mother's womb at the point of conception, acquires a physical body, lives a certain lifetime, leaves the body at death, goes into a transit phase, and then takes a new birth.

Derivative Right Way of Living

The Soul is a very fine entity made of pure energy, which is not perceptible to us all, but this does not mean that the soul does not exist. We do not see air, but air exists. We do not see atoms and molecules, but atoms and molecules exist. Their existence has been brought to light by scientists. Similarly the soul exists. Its existence has been brought to light by People's experiences, Soul scientists—mystics and sages of all times— and major religions of the world.

We do not see air, but we feel the air. We feel its blow, its chill, and its warmth. Similarly we do not see soul but we can feel the Soul—our deep selves—by self-search, by staying attuned to it, and by accessing its immense depth and sheer bliss by meditation.

Soul is the deepest "Self," "Ahm" or "I" of a person, located in the center of one's body, a little below her navel, in the form of a bunch of pure energy. It is conscious—"I,"—who feels, thinks, and pushes one to act in a certain way. It is eternal—lives through many lives of a human. And it is divine— connected to the divine in its deepest depth, as I will show in my next chapters on "God" and "Truth," and also as confirmed by major religions of the world.

Genuine Self-search is one of the ways to access one's Soul and thereby access the eternal Truth or divinity to which one's soul is connected. Self- search is a deep contemplative way to explore one's true Self. It involves going deep down within one's Self and questioning "who am I?" Such a query arises from the genuine quest to know the truth about one's true Self or being. Self-search is the pathway to the eternal Truth too, since eternal Truth lies hidden in One's deep Self or Soul.

Genuine Self-search is rare and available to very few, exceptional individuals. These were the sages and mystics of their times, who, perturbed by life's fragility and queries, searched for the eternal Truth. They searched it out, and they searched it deep within themselves. It was after years of hard, persistent search that they ultimately found their true selves—their souls—and the eternal Truth or divinity that is a part and parcel of one's Soul. This is what Buddha did—left everything in the search for Truth, and after years of hard, persistent searching, Self-search, and meditation ultimately got enlightenment—knowledge of his soul and the eternal Truth. In this process he realized his true Self—the soul, its eternity, and its bliss. This is what Muhammad, the Founder of Muslim religion, did. After years of searching and deep contemplation, he ultimately realized his true Self— his soul, and the divinity within it. He experienced its light, purity, and power and called it God.

Genuine Self-search includes both—deep contemplation of the nature of one's true Self, and meditation.

Meditation is the way to access one's soul. There are primarily two types of meditation—Contemplative meditation and Concentrative meditation. Contemplative meditation is a part of genuine Self-search where the seeker sits in solitude, goes deep down within one's self, and questions "who am I?" She probes, observes, and analyses her Self—her mind, its feelings, and thoughts. Constant practice of this takes her deeper into her "Self," and finally to its deepest depth—the point where it is connected to the divine.

Concentrative meditation, on the other hand, aims at stopping one's mind and focusing it on a single object or activity. Doing so calms one's mind and helps one go deeper into one's Self. Meditation is taught by different religions and others in different ways. Some of the popular meditation techniques are *Mantra* meditation and Breath meditation. In *Mantra* meditation, one repeats a *mantra*—a set of a few words—for some thirty minutes. In Breath Meditation one focuses one's entire attention on one's breath—it's going and coming. Each of these techniques ceases one's constantly chatting mind and helps one focus on one activity and thus calms it. Out of these the Breath meditation helps one go deeper into One's Self, because one's breath is totally inner and originates from one's inner center— one's Self. Either of these meditation techniques, if done every day for thirty minutes or so, makes one calm and balanced.

The purpose of meditation is to access one's soul. Since one's soul is located in the center of one's body, the right physical posture of meditation is to sit cross-legged on the floor, preferably in a lotus style. This keeps one's backbone straight and helps one access her center—her soul.

Daily practice of meditation controls and calms one's mind more and more and makes one more balanced and joyous by connecting her to her own Soul—the source of all joy, wisdom, and divinity. It is through meditation that sages and mystics gained immense control of their minds and felt the sheer depth and vastness of their souls and the divinity within it.

Meditation is hard and demands extreme discipline of body and mind, but its results are sheer bliss and joy. Daily meditation is required to stay calm, joyous, and connected to one's soul on a daily basis.

Meditation is the way to access your soul. But merely accessing your soul is not enough. You ought to stay attuned to it throughout the day. Since Soul is the deepest self—*"Ahm"* or *"I"* of a person—staying attuned to it means staying attuned to my "I," my Self—be aware of what is going on inside my Self—my mind—its feelings and thoughts. If I observe my Self a little, I will find that at any given time there are hordes of feelings and thoughts going on inside my mind without my being aware of them. They are important because they constitute the quality of my Self and motivate my actions. I ought to be aware of them.

Now, *"I"* is a word that envelopes different aspects of my being into one. It gives me one single identity. The moment I say "I," I stand out as a single individual to myself and to the world.

A human ought to stay attuned to her Self by observing her inner Self/mind all the time and by correcting it. The way to do this is to ask myself constantly, "What am I doing?" The moment I say this to myself, I become aware of my action. This awareness makes me concentrate on my action. For example, I may be doing anything at that time like making coffee, writing, or going for a walk. Asking myself, "What am I doing?" makes my action distinct and makes me focus on that action.

A human does a number of tasks at any given time. Her actions tend to get mixed up the way her feelings and thoughts do. For example, I am writing at this time, deeply engrossed in my thoughts and writing. A little while ago, I got up to warm my coffee. Right at that point, I asked myself, "What am I doing?" I answered, "I'm warming my coffee." Merely saying this to myself made my action distinct and made me focus on that. I warmed my coffee for the required time, came back, and resumed my writing.

Now it may be that I am not doing anything at that time. I might be sitting or standing. At this time if I ask myself, "What am I doing?" I will get the answer—Nothing. But a little peek into my mind will show to me that there is a lot going on inside there—crowds of feelings and thoughts, all mixed up. I may be remembering, imagining, feeling anxious, being assailed by pangs of jealousy and hatred, or being soothed by goodwill or love, or thinking—which is not often. Knowing what am I feeling or thinking helps me distinguish my feelings and thoughts and categorize them. If I am remembering—lost in memories, I may not want to do that for long but instead do something else. If I am imagining, at least I will know that I am imagining, and this is not real. And if I am fearing something, I may tell myself not to fear and plan an action on that. Similarly, if I am panged by jealousy or hatred, I will know this and its ill effects and try not to feel it. Or if I am feeling goodwill or love, then at least I will know it and its excess too.

A human ought to stay attuned to her Self by asking herself constantly "What am I doing? What am I feeling? And what am I thinking?" Constant practice of this makes a person aware of herself, her feelings, thoughts, and actions. This awareness makes her more focused on her action and helps her to stay attuned to her Self.

A human's Soul is her deepest, eternal Self that remembers, feels, thinks, and pushes one to act during her lifetime and after death too. It contains her deepest feelings, thoughts, memories, and effects of her lifelong karmas— actions. These things altogether shape the quality of a human's inner, deep Self. Also, a human's Self is her constant companion—it is with her every minute during this lifetime and afterlife too. You can run from the world but not from your own "Self."

A human ought to make her deep Self—her Soul—beautiful and noble by practicing *"Subhava," "Suvichara,"* and *"Sukarma."*

Subhava is a Hindi word made of two separate words: *"Su"* and *"bhava." Su* means "beautiful," and *bhava* means "emotions." *Subhava* means beautiful and positive emotions. An emotion is something I feel. It is deeper than a mere feeling and lasts longer. Emotions build over a long time and get deep in our psyches. They motivate our actions—Karmas.

A human feels a vast range of emotions, both positive and negative. Positive emotions are those of love, happiness, compassion, and goodwill. Negative emotions are those of hatred, sadness, antipathy, and jealousy. Feeling negative emotions makes a human suffer in her Self and life, while feeling positive emotions nourishes her Self and makes her enjoy her existence in this life and the afterlife too. Moreover, the constant quality of these emotions shape and define her Self—her inner being.

Though we have no control of how we feel, what circumstances befall us in our lives, and what types of people we encounter, we can still control our emotions, season them with thoughts, and practice feeling *Subhava.* When in the grip of emotions, we ought to never act out of mere emotions, but try to think logically and then act. Instead of feeling negative emotions, we should try to replace them with positive emotions, like love, happiness, compassion, and goodwill. Love your family and friends. Instead of feeling anxious and angry, try to feel calm and happy. Try to do things that make you happy.

Compassion and goodwill are two uniquely human, noble emotions which nourish your Self and make you feel generous and joyous in this life and afterlife too. Compassion is a unique human capacity to feel other's situation and pain and a willingness to help her. Feeling goodwill toward others means you want to see other persons and living beings happy. Feeling compassion and goodwill toward all humans and all living beings enlarges your Self, and makes it beautiful. They nourish you from deep inside and make you feel happy and well adjusted to others. Instead of living in the cocoon of "I," "me," and "mine," a human ought to enlarge her Self and include others in it. This is possible only by feeling compassion and goodwill toward others.

They are hard to practice, but the constant practice of *Subhava*—feeling compassion and goodwill toward all humans— makes your Self beautiful in this life and the afterlife too.

Suvichara is made of two words: *Su* and *Vichara*. *Su* means beautiful, and *Vichara* means thoughts. The thoughts we harbor deep inside us define the quality of our Selves. If negative, they make us suffer, and if positive, they nourish us and make us enjoy our existence.

Different thoughts keep arising in my mind, for example, thoughts of doing something, like going to my favorite restaurant tonight or calling my friend et cetera. Thoughts are also a way to view others. For example, how I think of you, how I think of the world around me—my "people view," my "world view." There are also pure thoughts arising in one's mind—a totally novel way to view something. They are rare and available to very few, deeply contemplative individuals.

Our thoughts are affected by our feelings and actions. They are born out of our actions, and they motivate our actions too. What I think affects my actions. What I do affects my thoughts.

A human ought to practice *Suvichara*. *Suvichara* means practicing *Vipassana*, and harboring high and noble thoughts inside her Self.

Vipassana is a Sanskrit word meaning pure view or seeing a thing the way it is, in its totality, with all its good and bad points. We often tend to view others on the basis of how they affect us or on the basis of our prejudices of caste, color, and creed or how we have been taught by others. For example, I may hate you because in the past you tried to harm me. Or I may dislike you because of your skin color or religion. Consequently I may think of harming you and eventually may harm you. Instead of viewing you through my glasses of personal experience and prejudices, I ought to view you by *vipassana*—seeing you not only as a bad person who tried to harm me but seeing you in totality with your good and bad points together. This will give me an overall, complete view of you and will pacify my negative emotions toward you. Blinded by my negative emotions, I may not see your good points. Similarly, seeing another human as a "Black" or "White" or as a "Muslim" or "Hindu" etc. is wrong—an impure view of a human. Skin color, caste, and creed do not tell me much about a person, like her inner make—her intelligence, her knowledge, and her potential et cetera. A Black human may be more intelligent, more knowledgeable, and more compassionate than a White human. Similarly a Muslim human may be highly intelligent, wise, and do more good to others than a Hindu.

View a thing the way it is. View a human the way he is, just as a human with her inner make and with both her qualities and flaws. This is *vipassana*—a pure view of things and people.

Another way of practicing *Suvichara* is thinking big, and having high and noble thoughts. A human ought to think big—think of people around her, think of the world, think of the Universe. We are born humans, but many of us live like animals trapped in their tiny cocoons of "I," "me," and "mine." They don't see people around them, their problems, their pains. They ignore other living beings and their pains. Such people are deeply miserable, living in their tiny, dark worlds. They don't read, don't travel, and don't know the vastness of the world they live in. They never lift up their heads and see stars and wonder about the mystery and the vastness of the Universe.

A human ought to think big. Thinking big means being sensitive to other people and living beings around me and knowing their pains and problems. Doing so enlarges my worldview. My own problems seem so trivial in front of others' problems. A human ought to make friends, keep in touch with family and friends, join some organization, and share with others.

This is a big world we live in. Every country is different; every society is different. A human ought to read, travel, and learn about the vastness and beauty of the world she lives in.

This is a vast and mysterious world we live in—too vast and too mysterious. Lift up your heads, look at the stars, and look at the sheer vastness of space, its mystery. Read and think about it. Doing so enlarges your mental world and illuminates it with knowledge.

Also, a human ought to think high. Thinking high means thinking noble thoughts—thoughts of purity, justice, truth, and beauty. Cap your night with some good book of literature, poetry, or noble thoughts. Read and think about deep human sentiments, the human fight for justice, her quest for truth and purity. Doing so raises you higher—much higher above the animal life of mere survival.

Constant practice of *Suvichara* gives you affinity with others, a pure and vast worldview, and enjoyment of your human existence.

Sukarma is another way to make your Self—your Soul—beautiful and noble. The word *karma* is a Sanskrit word made from the root *kri,* which means to do something. Any action, big or small, is a Karma, for example, walking, talking, reading, writing, or playing et cetera. Human actions, feelings, and thoughts are all mixed up. My feelings and thoughts motivate me to act. For example, if I feel contempt or anger toward you, I will look down at you, speak bad words to you, and may try to harm you. My action—behavior toward you will be affected by my feelings. Similarly, if I think of you as a low, contemptible person, I will behave the same way with you. Thus an action is a product of one's feelings and thoughts. I feel, I think, I act.

At the same time, one's feelings and thoughts are deeply affected and shaped by one's Karmas. Every Karma is different and evokes its own distinct feelings and thoughts. For example, walking is a good physical activity that speeds up my blood circulation and makes me feel active and energetic. Talking to another person connects me to that person, makes me share and learn new things, affects my thinking, and makes me feel good. Reading affects one's feelings and thoughts. For example, reading a sad narrative makes you feel sad and depressed, while reading an inspiring and happy account makes you feel inspired and happy. Reading builds our thoughts. You learn new thoughts and new ways of thinking from reading. Thus our Karmas shape our feelings and thoughts.

Human life is all a series of Karmas. We live our Karmas. We feel our Karmas, think our Karmas during their duration, and live their effects too. I feel good during walking, and after walking too. Its effects are good. If engaged in a happy conversation, I feel happy during talking, and after talking too. Reading high and noble thoughts makes me enjoy the process of reading, as well as it beautifies my thoughts too.

In order to make one's life and one's inner world—Self or soul, more beautiful, a human ought to choose one's Karmas carefully and do *Sukarma*.

A Sukarma is a Preconceived, Preplanned Karma with Positive Effects.

A human ought to do those Karmas that cast positive effects for her and for others too. For example, doing good physical exercise, and reading high and noble thoughts will make you feel good, and ennoble your thoughts. Engaging in a happy conversation with someone will make you and the other person feel happy. Helping someone in need will benefit the other person and will satisfy you too.

Thus *"Subhava," "Suvichara,"* and *"Sukarma"* help one live a good life and beautify one's deep Self—Soul.

The Soul is the eternal divine Self of a human that a human ought to access by constant Self-search and meditation; stay attuned to it by self observation—asking oneself constantly: "What am I doing?" "What am I feeling?" "What am I thinking?" and make it beautiful and noble by indulging in *Subhava, Suvichara,* and *Sukarma.*

CHAPTER 7

GOD

Our discussion on Soul leads us to God. Soul is a very fine, eternal entity, connected to the divine in its deepest essence. All religions proclaim it so, and I do too on the basis of my own personal experience. The Divine is associated with God. What is God?

This book is about Human Dharma—a Code of Conduct to be adopted by a Human or a Human's Right Way of Living. I have derived it from the analysis and definition of "What is a human?" "What is human life?" and certain core issues of human life, like "Death," "Soul," "God," and "Truth." These issues are interrelated too where one issue leads to the other.

God is one of the core most issues in a human's life. Belief in God or disbelief in God rules a human's life. When a human believes in God, together with him he believes in a Godfather, Mentor, Dad or Mom like figure over him who watches him, teaches him right things, and is there for him all the time. He believes in his absolute and total love for him. With God he believes in the oneness of us all; he believes in love and charity for others; he believes in compassion for the weak and poor; he believes in eternal Truth; he believes in eternal justice; he believes in morality; he believes in one Power above us all, holding the whole universe together, loving us all, caring for us all, and being there for us all the time. When a human believes in God, he believes in one absolute Truth—its purity, power, and justice.

When a human does not believe in God, he does not believe in any one Power above us all, loving us all, caring for us all; he does not believe in one absolute Truth; and with that goes away his belief in one universe, in the oneness of us All, in his love and compassion for others, in any one Power over him watching him and his actions, in morality, in truth, and in justice. He feels alone in this world and free—free to do whatever he wants. With God a human believes in heaven or hell—in an ultimate judge of his actions and the kind of life (s)he leads. Without God there is no one to judge his actions and the kind of life he leads.

God is a very important—core issue in a human's life. My purpose in this chapter is to analyze the whole concept of God, and the whole truth of God —What is God? define God, and then see how to incorporate God in our lives and how to live it.

Analysis

God is an English term with its synonyms in every human language, for example, *Allah* in Muslim, and *Ishwar, Bhagwan,* or *Parmatman* in Hindi etc. When we say God we mean an abstract entity who creates and runs the universe, loves us all, watches us and our actions all the time, and knows All. Such an entity is believed in and worshipped by the majority of humans all over the world, though in different forms. Does such an entity actually exist? Is there a God? In order to find answers to this question let us first trace the origin of God. Where did the concept and the term called "God" come from? This will throw some light on the truth of our existing God(s).

The very first origin of God lies in the human psyche, human fear, and human's need of God. A human, like any other living being, is a very weak being who needs lots of things and positive circumstances in order to survive and enjoy his life. In fact, a human at birth and during his long childhood years is the most helpless living being, who cannot survive without the care of others. Even as an adult a human needs the constant love and support of his family and friends in order to live on. A human by his weak and tender make feels very alone and helpless in the rough, hostile world. He needs a dad, a mentor throughout his life who will pick him up in his arms, fulfill all his needs, take care of him, be there for him all the time, love him, and love him always, no matter what—a dad on whom he can rely all the time.

This weak human psyche especially back in ancient times gave birth to the whole concept of God and sustained it till date. A human needs a God.

Another major source of God is a human's fear and awe of nature.

Nature is vast and gigantic, too powerful in front of a fragile human. It is varied and beautiful too. Human of ancient times lived and roamed amidst raw nature. He had to climb great heights and swim great distances to reach his destination. He feared nature. He feared its moods and temper. He feared sky-high mountains, their tough jungles, and their dangerous crevices. He feared the fury of roaring rivers and their all-destroying floods. Somehow in this process he came to pray—pray to please all-powerful Nature, its tough mountains and angry rivers. He made the god of a mountain and the goddess of a river. In old civilizations, especially in India, till date almost every mountain and river is worshipped like a god or goddess, for example, Mount Himalayas—the residence of Lord Shiva, and the river

Ganges— "Mother Ganges," Goddess, the holiest of all rivers, etc.

Nature's variety and beauty are breathtaking and so are the beauty and order of the Universe. They awed and inspired a human since the beginning. Humans imagined a God—a Power who created such a vast and well- ordered, beautiful Universe; who not only created it but ran it too. Humans of every society thought so and came up with their God(s)—hence the different names of different God(s), but almost same functions—"Create and Run the Universe."

During the long course of humanity's history, many types of God(s) were created who well suited and supported the weak human psyche and fulfilled his need of a God(s).

God(s) flourished in an agricultural society. By now some humans had settled down and lived in one place. In this Society a group of humans lived in one place, grew crops, domesticated animals, and owned lands. A great need was felt to control the constantly changing weather, avoid droughts, have plenty of rains and sunshine. Only a benevolent God could have ensured that. Money and wisdom became highly desirable entities, and so did land. Poets' and writers' imagination ran wild and created different gods and goddesses for different purposes. For example, Plutus was the god of wealth, and Athena was the goddess of wisdom in Greek religion. The god *Indra* in Hindu mythology was the god of weather and rains. He was worshipped and pleased to ensure good rains and good weather. Since sunshine was imperative to good crops, the Sun was worshipped too to ensure that. The goddess *Lakshmi* was created to bestow the blessings of money, while the goddess *Saraswati* was created to bestow one with wisdom and knowledge. A large number of pictures, paintings, and sculptures were created to symbolize each of these gods and goddesses. Believers worshiped their favorite god or goddess to earn his/her blessings.

Land was recognized for its fertility and utility. A plot of land was worshipped too to please unseen powers and is done so till date.

Form of God worship was almost the same everywhere for all gods and goddesses. A symbol of God was created in the form of a piece of stone, a painting, or a statue. The devotee kept it on a high, clean platform; lit candles and incense in front of it; offered it flowers, food and water; bowed down in front of it to please it; and tried to please it more and more with fasts and celebrations so that God would bestow the best of money and other resources to that devotee. Just as a weak and poor human does to please a rich and powerful human. Human created God in the form of a human.

All gods and goddesses of agricultural society were products of pure human imagination.

One major source of God is religion. A Religion is a body of certain Turth(s) and its Derivative Right Way of Living as per-ceived by its Founder. Some of the major religions of the world introduced and propagated God as their Central Truth, namely Hinduism, Christianity, and Muslim.

A little peep into the God(s) of major religions will help us unravel the truth of our existing God(s).

Let us start with the Hindu religion— one of the most ancient and popular religions of the humanity's history. Hindu religion is not one religion. It has many branches and cults within it. Each cult teaches a different type of God. In fact each geographical region in India has its own god or goddess.

Basic Hinduism teaches Tri-God—a set of three gods, namely *Brahma, Vishnu,* and *Mahesh,* where *Brahma* is the Creator, *Vishnu* is the Sustainer, and *Mahesh,* the Lord Shiva, is the Destroyer. As per Hinduism, it is the set of these three gods who creates, runs, and destroys the world. *Brahma* creates the world, the Universe; *Vishnu* maintains the world; and *Shiva* destroys the world. Different versions of these gods are worshipped in different parts of India. A large number of temples have been built all over India to house these gods and worship them. Maximum numbers of temples have been built to house Lord *Vishnu.* Lord Vishnu is one of the most useful and hence most popular gods, who sustains the world, blesses his devotees with riches and children, and fulfills their all worldly desires. There are very few (barely three or four) temples to house Lord *Brahma,* The Creator; and few to house *Shiva,* The Destroyer. People love *Vishnu,* who blesses them with riches and fulfills all their desires. *Brahma*— The Creator, is not of much use to them, and *Shiva*—The Destroyer, is feared by people and is very hard to please. Lord *Rama* and Lord *Krishna*—the two most popular gods of northern India— are considered reincarnations of Lord *Vishnu.* Lord *Balaji,* an extremely popular god in South India, is a version of Prime Lord *Vishnu* only.

A large number of devotees visit the temples where their statues are kept, venerate them, bow down their heads, lie prostrate in front of them, say their prayers to them, beseech them, and beg them to bestow their blessings upon them and fulfill their deep desires. People try hard to please their gods. In order to earn their blessings, they give many expensive gifts to their gods, like money, gold, and jewelry etc.; and they pray for hours.

People keep their gods' statues or pictures in their homes, pray to them every day, fast for them, and offer food and other valuables to them to earn their blessings.

People do so because people believe in them. They believe that if they please their gods enough, their gods will shower their blessings on them, fulfill their all desires, absolve them of their sins, and will give them a great rebirth. They believe in these gods because either they have been taught to believe or they simply follow other believers.

People's belief in God amounts to faith—a deep trust that their god exists, watches them, and will always take care of them, no matter what. In their sufferings, pains, and lone moments, they turn to their God(s), and request for his understanding and help. They treat their God(s) as their friend, a confidant, who will understand them and help them. Thus God emerges as a big emotional support for a human.

This trio of prime Hindu gods is a product of pure human imagination. In ancient India some highly imaginative religious writer came up with the brilliant idea of this trinity—three gods in one, who creates the world, sustains it, and destroys it. Other religious writers and poets liked the idea, supported it, and composed more stories and poems about them. Priests taught this concept to their followers. Soon temples were built to house these gods. With time this belief spread. More and more stories and poems were composed, and more and more temples were built. Their belief was passed down from generation to generation. Gradually over centuries, this concept and belief became deeply rooted in the psyches of Hindus to the extent that they deemed these gods as absolute Truth without questioning their truth.

Lord *Rama* and Lord *Krishna* are other two famous Hindu gods, who are worshipped in almost every Hindu home in northern India. Both are historical figures—heroes of their times. *Rama* was the king of Ayodhya, a town in the Uttar Pradesh province of India. He was a great king—brave, charitable, and exemplary in his behavior and deeds. He was highly respected and admired by his subjects—almost like a god. In ancient times, people tended to view their king as a god—one who provided for them and protected them. The epic *Ramayana*—till date a highly venerated religious text in Hinduism, was composed about his bravery and high character. Volumes of other stories and poems were written about him. Temples were built to house him and his family. All of these passed off from generation to generation, deepening and strengthening People's belief in him. With time, King Rama became a god. All historical records point to this fact.

Similarly, Lord Krishna was a unique human being in ancient India. He was an extraordinary person—very attractive, endearing, charming, brave, outgoing, and knew yoga and religion. Starting as a shepherd, he later became a diplomat and then a king. He had a tough childhood, grew up fighting his enemies, played a major role in shaping the politics of India at that time, and later became a king. He is said to have spoken/composed the *Gita*— another prime Hindu religious text. A great Hindu epic, Mahabharata, describes politics of that time, the great war of India, and Krishna's role in it. Countless other stories and poems were composed about Krishna—the King of Dwaper—now an island in the Gujarat province of India. Krishna was honored and worshipped during his time. People loved him and believed in him. Later, with time, with more and more stories, poems and folklore about him, belief in Krishna was further strengthened. Krishna—a human—became Lord Krishna—a god. Again, all historical records prove this fact.

Thus Rama and Krishna were two extraordinary human beings—heroes of their times—who were made gods by their admirers and followers over time.

The *Upanishads*, the sacred philosophical treatises of Hinduism discuss the nature of the universe, and everything in it, and by philosophical discussions reach the theory of *"Advaita."* *Advaita* is a Sanskrit word meaning no division—no division between the Universe and God—or The Created and The Creator. It means there is only one Prime truth—named Brahma—the seed of All who gives birth to All (The Universe), lives in everything in it, and runs All. Its belief is summed up and lived by the phrase *"Ahm Brahmasmi"*—"I am Brahma" or I as a human (or any living being for that matter) hold *Brahma*—the Prime Power and The Seed of All inside me. In the Upanishads there are many short discussions written by unnamed philosophers and sages who tried to access and define the Basic Reality— the Prime Truth—by thought and contemplation. As per them, *Brahma* is the Prime Truth, or God, in other words.

Thus Hinduism propagates and defines God by both—by imagination and by thought.

God is the central theme of two other major religions in the world: Christianity and Muslim. Both of them propagate God as the Creator and the Sustainer of The Universe.

The Bible is the holy book of Christianity, and Jesus Christ is the son of God. Deep concepts of Christianity are derived from the Bible—how God created the universe in a few days, and how we humans are primarily sinners et cetera. Jesus Christ, the son of God, is the Messiah to whom we humans— the sinners, have to pray constantly throughout our lifetimes so that he can forgive us; and if we please him enough by our prayers and faith in him, he will send us to heaven; otherwise we will be damned and go to hell.

The Bible is a book written by human beings. Many of its stories are the products of pure human imagination. Its stories, like any other religious stories, are "believed in."

Jesus Christ was a human being who was born sometime in 4 BC in Bethlehem, five miles away from Jerusalem (currently the capital of Israel). He was a Jew, a highly compassionate man, a healer, and a man of exemplary character. He was a man of humble origin, lived a tough life, and was crucified to death. He lived and taught Christianity. He earned a large number of followers during his lifetime and was revered and worshipped by many. After his death his teachings and stories with beliefs about his being the son of God were passed off to future generations. Slowly, with time, Jesus Christ became a god.

Thus Jesus Christ, like Lord Rama and Lord Krishna of Hinduism, was an extraordinary human being—a hero of his time—who was raised to the level of god by his followers.

Along with believing in Jesus Christ, Christianity propagates one Prime God as an eternal, all-powerful, compassionate person who sees, feels, thinks, and wills. A disciple can talk to "God," tell him about his deep concerns and worries, confess to him his sins, and expect to be understood and helped by him— the God. In Christianity, God is a father figure who watches us, helps us in need, and is a true confidant—a friend with whom we can share. Such a god is also the product of pure human imagination.

Concepts of God are similar in Christianity and Islam.

A Muslim is a person who follows the Islam (Muslim) religion. The Muslims' God is *Allah,* who as per their belief creates and sustains the universe and is all-powerful, compassionate, and just. The concept of *Allah* was first introduced and propagated by Muhammad-Ibn-Abdullah. Muhammad was the founder of the Muslim—Islam religion, who taught that there is only one God—*Allah,* and taught other basic tenets of the Muslim religion. His sayings form the verses of the Koran— the holy book of Muslims. Muslims view Muhammad as the Prophet of God.

Muhammad had a very tough childhood, and a life full of struggle. As per historical accounts, Muhammad was born in 570 AD at Mecca. He was orphaned during childhood and worked as a shepherd, as a merchant, and later as a diplomat and a military general. He was a great orator too. During his early youth he used to be a highly anxious man who often sought solitude and retired to nearby mountains for prayer and meditation. It was during one of his phases of deep, lone prayer and meditation inside a cave that he heard an inner voice and witnessed a very bright light around him. He deeply felt the presence of some strong Power. He named it *Allah*—The God. This profound, personal experience of Muhammad calmed him from deep within and filled him with a sense of certainty that some Power—God—existed. He came out and started preaching the concept of *Allah*— God to all.

At that time Mecca, the city where Muhammad lived, was full of fighting tribes. Muhammad started teaching the concept of *Allah* and other truths to them. Soon he got a good number of followers, but also there were others who did not like him. For fear of persecution, he left Mecca and went to Medina, another city. He kept teaching his gospel and earned a large number of followers. By the time Muhammad died at the age of sixty-two, he had conquered Mecca, Medina, and surrounding cities and had united a large number of conflicting tribes in one political union. Even after his death, his religion spread by leaps and bounds and brought together a major part of human population under the flag of one Muslim empire. The Muslim empire during its golden period in Medieval Times dominated a major part of the world, extending from Asia to Africa and to certain parts of Europe. It was an empire of magnificence, riches, and great cultural and scientific achievements.

The Muslim religion is an excellent example of how a religion connects diverse, conflicting people into one bond and leads them to growth and prosperity. Also, from the example of Muhammad, we infer that Muhammad, like Buddha and other sages and mystics, underwent a personal experience of Prime Truth or God. This makes God a matter of personal experience.

Muhammad in his deep meditation heard an inner voice, saw a bright light, felt its truth and power, and named it *Allah—* the God. Muhammad's experience was like Buddha's experience of Revelation of Truth; except, Buddha named his experience Nirvana—Enlightenment—a state of sheer bliss. What Muhammad and Buddha experienced has been experienced by true sages and mystics of their times. Each of them named it different.

Our search into the origin of God leads us to conclude that each god in the history of humanity was either *a product of human imagination*, like gods of Hindu and Greek mycology, and nature gods etc; or *a hero human of his* time, like Lord Rama, Lord Krishna of Hinduism, and Jesus Christ of Christianity; or *a matter of personal experience—Allah—* as experienced by Muhammad.

Now, imagination is fake. A human's imagination is a creative ability to create something in her mind in sharp contrast to reality of her outside world. An imagination is never true. A God produced by human imagination cannot be a true entity. Such a God exists in a human mind only.

A hero human, however heroic she or he may be, is still a human. A human cannot be a god.

And personal experience, howsoever profound it may be, is still a person's personal experience. One person's personal experience cannot be the truth for all. Also, people's personal experiences vary. We cannot define a God on the basis of any one of the above.

Many of us believe in God. We believe in God because we have been taught to believe in God. We pray to God, offer food to her/him, try to please her/ him, and do other rituals because we believe that doing so will keep my god happy who in turn will make me happy. This belief has been instilled into us by our well-wishing elders and teachers since our childhood. We grow up believing in God, doing our daily rituals, never questioning the logic of what are we doing, and never questioning the existence of God. Some of us believers may be highly intelligent people, highly logical and thinking human beings, but we close our thinking when it comes to our gods. We just believe blindly in gods. It is gods because Hindus mostly worship a set of four or five gods, where each god performs a specific function.

What is it with belief that we do not question our belief? What is it with God that we never think about the truth of God?

Belief is trust or faith in a person or an entity that no matter what happens, this person or this entity will always be there for me. It is a mental act, more like a habit, which builds over time and works for the believer. It is an unthinking and illogical mental act. It may or may not be true. But it gives the believer a certainty, a strong emotional support, and inner strength. That is why one's beliefs last. Belief in God is the belief in an unchanging power/entity who remains constant amid all this flux and change and who will always be there for me, no matter what I do. This is how everyone believes in her/his God. Belief in God works because our belief in God is not like our belief in a person, which may get shattered with our bad experience of that person. When we believe in God, we believe in an abstract, stable entity who will always be there for me no matter what. So even if my god ditches me one time, I hope that next time he will not. God is our everlasting hope.

But belief is belief. Belief is an unthinking, unknowing act of following others and hoping or wishing something to be true. Belief is not truth. What I believe to be true may or may not be true. People's belief in God does not tell us anything about the truth of God—whether God exists or not. Such a God exists in the Believer's mind only.

In the absence of any prior religious training or belief, where a person has not been taught about God at all, can she still seek and find God? There are some rare, deeply sensitive and highly intelligent humans who are deeply perturbed by life and its sufferings. Amid all this flux and stark nakedness of life, they seek stability, truth, beauty, and justice. It is as if they have an intuition that there is an entity that has all these traits—which is stable, true, beautiful, and just. They seek "it."

Depending upon how genuine and how intense their search is, they seek it all the time, everywhere, outside themselves, and within themselves. Rare are such individuals. They read, they think, they go to other religions, they meditate, they contemplate, and they choose any and every path leading them toward it. Very few of them, after a lifetime's or maybe many lifetimes' deep search, find "it."

They experience this entity deep inside their Selves—Souls in the form of "an inner voice," or "the presence of a very strong Power," "or "pure, golden light" around them. Different Seekers experience different aspects of this entity. But it is a profound, personal experience in which the Seeker has a direct experience of some very strong power, its truth, and its purity. After this experience, the Seeker _knows_ beyond any doubt that there exists an entity that is stable, all-powerful, pure, and true. This personal experience of the Seeker fills her/him with joy and certitude. For all Seekers it is a personal, spiritual, and blissful experience. Every Experiencer names it differently. Krishna named it Soul; Muhammad named it _Allah_— "the God"; and Buddha named it _Nirvana_— the ultimate bliss and wisdom. These were famous religion founders. There have been less famous and less known sages and mystics in the history of humanity who experienced this entity deep within their Selves. Some named it "God," others "Prime Truth," and so on.

Thus God is a matter of inner spiritual seeking and finding too.

Also, we can infer some common characteristics of "God" or "Prime Truth" from all these religion Founders' and sages' experiences. Many of them experienced it as "an immense bright light"—a form of pure energy. Some of them experienced it as "a voice within"—therefore conscious—and for all of them it was a "very clear, direct experience of some Power and its truth." So as per their experiences, there is an entity that is true, conscious, all- powerful, and a form of energy. This could be "God" or "The Prime Truth."

All religion founders experienced God or Prime Truth. Believers in God claim that they feel God's power, energy, healing, and direction during their prayers and their troubled times.

Personal experience of "God" or "Truth," howsoever profound it may be, is still a personal experience. One person's personal experience cannot be the Truth for all. Moreover, personal experiences of "God" or "Truth" vary. They are not the same for all.

God is not a material entity that we can see, touch, or feel but is "a matter of personal belief and personal experience."

Now, we cannot define an entity on the basis of people's personal beliefs because people's beliefs vary, and a belief may or may not be true. Also, we cannot define an entity on the basis of people's personal experiences because people's personal experiences vary, and one person's personal experience cannot be the truth for all. All these factors associated with God make it hard to define God. We do not know if such an entity exists, and if it does, we cannot determine its exact form and functions. Therefore I would like to leave God Undefined

Definition of God

UNDEFINED.

Derivative Right Way of Living

Since God is an undefined entity, in other words we do not know the exact form and functions of God—what it looks like and what it does—we will not know how to view God and how to live her/him/it in our lives. We cannot deal with an undefined entity. A human ought not to deal with an undefined entity. I as a human do not deal with God.

But God does exist for its Believer. For a Believer her or his God is the highest, abstract entity—the purest symbol of love and faith, whom she or he trusts deeply and holds in the highest esteem. We as humans ought to respect each other's God(s).

CHAPTER 8

TRUTH

Our discussion of God leads us to Truth because God and Truth are two akin issues. One is connected to the other.

Truth is a core issue in a human's life. A human has always grappled with the issue of truth—be it truth in speech, truth in work, truth in relationship, truth about nature and its laws, or The Prime Truth—Truth of All—Basic Reality—the way things really are.

My objective in this chapter is to analyze and define The Prime Truth—The Basic Reality—the way all things are in their basic make. My approach is the same as with other issues—to analyze the issue of Truth, list its derivatives, define it, and then derive the Right Way of Living from it—see how a human ought to view the Truth and live it in her everyday life.

Analysis

Things are not what they seem to be. Reality lies hidden behind many veils. For example, I, as a human, see a flower with two colors—yellow and orange. As per the scientific findings of Biology, a bird watching the same flower sees some 250 colors in it, and a dog watching the same flower sees only black and white.

Now, one thing cannot "be" so many ways. It is only one way, but its perceptions are different to different living beings. That "one way" is the truth of that flower—the way that flower "is."

The issue of "The Truth of All" or "The basic scheme of things" or "the way all things really are" has been a core issue of human curiosity. It has been an intellectual query with philosophers and scientists; a spiritual query with mystics and sages, some of whom later founded their own religions; and an intuition with many humans. Each of them searched for The Truth his own way: a Philosopher by thinking; a Scientist by thinking and experimenting; and a Sage or a Mystic by both—thinking and an inward search of one's own Self. Surprisingly, the answers found by all of them indicate at the same fundamental reality or Truth of All—The Prime Truth. It is just that each of them named it different.

Here I will not go into various findings of Philosophers, but I will limit my discussion to the findings of scientists, sages, and mystics. Also, I will discuss my own search for Truth and my own findings. It is on the basis of these findings that I will define the Truth and derive the Right way of living it.

Truth As Per Science

Though all human knowledge aims at finding the truth, it is Science that gives the most objective and trustworthy truth of a thing. A scientist observes a natural phenomenon; asks questions; searches for an answer with deep studies, research, and experiments; and comes up with a hypothesis, which if proved correct by repeated experiments becomes a Scientific theory/ Law or truth of a thing. Science deals with truth. The test for scientific truths is that they can be proved true all the time by experiments.

Though all sciences deals with truth—the way a thing really is, it is the branch of Physics that deals with "The Truth of All," "the physical reality," or "the way all things are" in their basic make.

Truth As Per Physics

Physics deals with the study of the material world—all matter and its movement. It is a branch of science with its long history of scientific research and findings. Its study started over 2000 years ago during the Greek and Eastern civilizations. Democritus, a Greek Philosopher & Scientist (460 BC), started a chain of thought. He suggested that if you break any matter, a piece of stone for example, separate a part of it, break that part again, separate a part of it, and break it again; very soon you will be left with a very fine part, which you can not break down any more. He called this unbreakable part an atom. An atom—*atomos* in Greek —means unbreakable or indivisible.

This study of the constant division of matter into its finer and finer forms was taken over by other scientists in the same field. Years of persistent research by a number of scientists finally led to the theory of atom and energy sometime in the late 19th century.

Atom is a basic, irreducible unit of matter. It cannot be broken down any further. Every material object in the world—be it a plant, a lamp, or the body of a human—in its basic form exists in the form of atoms. An Atom—the smallest unit of matter—is made of three types of subatomic particles: neutrons, protons, and electrons. A nucleus is the Center of the atom surrounded by neutrons and protons. Neutrons have no charge, while protons have a positive charge, and electrons have a negative charge. Energy is trapped inside the atom in the form of positively charged protons and negatively charged electrons. This trapped energy moves the matter. Electrons lying in the periphery of an atom, and being very lightweight, combine with electrons of other atoms and thus give rise to a molecule. A molecule is a collection of two or more atoms. A molecule combines with other molecules and results in a cell. A cell is a collection of different molecules. That is how different material objects come into being and live. A lamp is a collection of atoms and molecules. A plant is a collection of atoms, molecules, and cells. And a human body is a collection of atoms, molecules, and cells too. But each of these in its very basic form exists in the form of atoms and energy.

An atom is an extremely fine entity. It is so fine that we cannot see it with our bare eyes. For example, a pinch of salt contains trillions of atoms inside it.

So, as per the theory of the atom and energy, all things in the universe—all gases, stars, planets, Earth, a plant, you, and me—in their basic make exist in an extremely fine form of atoms and energy. Its finesse is unimaginable— purer than a dewdrop and whiter than snow.

Further research in Physics was focused on finding the relationship between energy and matter. For this, scientists studied the behavior of both: light—a form of energy, and subatomic particles—very basic units of matter. After a number of "blind slits" experiments, they discovered that both light and particle exhibit the dual pattern of "wave/particle." A ray of light passed through a hole moves as a wave, changes into a particle, and then changes back to a wave form. And a subatomic particle, when passed through a hole changes to a wave form and then back to a particle form. As per this theory of wave/particle duality, both matter and energy in their basic forms are interchangeable—where matter becomes energy or energy becomes matter or where energy itself seems to create matter.

This gave birth to the theory of "quantum mechanics"—the latest theory of Physics describing the Basic Reality. A quantum is a bit of energy that behaves both like either a wave or a particle at different times. It is as if the energy itself becomes a particle—the basic unit of matter. (Each of these theories— "atom and energy," "wave/particle duality," and "quantum mechanics"—can be verified by any Physics College Textbook or a reputed Encyclopedia.)

In sum, as per Physics the whole universe is a vast ocean of pure, bright moving energy creating and regulating all material objects in the universe. This energy, being very fine, permeates All and connects All. It is the dance show of One Energy. The Universe is One.

Since this One Energy creates, moves, and destroys all matter, maybe it is "conscious." And since light is a form of energy, the universe in its basic form exists in the form of a very fine light. Both of these deductions— conscious aspect of Truth— Basic Reality, and its light like form perfectly match the findings of Soul Scientists—sages and mystics of humanity.

Truth As Per Sages and Mystics

The search for truth was not limited to scientists only. There is another breed of humans who in all ages searched for "Eternal Truth" or "the Truth of All." These are sages and mystics of their times. A Sage or Mystic is a super sensitive, highly intuitive, and intelligent person who has a talent for deep contemplation, meditation, and inward search. Such a person, when deeply perturbed by life's fragility and sufferings, begets certain queries, and proceeds to find answers to them—not only answers, but The Truth too. Being a deeply sensitive and intuitive person, (s)he can somehow intuit that this is not all; the world she sees is not all truth; there is some truth much deeper and finer than what she sees around her. Hers is a perturbed, restless soul who cannot find peace unless she finds answers to her queries, and the Truth of All.

Just like a Scientist, a Sage has questions, and she searches for truth, but her ways to find answers are different. She looks outside as well as inside her Self too. Her search is more inward than outward. Her ways are those of Self -search and meditation. She seeks solitude, goes deep down within her Self, probes it constantly, talks to herself, cries and laughs with her Self. She reads, masters her era's knowledge, thinks, and synthesizes all knowledge. By reading and thinking, she finds some of the answers, but not all, and still not the Truth—The Truth of All.

She meditates. Meditation comes naturally to her. She meditates her own way, diving deep down in her Self, going deeper and deeper into it, until one day she suddenly encounters Truth—Truth of All or Basic Reality. That is the moment of bliss for her because that is what she was searching for through her whole life and maybe many a lifetimes. Now she "knows" *The Truth.*"

The Experience of "Truth" or "Prime Reality" has been more or less the same for all sages and mystics. All of them report having seen a very bright light and everything shining in it and feeling the presence of a Great Power. Some of them heard an inner voice in the deepest abyss of themselves, which they called the "Voice of Truth," or "God."

Some of these sages and mystics, after their experiences of Truth, founded their own religions. Most notable among them are Gautam Buddha, the Founder of Buddhism, and Muhammad-Ibn-Abdullah, The Founder of the Muslim religion.

Gautam Buddha, born as a prince in India in 570 AD, was deeply perturbed by life's miseries, old age, and death et cetera. He sought answers to these queries and Truth. In search of Truth, he left his Palace, his wealth, his family, his beautiful wife and child, and wandered from place to place. He read, meditated, and did a lot of self searching. He went deep into his Self, and meditated for hours. He lived in jungles, hardly ate, his whole being focused on finding The Truth only. He did so for years, until answers— truths— started revealing to him.

Then one day during one of his deep meditation sessions under a tree, while he was deep down within his Self / Soul, that he realized the ultimate Truth—the basic make of All. Buddha named this experiences "Bliss"—a moment of deep joy; "Nirvana"—freedom from all worldly desires; and "enlightenment"—a moment when you know All, or "Truth." (This is a historic account of Buddha's search and findings verifiable by all history books on Buddha.)

As per Buddha, the world is not the way we see it, not so gross and crude. The entire world or the universe in its basic make exists and moves as "One All abiding Pool of Conscious Energy, which gives rise to many forms and takes them back within it." This is the "Truth" or "The Prime Reality" or "the Way things are." And this Truth or Prime Reality can only be realized through meditation. The continuous practice of meditation takes one deeper and deeper into her Self/Soul, until she finally realizes The Truth—the Basic Reality, its bliss, and Nirvana. Buddha taught meditation and a whole new Religion called Buddhism.

After Buddha there came Muhammad in 570 A.D. Muhammad was a deeply sensitive Sage and mystic, who, perturbed by life's miseries, searched for Truth. His ways to find it were like those of other sages and mystics. He often sought solitude, retired to nearby mountains, and indulged in deep reflection and meditation. After long years of outward search and deep inner, self-search and meditation, one day while he was in deep meditation, he heard an inner voice from his deep "Self," and saw a very bright light. This was his moment of experiencing the "Truth"—its power and purity. In this one moment, he knew beyond any doubt that there existed a deep Power above all. He called it *Allah*—The God—and started his own religion—Islam or the Muslim religion—one of the greatest religions of the world. His religion bound thousands of different fighting tribes into one and gradually gave rise to the magnificent Muslim Empire. (All historical accounts of Muhammad attest to this fact.)

Besides these two great religion founders, there have been a few other mystics and sages who experienced the ultimate "Truth" and recorded their experiences.

In recent times Swami Rajneesh or Osho of India was a well renowned Mystic, who experienced "The Truth" and wrote about it. Like other mystics and sages, driven by his search for Truth, Rajneesh left his home and its comforts and wandered from place to place. He read, studied other religions, meditated, and fasted for days at a stretch. Nothing happened. He finally gave up looking or searching for anything. It was during such a phase that one night Rajneesh suddenly felt a very strong presence in his room. It was so strong that he almost felt suffocated and breathless. He could not stay in that room any longer. He came out and saw that everything was shining. There was a big tree shining the brightest. He went and sat under that tree.

Slowly things started settling down. It was all very calm and peaceful. He kept sitting there for some time. (This experience was reported by Rajneesh in many of his books and lectures.)

After that time Rajneesh's whole life transformed. His personality took on a glow and hypnotism available only to very few, rare individuals who go through such an experience.

Rajneesh's experience of 'Truth' was like that of Buddha and Muhammad— a profound, inner experience in which he felt the presence of a Great Power, and saw everything shining—a light-like energy make of ALL things.

Though each of these three mystics—namely Buddha, Muhammad, and Rajneesh—gave his own version of 'Truth,' there are some common elements ringing through all of them. Buddha's "Bliss," and "All abiding pool of conscious energy," Muhammad's "inner voice" and "seeing the bright light" and Rajneesh's experience of "a strong Power" and "light make of ALL things"—all indicate at some Supreme Power residing in our deep Selves, and at the energy/light (a form of energy) make of All things. This energy is True, Conscious, is All abiding, and One. It creates All and moves All.

Thus the mystics' description of "Truth" or "Basic Reality" is similar to Physics' description of "Basic Reality." As per Physics' theories of "atom and energy," and currently "quantum mechanics," all things in the universe primarily exist in the form of extremely fine, moving energy that gives rise to a material entity, gets trapped inside it, moves it, and leaves it at its destruction.

Since Physics examined things from outside, it could not capture Reality's— Truth's—"bliss" and "conscious aspect," as experienced by Buddha, Muhammad, Rajneesh, and other Mystics who searched the Truth inside their Selves too.

On the basis of Physics', and Mystics' version of Truth or "the Basic Reality," it can safely be concluded that "All things—the Universe in its basic make—exist and move in the form of a One vast pool of conscious energy—energy that creates all material entities, moves them, and destroys them at its will."

Truth As Per Me

Truth is twofold. It lies outside me as well as inside me. Truth outside me is so fine that it cannot be grasped by mere senses. Nor can truth inside me. Truth outside me has been grasped by scientists by their microscopic devices; and Truth inside me has been grasped by mystics and sages by their intuition, self searching, and meditation.

The search for Truth is so abstract and complex that when you are searching it, you don't even know what you are searching for. It is only when you find it that you know what you were searching for. As the search for Truth is complex, so is its finding too. When you first find it, you don't even comprehend it completely. It is a sudden revelation of some truth in the deepest of your consciousness or a deep inner voice speaking from within. Slowly and gradually as you live on, think more, and incorporate it with other knowledge, then you know exactly how to define it. But its knowledge is so certain that nothing can waver you from it.

I did not know what I was looking for when I started looking. But I was looking all right. I was born in India and that too as a deeply sensitive child. I was born different. Since childhood, sights of death shook me from deep within and made me detest life and its every offering. As I grew up, I was constantly pained and perturbed by life around me—by masses of humans and their base living conditions; by sights of poverty, slums, and filth; by the sheer, naked misery of hungry, helpless animals; and by the total hopelessness around me. Somewhere in the process, I started searching, knowing not what I was searching. I was restless, angry, and anxious all the time. Nothing made sense to me. You know how you feel when you have queries like these.

I read, I thought, and I meditated. I read at length all religious Scriptures and books. They did not satisfy me and felt totally out of place. Then I came to the USA. Here I saw a totally different kind of life around me—few people, all well dressed and well behaved; big, beautiful houses; rows of cars; dazzling lights. Its order, beauty, and wealth soothed my psyche. Human life could be different and (perhaps) beautiful too.

My reading continued. I joined a college and took classes in different disciplines: Math, Science, Humanity, and Law. I spent hours in the library reading books on Philosophy, Humanities, and Sciences. Western Philosophers thought so differently. They questioned everything, reasoned, and tried to assess Truth by thinking only. Their rationality was totally novel to me, but very impressive. World history opened my eyes to the vastness of our human world—some 200 different countries, each with its own past and unique culture. Astronomy gave me a concept of the Universe. Anthropology with its well-supported theories taught me how a human evolved from an ape to a human. Combining it with Biology, a magnificent Science, I learned all about human evolution—how a human evolved from elementary forms of life—from an amoeba to a fish, a fish to a reptile, a reptile to a mammal, a mammal to an ape, and finally from an ape to a human. Biology also taught me about the origin of the whole "Life"—how it started on the Earth some 3.8 billion years ago; its history, its vastness, and variety; and the close connection of all forms of Life. It showed how Flora— the entire plant life, together with Fauna—all living beings, form One Closed Whole—"The Whole of Life," where all forms of life depend on one another and All are required to make The Whole run. Science of Physics unraveled the atom and energy make of the universe—the sheer finesse of ALL—The Basic Reality.

It was within the pages of the Science and Humanity books—the ocean of knowledge, that I found part answers to my queries. Lucid and clear knowledge of these books helped me understand the depth of a human's make; the Oneness of us All and Life around me; the vastness and finesse of the Universe. This knowledge formed part of my Truth—the truth outside me. It gave me concepts of "The Human Whole," "The Whole of Life," and "The Universe," which formed "U" of Om—The Prime Truth of The Human Dharma.

Still it was part of the Truth—the truth outside me. There was another aspect of the Truth—the truth inside me, which I had yet to discover.

Together with reading I meditated. Meditation came naturally to me. I never learned it—maybe it was a purely genetic gift to me from my Brahman ancestors. (My father was a deeply religious man.) I sought solitude. I contemplated deeply and tried to synthesize all knowledge. I talked to my Self all the time. I never left it. I sat in silence and probed my Self constantly. I still had queries within my Self —Who am I? What is this life? What is death?—Many unnamed queries. It was as if I could see through the fragility and seeming futility of life so clearly. I felt as if I had lived many a lifetimes. I talked to my Self for hours. I cried bitterly. Nothing gave me peace.

Meditation is an inner journey into one's Self. Through my constant, everyday meditation—deep reflection, contemplation, gazing inward into my Self—I was going deeper and deeper into the abyss of my Self.

It was during such moments of deep meditation that answers started revealing to me. Then one day while in deep meditation, when I was still questioning my Self—Who am I? there arose a voice within me that said, **"I am The One. It is from _Me_ that All originates, and it is into _Me_ that All comes back."** It was such an inner voice arising from my own Self that I just knew this was true. At that very moment I was one with my true Self. It was such a clear, definite knowledge of my Self that nothing could shake me from it. I had found my Self. I had found the base point of my Self, and the base point of ALL. Now I knew where to start from and where to come back to.

Later on I tried to unravel it. I knew I was an individual human and an individual soul. I knew about individual souls from my personal experience. I knew that individual souls existed and my soul was one of them. This definition of Truth— "One from whom it All emerges and One into whom it All comes back"—could not be the definition of only my Soul. This was the definition of the Soul of ALL—the Origin Point of All—from whom All originates and to whom All comes come back. This was the PowerPoint of The Whole. And this PowerPoint of The Whole (from whom it All originates and to whom All goes back) resides in the deepest depth of one's Self/Soul, whom one can access by a genuine search for Truth, and by meditation. I say "whom," because "it is _conscious_. It spoke to me."

This PowerPoint is the Center of The Whole as well as the Center of each and every entity in The Whole. It resides in the Center of every entity's true Self—one's Soul.

From this I derived the "Ahm" of "Om"—the base point of my "Self" and the base point of All—The Whole. This completed Om—The Prime Truth of The Human Dharma.

This was my experience of Truth—Truth which I was searching for without knowing what I was searching for. But once I found it, it calmed me from deep within and gave me a point of certitude—the base point of my Self and the base point of All.

It was after this personal experience of Prime Truth that I could synthesize all my all knowledge. Now I knew where to start from and where to come back to. Now I had this point of certitude—my own Center, residing in the deepest depth of my Soul; and the Center of All—The Whole—from whom the Whole originates and into whom The Whole goes back. This Center formed the "Ahm" of Om—which means "I" or my deep Self—my Soul.

Now I knew both aspects of Truth—truth outside me and the truth inside me. From this emerged "Om"—the Central Truth of the Human Dharma, and its three Sub-Truths—First, "Om is The Whole"; Second, "Om is The Prime Energy channel within which The Whole moves"; and Third, "Om is The Prime Principle of living." *Om* forms the Central Truth of the Human Dharma which I will discuss in Part Two of this book—"Om—The Prime Truth, and The Human Dharma way of living."

As far as "the Prime Truth"—"The Basic Reality," or "the way things are" is concerned, I will say things are not the way they look. The Universe is not the way it looks. All things and the universe actually exist in the form of an extremely fine, pure, moving, *conscious* energy (lightlike), originating from One Center and coming back to it. This is the Center of The

Whole as well as The Center of each and every entity in The Whole. This Center resides in the deepest depth of one's Self/ Soul whom one can access by genuine search for truth and by meditation.

This Truth, the energy make of all things, is extremely fine—not visible to our senses. Its finesse and truth can only be seen by scientists with their microscopic devices; and its inner truth—its conscious energy, its purity, and bliss—can only be experienced by sages and mystics in their deepest moments of meditation, often after an intense, genuine search for Truth.

Derivatives

From the above analysis of "Truth" or "Basic reality"—"the way things are," there emerge certain common characteristics on the basis of which we can define the Truth or Basic Reality.

Starting from the Science of Physics—one of the most authentic ways to know the outside world—all things in the universe in their basic forms exist as atoms and energy, where energy is trapped inside an atom in the form of particles, moves an atom or matter, and leaves it at its destruction. An atom is an extremely fine unit of matter not visible to our eyes. As per this the entire universe in its basic form exists and moves as One vast pool of extremely fine, moving energy. Since light is a form of energy, the universe in its basic form exists in an extremely fine, lightlike form.

Further, "quantum Mechanics" theory tells us that both matter and energy are interchangeable. As proved by all experiments, "a particle"—basic unit of matter, and light—a form of energy, both behave like a "wave" and "a particle" at different times. As per this the moving energy itself becomes a particle or creates a particle—a basic unit of matter. Maybe this energy is "conscious," creates matter at its will, moves it, and destroys it.

Physics missed the conscious aspect of the Truth or Basic Reality, because Physics checked it from outside. The conscious aspect of The Prime Truth has been caught by sages and mystics in their deepest, best moments of meditation. These Sages and Mystics in their search for "Truth," dived deep down in their "Selves," went in and in, and finally arrived to their Centers, located in the deepest depths of their Selves—the very point where they caught the current of the Truth, and felt one with It. Some of them heard an inner voice, like Muhammad (the Founder of Islam religion) did; or saw a very bright light or the light/energy make of all things, like Muhammad, Buddha, Rajneesh, and many others did. And all of them felt the presence of a Great Power and felt its truth and purity. It was a moment of utter bliss for them when they felt the joy of being one with the Prime Truth or the Supreme Power and a moment of enlightenment when they knew "The Truth" —when they knew it "All."

So as per sages' and mystics' experiences, all things and the entire universe in their basic forms exist and move in the form of a pure energy—they saw it in bright light-like form; and this energy is *conscious*— they heard an inner voice—and there is some Great Power residing in the deepest depth of our "Selves" who is in All, and runs it All.

In my personal experience of "Truth"—I heard an inner voice saying, "It is from _Me_ that All originates, and it is into _Me_ that All comes back." I define this "_Me_" as the base point of my "Self," and the base point of All—the Universe. So as per me, "Truth" resides in the deepest depth of one's Self—in one's Soul, in the Center of one's Self, and the Center of All—the very PowerPoint from whom it All originates, and into whom it All goes back. This Center—the Power Point of All—the "Truth"—is conscious, because it spoke to me. It can be accessed by genuine search for Truth and by meditation.

On the basis of Physics' findings, sages' and mystics' experiences, and my own personal experience, it can safely be concluded that All things in the universe, in their basic makes exist in the form of an extremely fine, pure conscious energy that is all One, is moving, and has a Central point from where it All originates and into whom it All goes back.

Definition of Truth

In Truth or in Basic Reality, All things in the world—the entire universe—exists as One vast pool of extremely fine, pure, conscious energy that is all One, is moving, originating from One Center point, going out, and coming back into it. This Center is the PowerPoint of the Whole, from whom the Whole originates and into whom the Whole comes back. This is the Center of the Whole as well as the inner center of each and every entity in the Whole. This is your center and my center too, residing in the deepest depth of yours and my soul. This Center—The Truth—can be accessed by genuine search for Truth, intense Self-searching, and by meditation.

Derivative Right Way of Living

A human with her regular senses does not see or perceive "the Truth," or "the Basic Reality"—the way things are. A human sees colors, while there are no colors. A human sees solids, shapes, and sizes, while in reality there is no such thing. In Basic Reality all things exist and move in the form of pure energy, which is Conscious, is All, and is One. A human does not have senses to perceive this reality.

But Truth exists whether a human sees it or not. Things are the way they are whether we see them or not. The entire universe with all things in it exists and moves as One vast pool of pure, conscious energy originating from one Center—the PowerPoint of All—and coming back into it. This prime make of all things—the ultimate Truth—has been brought to light by the Science of Physics, by sages' and mystics' personal experiences, and by my own personal experience of Truth.

A human, though not able to see truth, ought to accept others' proofs and understand the Truth or Basic Scheme of All things. Also, this Truth or the Prime Reality of things, though not available to human senses, can be accessed and known.

A human ought to understand this fact—the prime energy make of All—thus the Oneness of us All. A human ought to know that in reality, every entity is created and run by the same Power and houses that Power within its Center. In view of this fact, a human ought to see the divine in All, feel her connection to All, and respect All.

In Reality, the universe is One vast pool of extremely fine, pure, conscious energy originating from one center and going back into it. This center is the PowerPoint of all, is conscious, is the Center of All, and the Center of each and every entity in it. This is my Center and your Center too. A human can access this Center—the PowerPoint of All—by accessing her own center. In the deepest depth of a human's Soul, there resides this Center—the PowerPoint of All—at which a human is connected to this PowerPoint—the Supreme Soul, and the ALL. A human's genuine search for Truth leads her to this deepest point in her center—her Soul. Also, a human can access it and feel its sheer purity and bliss by meditation.

Accessing one's Self/Soul by meditation connects one to the PowerPoint of All—the Soul of All, and the All. It is at this point of connection that a human experiences her own connection to the PowerPoint and connection to the All—The Whole. She feels the sheer depth, purity, and bliss of her own Soul; and ever-flowing joy, wisdom, and creativity of the Supreme Soul— the Center, the PowerPoint of All.

Meditation is a technique to access one's Self or Soul. To meditate is to contemplate, to reflect, to focus on one's Self, to go deep down within it by an inward gaze and inner search. It requires years of practice, solitude, silence, and an inner journey marked by constant self-search, self-talk, deep reflection, and focusing on one's Self. Only a genuine Truth Seeker—perturbed by life's queries, who demands Truth and only Truth—can meditate truly, access her Self/Soul, and find answers to her life queries and finally the Truth. Rare are such individuals—the gems of humanity, born once in a while—who undertake such a search and complete it.

There are other simpler ways to meditate. Adopting one of them and practicing it every day balances a human physically and mentally, calms her mind, and helps her access her center— her Soul.

Since meditation is a way to access one's Soul, which is located at the Center of one's body a little below her navel, the right way to meditate is to sit cross-legged in a Lotus Posture, with a straight backbone; calm one's mind, and focus one's entire attention onto one's inner Self/Soul. This requires an inward gaze, going deep down into your Self, to the point where your true Self or Soul lies.

There are certain meditation techniques to help one calm her mind and focus onto her deep Self—Soul. These are gazing at one single object or point in your front center *or* repeating a single word or Mantra *or* focusing your entire attention onto your breath—its coming and going. Practicing any of one these techniques for twenty minutes a day calms one's constantly chatting mind and takes one into her deep Self—her Soul.

Daily continuous practice of meditation calms one's mind more and more and takes one deeper and deeper into one's Soul, finally up to the very point at which one's Soul is located and is connected to the divine—the Center of All—the Supreme Soul. It is at this point that a human feels the sheer power and bliss of "Truth" and becomes one with it. This is the purpose of meditation—its high point. Reaching this point in meditation requires years of constant practice and the genuine search for Truth.

The best meditation is more mindful meditation, where the Meditator also employs her mind. This is complete yoga—the union of one's body, mind and soul.

Based upon my own definition of Truth, I have devised my own Meditation technique in which the Meditator contemplates upon the Prime Truth of "Om—The Whole," and by thought, breath, and sound tries to access and feel the Eternal Truth of Om and be one with it. I will discuss it in detail in Part Two—"Om—The Prime Truth, and The Human Dharma Way of Living."

PART TWO

_____

THE WAY OF LIVING

(Om: The Prime Truth

and

The Human Dharma Way of

Living)

CHAPTER 9

Introduction to Part II

Before going into Part Two, "Om—The Prime Truth, and The Human Dharma Way of Living," I would like to do a little review of the term *Dharma* and the preceding work.

Dharma is a Sanskrit word derived from the root *dhra* which means "to wear" or "to adopt." Inherent in its meaning is the term duty—an obligation or the Right thing to do for a person. Starting from this, the term *Human Dharma* means "A Code of Conduct to be adopted by a human, how a human ought to live or a human's Right Way of living."

Svadharma goes with Dharma. *Svadharma* is another Sanskrit word made of two words: *Sva* and *Dharma*. *Sva* means "I," "my," and *Dharma* means "Duty" or the Right thing to do. Thus *Svadharma* of an individual means doing "my Dharma"— my duty—my doing the right thing even if others don't do so. It means my taking an initiative to doing the right thing and sticking to it even if others do not do so. (I have explained *Svadharma* in detail in the latter chapter of this book as the proper ending of the Human Dharma).

The Human Dharma is one single individual human's (a woman's or a man's) Dharma—The Right Way of Living.

The Human Dharma is not a set of my personal opinions or preferences but is a total derivation—derived from the hard, core facts of a human's make, human life, and certain major issues of a human's life—facts brought to light by and well supported by scientific theories too.

As discussed in the beginning of this book, the Human Dharma is a human's Right Way of Living. There is a Right way to do everything. Name any task, it has the Right way of being done. Similarly there is the Right way to live. The Right way of doing a task is to be derived from the nature and objective of the task itself. Starting from this premise, I derived the human Dharma—"a Human's Right Way of Living" from the analysis and definition of "What is a human?" "What is human life?" and certain major issues of a human's life like "Death," "Soul," "God," and "Truth." All of these issues are interrelated too where one issue leads to the other.

In Part One of this book, I analyzed each of these issues in detail. From a thorough analysis, there churned up certain truths about each issue. It was on the basis of these truths that I defined each of these issues. Then, from the definition, I derived the Right Way of Living that issue or how a human ought to view each of these issues—her/his basic identity, her/his life, death, soul, God, and Truth—and incorporate it into her/his living.

So far these derivatives were scattered—the derivative Right Way of Living from each issue.

As I was reading and contemplating on each of these issues, there was another realm of mine in which I was searching too. This was my deep inner Self. I was searching my Self by constant probing, self talk, and by meditation. As described in my discussion on Truth, one day during my deep meditation, I heard an inner voice that said, "It is from _Me_ that All originate and it is into _Me_ that All come back." This was such a spontaneous, true voice coming from my own Self. At that very point I came to know my Self, and I came to know the Truth—the Truth of _ALL_. Now I knew beyond any doubt that in the deepest depth of my Self/Soul there resides an entity "who" (it is conscious, since it spoke to me) is the First Source of All—The Origin Point of All. I had found my Self, I had found my base, and the base point of each and All. Now I knew where to start from and where to come back to. This became "Ahm" ("I") of "Om—The Prime Truth."

It was after this personal experience that I was able to synthesize all my knowledge into one. It was after this experience that there emerged Om—the Prime Truth, and the Central Truth of The Human Dharma. Om somehow beautifully encompassed all derivatives into it and came up as One compact Truth containing the gist of All.

Om is the Prime Truth that exists by itself. It is the basic, fundamental Truth—true for All beings and true for a human.

Om is the Central Truth of the Human Dharma. Om has three Sub-Truths:

- **First, "Om is The Whole";**

- **Second, "Om is the Prime Energy Channel within which The Whole moves"; and**

- **Third, "Om is The Prime Principle of Living."**

Each of these is a Truth by itself as well as related to the other. And Each has its own derivative Right Way of Living.

347

Following from Om, there also emerged the total Human Dharma Way of Living.

<u>The Human Dharma Way of Living is a Value-Oriented Life with Short-Term goals, and Daily Objectives of a Rich, Healthy, Happy, and Meaningful Life.</u>

The human Dharma is a human's everyday Dharma. A human lives a long life but (s)he lives it on an every day basis. It is on the basis of a human's everyday Karmas that a human builds an Edifice of her life in which she lives, rejoices her existence, and which she leaves to The Whole at her death. I have summed up the entire Human Dharma in the form of a daily prayer, which a human remembers the first thing in the morning, plans her day as per it, and lives her day as planned.

The Human Dharma is a human's Right Way of Living, which if followed helps a human (an individual) live a good life herself, and enrich her Whole too. This, in turn, leads to a happy and prosperous human society and a happy and prosperous humanity.

In the next few pages I will discuss "Om—the Prime Truth," and "Om—the Central Truth of the Human Dharma," followed by the total "Human Dharma Way of Living," which includes how a human (An individual—a woman or a man) ought to view herself and her life and live it in the richest and fullest terms.

CHAPTER 10

OM—THE PRIME TRUTH

Om is the basic, fundamental Truth that is true for every being. Om exists. The Truth of Om stands by itself. It is for a human to try to understand its finesse, its totality, and its perfection, to live as per it, and experience the sheer bliss and joy of living.

Om is the Prime Truth, which has three Sub-Truths:

- **First, Om is The Whole;**

- **Second, Om is The Prime Energy Channel within which The Whole moves; and**

- **Third, Om is The Prime Principle of Living.**

These three Sub-Truths are interconnected and complementary. But at the same time, each of these Sub-Truths stands by itself and has its own derivative Right way of living.

Also, as we will see, Each of these is a self-evident Truth, further verified by Sciences, common observation, and a little insight—a truth to be felt and practiced. Let us analyze Each of these Sub-Truths separately one by one.

First Truth: "Om is The Whole"

Om is a Sanskrit word made of two letters, *"Ahm"* and *"U."* Ahm means "I," and U means "everything other than I."

The letter *Ahm* in English can be translated as "I" or "I am." Meaning wise, the letter *Ahm* within itself contains the basic ego of an entity—"I am," its inner Self—"I" and "my"; and its deep Self—Soul located in that entity's center connected to the very origin point from where that entity arose—The Origin Point of All—The Whole. When a Being says "Ahm" ("I"), the word *"Ahm"* arises from the very center of that Being—her origin point—The Point from where that being arose—and The Point from where All beings arise. It is the Center of The Being, and the Center—the Power Point of All beings, from where All arise, and into whom All go back.

The letter *"U"* in English means "everything other than I" or "the world outside me." While "Ahm" means the inner Self of a being, "U" means the world outside that being. Every being exists by itself, alone, in a vast vast world inhabited by multitudes of other beings and things. This is the outer world—the world outside the Being, in which the Being exists, and with which the Being has to cope.

The above holds true for every being in the world—living and nonliving. Even a nonliving being has its own Center from which it operates—"Ahm," and has its own outside world—"U"— in which it exists, and with which it has to cope. Examples of this can be seen around us in every entity. A tiny ant has its own Center—its own physical center, and her own inner Self— Ahm— I, which feels, thinks, and pushes her to act. She lives in a vast vast world—the world outside her—her "U." Similarly a human has her own physical center and her own inner Self—Ahm—I.

(S)he lives in a vast world with which (s)he has to cope—the world outside her/him—her/his "U." The Earth, a non-living being, has its own Center of gravity—its own "Ahm"—"I" from which it moves. It exists in a vast universe—world outside it—its "U," with which it has to cope.

Combining these two letters *"Ahm"* and *"U"* creates the word *Om*. Thus Om is The Whole containing within itself the "Ahm"—"I" of an entity, and its *"U,"*—the world outside that entity.

Om is a Primordial word—a sound originating from the inner Center—the Origin Point of a Being—Ah(m), going out—"U..," and coming back to the same center—"M.." of her Ahm. When a being says "Om," the word Om envelops that being's inner Self—"Ahm," and her entire outer world—"U" in it. **_Thus, Om is The Whole. There is nothing that exists outside Om._**

Second Truth: "Om is The Prime Energy Channel within Which The Whole Moves"

The Whole is moving. The Whole—a being's inner Self, "Ahm," and the being's outer world—"U" are constantly moving. The Whole is not outside me; the Whole by its very definition includes me—"Ahm"—"I," and my "U"—the world outside me. There is a constant movement inside me—my breath, my feelings, and my thoughts are constantly moving, and so is there a constant movement in the world outside me—everything is moving and changing.

As proved in my earlier discussion on Truth, The Whole in its prime form exists and moves in the form of pure conscious energy—All originating from one Center—the PowerPoint of All—"Ah(m)," going all the way out—"U..," and coming back to the same Center—"M.." of (Ahm). Thus O..m.. is the Prime Energy channel within which the Whole moves. The Whole's energy rises from this center—Ahm, goes out—U.., and comes back to it—"M" of Ahm. This is the Center of the Whole, as well as the Center of each and every entity in the Whole. This "Center" of The Whole resides in the deepest depth of a being's inner Self—I—her Soul.

A being moves/breathes from her center. This is the being's Center as well as the Center of The Whole.

Since The Whole exists and moves in the form of pure, conscious energy, The Whole inside a being moves in the form of her breath. A being's breath is pure, conscious energy. A being's breath is closely interlinked with her consciousness. It is affected by the being's feelings and thoughts, and affects them too. And, a being's breath is pure energy. It enlivens and invigorates the Being.

Thus The Whole inside me moves in the form of my breath. When I watch my breath, I am watching the movement of the Whole inside me. When I feel my breath, I am feeling the movement of The Whole inside me.

A Being's breath originates from her center—"Ah(m)," goes all the way out—"U..," invigorates her whole body, and comes back to the same Center—"M" of Ahm. The Whole inside a being moves within the channel of O..m... If I breathe by O..m.., I can feel one with the movement of The Whole inside me.

The same holds true for every entity—Living and Non-Living being. Every entity in its center is connected to the Center of the Whole. The Whole within a living being like an ant or a human moves in the form of her breath —pure conscious energy that arises from her center (The Center of The Whole)—"Ah(m)," goes out—"U..," invigorates her whole being, and comes back to the same Center—"M" of her Ahm. The Whole inside The Earth moves in the form of pure energy that arises from its center— "Ah(m)," goes out —"(ah)U..," and comes back to the same center "M" of Ahm.

Om is the Conduit within which The Whole moves.

Third Truth: "Om is The Prime Principle of Living"

The word "*Om*" is made of two letters "Ahm" and "U." "Ahm" means "I," and "U" means "everything other than I"—"the world outside me." Every entity in the Universe primarily exists for its own "survival" and "happiness" —"Ahm"—"I." These are two prime triggers that move an entity. Every entity primarily moves/lives to fulfill its basic survival needs of energy, food, and protection et cetera. Secondly, it seeks happiness consciously or unconsciously. It tends to do what makes it happy. This is true for every entity—living and nonliving. An entity cannot live without following this principle.

The entity at the same time is a creation and a part of the Whole in which it lives. This is "U"—"the world outside the entity." An entity by its living, and during its living has to enrich the Whole of which it is a part. It has to relate to its Whole—the world outside it—be a part of it, and enrich it. If it does not do so, the Whole will not let it survive. The Whole is far too powerful.

Thus Om is The Prime Principle of Living, where "Ahm"—"I"— means every entity primarily seeking its own survival and happiness; and "U"—"everything other than I" or "the world outside me"—means an entity's need to relate to and enrich its Whole.

This principle is true for every entity—living and nonliving. A teeny-tiny ant moves/lives to fulfill her own basic needs of food and protection—"Ahm"— "I." While doing so, she has to enrich her colony of ants, of which she is an integral part—"U"—"the world outside her." She carries food to it and communicates with other ants et cetera. Similarly a human primarily seeks her own survival and happiness. She lives and works in order to fulfill her basic needs of food, clothing, and housing et cetera; and she tends to do what makes her happy—play, sing, read et cetera—"Ahm"—"I." During her living she has to relate to and enrich her Human Whole—her family, and her society et cetera, of which she is a close part —her "U"—"other than I"— "the world outside her." The Earth—a nonliving entity, primarily moves by its own Center in a way so that it can survive as a separate entity, maintaining its "Ahm"—"I." While doing so, it nurtures The Whole of life within its lap, gives light to its Moon et cetera. Thus it enriches its "U"— "the world outside it."

Thus Om is the Prime Principle by which every entity moves/ lives.

Om is the First, Fundamental Truth—true for every entity. I discovered "Om" in my journey of seeking Truth and in my endeavor to define the Human Dharma—a human's Right Way of Living. While analyzing a human, human life, and the core issues of human life, Om emerged as the key Truth encompassing all other truths within it, and as The First, Prime Truth—true for every entity, and true for a human.

CHAPTER 11

OM—THE CENTRAL TRUTH OF THE HUMAN DHARMA AND ITS DERIVATIVE RIGHT WAY OF LIVING

Every Religion has a Central Truth from which it derives its philosophy and way of living, for example, the "God" of Christianity and Islam, and the "Enlightenment" or "Nirvana" of Hinduism and Buddhism. The Central Truth of the Human Dharma is "Om." **The entire Human Dharma is derived from "Om" and its Three Sub-Truths, namely:**

1. **"Om is The Whole";**

2. **"Om is The Prime Energy Channel within which The Whole moves"; and**

3. **"Om is The Prime Principle of Living."**

Each of these is a Truth which stands by itself, independently of others, and has its own derivative Right Way of Living for a human. Let us look into each of these Sub-Truths of "Om" to see how it is a truth in the context of a human, and its derivative Right Way of Living for a human.

The First Truth of OM: "Om is The Whole," and Its Derivative Right Way of Living

Om is a Sanskrit word made of two letters *"Ahm"* and *"U."* In English *"Ahm"* means "I," and *"U"* means "everything other than I" or "the world outside me."

Ahm—I am a Human

The letter *"Ahm"* well translated into English as "I am," contains within it the Prime Ego of an entity and the inner sense of its basic make, its power and its potential. It is the declaration and affirmation of an entity's existence, its self-awareness, and its self pride— "Ahm"—"I am."

The "Ahm"—"I"—The Prime ego of a human—lies in her/his basic identity of being a human, her/his self-awareness, and self pride of being a human. A human does not derive her identity from her mere name. A name is just a way to address an entity; or from her citizenship—that is the country she is born in and lives in; or from a relationship—"wife" or "daughter" of so and so; it is just a relationship she shares with another human. A human derives her/his basic identity from the fact of her/his being a human, from her human make, and from her human power and potential lying deep inside her. When a human says "Ahm"—"I am," it is a declaration of being a human— "I am a human."

What does it mean to be a human? What is a human? Our inquiry into this issue (Part 1, Chapter 2) led us to define a human as "Evolved, Multi-Dimensional," and "A Part of The

Whole living being." As proved by Sciences of Biology and Anthropology, the human form evolved from other forms of life over millions of years. A human stands at the tip of evolution, containing within her "Self"—"Ahm"—"I" the psyche, memories, basic emotions and intelligence of all forms of life. A human by her very make has lived through all forms of life. When a human says "Ahm," she declares this aspect of her being—"**Evolved**."

But, a human is a human. Since her branching out from a chimp form some five to seven million years ago, and after that, since the inception of human civilization, and especially during the last ten thousand years of humanity's history, the human form evolved further—a human evolved as a human. During this period a human form diversified, developed, perfected its each dimension, and emerged as a **Multi-Dimensional Living Being**—a form very distinct from any other living being, with various dimensions of her being—Physical, Emotional, Intellectual, Moral, and Spiritual.

During the stupendous growth of human civilization, especially during the last ten thousand years, the human developed a distinct physical form—very different from any other living being—and became a Bipedal walking being with a straight backbone, highly agile and capable hands, and a very strong brain. (S)he developed and sustained distinctive human emotions, like love, compassion, tender affection, and respect et cetera, rare to any other living being. Above all, there emerged three dimensions of a human form that make her a unique and truly noble living being. These are Intellectual, Moral, and Spiritual. It is human intellect that created the Human Whole—a human made world for the humans—and sustains it till date. Human intellect is marked by an immense capacity to learn, acquire a vast amount of knowledge, retain it, and use it; strong memory, thought, reasoning, affinity with numbers, and problem-solving ability et cetera. The Moral Dimension, higher than the intellectual is uniquely human too. It is only a human who questions the right and wrong of her own and others' actions, defines Right and tries to follow it. The Spiritual dimension is the highest dimension of a human's being. It is related to the unique human spirit—"Self"—seeking answers to basic questions of existence, the meaning of life, truth, and God et cetera. Every human has access to these dimensions of her being. Exercising each dimension and incorporating it into her daily living helps a human live a good and wholesome life.

When a human says "Ahm"—"I am" (S)he declares this aspect of her being too—its Multi-Dimensional aspect—its power and potential.

Human—A Part of The Whole

A human (an individual) is not alone on this Earth. As noted in my earlier discussion on "What is a human?" and "Human Life," a human is born, lives, and dies as a part of The Whole. There is a vast world around a human of which (s)he is a close part. Therein we saw, how starting from a human as the Center, the world around a human can be viewed as three gradually increasing Sub-Wholes, one merging into another and leading to One Whole. These are The Human Whole; The Whole of Life; and The Universe.

The Human Whole is the immediate world around a human in which a human is born, lives, and dies. "The Human Whole is a network of a human's Family, Society, Country, Humanity, and their Cumulative Achievements in all aspects of the human life, ranging from a needle to an airplane, from a thatch-roof hut to a skyscraper, from one single alphabet to the most complex Philosophical treatise, from one single number to Advanced

Calculus, our sprawling cities, our monuments, our universities, our libraries, our hospitals etc.—in sum each and everything we humans have ever achieved and live by on the face of this Earth." The Human Whole is a product of humanity's cumulative labor of millions of years, especially of the last ten thousand years where each new generation of humans came in, contributed its best to "The Human Whole," and departed, somehow making it more beautiful than they found it.

A human is a very close and intrinsic part of The Human Whole—the human made world around her. A human is born in the Human Whole, lives in the Human Whole—uses, and depends upon its relationships, products, and services, and dies in the Human Whole. A human is born and lives in her family—a group of people related to her by blood or by marriage. A human is an integral part of her society—the people she lives amidst and works with. A human is a part of her country as its citizen. And, a human is an integral member of the Humanity simply by being a human. A human is a part of the "Cumulative Achievements" of the Human Whole. A human throughout her lifetime needs and uses its various products and services. A human lives, works in some field of human labor, and leaves her best to the Human Whole in the form of her "Work." A human marries, produces children, raises them, and leaves them to the Human Whole as future members of humanity. Thus a human is a very close part of The Human Whole.

A human is affected by the Human Whole—kind of human world she is born in— and she affects it too by her own actions.

A human and her Human Whole (7 billion humans and their human made world) nestle in the lap of "The Whole of Life." The Whole of Life is "The vast blue-green Earth with its Flora—acres of greenery on its lands and inside its oceans; and its Fauna—trillions of flying beings in its air, trillions of crawl-ing and walking beings on its lands, and trillions of swimming beings in its oceans, where humanity is just a thin streak of walking beings on it lands amid multitudes of other crawling and walking beings."

A human is a close part of the Whole of Life. A human is affected by the Whole of Life—its climate, its weathers, its rains, its sunshine, the kind of air she breathes, and the kind of food she eats et cetera. And a human affects it too by her own actions. Every human by her living affects the Whole of Life—whether she causes pollution or grows more plants; whether she is com-passionate toward other living beings—lives and lets them live or kills them mercilessly; whether she mindlessly produces many children or has one or two well-raised children. Every human by her living either enriches the Whole of Life or harms it.

The Whole of Life—The Earth with its flora and fauna—is a part of the bigger Whole, our Solar System—a group of planets with one center Sun. Our Earth nursing the Whole of Life in its lap moves around our Sun with seven other planets moving around it (the Sun). Our solar system in turn is a part of the bigger Whole—our Galaxy—"the Milky Way"—a still bigger group of many solar systems with one center Sun. Our sun moves around the Center Sun of our Galaxy— the Milky Way—with millions of other solar systems' Suns moving around it—the Center of the Galaxy. Our Galaxy the Milky Way, is a part of the bigger Whole—our Cluster—a group of galaxies with one center Sun. The Center Sun of our Galaxy, the Milky Way moves around the Center Sun of our Cluster, with millions of other galaxies' suns moving around it—the Center of the Cluster. Our Cluster, in turn, is a part of the biggest Whole—The Super Cluster—the big-gest group of clusters with one center Sun. The Center Sun of our Cluster moves around the Center Sun of the Super Cluster with millions of other Clusters' Suns moving around it —the Center of The Super Cluster. *This is the Universe—one verse, one song, a vast organization of all suns, stars, and planets moving around one Center.*

A human is a close part of the Universe both indirectly and directly. First, A human is a resident of The Earth, where Earth is just a small planet moving around our Sun, and where all suns and planets are ultimately moving around One Center—all controlled and regulated by the same moving force. Second, a human is a creation of the Universe. *I view the Universe as a moving Potter's Wheel with one Center that is creating and moving All.* This Potter's Wheel is constantly moving, creating new and new artifacts, and throwing them in the Whole, where each artifact is a totally novel and unique creation of The Whole created in a very special way to enrich it. Where every single human is an individual—a totally novel, unique creation of The Whole, created as a part of the Whole to enrich it.

A human is affected by the Universe and she affects it too by her living. A human by living true to her special nature and talent fulfills the deep purpose of the universe behind her creation and enriches it.

Thus a human is a close and intrinsic part of her Whole—the world around her, and its each Sub-Whole—The Human Whole, The Whole of Life, and the Universe.

When a human says "Ahm"—"I" (S)he declares this aspect of her "Ahm"—"I" too as "a Part of The Whole." A human understands the nature of the Whole—the vast world around her, and her close relationship to each Sub-Whole, and The Whole, her part in it, and her play in it.

This is "Ahm"—"I" the human identity of a human. When a human says "Ahm"—"I," (S)he declares, "I am a Human—Evolved, Multi-Dimensional, and a Part of The Whole."

The Ahm—I of a human also includes a human's awareness of her inner Self —her Soul—the very origin point from where she came. This is the core identity of a human. When a human says "Ahm"—"I" she also declares, "I am a soul."

"Ahm"—I Am a Soul

Every human has an inner Self—a Self marked by her "I," "me," and "mine." This is a very private part of a human, where (S)he roams alone—a part made of a human's deeply personal, innermost memories, attachments, and desires. The Self of a human is very deep, deeper than anything we know. A true and persistent journey into her inner Self leads a human to the depth of her Self—to the deepest depth where her soul resides and is connected to the Supreme Soul—the Soul of All—the Center, and the Power Point of the Whole. This is the Origin Point of her Soul and All—the point where her Soul is diversified from (but is still connected) to The Supreme Soul.

"The Soul is one's deepest Self, located in the Center of one's body, a little below her navel, containing the deepest memories, attachments, and desires of all her previous lives and this life too." I arrived at this definition of soul after analyzing People's experiences of soul, various religions, and my own personal experiences of soul. Same also revealed that one's soul is a non-material entity, which enters her mother's womb at the point of conception, takes up a body, lives inside it as a person's deepest Self—"I," motivates her to act/live in a certain way, and leaves the body at death. The word *"Ahm"* originates from a human's deep Self—her Soul, the very Origin Point of herself, and the

Origin Point of ALL, the point where (s)he knows that (s)he exists. It is the true Self of a human, a Self that is eternal, that lives with a human always—from one life to another; her deep inner Self which a human cannot negate.

Thus letter "Ahm" of Om denotes both—a human's identity as a human and her inner Self/Soul. When a human says, "Ahm," she states, "I am a Human —Evolved, Multi-Dimensional, and a Part of The Whole. I am a Soul. My soul is my deepest Self located in the center of my body, a little below my navel, containing the deepest memories, attachments and desires of all my previous lives and this life too."

"U"

The second letter of Om is "U," which means "everything other than I" or "the world outside me." (It is by combining these two letters—Ahm and U that the word Om is formed.) While Ahm—"I," the first letter of Om, denotes a human's individual, basic identity—"I am a human, I am a Soul," "U"— the second letter of Om, means "everything other than I"—"the world outside me."

Every entity in the universe exists and lives as an individual entity, but at the same time it is a part of and lives in a vast world. The same is true for a human. Though a human is born as an individual and lives as an individual, but (s)he is born in, lives in, and dies in the vast world of which (s)he is an integral part.

The world outside a human is too vast, with multitudes of living beings, things, and places in it. But taking a human as the Center, if we look closely, we find there are three gradually increasing Sub-Wholes, the one merging into another, of which a human is a close part. These are "The Human Whole," "The

Whole of Life," and "The Universe." Starting from a human as the Center, each of these is a bigger Sub-Whole, a part of another, and closely interlinked to a human's make and survival. The entire world outside a human fits into these three Sub-Wholes.

My earlier analysis of "What is a human?" and "Human Life" in Part One brought forth the definition of these three Sub-Wholes, which altogether constitute a human's "U"—"the world outside a human." Therein, while tracing the origin of a human and a human's life journey from birth till death, we saw how a human throughout her lifetime remains a close part of her Family—"a group of people related to her by blood or by marriage." Then we saw how a human and her family depend upon and live amid a bigger group of humans, a human Society—"a group of people tied to each other by living together and by personal and business relationships." A human, her family, and her society depend upon and live in a Country of which they are close parts. "A Country is a vast tract of land enclosed within a boundary line, having its own territory, resources, and people tied to one another by the same country citizenship."

A human, her family, her society, and her country, in turn, are parts of a bigger Whole in which they live together, need one another, and help one another—"The Human Whole." The Human Whole is a group of All— some 196 countries tied to each other by mutual need, mutual aid, and their common sharing of One Earth and its resources. They altogether form The Human Whole—the First Sub-Whole of a human's "U"—the world outside a human. "The Human Whole is a network of a human's Family, Society, Country, Humanity, and its cumulative achievements in all aspects of the human life—ranging from a needle to an airplane, a thatch-roof hut to a skyscraper, from one single alphabet to the most complex philosophical treatise, and from one single number to Advanced Calculus, our sprawling Cities, our Monuments, our Museums, our Libraries—in sum each and everything we humans have ever achieved and live by on the face of this Earth."

A human is affected by her Human Whole, and she affects it too by her own actions.

The Human Whole—the entire humanity with its Cumulative achievements—nestles in the lap of "the Whole of Life." As we saw in our analysis of a human and a human's life, a human like any other living being needs oxygen to breathe, water to drink, and food to eat. She also needs Earth's other resources to survive. It is the fine co-working of Earth's atmosphere, its Flora—the entire plant life, and its Fauna—the entire animal life which fulfills a human's needs for these things. Also, we saw a close connection amid the Earth's atmosphere, its flora, and its fauna—how each and every living being on the Earth—each plant, and each animal by its very living helps one another to flourish. And how all of them—the Earth with its atmosphere, the entire flora, and the entire fauna—altogether construct the Whole of Life, One close-knit Web in which the entire Life and its all forms subsist and flourish. It was from these scientific facts that I derived the definition of "The Whole of Life."

The Whole of Life is the second bigger Sub-Whole of a human's "U"—the world outside her (a human). "The Whole of Life is the Earth enclosed within its veil of atmosphere, with its entire Flora—acres of greenery on its lands and inside its oceans—and its entire Fauna—trillions of flying beings in its air, trillions of crawling and walking beings on it lands, and trillions of swimming beings in its waters—where humanity is a thin streak of walking beings on it lands amid multitudes of other crawling and walking beings." It is The Whole of Life which nurtures the Human Whole in its lap.

A human is affected by the Whole of Life, and she affects it too by her own actions.

The third Sub-Whole of a human's "U"—the world outside a human—is the Universe. As per the Sciences of Physics and Astronomy, the Earth housing the Whole of Life is a part of the bigger Whole—our Solar System. Our Earth moves around our Sun, takes its sunshine and energy, with which it nurtures its Whole of Life. There are seven other planets moving around the Sun. All of them altogether form our Solar System. Our Solar System, in turn, is a part of the bigger Whole—our Galaxy, the Milky Way. Our Sun moves around the Center Sun of our Galaxy with millions of other solar systems' Suns moving around the same Center of our Galaxy. Our Galaxy, the Milky Way, in turn, is a part of the bigger Whole—a Cluster. The Center Sun of our Galaxy—Milky Way moves around the Center Sun of our Cluster, with millions of other galaxies' Suns moving around the Center of our Cluster. Our Cluster, in turn, is a part of the bigger Whole—the Super Cluster—the biggest of all. The Center Sun of our Cluster moves around the Center Sun of the Super Cluster, with millions of other clusters' suns moving around the Center Sun of the Super Cluster.

This is the Universe—one verse, one song, a highly organized collection of all physical bodies moving around one single center—the Center of the Super Cluster. This is the third biggest Sub-Whole of a human's "U"—the world outside a human.

A human is a creation of the Universe. She is affected by it, and she affects it too by her own actions.

This is "U": the world outside a human, neatly divided in three Sub Wholes—"The Human Whole," "The Whole of Life," and "the Universe," with one Sub-Whole merging into another, and all together forming a human's Whole.

Combining these two letters "Ahm"—"I," and "U"—the world outside me creates the word Om. Thus Om is The Whole. When a human says "Om," the word *Om* includes within it her "Ahm"—"I", her basic human identity— "I am a human," and her deep Self/ Soul—"I am a Soul"; and her "U"—the world outside her as neatly divided in three Sub-Wholes of "my Human Whole—a network of my Family, Society, Country, Humanity, and our Cumulative Achievements in all aspects of the human life"; my "Whole of Life—the Earth enclosed within its veil of atmosphere, with its Flora—acres of greenery on its lands and inside its oceans, and its Fauna—trillions of flying beings in its airs, trillions of crawling and walking beings on its lands, and trillions of swimming beings in its oceans, where humanity is just a thin streak of walking beings on its lands"; and "my Universe—our Earth moving around the Sun with seven other planets moving around the Sun— our Solar System, our Sun moving around the Center Sun of our Galaxy— the Milky Way with millions of other solar systems' Suns moving around it (the center of our galaxy), the Center Sun of our Galaxy moving around the Center Sun of our Cluster with millions of other galaxies' Suns moving around it (the center of our Cluster), and the Center Sun of our Cluster moving around the Center Sun of the Super-Cluster with millions of other Clusters' Suns moving around it (the Center of the Super-Cluster), All moving around one single Center. This is the Center of the Whole as well as the Center of each and every entity in the Whole. This is my Center too residing in the deepest depth of my "Ahm"—"I"—my Self/Soul.

Thus Om is The Whole. There is nothing which is outside Om. The word Om said by a human envelops both—her "Ahm"—"I," and her "U"—All other than I—the entire world outside her.

Om—The Whole, is a Truth, a Truth not only verified by sciences, by sages' and mystics' personal experiences and my own personal experience, but also a Truth that a human can access, and feel one with by meditating upon Om.

Meditation upon Om

It is not enough to merely know a truth. Living a truth is as important as knowing a truth. The derivative Right Way of Living from the Truth of "Om—The Whole" is to meditate upon Om. Meditating upon Om helps a human internalize the Truth of "Om—The Whole," feel the power and potential of being a human individual; feel the vastness and richness of her Whole; feel the depth and purity of her Soul; feel one with her Soul, The Super Soul, and The Whole. It is a total experience of extreme spiritual richness and purity. Also, daily practice of "Om Meditation" makes a human healthy, happy, and joyous from within.

To meditate upon something is to focus completely upon it, reflect upon it, contemplate upon it, and be one with it.

"Om—The Whole" is a mental concept, a totally novel way for a human to view herself, "Ahm," "I"—as a human and as a soul—and to view her "U"—the world outside her as neatly organized in three Sub-Wholes of the "Human Whole," "The Whole of Life," and "The Universe." In Om meditation, the Meditator starts from herself as the Center—"Ahm"—"I am a human," then views her "U"—the world outside her as three gradually increasing Sub-Wholes of "The Human Whole," "The Whole of Life," and "The Universe" around her, and then comes back to her "Ahm"—her inner Self—her Soul, her own Center, and the Center of The Whole. This is how the Meditator builds the concept of "Om—The Whole" in her mind, and meditates upon it.

The First two steps of Om meditation are Concept-building meditation. In the first step, the Meditator meditates in detail upon each separate aspect of "Om—The Whole": first, Ahm—I am a human; then, First "U"—my Human Whole; Second "U"—my Whole of Life; Third "U"—the Universe; and then "Ahm"—I am a Soul, all into one count of O..m.. on her finger. The Meditator does five counts of this. Doing so helps the Meditator build the concept of "Om—The Whole" in her mind.

Then, in the Second step, the Meditator combines all distinct aspects of "Om—The Whole" into one and meditates upon the total concept of Om—The Whole, all into one count of the word O..m... The Meditator does 15 counts of this. By now the Meditator gets a strong concept of Om—The Whole in her mind.

Om is a primordial word. The word "Om" contains within it "Ahm"— "I"—the basic Self of an entity, and her "U"—the world outside her. When a human says O..m, the word Om originates from her Center—her deep eternal Self—"Ahm," goes all the way out—"(ah)U..(nasal O..)," and comes back to the same Center—"M" of Ahm—Ou..m.. It is at her Center—her Soul, that a human is connected to The Center—the PowerPoint of the Whole—the Super Soul. As proved in my discussion on Truth, in Reality, the Whole—the entire universe—exists and moves in the form of pure conscious energy. The Whole inside a human moves in the form of her breath. A human's breath is pure, conscious energy containing within it, and moving within it her feelings and thoughts. When a human says "O..m..," her voice contains her breath in it—the Whole's conscious, moving energy in it, rising from her Center and the Center of The Whole. Saying a long slow O..m.., and focusing upon the sound of it is like focusing on the movement of The Whole inside her.

In the Third step of Om meditation, the Meditator says a long, slow "O..m..," and focuses her entire attention on the sound of the word *O..m..* —its rise from her Center—Ah(m), its pitch, its tone—(Ah)U.. (nasal Ou...), and its fall back to her center—M..of her Ahm. Doing so helps the Meditator align to the Pre-Existing Truth of "Om-The Whole"—its pure, conscious energy moving inside her the O...m way. The Meditator does 15 counts of this.

Om exists. Om is The Prime Truth that exists by itself. As defined in my earlier discussion on Truth, The Whole (the Entire Universe with all beings in it) exists in the form of pure, conscious energy, moving the O..m.. way—All originating from one single Center—the PowerPoint of the Whole—Ah(m), going all the way out—"(ah)U..," and coming back to the same Center—"M" of Ahm. This Center, the PowerPoint of the Whole, resides in the deepest depth of every entity (a human too) as her basic, eternal Self—her Soul—"Ahm"—"I."

In the Fourth step of Om meditation, The Meditator remembers this Prime Truth of Om—"It is from *Me* that All originates and it is into *Me* that All comes back"—and combines this Truth with the concept of "Om—The Whole," and the sound of Om. While saying a long slow O..m.., she remembers and mentally visualizes the concept of Om—The Whole: her Self—Ahm—I—and her "U"—the world outside her—as All originating from her own Center—the Center of The Whole—Ah(m), going out— (ah)U..., and coming back to her Center—M... of (Ahm)—All bound and moving within one word O..m... Thus she tries to access the vastness and finesse of the Whole moving inside her in the sound of the word O..m. Because that is how The Whole moves. The Meditator does 15 counts of this.

This is the high point of Om meditation, where the Meditator gets aligned to the movement of "Om—The Whole" inside her, its flow, and its blissful energy, and feels one with it—The Whole, and her Soul. Feeling one with Om—The Whole and its inner flow—is like sipping nectar for your soul. Its sheer purity, perfection, and divinity are inexplicable. At times during meditation you may just happen to pass by this flow and not be able to get into it. Even that feeling is like passing by a canal of nectar— a route of extreme purity, beauty and divinity, where you just get its glimpse and a little fragrance.

If done Right—in the manner prescribed above, the Meditator gets set in the conduit of Om —The Whole moving inside her the O..m.. way.

In the Fifth—final step of Om meditation, the Meditator tries to remain in the conduit of Om—The Whole, and enjoys its bliss. Reaching this high point in Om meditation is very hard. It requires extreme concentration and years of daily practice. Only a true Seeker can take this path, and reach this point in her soul's evolution, and feel its bliss and purity.

Technique of Om Meditation

Meditation upon Om is a 40 minute exercise to be done preferably twice a day, once in the morning and once in the evening, and only on an empty stomach.

As the Earth has its own Center and gravity, so does a human. Every human has her own Center and gravity. Meditation upon Om connects a human to her Center—her Soul, the PowerPoint of The Whole—the Supreme Soul—balances her, energizes her for the day with the Whole's blissful energy, and makes her healthy, happy, and joyous from within.

Posture

The Meditator sits cross-legged in a Lotus posture by plac-ing her right foot above her left thigh, and her left foot above her right thigh. Sitting this way, her both feet encircle her center and help her to keep it steady. Then she places her both hands in the center of her both feet, with her left hand placed above her right hand, with both hands touching and pressing the lower part of her center (This is the point where her Self/Soul is located.) She does all counting on her left-hand fingers, counting one "Om" on her each finger joint. She starts the count from the first, lowest joint of her left hand little finger and ends the count at the lowest joint of her left hand thumb. Lotus posture is a hard but ideal pos-ture for meditation. It helps the Meditator access her Center. If The Meditator finds it too hard, she can choose to sit in a simple cross-legged posture with her both hands placed on the lower part of her Center. But the ideal posture is lotus posture.

Figure 5

Om Meditation Posture

Breath

As I said earlier, The Whole inside a human moves in the form of her breath. Her breath is the thread by which she is connected to her Center, and the Center of The Whole. During Om meditation when the Meditator says the word O..m, it contains her breath in it. Her *Ou...* is going out of her breath from her Center, and her *M...* is coming in of her breath back to her Center. By Law as much goes out, as much ought to come in; hence as long the *Ou...*, as long is the *M...* The Meditator says a long *Ou...*, then as long an *M...* This *M...* takes the Meditator directly back to her Center—"M" of her "Ahm." It is at *M*—the end of the word O..m— that the Meditator pauses, inhales deeply from her Center, then says her next word O..m. It is important that at this point the Meditator inhales very deeply, so that she can say a long O..m...

Thus, The Meditator controls, regulates, and makes her breath move the O..m way because that is how The Whole is moving—O..m way. And at every O..m she comes closer to her Center, and inhales and exhales from there. This is the purpose of Om meditation—to access your Center, the Center of The Whole, and get into the flow of "Om—The Whole" inside you.

By the end of Om meditation, The Meditator gets set in the conduit of O..m, which is The Whole moving the O..m way inside The Meditator in the form of her breath. It is within her breath that The Meditator feels the sheer finesse, purity, and perfection of The Whole.

During Om meditation, The Meditator, together with the concept of "Om—The Whole" ought to focus part of her attention on her breath too. Because, it is her breath through which she accesses her Center, and it is her breath into where she feels her connection to The Whole.

Meditation upon Om is a deep meditative exercise that requires complete silence and solitude. The Meditator seeks a solitary place, and sits cross-legged on the floor in the Lotus posture. She keeps an alarm clock near her and sets an alarm for 40 minutes. The Meditator must time her meditation and say each O..m.. as prescribed.

Meditation upon Om is a five-step exercise with one step leading to another and finally all culminating in the Meditator's being centered on her Center, feeling one with her Soul, and The Whole. If done Right and with complete concentration, it is at the final step, that the Meditator in her breath gets aligned with the Pre-Existing conduit of Om—The Whole and its moving conscious energy inside her. If she catches its current and remains in it, she feels the sheer, blissful energy of the Whole bathing her entire being.

Sitting in a Lotus posture with her both hands placed below her center, as prescribed above, the Meditator starts her Om meditation.

First Step: Concept Building of "Om—The Whole" (5 Counts)

The First five counts of separate Concept meditation help The Meditator build a mental concept of each aspect of Om—The Whole: First, her *"Ahm"*—"I"— as a human self, then her *"U"*—the world outside her as neatly organized in three Sub-Wholes: "The Human Whole," "The Whole of Life," and "The Universe," and at the end her "Ahm" as her deep eternal Self—her Soul—her own Center, and the Center of the Whole.

The Meditator sitting in a cross-legged posture with her eyes closed, counts one on the bottom joint of her left hand's little finger by her left hand thumb, and says a long, slow "Aham…" While saying "Aham..," the Meditator remembers her human self as "I am Jane (her/his first name), a human woman (or a man as applicable)—Evolved, Multi-dimensional, and a Part of The Whole." Thus she gets a mental concept of herself as a human individual.

Then in this same count of one on her finger, the Meditator says her first "U…" While saying a long slow "U..," the Meditator remembers (says in her mind), and mentally visualizes her first "U"—her immediate outside world—as "my Human Whole—a network of my Family—my First Family, my Second Family; my Society—people I live amid, and work with; my Country—USA (name of the Country where the Meditator lives); my Humanity—some 200 countries with their 7 billion humans; and our Cumulative Achievements in all aspects of the human life ranging from a needle to an airplane, from a thatch-roof hut to a skyscraper, our cities, our monuments, our libraries, each and everything we humans have ever achieved on the face of this Earth." While saying "U..," and remembering the definition of the Human Whole in her mind, the Meditator mentally visualizes each aspect of her Human Whole around her—her Family—as a group of people related to her by blood and by marriage; her Society as a bigger group of humans among whom she lives and works with; her Country as a bigger group of millions of humans; and her Humanity as the biggest group of billions of humans around her with their Cumulative Achievements spread amidst them in the form of a needle, a plane, dazzling cities, some world famous monuments like Eiffel Tower, Statue of Liberty, the Taj mahal; books etc.

This is hard. The Meditator, while saying "U..," has to focus her entire attention on the definition of the Human Whole and imagine its each aspect around her. It requires good memory, concentration, and imaginative ability. But it is quite enjoyable too—to feel the vastness of The Human Whole around her and her connection to it.

After finishing her first "U"—The Human Whole, the Meditator pauses, inhales deeply, and then remembers her second "U"—The Whole of Life—that houses her as a human, and her entire Human Whole in its lap. In the same count of One, on the bottom joint of her left's hand little finger, the Meditator says her second "U..." While saying a long, slow "U..," she remembers (says in her mind), and mentally visualizes her second "U.."—"The Whole of Life" (see figure # 4, The Whole of Life) as "my Human Whole nestles in the lap of the Whole of Life. My Whole of Life is the vast blue-green Earth with its Flora—acres of greenery on its lands and inside its oceans; and its Fauna—trillions of flying beings in its air, trillions of crawling and walking beings on its lands, and trillions of swimming beings in its oceans, where our entire humanity is just a thin streak of walking beings on its lands." While remembering so, and focusing her entire attention on the Whole of Life, the Meditator mentally visualizes the picture of the Whole of Life as a vast, blue, green Earth with an expanse of greenery on its lands and inside its oceans, with vast flocks of colorful birds in its airs, with multitudes of crawling and walking beings on its lands—like snakes and lizards, elephants, lions, and humans— with trillions of swimming beings in its oceans, such as big and small swarms of colorful fishes in its waters; and amid all this, the entire humanity as a thin streak of walking beings on its lands. Doing so gives the Meditator a mental picture of the Whole of Life, and her and humanity's place in it. Thus the Meditator finishes her second "U"—The Whole of Life.

At the end of her second "U..," the Meditator pauses, inhales deeply.

Then, in the same count of One on her left hand's little finger, the Meditator remembers her Third "U"—the Universe that houses her, her Human Whole, and her Whole of Life—and All inside it. While saying a long, slow "U.." the Meditator (with her eyes closed) remembers the definition of the Universe, and mentally visualizes it as "my Earth moving around our Sun—our Solar System; our Solar system moving around the Center of our Galaxy; our Galaxy moving around the Center of our Cluster; and our Cluster moving around the Center Sun of the Super-Cluster—All moving around one Center—this is Universe." While saying so, the Meditator in her mind tries to see the picture of each aspect of the Universe—our Earth, our Solar System, our Galaxy—the Milky Way, our Cluster, and the Super Cluster—all moving around one Center. Thus the Meditator finishes meditating upon her third "U"—the Universe. At the end of the third "U," the Meditator pauses, and inhales deeply.

Still counting One on the bottom joint of her left hand's little finger by her left hand thumb, the Meditator then says her Second "Aham," and remembers her deep Self—her Soul— her own Center, and the Center of the Whole. While saying a long slow "Aham...," she remembers and mentally visualizes her deep Self—her Soul as, "I am a soul. My soul is my deepest Self, located in the Center of my body, a little below my navel, containing my deepest memories, attachments, and desires of all my previous lives and this life too—my own center, and the Center of the Whole." While remembering so she gazes inward, pauses at "M..," and focuses her entire attention on her inner Self—her Soul as a point in the center of her body a little below her navel—her own Center, and the Center of The Whole.

This completes one count of meditating upon each distinct aspect of Om —The Whole. In this one count of "O..m," the Meditator starts from herself in the Center as a human, remembers her first "Ahm,"—"I am a human"; then her "U,"—the world outside her as neatly organized in three Sub-Wholes of "The Human Whole," "The Whole of Life," and "The Universe"; and then comes back to herself in her center, remembers her second "Ahm"—her deep, eternal Self—her own Center, and the Center of The Whole—The Universe. This is "Om —The Whole" containing a human in the Center, and her Whole—her entire outside world in one word of O..m.

The Meditator does five counts of this step of Om meditation, counting on her left hand's fingers by her left hand thumb in the manner prescribed above.

Doing so for five counts—remembering and mentally visualizing each aspect of "Om—The Whole"—her Human Self, her entire outside world, and her Soul Self creates a mental picture and a clear concept of each aspect of "Om—The Whole" in the Meditator's mind. This is the First—concept building phase of Om meditation. Now the Meditator has a clear concept of "Om—The Whole" in her mind.

Next, the Meditator starts the 2nd phase of Om meditation—meditating upon one single concept of "Om—The Whole."

Second Step: Meditating upon the Single Concept of "Om—The Whole" (15 counts)

After finishing five counts of separate "Ahm" and "U" meditation, the Meditator then meditates upon the total concept of Om—the Whole—all into one word O..m... In this phase, she combines all three distinct aspects of Om—The Whole, i.e.,

Ahm—I am a human; U—my Human Whole, my Whole of Life, and my Universe; and Ahm—I am a Soul—all into one single concept of "Om—The Whole"; remembers and mentally visualizes a summary of its each aspect, and the total.

The Meditator, sitting with her eyes closed, starts a fresh count of Om on the bottom joint of her left hand's little finger by her left hand thumb. She counts One, and says a long, slow "O..m..." While saying O..m.., she remembers each distinct Concept of Om—The Whole, as built in her first step of Om meditation, and mentally visualizes it. She starts from herself as the Center; says "Ou...," remembers, "Aham—I am a human—Evolved, Multi-Dimensional, and a Part of The Whole"; views herself as a human woman (or a man as applicable) sitting; then remembers her First "U" as "my Human Whole—a network of my family, society, country, humanity, and our cumulative achievements," mentally views the picture of the Human Whole as some seven billion humans around her with their cumulative Achievements spread amid them. She then remembers her second "U"—The Whole of Life, and says to herself, "My Whole of Life is the vast Earth with its flora and fauna." Saying so, she mentally visualizes the picture of the Whole of Life as the blue green Earth with its entire flora and fauna, with a thin row of humans amid its fauna. Then she remembers her Third "U,"—The Universe, as "My Earth, all stars and planets—moving around One Single Center." The Meditator then comes back to herself, M..; remembers her Ahm—her Soul—as, "I am a soul. My soul is my deepest Self located in the center of my body, a little below my navel, containing my deepest memories, attachments and desires of my all previous lives and this life too—my own Center and the Center of the Whole."

Thus in one word of O..m.., the Meditator remembers each of these concepts and its mental picture: first "Ahm"—I am a human; then "U"— my Human Whole, the Whole of Life, our Solar System, Galaxy, Cluster, Super-Cluster—the Universe; and last, her Ahm—I am a Soul. While doing so the Meditator links each distinct concept of "Om—The Whole" to the other in one order and creates one single concept of "Om—The Whole" in her mind, starting from herself as the Center—Ah(m)—I am a human; viewing her "U"—the outside world as her Human Whole, The Whole of life, and The Universe; and then coming back to herself in the Center—(Ah)m—I am a soul—my own Center and the Center of the Whole—all in one count of one word O..m...

The Meditator does 15 counts of this, meditating upon one single concept of Om—The Whole—all in one word of O..m... After saying every O..m.., at M, the Meditator mentally says to herself, "I pause at my center," feels a short pause, and then says, "Inhale," inhales deeply from her center, and then says her next O..m...

This phase is hard—harder than the First Phase of Concept building meditation—but is highly enjoyable and mentally challenging too. The Meditator has to say a long, slow O..m.., remember each distinct aspect of Om—The Whole in quick succession, and focus on it. This requires good memory, imagination, and extreme concentration.

Third step: Meditating Upon the Sound of the Word Om (15 counts)

After doing 15 counts of "Om—The Whole" Concept meditation, the Meditator by now gets a clear concept of Om—The Whole in her mind. Next, the Meditator meditates upon the sound of the word O..m.. as she says it.

O..m.. is an eternal sound. As proved in my discussion on "Truth," The Whole in its prime make exists in the form of pure conscious energy and moves the O..m.. way—all originating from one Center, Ah(m), going out "(Ah)U..," and coming back to the same Center—"M.." of Ahm. This is the Center of The Whole as well as the Center of each and every entity in the Whole, located in the deepest depth of an entity's Self—her Soul. The Whole inside an entity moves in the form of her breath, which is pure conscious energy. It is by her breath that an entity is connected to her own Center and the Center of The Whole.

Similarly, The Whole inside the Meditator moves in the form of her breath. When the Meditator says, "O..m..," the word *Om* arises from the Center of the Meditator—Ah(m), goes all the way out—O(u)..., and comes back to the same Center of the Meditator—M... of Ahm. Also, speech and breath are interconnected. When you speak something, your speech contains your breath in it. The Whole inside the Meditator moves in the form of her breath as pure conscious energy. When the Meditator says, "O..m.." the word "O..m.." contains her breath in it, is modulated by her breath, and modulates her breath too.

After having done 15 counts of Single Concept of Om meditation, the Meditator pauses, and remembers (mentally says to herself), "The Whole inside me moves in the form of my breath. When I say the word *Om* and focus on it, this is like focusing on the movement of The Whole inside me. I will say the word *O..m..*, focus on its rise from my center—Ahm, its pitch, its tone—Ou..., and its fall back to my center—"M." After having remembered so, the Meditator starts her Sound Meditation.

In Sound Meditation, the Meditator counts One on her left hand's little finger by her left hand thumb, says a long slow

"O..m.." While saying "O..m.." the Meditator focuses her entire attention on the sound of the word "*O..m..*"—its rise from her Center—(Ah)m, its pitch, its tone—Ou...; then its fall back to her Center—M... of Ahm—its whole movement. By law, as much goes out as much ought to come in. Hence as long the *Ou...* as long is the *M...* By doing so the Meditator gets connected to her Center—Ahm, The Center—the PowerPoint of the Whole, follows the movement of The Whole moving inside her in the form of her breath, and tries to align to the movement of The Whole which is moving the "O..m.." way inside her.

Focusing upon the sound of the word *O..m* is like focusing on the movement of The Whole inside her. The meditator does 15 counts of Sound meditation, counting each "O..m.." on her left hand's fingers by her left hand thumb, pauses after every O..m.., says to herself, "I pause at my center," inhales deeply, and then says her next word O..m... While doing so, the Meditator feels the sheer finesse and perfection of the Whole's movement in the Sound of the word O..m.. inside her.

Fourth Step: Meditating upon the Prime Truth of Om—The Whole (15 counts)

After finishing 15 counts of sound meditation, The Meditator then starts the Fourth Step of Om meditation. During this phase the Meditator meditates upon the Prime Truth of Om—"It is from *Me* that All—The Whole originates, and it is into *Me* that All—The Whole comes back." As defined in my discussion on "Truth," The Whole originates from one Center—Ah(m), goes out "O(u)..," and comes back to the same Center—M of Ahm. This is the Center of The Whole, the Center of each and every entity in the Whole, and the Center of The Meditator too.

In this step of Om meditation, the Meditator combines the concept of "Om—The Whole" and the Sound of the word *Om* with this Prime Truth of Om. The Meditator sitting with her eyes closed, starts a fresh count of One on the bottom joint of her left hand's little finger by her left hand thumb, and says a long slow "O..m..." While saying "O..m.." the Meditator remembers (says mentally to herself) and mentally visualizes the concept of Om—The Whole: First, her Ahm: "I am Jane—a human woman (or a man and his name as applicable); then, "U...—My Human Whole, My whole of Life, and the Universe; All this— the entire moving Universe originating from my Center— Ah(m), All going out within O(u)..; and All coming back to my Center—M..—All bound and moving within one word—*O..m...*" While saying and remembering so, the Meditator tries to see a quick mental picture of each one: first herself as a human woman (or a man as applicable) in the center; then her Human Whole as a very large number—some 7 billion humans around her with their Cumulative achievements spread amid them, then her Whole of Life as the vast Earth with its blue oceans, green lands and its fauna, then the Universe as all stars and planets moving around One Center—All this arising from her center, Ah(m), going out—Ou.., and All coming back to her center—M of her Ahm, all within one word Om. Also, while remembering so the Meditator also tries to focus on the sound of the word *O..m..*, and her breath because it is within her breath that the pure conscious energy of the Whole is moving the *O..m..* way.

This finishes one count of one word of *O..m*. The Meditator does 15 counts of this—meditating upon the Prime Truth of Om, counting each O..m.. on her left hand's fingers by her left hand thumb.

During this phase of Om meditation, the Meditator fully equipped with the Concept and Truth of Om, tries to access the flow of Om—The Whole—The Pre-existing Truth that moves inside her in the form of her breath. Accessing its flow and getting into the flow of the Whole is very hard—hard to access and harder to hold. But even if you just happen to pass by it, you feel as if you passed by a stream of pure nectar which you just got a fragrance of, which you just glimpsed by. And if you manage to get into the flow, be one with it, you feel connected to your Center—the Center of the Whole, feel the flow of the Whole inside you, and feel such an inner surge of sheer bliss and energy bathing your whole being. For your deep Self—your Soul—this is like dipping into the nectar of The Whole. Its sheer perfection, purity and bliss are inexplicable. This is the high point of Om meditation. Reaching this point is very hard. It takes complete concentration and years of daily practice of "Om meditation."

Fifth and Final Step: Meditating Upon the Conduit of "Om—The Whole" (15 Counts)

If done Right—in the manner prescribed above—the Meditator by now gets set into the Conduit of Om—The Whole moving inside her the O..m way. Remember, Om is the Conduit, the Capsule within which the Whole moves. Next, the Meditator does 15 counts of saying the word O..m. The Meditator counts one on the bottom joint of her left hand's little finger by her left hand thumb, says a long, slow O..m.., and focuses her entire attention on the word "O..m.."—its rise from her Center, Ah(m), its all the way going up, Ou.., and its coming back to her Center, "M.." (of Ahm). During this phase she does not think about anything—no mental visualization, no image. Thus she enjoys the bliss of being inside the conduit of Om—The Whole, where there is no form; there is only pure conscious, divine energy moving inside her the O..m.. way. At the end of the word O..m.., at M, the

Meditator pauses, inhales deeply, and then says her next word O..m.. The Meditator does 15 counts of this—saying O..m.., and trying to remain inside the conduit of Om—The Whole, The Prime Truth.

If well set, its bliss is such that your eyes don't open, and you don't want to get out of it.

After the 15th count, at the end of Om meditation, the Meditator opens her eyes, then her both legs, rubs her both thighs from her knees upward, places her both feet on the floor, rubs her both legs from her knees downward to her feet, and then rubs her both feet. Then the Meditator stretches her both legs long, leans back on her both hands, and ponders on the Prime Truth of Om—The Whole, which exists and moves inside her in the form of pure conscious energy: All arising from her Center—Ah(m), going out—U...; and All coming back to her Center—M... of her Ahm—All bound and moving within one word of O..m. The Meditator sits in this posture for two minutes. Sitting so allows the blood flow freely to her both legs and down to her feet, which most probably are numb and asleep by this time. (Mine still do this after years of daily practice.) Sitting in a Lotus posture is hard. After two minutes of relaxing, at this point, the alarm clock should beep. This completes 40 minutes of Om meditation.

A Word of Caution

Meditation upon Om is a hard process. It is hard to sit in a cross-legged Lotus posture with a straight backbone for 40 minutes. It is hard to remember the Concept of "Om—The Whole," mentally visualize it, and focus on it constantly. It is harder to stay focused on the sound of the word *Om* and inside its conduit. It requires intense physical discipline, pinpoint mental concentration, and good imaginative ability. But its effects are stupendous.

Effects of Om Meditation

Meditation upon Om is a true *Yoga*. *Yoga* is a Sanskrit word that means "union of one's body, mind, and soul into one." In Om meditation, the Meditator sits in a cross-legged Lotus posture with a straight backbone, which centers her physically. When she says "*O..m..*," the word *Om* originates from her Center—her physical Center and her eternal and Spiritual center too. It entails her "Ahm"—her Prime, basic ego—her deep Self, her Soul, and the Super Soul. It also entails her remembering the Concept of Om—The Whole, mentally visualizing it, and focusing upon it. Thus meditating upon Om—The Whole unites the Meditator's body, mind, and soul into one.

Since the word *Om* originates from the Center of the Meditator, saying "Om" balances her physically and mentally. After meditating upon Om for 40 minutes, you emerge as a more balanced and centered person.

Meditating upon Om orders your breathing. Saying a long, slow "O...m..." makes you breathe long and deep. It makes the Meditator access her Center—the Origin Point of her breath, and makes her breathe from there. That is the Source of one's breath—one's life energy. Also, it helps one access and get into the flow of the Whole's energy. This is like partaking from the Whole's divine and creative energy. Consequently it makes the Meditator feel blissful, energetic, and creative throughout the day.

Meditating upon Om is food for the Meditator's human spirit and her Soul. "Ahm—I am a human" reminds her of her individual human identity and the immense power and potential of being a human; "U— my Human Whole," "The Whole of Life," and my "Universe" gives her a vast, neat, and orderly worldview. It satisfies her human spirit. And the last "Ahm—I am a soul" reminds her of her deep Eternal Self—her Soul. Meditation upon Om makes a human view herself as an individual, as well as makes her relate to the whole world and see her place in it. It connects her to her deep, eternal Self—her Soul—The Whole, and its constantly flowing divine, conscious energy inside her. It satisfies her from within and makes her joyous from within.

Daily practice of Om meditation for 40 minutes makes you feel balanced, energetic, and deeply joyous. It ought to be done twice a day, once in the morning and once in the evening, but if not possible, once a day is a minimum and a must.

The Second Truth of Om: "Om is the Prime Energy Channel within Which The Whole Moves," and Its Derivative Right Way of Living

The Whole is moving.

As defined in my discussion on "Truth," the Whole (the entire universe with All things in it) in its prime form exists and moves as pure conscious energy—All arising from one Center—"Ah(m)"; going out—"Ou."; and coming back to the same Center—"M" of Ahm. This is the Center of The Whole, the very PowerPoint from whom All come into being and into whom All go back. This PowerPoint is Conscious, is the Center of The Whole, as well as the Conscious Center—Ahm—deep Self and Soul of each and every entity in the Whole. This is your Center and my Center too.

The Whole moves within the Channel of Om—All arising from one Center, Ah(m)—(my own Center), going out "Ou...," and coming back to my same Center—"M" of Ahm. Thus Om is the Conduit within which The Whole's Conscious energy moves.

Now the Center of the Whole is my Center too. In the deepest depth of my Self—my Soul, there resides this point at which I am connected to this PowerPoint—the Center of The Whole. Since The Whole exists and moves in the form of pure, conscious energy, The Whole inside me moves in the form of my breath. My breath is pure conscious energy. My breath gives me life, energizes me, and contains my feelings and thoughts within it. My pattern of breathing directly affects the quality of my feelings and thoughts, and the quality of my feelings and thoughts directly affects my pattern of breathing. Since The Whole is moving the "O..m.." way, if I breathe by O..m.., I can align the movement of my breath with the movement of The Whole; I can align the movement of my conscious energy with the movement of The Whole's conscious energy; I can align the movement of my consciousness with the consciousness of The Whole. Also, as we will see, when I breathe by Om, I breathe from my Center: my breath starts from my Center, Ahm, goes out Ou.., and comes back to my Center, "M" of Ahm. This connects me to my Center and the Center of The Whole. Being connected to my Center keeps me grounded and makes me calm, balanced, and joyous.

Breathing by Om

A human's breath is in three parts – Inhale, Retain, and Exhale. Inhaling is a process by which a human draws in fresh air—oxygen that enlivens and invigorates her body. Retaining is a short pause during which a human holds the inhaled fresh air—oxygen inside her lungs. And, by exhaling, a human throws out carbon dioxide—stale, toxic air—from her body.

The quality of our breath directly affects our health, feelings, and thoughts, and in turn is affected by them too. We humans breathe anyway, often without being conscious of it at all. Our breathing is mostly diffused where both inhaling and exhaling are mixed up. When anxious, we tend to breathe shallow, and take short breaths. Such shallow, broken breathing ill-affects our health, and leads to broken consciousness—fragmented feelings and thoughts, and lack of focus. A human ought to breathe long, deep, and in one breath, where her both inhaling and exhaling are distinct with a pause in between. Breathing this way keeps a human calm, alert, and healthy.

Breathing by Om is an Art, a symphony of one breath where you exhale from your Center while saying a silent "O..m..," pause at "M" at your inner Center, feel your Center, and then inhale from your Center. Breathing this way keeps your both inhaling and exhaling distinct with a pause in between. Also, when you breathe by Om, you try to align your breath with the movement of The Whole's conscious energy inside you that moves the O..m.. way.

Breathing by O..m is an Achievement—a Sagelike mental state. When you come to this stage, you breathe naturally by O..m.. all the time; you breathe from your Center, "Ahm," are connected with your Center—your Soul—the Center of The Whole, partaking the Whole's energy and consciousness from it, and if perfected, you feel one with the Whole and its conscious energy all the time. Your consciousness becomes a part of The Whole's consciousness. You feel calm, serene, and joyous from within, and you are alert—totally aware of your surroundings too.

This stage can be partially reached by breathing by Om exercise. Breathing by Om is an early morning exercise. It supplies your body with plenty of fresh air, oxygen, energizes you, strengthens your breathing organs, and makes you aware of what it means to breathe by Om—the oneness of your breath, its purity and serenity, and its immense energy flowing throughout your whole body. Breathing by Om exercise invigorates you for the day. But throughout the day it is important that you maintain your state of breathing by Om—a calm and serene mind. You achieve this by living by asking yourself constantly, "What am I doing?" "What am I feeling?" "What am I thinking?" and the rest of the time saying a silent O..m to yourself. Since your breathing and consciousness are interconnected, living this way helps you order and organize your consciousness which in turn orders your breathing too. Also, doing 300 *japas* of Om thrice a day brings the flow of your consciousness back to yourself, orders your consciousness, and thus orders your breathing too. Practicing all of these three help one breathe by Om, and make her feel calm, healthy, and alert.

In the next few pages I will discuss each of these 3 techniques in detail.

1. Breathe by Om Exercise

Breathing is vital to human life. You breathe and you live. The quality of your breath directly affects your physical and mental health. It is by breathing that you inhale oxygen which is required for the overall running of your body and brain, and it is by breathing that you exhale carbon dioxide, a gas toxic to your body and brain. As proved by medical studies, poor breathing leads to premature ageing, heart disease, cancer, stroke, and many other diseases.

Since breathing is conscious energy, the quality of your breath directly affects your feelings and thoughts. A human who breathes in long, deep breaths is often a calm, balanced, and joyous human. And a human who breathes in short, shallow breaths is mostly an anxious, unstable and perturbed human. Thus it is vital that a human breathes the Right way.

A human's breath is in three parts: Inhale, Retain—pause, and Exhale. These three parts altogether compose one full cycle of a human's breath. Each of these parts has its own importance. By inhaling, a human draws in fresh air—oxygen which moving through her nostrils, and from an inner Path, the trachea inside her throat goes to her lungs. Then there is a short pause, during which the Breather retains the inhaled air—oxygen inside her lungs. During this phase the inhaled oxygen gets stored in millions of tiny air sacs called alveoli inside her lungs, to be taken by blood to all parts of her body and brain. Then the breather exhales. By exhaling, the Breather throws out stale, toxic gas— carbon dioxide—from her body. During inhaling, if the Breather releases her stomach, center loose she can take in a lot of fresh air—oxygen. And during exhaling, if the Breather contracts her center, she can throw out the bad air—carbon dioxide strongly. Right breathing requires that you inhale as fully as possible, pause—retain your breath for a while, and then exhale as fully as possible. Doing so requires conscious breathing, strong breathing organs—such as the lungs and diaphragm—and above all, a strong center.

A daily "Breathe by Om exercise" energizes a human, tones and strengthens her breathing organs, and trains her body and mind to breathe by Om. The "Breathe by Om" exercise is my own creation. It came to me as the derivative Right Way of Living from the Second truth of Om. I planned and perfected it further by my thorough study of the subject of human's breathing, by my own daily practice, and many personal and other experiments.

The Breathe by Om exercise is a fine interplay of the three parts of your breath: inhale, retain, and exhale, where you watch your breath, control it, and regulate it to move the O..m way. It is a 35 minute, daily morning exercise that helps a human breathe fully and deeply. It also strengthens one's center and all breathing organs. Above all, the Breathe by Om exercise makes you watch your each breath, feel its movement, and practice breathing in one breath; and gradually brings you to the point where you breathe by Om in one full breath—exhaling from your Center, Ah(m)—Ou..; stopping at your center, "M" of Ahm, pause, and then inhaling from your Center. In short, you learn to breathe by Om.

The Breathe by Om exercise is performed in three steps. First is the warm-up and Concept-building step, where the breather breathes very slowly and gets a mental concept of "inhaling" fresh air oxygen, "retaining" it inside her lungs, and then "exhaling" dirty, toxic air carbon dioxide from her body. This warms up her breathing organs and gives her a mental concept and feel of each breath and its importance.

In the Second step, the breather does faster strokes of the "exhale-based" exercise in which she first exhales strongly from her both nostrils, pauses, releases her stomach, and then inhales full and deep from her both nostrils. Forceful exhalation in this step helps her throw out the mucus and stale, toxic air carbon dioxide that gets accumulated inside her body. Thus it cleans up her breathing organs. Also, deep inhaling helps her take in plenty of fresh air—oxygen. After a few counts of this exercise, the Breather starts to feel an inner surge of fresh energy inside her lungs and her body.

In the Third Step, the breather practices breathing by Om. She says a long slow "O..m.." silently to herself and exhales with it. At "M" of O..m she stops, feels her center, and then inhales while telling herself, "take the same breath up." It is in this last leg that she starts feeling the oneness and finesse of her breath—the same breath going out from her center as "exhale," and rising from her center as "inhale." By the end of this step, the Breather feels a strong surge of energy—an inner tingling and a movement of fresh air inside her whole body, in her cheeks, very vigorously inside her lungs—from her tip to her toes.

The Breathe by Om exercise must be done after meditation and always on an empty stomach. If done during the day, it should be a minimum of five hours after eating anything.

Technique of Breathe by Om Exercise

The "Breathe by Om" is an early morning exercise that ought to be done in the open space amid nature—on a lawn, in the woods, or by a beach or a riverside, where there is plenty of fresh air oxygen.

This is a timed exercise of 35 minutes. The Breather must use an alarm clock and set the alarm for 35 minutes. The whole exercise is done by counting on one's hand fingers.

The Breather stands straight with her both knees joined together, folds her both arms sideways, and places her both hands on her navel, with her both hands' middle fingers touching each other. The Breather, throughout the whole exercise stands straight in this posture at the same spot, and looks far ahead in the distance at some central point. This is an excellent posture that keeps her backbone straight and her all inner body organs in place, and helps her breathe well and stay focused on her breathing.

Thus the Breather standing straight with an alarm set for 35 minutes starts her "Breathe by Om" exercise.

Step One: Warm-Up and Concept-Building Exercise

This is the First Phase of the Breathe by Om exercise in which the Breather breathes very slowly while mentally visualizing and feeling each breath. This warms up her breathing organs and gives her a mental concept of each breath.

This phase is made of two parts: Part A—breathing by Alternate nostrils, and Part B—breathing by Both nostrils.

Part A: Breathing by Alternate Nostrils

In this Part, the breather breathes by alternate nostrils. First she does Inhale-based exercise in which she starts her every breath by inhaling first. Next, she does Exhale-based exercise in which she starts her every breath by exhaling first.

(i) Inhale-Based Exercise by Alternate Nostrils (15 counts)

The Breather, standing straight with her both arms folded sideways, with her both hands placed on her navel, counts One on the lowest joint of her left hand little finger by her left hand thumb. Then she pulls in the three middle fingers on her right hand, keeping her thumb and little finger out. While counting "One" on her left hand, the Breather, by her right hand thumb presses her right nostril, leaves her belly (stomach) loose, and says quietly (in her mind) to herself, "Inhale fresh air oxygen inside my lungs," and while saying so she inhales from her left nostril. While doing so she mentally visualizes and feels the fresh morning air going inside her lungs. At the end of "inhale," she removes her thumb from her right nostril and says quietly to herself, "Retain fresh air oxygen inside my lungs." While saying so she holds her breath inside her and imagines fresh air oxygen being retained inside her lungs. This is a short pause of a few seconds. After this, she presses her left nostril with her right hand little finger, says to herself, "<u>Contract</u>" and contracts her Center. Then with her contacted center, she says to herself (in her mind), "Exhale toxic air carbon dioxide from my body," and while saying so she <u>exhales</u> strongly through her <u>right nostril</u>. At the end of "Exhale," the Breather <u>counts 1,2,3,4,5</u> in her mind. This gives her a short pause after exhaling. Then the Breather says silently to herself, "<u>Release</u>," and leaves her belly loose. This is one complete cycle of breathing starting from "inhale," then "retain," and ending at "exhale" with each breath accompanied by its own pause.

In the "Breathe by Om" exercise, each cycle of breath is made of six points—<u>inhale, retain, contract, exhale, Count 1,2,3,4,5, then release;</u> and inhale again. They may seem hard in the beginning, but as the Breather practices them, she realizes the importance of each point in breathing. Inhaling with loose belly helps the Breather inhale fresh air full and deep. Retaining strengthens her lungs, making them hold the inhaled air. Exhaling with a contacted center helps the breather throw out toxic air as forcefully and as fully as possible. Counting 1,2,3,4,5 with the contracted center strengthens her center and gives her a pause after "Exhale."

Next, the Breather starts her Second cycle of breathing from her Right nostril. Standing straight with her belly lose, the Breather, still pressing her left nostril with her right hand little finger, counts Two on the middle joint of her left hand little finger by her left hand thumb and says quietly to herself, "inhale fresh air oxygen inside my lungs." While saying so, she <u>inhales</u> deeply from her <u>right nostril</u> and feels fresh air going inside her lungs. Then she says, "<u>Retain</u> fresh air oxygen inside my lungs," holds the inhaled air inside her, and mentally visualizes holding fresh air inside her lungs. At the end of "retain" she says quietly to herself, "contract," presses her right nostril with her thumb, and contracts her center. Then she says to herself, "Exhale toxic air carbon dioxide from my body," and exhales from her left nostril. Then she counts 1,2,3,4,5 in her mind. This completes one full cycle of breathing from her Right nostril.

This is inhale-based alternate breathing where the breather starts her every breath by inhaling first, and breathes from each nostril one by one. The breather does this exercise for 15 counts starting her each count on each "inhale" on her left hand fingers by her left hand thumb. She starts the count on the first—lowest joint of her left hand little finger and ends it at the lowest, last joint of her left hand thumb. (She counts 3 joints on her thumb.)

(ii) Exhale-Based Exercise by Alternate Nostrils (15 Counts)

After finishing her inhale-based exercise, the Breather gives a short pause, leaves her belly lose, and starts exhale-based exercise. In this part, the breather repeats the whole exercise of Part one, except that she starts her each breath by exhaling first.

The Breather, standing straight with her both arms folded sidewise, and with her left hand on her navel, presses her right nostril with her right hand thumb, says quietly to herself, "Contract" and contracts her center. Then she says, "Exhale toxic air carbon dioxide from my body" and exhales from her left nostril. At the end of exhale, she counts 1,2,3,4,5 in her mind. This gives her a short pause after Exhale. Then she removes her thumb, says, "Release" to herself, and leaves her belly lose. Next, she presses her left nostril with her right hand little finger, says, "Inhale fresh air oxygen inside my lungs" to herself, and inhales full and deep from her right nostril. Then she says, "Retain fresh air oxygen inside my lungs" and holds her breath inside her lungs. This is one complete cycle of exhale-based exercise by alternate nostrils.

After retaining her breath for a few seconds, the Breather presses her right nostril with her right hand thumb, says to herself, "Contract," contracts her center, then says, "Exhale toxic air carbon dioxide from my body," and <u>exhales</u> from her <u>left nostril</u>. Thus she repeats the whole exhale-based exercise from her alternate nostrils. The Breather does 15 counts of exhale-based exercise, counting each exhale on her left hand fingers. She starts the count on the lowest joint of her left hand little finger, and ends it at the lowest joint of her left hand thumb. Throughout the whole "Breathe by Om Exercise," the Breather focuses her entire attention on her each breath.

This exercise cleans up her each nostril and the breathing pipe—trachea, lungs, and other breathing organs. Next, the Breather starts her breathing by Both nostrils exercise.

Part B: Breathing by Both Nostrils

Like the previous exercise, this exercise also has two subparts: first, an inhale-based exercise by both nostrils; and, second, an exhale-based exercise by both nostrils with the same six points of each cycle of breathing. This is a 15x1 count exercise in which The Breather counts each individual stroke of 15 on her Right hand fingers and counts the total of 15 strokes as 1 on her Left hand fingers.

(i) Inhale-based exercise by both nostrils (15 Counts)

The Breather, standing straight with her both arms folded sidewise, and with her both hands placed on her navel, counts 1 on the lowest joint of her Left hand little finger by her Left hand thumb to mark the beginning of her "Inhale based exercise." Then she counts 1 on the bottom joint of her Right-hand little finger by her Right-hand thumb, leaves her belly loose, and says quietly to herself, "Inhale fresh air oxygen inside my lungs" and <u>inhales</u> full and deep from her both nostrils. While inhaling so she focuses her entire attention on her breath and feels the fresh morning air going inside her lungs. Then the Breather says to herself, "<u>Retain</u> fresh air oxygen inside my lungs" and holds the inhaled air inside her lungs for a few seconds. During this she feels and imagines the fresh morning air inside her lungs. Next, the Breather says to herself, "<u>Contract,</u>" and contracts her inner center. Then she says, "<u>Exhale</u> toxic air carbon dioxide from my body" and exhales strongly from her both nostrils, imagining the dirty toxic air going out of her body. At the end of "exhale," she <u>counts 1,2,3,4,5</u> in her mind. This gives her a short pause after exhaling. Then, still counting 1 on her Right hand, she says to herself, "<u>Release</u>" and leaves her belly lose. This finishes count one of her one full cycle of breathing.

Next the breather starts the count of 2 on the middle joint of her Right- hand little finger by her Right-hand thumb, and repeats all six points of her next cycle of breathing. Standing with her belly loose, she says to herself, "<u>Inhale</u> fresh air oxygen inside my lungs," inhales full; then says, "<u>Retain</u> fresh air oxygen inside my lungs," holds her breath inside her lungs; then says, "<u>Contract</u>" contracts her center; then says, "<u>Exhale</u> toxic air carbon dioxide from my body," and exhales strongly from her both nostrils; <u>counts 1,2,3,4,5</u>; then says, "<u>Release,</u>" and leaves her belly loose.

Thus the Breather performs 15 counts of "inhale-based exercise by both nostrils" counting each count on her Right-hand fingers. She starts the count on the lowest joint of her Right-hand little finger, and ends the count at the lowest joint of her

Right-hand thumb. Throughout this whole count of 15 on her Right-hand fingers, the Breather keeps holding her Left-hand thumb on the lowest joint of her Left-hand little finger to mark her Inhale-based Exercise.

After finishing 15 counts on her Right hand fingers, the Breather starts her Exhale-based exercise by Both Nostrils. She moves her Left-hand thumb to the middle joint of her Left-hand little finger to mark the start of her "Exhale-based Exercise by both nostrils."

(ii) Exhale-Based Exercise by Both Nostrils (15 counts)

In this part, the Breather repeats all six points of the previous exercise, except that she starts her each breath by exhaling first. The Breather, standing straight with her both arms folded sidewise and both hands placed on her navel, starts a fresh count of one on the lowest joint of her Right-hand little finger. At the count of one, she says, "Contract" to herself, and contracts her inner center. Then with her contracted center, she says to herself, "Exhale toxic air carbon dioxide from my body," and while saying so, exhales strongly from her both nostrils. Then she counts 1,2,3,4,5, in her mind, which gives her a short pause after exhaling. At the end of 5 she says to herself, "Release" and leaves her belly loose. Still counting one with her belly loose, next she says, "Inhale fresh air oxygen inside my lungs" and inhales full and deep from her both nostrils. Then she says, "Retain fresh air oxygen inside my lungs" and holds her breath inside her lungs.

This completes one full cycle of Exhale-based exercise from Both Nostrils. The Breather does 15 counts of this, counting each count at the start of each "Contract" on her Right-hand fingers. She starts the count on the first-lowest joint of her Right-hand little finger, and ends the count on the last—lowest joint of her Right-hand thumb.

At the end of count 15 on her Right hand thumb, the Breather removes her Left had thumb from the middle joint of her Left hand little finger to mark the end of her "Exhale-Based Exercise by Both Nostrils."

Next the Breather starts the second step of "Breathe by Om Exercise."

Step Two: Exhale-based Exercise, Faster Strokes (15x1x5 Counts)

This is the longer step of the Breathe by Om exercise. This is a 15x1x5 counts exercise in which the Breather breathes from her both nostrils by exhaling first, in faster strokes, counting each stroke on her Right hand fingers. The Breather, standing straight, <u>contracts</u> her center, <u>exhales</u>, <u>counts</u> 1,2,3,4,5 (pauses), <u>releases</u> her center, and then <u>inhales</u> deep, and <u>retains</u>. This one full cycle of breathing forms the count of one on her Right hand. The Breather does 15 counts of this exercise, counting all 15 on her Right-hand fingers. At the end of count 15, she counts them as *One* on her Left-hand fingers. Then, again, she does 15 counts of this exercise, counting all 15 on her Right hand, and counts them as *Two* on her Left-hand fingers by her Left-hand thumb. Doing so, she finishes 5 counts of this exercise on her Left hand.

The Breather, standing straight at the same spot with her both arms folded sidewise and both hands placed on her navel, counts 1 on the lowest joint of her Left-hand little finger by her Left thumb to mark the beginning of the first 15 counts. While holding her Left-hand thumb so, she starts a fresh count of 15 on her Right-hand fingers. She counts 1 on the lowest joint of her

Right-hand little finger by her Right-hand thumb, says silently to herself, "Contract," and with it contracts her center. Then she says, "Exhale" and exhales strongly from her both nostrils. At the end of the exhale, she pauses and counts 1,2,3,4,5 in her mind. Then she says to herself, "Release" and with it she releases her belly lose. Still counting 1 on her Right-hand, she then says to herself, "Inhale" and inhales full and deep from her both nostrils, feeling the fresh air going inside her lungs. Then she says a silent "Retain" to herself and holds her breath inside her lungs. This is one full cycle of breathing starting from "Contract" and ending at "Retain."

Next, the Breather starts her Second count of exhale-based exercise on her Right hand. She counts 2 on the middle joint of her Right-hand little finger by her Right-hand thumb and completes one full cycle of exhale-based exercise—contracts; exhales; counts 1,2,3,4,5; releases her belly; inhales; and retains—all on the count of 2 on her Right hand. Thus the Breather finishes 15 counts of this exercise, counting each count at each "Contract" on her Right hand. At the end of count 15 on the lowest joint of her Right-hand thumb, the Breather counts this as the end of count 1 on her Left-hand little finger. This is a 15x1x1 count.

Next, the Breather starts her Second count of the exhale-based exercise on her Left hand. She moves her Left hand thumb to the middle joint of her Left hand little finger to mark the beginning of the next 15 strokes. Then she counts 1 on the lowest joint of her Right-hand little finger by her Right-hand thumb and repeats the whole exhale-based exercise: she says "contract" and contracts her center; says, "exhale," and exhales fast and strongly from her both nostrils; counts 1,2,3,4,5 in her mind; says, "release" and leaves her belly loose; says, "inhale" and inhales full and deep from her both nostrils; says, "retain" and retains her breath inside her lungs. This finishes one count of one full cycle of breathing. The breather does 15 counts of this exercise, counting each count at the start of each "Contract" on her Right hand. At the end of count 15 on the lowest joint of her Right hand thumb, she counts this as the end of count 2 on her Left-hand little finger by her Left thumb. This completes 15x1x2 counts of this exercise.

The Breather does 15 counts of this exercise on her Right hand, counting each of 15 as One on her Left-hand fingers by her Left-hand thumb. Thus the breather finishes 15x1x5 counts of this exercise.

If done Right—as prescribed above—it is during this exercise that the Breather starts feeling an inner surge of fresh energy in her cheeks, in her lungs, and in her arms, from her tip to her toes. This is the effect of exhaling stale, toxic air—carbon dioxide from her body and inhaling plenty of fresh morning air—oxygen. Also it is during this exercise that the breather starts feeling a slight pressure on her center. Thus she is able to locate her inner Center. This is the Breather's physical and spiritual Center, and the Center of the Whole's conscious energy inside her. Actually it is from this Center that the Breather ought to breathe—both exhale and inhale.

Step 3: Exhale by Om Exercise (15x1x5 counts)

At the end of the second step, the breather then starts the third—the last leg of this breathing exercise. This is the cooldown phase. In this exercise, the Breather exhales by saying a silent O..m.. to herself, pauses at "M" at her Center, and then inhales—while taking the same breath up. Doing so, the Breather feels the play of one breath inside her. The Breather does 15 counts of this exercise, counting each stroke on her Right-hand fingers. At the end of count 15, she counts this as One on her Left-hand fingers. Then she does 15 counts on her Right hand and counts this as Two on her Left-hand fingers. Thus she completes 15x1x5 counts of this exercise. (As a reminder, in the "Breathe by Om Exercise" the Breather counts all individual breathing strokes on her Right hand fingers, and all composites on her Left hand.)

The Breather, standing straight in the same spot with her both arms folded sidewise and both hands placed on her navel, counts 1 on the lowest joint of her Left-hand little finger by her Left-hand thumb. While holding her Left-hand thumb so, she says a silent "O..m.." to herself and exhales with O..m... While doing so with her full attention on her breath, she mentally watches the inner flow of her exhale breath. At "M"—the end of "O..m..," she pauses and counts 1 on the lowest joint of her Right hand little finger by her Right-hand thumb. At this point she feels a slight contraction at her inner Center. Then, with her contracted center, she says to herself, "1,2,3,4,5." At 5 she says, "Release" to herself and leaves her belly loose. Then she says quietly to herself, "Take the same breath up," and while saying so she inhales full and deep from her center. While inhaling so, she mentally watches and feels her inner breath rising from her Center. This completes one full cycle of the "exhale by Om" exercise.

At the end of "inhale," still counting 1 on her Right hand little finger, the Breather again says a silent O..m.. to herself and exhales with it. At "m" of Om she stops, counts 2 on the middle joint of her Right-hand little finger by her Right-hand thumb. Then at the same count of 2, she mentally counts 1,2,3,4,5. At 5 she tells herself, "Release" and leaves her belly loose. Then she says to herself, "take the same breath up" and inhales with it. Thus she finishes the second count of the "Exhale by Om" exercise.

It is at the second or third count on her Right hand that the breather starts feeling the oneness of her both breaths—the same breath going out from her Center as "exhale" and rising from her Center as "inhale." It is at this step that the Breather can now combine three parts of her breath into one —she exhales, pauses, and then inhales, taking the same breath up. She does not let her breath break up in between the three parts. She keeps it as one breath. This is "breathing by Om."

The Breather does 15 counts of this exercise, starting the count on the lowest joint of her Right-hand little finger by her Right-hand thumb, and ending the count on the lowest joint of her Right-hand thumb. At the end of count 15, the Breather counts this as the end of count 1 on the lowest joint of her Left-hand little finger by her Left-hand thumb. This is a 15x1x1 count.

Next, the Breather repeats the whole "breathe by Om" exercise, counting each cycle of breath as 1 on her Right hand fingers. She finishes 15 counts of this exercise on her Right-hand fingers and counts them as 2 on the middle joint of her Left-hand little finger by her Left-hand thumb. This is a 15x1x2 counts. Thus The Breather finishes 5 counts on her Left- hand fingers counting 1 for each 15 counts of the "Exhale by Om" exercise. Thus it is a 15x1x5 counts of the "Exhale by Om" exercise—the last leg of the "Breathe by Om exercise."

It is during this last step that the breather learns—realizes what it means to breathe by Om. She feels the finesse and oneness of her one breath playing both as exhale and inhale inside her.

At the end of the "Breathe by Om exercise," the Breather feels a tightness in her center, and an inner tingling and vibrating energy throughout her whole body—in her left temple, right temple, in her cheeks, very vigorously inside her lungs (where she has stored lots of fresh morning air oxygen), from her tip to her toes. She can feel the fresh blood flowing to all parts of her body. This is the effect of the whole "Breathe by Om exercise." Standing straight in one spot strengthens the Breather's inner center, balances her, and helps her breathe from her Center. Exhaling forcefully clears her body of stale, toxic air—carbon dioxide that gets accumulated inside her body through the whole night. Inhaling fresh morning air full and deep fills her lungs and body with oxygen. Giving a pause between two breaths rests her breathing organs and helps her retain fresh air inside her.

Overall, the "Breathe by Om exercise" fills the Breather's body and mind with all pulsating vigor. It also tones and strengthens her Center and her breathing organs, which help her breathe well all the time. At the end of the "Breathe by Om exercise," for about 1 minute, the Breather keeps standing straight in the same spot in the same posture and feels the inner effects of her breathe by Om exercise. Doing so also balances her overall system.

At this point after finishing the full "Breathe by Om exercise" and some 1 minute of standing, the alarm should beep. If done Right—in the manner prescribed above—the whole exercise takes 35 minutes.

Like any other exercise, the "Breathe by Om exercise" is a hard exercise but quite enjoyable too. It requires good physical and mental discipline. The Breather throughout the whole exercise has to stand straight in one spot in the same posture and has to focus on each count and on her breath all the time. But, if done Right—as prescribed above—the Breather enjoys the whole process—the process of inhaling fresh morning air, its soft feel and sheer vigor throughout her whole body; feel of exhaling stale, dirty air from her body; and at the end the symphony and finesse of breathing by Om.

Breathe by Om Exercise makes a human calm, alert, and aligned to The Whole's consciousness inside her. But it is not possible to breathe by Om all the time. A human, throughout the day deals with other people and goes through several problems and experiences. They create different feelings and thoughts in her, affect her consciousness, and thus affect her breathing too. Stress, anxiety, fatigue, and concentration constrict a human's breathing and make it short and shallow—far away from the harmony of breathing by Om. Besides, an average human throughout the day does some 1,620 tasks—ranging from walking, talking, driving, reading, and writing to performing the complex duties of her profession. Each of these tasks has its own importance and requires full attention. It is not possible to pay full attention to the task at hand and breathe by Om too. Every task must be done with complete concentration.

A human's stream of consciousness—her feelings and thoughts—are constantly moving. And they mostly move in a very disorderly and scattered way. If I watch myself a little, I find that at any given time I am either feeling or thinking or acting or doing them all together. But rarely do they go together. For example I may be driving and thinking of my family, or I may be eating and thinking about my work. Living this way gives rise to a fragmented consciousness. A human's consciousness is like a pile of hay being blown in different directions by the winds of the world. Such unregulated, constant running of my feelings and thoughts consumes my physical and mental energy. If I bind this blowing hay of my consciousness, control it, and streamline it, I can avoid its wastage— wastage of my conscious (and physical) energy—and utilize it well. If I live by asking myself constantly, "what am I doing?" I can focus on the task at hand, bring order in my consciousness, regulate it well, and help it move The Whole's way. Because that is how The Whole's consciousness moves—in an extremely calm and concentrated way. It is a very hard practice, but doable. A human's brain is a product of millions of years' evolution. It runs its own way. Trying to control it and making it run your way is very hard indeed.

2) Live by Asking Myself Constantly, "What am I Doing?" "What am I Feeling?" "What am I Thinking?" and the Rest of the Time Saying a silent Om to Myself

As defined in my earlier discussion on 'Human life', "Living is a continuous process of feeling, thinking, acting, and facing the consequences of one's actions." This process goes on continuously without our being aware of it. Many a times we are not aware of even our own actions or inner feelings and thoughts.

The moment I ask myself, "what am I doing?" I become aware of my own actions. I can distinguish my action. Now it may be that at that moment I am driving. Now I know that I am driving. Once I become aware of my action I can focus on it, and do it well   drive well and follow all the rules. Or it may be that I am just sitting and not doing anything. Even at that time there is a thought process going on in my mind. If I watch my mind a little I will find that either I am RIFing— remembering, imagining, or fearing (a natural movement of one's consciousness)—or thinking. Asking myself "what am I doing?" helps me gaze in my mind also, and catch my own feelings and thoughts. Once I am aware of my inner feelings and thoughts, and I catch myself

"RIFing"—remembering, imagining, fearing, or maybe thinking in a disorderly way, I may decide to do something worthwhile—maybe get up and finish some task of the day or truly think—define, and sort out an inner issue that has been pending for long and requires my attention.

Also, once I am aware of my own feelings, thoughts, and actions, I can practice *"Subhava," "Suvichara,"* and *"Sukarma"*—a set of three highest virtues. Practicing these helps me enjoys my inner being and my life and move my consciousness The Whole's way.

Subhava is a Sanskrit word made of two words *Su* and *Bhava*. *Su* means beautiful and *bhava* means feelings or emotions. Practicing *Subhava* means viewing others—All beings—with compassion and goodwill, where compassion means viewing the other person/ being the way she is, understanding her problems and her situation in life; and goodwill means wanting to see the other person/being happy. Once I am aware of my inner feelings I can change them to *Subhava*. For example, at a given moment if I am feeling jealousy and ill will toward my colleague, I may replace those emotions with *Subhava*—feel compassion and goodwill toward her. Jealousy and ill will are negative, toxic emotions. They make me feel bad, while compassion and goodwill are positive, beautiful emotions. They connect me to the other person. Also, feeling *Subhava* aligns my consciousness to the Whole's consciousness because this is how the Whole's (Supreme) consciousness moves—feels compassion and goodwill for ALL.

Living by asking myself constantly, "What am I thinking?" makes me aware of my own inner thoughts. For example, by a little self-gazing I may find that all the time I am thinking of "I," "me," "myself"—thinking very selfishly or thinking low, animal thoughts. Once I am aware of my own inner thoughts, I can practice *Suvichara*—think noble and beautiful thoughts—and think about others/All beings and their wellness or think some beautiful thought. By living so I enjoy the higher realm of my being. Also, this brings me close to the Whole's (Supreme) consciousness. Because this is how the Whole's consciousness thinks—thinks high and noble for ALL—All beings, thinks beautiful and perfect.

Sukarma is another Sanskrit word made of *Su* and *Karma*. *Su* means "beautiful" and *Karma* means "an action." *A Sukarma is a preconceived, pre-planned Karma with positive effects (for All).* Practicing *Sukarma* is the highest of all virtues because my Karmas not only affect my life but others' lives too. Living by asking myself constantly, "What am I doing?" makes me aware of my own actions—Karmas. Once I am aware of my own action, I can change it to a *Sukarma*. This totally goes with the Whole's (Supreme) consciousness—do good to ALL.

Thus, living by asking myself constantly, "What am I doing?" "What am I feeling?" "What am I thinking?" makes a human aware of her own actions, feelings, and thoughts—orders and beautifies her consciousness and helps it move the Whole's way. Living this way makes one calm, alert, and joyous—connected to her Self and connected to the Whole.

Saying a Silent O..m.. to Myself

Once I start monitoring and organizing my consciousness by living by "What am I doing?" "What am I feeling?" and "What am I thinking?" I will find that often there are times when I am not doing anything. In between my actions, feelings, and thoughts there are short gaps—lapses when I am not doing anything. During such times—when I am not doing anything—saying a silent O..m to myself brings me back to my Self, my Center— the Center of The Whole.

Om is a powerful word. The moment I say O..m to myself, it brings the whole flow of my consciousness back to myself—at "m" of my "Ahm"—Self. It makes me grounded and alert. Also, when I say O..m it affects my breathing too. I will find that every time I say the word O..m, it tries to align to my breathing. The word O..m goes with my exhale—"Ou.."— and stops at my Center—"m"—then it is from this Center that I inhale. Thus saying the word O..m to myself stabilizes my breathing too.

3) Doing 300 *Japas* of Om Thrice a Day

The last and the most important way to practice breathing by Om is to do 300 *japas* of Om thrice a day. Repeating a word constantly is called *japa* in Hindi. Doing *Om japa* means repeating the word Om silently to yourself. Every O..m is an exhale. When you say the word O..m to yourself, you feel your breath being regulated by it. At every "m" of O..m.. you come back to your *Ahm*—your Self—your Center—and inhale from there. The word Om starts from your Center—Ah(m)—goes out— Ou..—and comes back to your Center—"m.." of your Ahm. Repeating it constantly 300 times connects you to your Center—your *Ahm* (Self)— your Soul, and the Center of the Whole. Also during this process, slowly and gradually your breath gets regulated by and gets aligned to O..m— the movement of the Whole and its conscious energy moving inside you the O..m way. This makes you feel calm, alert, and energetic.

During the hustle and bustle of the human life, coping with everyday life and its many demands may make a human perturbed and lost. Also, it is hard to control the constant chattering of one's mind. In such situations, and also during regular everyday life, doing *Om japa* makes a human calm and alert.

The human Dharma Practitioner ought to do 300 *japas* of Om thrice a day: once in the morning, once at noon, and once in the evening, each after a gap of four hours. *Om japa* must be done on an empty stomach or at minimum after three hours of eating anything. It takes 15 minutes to do 300 *japas* of Om. You may count each Om on your fingers or by counting beads on a bead string. If counting on fingers, you count 100x1x3 counts, where you count 100 on your Right-hand finger, and for each 100 counts you count 1 on your Left-hand finger; then again you count 100 on your Right-hand, and count it as 2 on your Left-hand. So you count 100x1x3, a total of 300 *japas* of Om.

Technique of Om *Japa*

The Right way to say Om is to say Ou...m...(nasal Om). As I explained earlier, in saying O..m.. as much goes out, as much ought to come in. Hence as long the "Ou..." as long is "m..."

The Practitioner seeks a quiet place, stands straight in one place with her both knees joined together, and places her both hands on her navel with the middle fingers of her both hands touching each other. She looks far ahead at one Center point. She holds her Left-hand thumb on the lowest joint of her Left-hand little finger to mark the start of the First 100 *Japas* of Om. Then she says a quiet Ou...m... to herself (with the Ou... as long as the "m..."), **pauses at "m..."** at her center (the pause is important), counts 1 on the top joint of her Right hand First (index) finger by her Right thumb, and then inhales with it. Next, she again says a silent O..m.. to herself, pauses at "m" of Om, counts 2 on the top joint of her Right-hand First (index) finger by her Right thumb, and inhales with it. Thus she does a 100 counts of Om, counting on her Right-hand First (index) finger by her Right hand thumb. The end of the count to one hundred (100) on her Right hand, she counts as the end of count one (1) on the lowest joint of her Left-hand little finger by her Left-hand thumb.

Next she moves her Left-hand thumb to the middle joint of her Left-hand little finger to mark the start of the Second 100 *Japas* of Om. Holding her Left-hand thumb so, she says a silent O..m.. to herself, pauses at "m" of Om, counts 1 on the top joint of her Right-hand First (index) finger by her Right-hand thumb, and inhales with it. Thus she completes a 100 *Japas* of Om counting each Om on her Right Hand First (index) finger; and counts this as the end of 2 on the middle joint of her Left-hand little finger by her Left-hand thumb. Then she moves her Left-hand thumb to the top joint of her Left-hand little finger to mark the start of the Third 100 *Japas* of Om. She holds her thumb there, and does the last 100 *Japas* of Om, counting each Om on the top joint of her Right-Hand First (index) finger by her Right-hand thumb. Thus she completes 100x1x3=300 *Japas* of Om. It requires concentration.

In odd situations, the Practitioner can do 300 Japas of Om while sitting straight or while walking. But the ideal posture is to stand straight and look ahead at some center point.

After finishing 300 *japas* of Om, the Practitioner keeps standing in the same posture for a few seconds, and feels the inner effects of Om *japa*. If done Right—in the manner prescribed above—the Practitioner feels an inner flow of vibrating energy in her face, very vigorously inside her lungs, and throughout her whole body. This is the effect of doing Om *japa*. Also she feels calm, centered, and energized to resume her day's work.

The purpose is to breathe by Om all the time. Breathing by Om keeps a human calm, grounded, alert, and connected to her Center—the Center of the Whole and to the Whole's conscious energy moving inside her in the form of her breath the O..m way. Each of the above three techniques helps you breathe by O..m. A "Breathe by Om exercise" done early in the morning strengthens your Center and breathing organs, teaches you how to breathe by Om, makes you feel its finesse and vigor, and invigorates you for the day. Then, during the day, while doing some 1,620 tasks of the day living by asking yourself constantly "What am I doing?" "What am I feeling?" "What am I thinking?" helps you order your consciousness, remember, and do each task well; practice *"Subhava," "Suvichara,"* and *"Sukarma";* and thus move your consciousness—feelings and thoughts—The Whole's way. Then during the gaps when you are not doing anything, saying a silent O..m to yourself brings the flow of your own consciousness back to yourself and calms you. Again, during the long day when the day's circumstances and events agitate and tire you, doing 300 *japas* of Om thrice a day makes you feel calm, alert, and energetic.

This is how a human internalizes The Second Truth of Om—"Om is the Prime energy Channel within which the Whole moves"—the Whole moving the Om way inside her in the form of her breath. And, this is how a human lives this Truth of Om in her everyday life. Thus these Three Ways constitute the derivative Right Way of Living from the Second Truth of Om.

The Third Truth of Om: "Om is the Prime Principle of Living" and Its Derivative Right Way of Living

"Om is the Prime Principle of Living." This is the Third Truth of Om— true for every entity and every being, including a human.

Om is a Sanskrit word made of two letters "Ahm" and "U." "Ahm" means "I" and "U" means "everything other than I" or "the world outside me." Every entity in the Universe primarily exists for its own survival and happiness—"Ahm"—"I" but somehow in the process it has to enrich its Whole too—its "U"—the world outside that entity. This is the Prime Principle of Living. No entity can survive without following this principle.

The term "Ahm"—(I) denotes an entity's basic Self, and its quest for survival and happiness. Every entity has an inner drive to survive. It strives to survive anyway possible. And every entity during the process of its movement/living seeks happiness consciously or unconsciously. It tries to do what makes it happy.

The term "U" means "everything other than I" or "the world outside me." There is a vast world outside an entity in which it is born and in which it lives. An entity by its very creation and living is a part of this world— her Whole—her "U." An entity is a product of her Whole. It is as if the Whole creates an entity with a specific purpose—to enrich the Whole. The entity during its movement/living needs her "U"—her Whole—the world outside it and its resources—has to relate to it, and has to somehow enrich it. It cannot survive without doing this.

Thus Om is the Prime Principle of Living.

Examples of this principle can be seen around us everywhere in both— nonliving and living entities. Our Sun moves in its own axis. By its constant movement, it produces immense heat and energy that keeps it going and by which it enriches its Whole—gives sunshine, life, and energy to its eight planets—including our Earth. Our Earth moves around the Sun, and on its own axis too. By its movement it ensures its own survival, and also nurtures The Whole of Life within its lap. The Flora— entire plant life of The Whole of life functions/lives in a way so that it blooms and blossoms itself, and also nourishes the entire Fauna—all animals/living beings within it. Amid the Fauna, a butter-fly flies from one flower to the other, drinks its nectar, gets its food and survives itself. While doing so, it pollinates the flowers and helps them to multiply and flourish. A roaming deer eats a fruit, walks off to a distant pasture, and excretes the fruit's seed. That seed germinates into a tree, blossoms, gives fruits. Thus, that deer by his natural living gets his food as well as enriches his Whole too. Similarly, a human— a Scientist, for example, by his natural living—by following his talent works hard in some field of Science, enjoys his work, earns his living, comes up with an important scientific discovery through which he enriches his Human Whole for ever. Another human—a Philosopher, for example—by living naturally works hard in his field, writes important philo-sophical works, enjoys the process himself, and enriches his Human Whole forever. Thus Om is the Prime Principle by which every entity in the universe moves/lives.

Translating this Principle of Om into a human's life means that *"Ahm"*— I as a human ought to live a good life myself, and "U"—enrich my Whole too.

A good human life is a Rich, Healthy, Happy, and Meaningful life. A human's life in keeping with human nature and intelli-gence ought not to be a mere quest for survival and happiness but ought to have a purpose, some meaning in it, too. A human like any other entity is born in and is a part of the vast world around her. This is her "U"—the world outside her—her Whole of which she is an integral part. In my analysis of "What is a human?" in Part one, I traced three Sub-Wholes—worlds around a human that she is a part of. These three Sub-Wholes are "The Human Whole," "The Whole of Life," and "The Universe," which taken altogether constitute a human's Whole—the world outside a human, her "U." A human is a creation of this Whole, lives in this Whole, and dies in this Whole. A human is an inseparable part of each of these Sub-Wholes. First, a human is a part of her Human Whole—a human-made world in which she is born, lives, and dies. A human and her Human Whole in turn are parts of a bigger Whole—The Whole of life. The Whole of Life is "the vast Earth veiled inside its atmosphere with its flora and fauna" that nurtures the entire Human Whole in its lap. A human, like any other living being, is a product and part of the Whole of Life. The Whole of Life—the Earth with its flora and fauna—in turn is a part of the bigger Whole—our Solar System. Our Earth moves around our Sun, gets its sunshine, life, and energy from it. Our solar system is a part of our Galaxy, with our Sun moving around the Center Sun of our Galaxy. Our Galaxy is a part of the bigger Whole—our Cluster, with the Center Sun of our Galaxy moving around the Center Sun of our Cluster. Our Cluster moves around the Center Sun of the Super Cluster—All of them altogether forming The Universe where All stars and planets are moving around one Center. The universe is like a constantly moving Potter's Wheel moving around one Center, creating new and new artifacts and throwing them in The Whole. Our Sun, our Earth, an ant, a human— each and everything in the Universe is a creation of this, created for a specific purpose—to enrich the Whole. This fact gives meaning to a human's life on this Earth—to enrich her Whole by giving her very best to it.

Thus a human is a part of each Sub-Whole of her Whole— "The Human Whole," "The Whole of Life," and "The Universe." A human, by her living and during her living, ought to enrich each of these Sub Wholes.

Next, we will see in detail how a human ought to live by Om—the Prime Principle of Living—which is to live a good life herself and enrich her Whole too.

Good life

A good human life is a Rich, Healthy, Happy, and Meaningful life. These four ingredients in a human's life make it an enjoyable process.

Rich

A human like any other living being needs to survive. Human survival is closely linked with money. A human of any society needs money to survive. Thus being rich is the first, prime requirement of a good human life.

"Rich" is a highly debatable term meaning different thing to different people. But in broad terms, *being "rich" means having "basic" plus "surplus" money.* "Basic" is one's survival money—a certain amount that one needs in order to pay for her basic needs like home, food, clothes, and medicine etc. This amount varies from person to person depending upon where she lives, the number and kind of dependents she has etc. "Surplus" is the money in excess of basic money that one needs in order to save some money for the future, and to buy certain goodies that add quality to a human's life and make it worth living, for example, some extra comforts like air-conditioning, a car et cetera; some quality entertainment—like TV, music, movies, theatre, and books—and some spare money for socializing and traveling et cetera. Every human ought to travel. It enlarges one's mental world, adds to her experiences, and makes her happy. Again, the amount of surplus money differs from person to person.

Money has been called a whore in old Hindu religion and rightly so. The race for more and more money often preoccupies a human and makes her sacrifice her ethics and other life Values like health, family, talent work etc. Money has a certain place in a human's life and it ought to be used for that—to buy her basic plus some surplus goods. A human ought to define her income target—a certain monthly income that she needs in order to live a decent human life.

"Work" and **"Money Management"** are two ways to become rich and remain rich. Work is a human's profession, job, or business that gives her money. If her work does not give her sufficient income, she may want to do two jobs or a combination of a job and some side business to meet her income target.

Money management is essential in order to remain rich. Whether you earn a thousand dollars a month or a million dollars a month, if you do not manage your money you will lose it all. Money management means managing one's income in such a way so as to be able to pay one's basic expenses, save some money, and also afford some surplus goods. This can be achieved by making a monthly budget and adhering to it.

A monthly budget is a logging of one's total monthly income (from work and other sources), deducting her basic expenses (which are required and fixed) from it, keeping some money aside for saving (which should be good), and then take out money for her surplus expenses. After all these deductions of basic expenses, saving, and surplus expenses, the last figure should be zero which means the right calculation. If it is plus or minus, that means the wrong calculation.

Once you make a monthly budget, the next thing to do is to strictly adhere to it—spend as per the budget, log down your daily expenses, and calculate your all income and expenses at the end of the month to see if your budget worked and if you adhered to it. Money management is a monthly and every day's work. One ought to make a monthly budget at the beginning of every month, follow it in her every day's expenses, and calculate at the end of the month.

Good money management helps one to control the flow of money, spend right, and save.

Healthy

Having a healthy body is another requirement for a good life. A healthy body houses a healthy mind and gives one a cheerful demeanor. A healthy life is a happy life too.

Being healthy means having a disease-free, slim, supple, and energetic body.

Many a human diseases can be prevented and even cured by adopting a healthy lifestyle. As evidenced by medical science, any excess fat on a human's body is an invitation to disease. Moreover, having a slim body makes one's body movements easy and keeps her active. A supple body is a body flexible enough for any kind of movement like moving one's neck, arms, and knees easily. An energetic body is a body full of vitality and vigor. A prime source of energy in a human's body is breath. It is through breathing that we inhale oxygen— a form of pure energy—and exhale carbon dioxide—stale and toxic air from our body. Food and an active life style are two other sources of energy.

"Right Diet" and **"Right Exercise"** are two prime ways to acquire good health and maintain it.

Right Diet

Right Diet means eating the right type of food in small portions and at the right time. Eating Four small, nutritious meals a day— breakfast, lunch, supper, and dinner—constitute the Right Diet. There should be a four-hour gap after every meal. Breakfast and lunch can be slightly heavy, but dinner must always be light and early. As per Science of Biology, every human body needs some amount of each of these— protein, carbohydrates, calcium, vitamins, minerals, and fibers. These are acquired by eating the right types of food—food that contains some lentils/chicken/fish/light meat for protein, some bread/rice for carbohydrates, some milk/yoghurt for calcium, some fruits for vitamins and minerals, and some vegetables/salad for fiber. All of them cannot be eaten at one time, but they can be had in the form of four small meals a day. A human before starting her day ought to plan her day's Right Diet and stick to it.

Together with the Right Diet, Right Exercise is another daily requirement for a healthy body.

Right Exercise

Right Exercise includes Right breathing exercise, Right organs-cum-stretching exercise, and Right walking or running exercise. A set of these three exercises done every day or five days a week keeps one's body disease-free, slim, supple, and energetic. Right breathing exercise exercises and strengthens a human's breathing organs, supplies her body with a good amount of oxygen, and makes her feel fresh and vigorous. Right organs exercise exercises one's main body organs, like the eyes, neck, arms, and legs et cetera, and makes their movement easy. Further, stretching exercise makes one's body muscles supple. Thirty to forty minutes of brisk walking or running exercises one's heart, stimulates her blood flow, and makes her feel energetic overall.

A human ought to exercise early in the morning in open space amid nature. Fresh morning air invigorates the body and the mind.

Right breathing exercise includes deep and long inhaling, good retaining, and strong exhaling first by alternate nostrils, then by both nostrils. "Breathe by Om" exercise as prescribed by me in my earlier discussion is a good breathing exercise. Right breathing exercise done for 35 minutes a day exercises and strengthens one's breathing organs like the lungs, and diaphragm et cetera; fills her body with oxygen; and helps her throw out stale, toxic air carbon dioxide. It invigorates her whole body and makes her feel fresh and energetic.

Right organs exercise is an exercise of one's main body organs, like the eyes, neck, arms, hands, legs, and feet. A good eye exercise is to move one's eyes *very slowly* clockwise and anti-clockwise for a count of 10 each, move them up and down for a count of 10 each, and then sideways for a count of 10 each. This strengthens one's eyes muscles and makes them flexible. Neck exercise is done by moving one's neck clockwise and anticlockwise for a count of 10 each, then up and down for a count of 10 each, and then sideways for a count of 10 each. This makes one's neck muscles and joints flexible and pain free. Moving one's each arm in a circular way for a count of 10 gives one a good arm exercise. Then comes hands exercise. Closing and opening one's each fist for a count of 10 gives one a good hand exercise. Legs exercise is well done by standing straight, lifting one leg, bending it inward from the knees, and straightening it. Doing so with each leg for a count of 10 gives one a good leg exercise. At the end comes one's feet exercise. Feet exercise is done by standing, lifting one foot off the ground, and bending it down and up from the ankle for a count of 10 each; and then, closing and opening one's toes for a count of 10 each. This whole set of organ exercises can be done at one time, starting from one's eyes and ending at one's feet.

Organs exercise accompanied by stretching exercise makes one's body muscles supple. Stretching exercise is well done by standing straight, then lifting one's both arms straight above the head, bending forward very slowly from the waist, standing straight, and then bending backward very slowly (toe-touching) for a count of 10 each. After this, keeping one's both arms straight above the head, and bending sideways from the waist, first to the left, and then to the right, for a count of 10 each. Doing so relaxes one's upper body.

The whole organs-cum-stretching exercise can be done at one time. It takes about 10 minutes to do this exercise.

Right walking or running exercise is a brisk walk or run of good 30 to 40 minutes to be done preferably outdoors amid nature. Going for an early morning walk or run amid nature— in a park or woods amidst lot of greenery heightens one's spirits and makes her feel energetic throughout the day. Also, it strengthens her heart and stimulates her blood flow.

Happy

Another Mark of a good life is to be happy. After survival, seeking happiness is the second basic drive of a living being. And, so it is for a human. Every human seeks happiness consciously or unconsciously. Since being happy is a prime human need, a human ought to make it an every day's conscious objective.

Happiness is distinct from short-term pleasure. Happiness is a constant, lingering feeling of self-satisfaction accompanied by feeling calm and joyous from within.

"Happy Work" and **"Happy relationships"** are two prime modes through which a human can be happy.

Happy Work

Work is one's profession, job, or business that one does for most of the day—some 8+ hours. Your work ought to be such that you like doing. Happy work makes one happy through most of the day. Choosing a profession as per one's talent or making work of one's hobby creates happy work for a human.

Every human is distinct by nature and temperament, and so is her talent. A talent is one's natural flair—a specialty by birth. Some people are rational, practical, good with numbers or in Science, while others are imaginative, speculative, and good in letters. Some are born scientists—seek solitude, observe, and like to solve puzzles, while others are born artists—like to sing, dance, or paint. A human ought to understand her true nature, her talent, and choose a profession that best matches that. If she is not able to do so, she at least ought to pursue her hobby.

A hobby is something you like to do naturally all the time. It is more of a creative nature. Some like to draw or sculpt, while others like to think and write. Actively pursuing one's hobby for an hour a day makes a person calm and happy from within. It makes her day. Also, with every day's effort, it develops to the point that she may eventually make a profession of it.

Happy Relationships

Maintaining happy relationships is another way to be happy. Happy relationships are those of family and friends. Having happy exchanges with others also makes one happy. Maintaining family ties and a set of few good friends is deeply satisfying to a human's psyche. It makes one feel safe, secure and happy. Family and friends are those people who care for you and support you in need. Talking to one's family and friends, and spending time with them makes one unwind, open up, share, and rejoice. ***"Care, Communicate, and Support"*** are three key ways to maintain one's personal relationships. A certain part of every day should be devoted to talking to one's family and friends, asking them about their well-being, meeting with them, and sharing some activity with them.

Happy exchanges with other people also make one happy. In relationships you often get what you give to others. Smiling at others, talking nicely to them, and avoiding arguments and unwarranted criticism of others makes them do the same to you. This creates a happy exchange—an exchange of pleasantries with others.

Meaningful Life

The last and the most important ingredient of a good human life is a Meaningful life. Every human needs and seeks a meaning in life—something that gives her a reason for living, a purpose in it—a thing she wants to live for. It can be her work, hobby, a deep relationship, or some cause or thing that transcends her temporary existence on this Earth. Different people find different meanings in their lives. For some it can be their "work" or a hobby that they find highly satisfying and rewarding; for others it can be a deep relationship with a spouse, child, or parent etc.

And there are some who find meaning in a transcendent cause like fighting for their country, the environment, or women's rights et cetera.

A human ought to devote some part of every day to the thing or relationship that she finds most meaning in. This satisfies her from deep within.

There is however a pre-giving meaning to every human's life on this Earth. A human is a creation and a part of the Whole. The Whole is like a constantly moving Potter's Wheel, which keeps moving and creating totally novel and unique artifacts—the Sun, the Moon, the Earth, a bird, an ant, a human et cetera. Each of these is distinct, unique, and each enriches The Whole by her own special way. Even among humans *every human is distinct and is a special creation of The Whole—created to enrich the Whole by her own special way.* Every human has a unique nature, temperament, and a set of talents through which she lives and enriches The Whole. Each human gives to the Whole that others cannot give. For example, a compassionate and cheerful human helps others and makes them happy, while a solitary, cranky writer enriches others' lives by her writings. A Scientist gives to the Whole that an Artist cannot. And an Artist gives to the Whole that a Scientist cannot. Each is a creation of the Whole, created in a very special way to enrich The Whole by her own way. And each human is required in the Whole and especially in our Human Whole to make it richer and more beautiful. This is the value and meaning of every human's life on this Earth.

Keeping this in mind a human ought to view herself as a special creation of the Whole, created in a special way to enrich the Whole. It is by living her own special way that a human enjoys her existence and enriches The Whole too. That way is the Right Way of Living. That is one's supreme Dharma.

A human ought to live The Right Way—the Dharma way—by recognizing her own true nature, special skills, and talent; choose a profession/work as per that, excel in that, and view her "work" as a way to enrich The Whole. That is "Right Work." Every human ought to find her own Right Work by following her talent/hobby/natural liking and make a profession of that. By doing Right Work a human enjoys her own existence, enriches "The Human Whole," and serves the deep purpose of the Whole behind her creation. This is the Right way of living—the Dharma way of living.

This is how a human lives a good life—a Rich, Healthy, Happy, and Meaningful life. These four ingredients in a human's life give it a certain quality, flavor, and make it an enjoyable process. A human ought to view each of these Four (4) as an everyday's conscious objective and try to achieve it. This fulfils "Ahm" of Om—the Prime Principle of Living.

Enrich My Whole

The second letter of Om is "U" which means "everything other than I" or "the world outside me." As proved in my earlier discussion, every entity in the universe is a product and a part of The Whole—the world around it. Being a part of the Whole, it has to enrich the Whole. The same is true from for a human. A human is a product and a part of her Whole—the world around her.

There is a vast Whole around a human of which she is a deep and intrinsic part. A human is a creation of this Whole; she lives in this Whole; and she dies in this Whole. Starting from a human as the Center, "The Whole" is made of three Sub-Wholes—The Human Whole, The Whole of Life, and The Universe. Each of these Sub-Wholes is closely related to each other and to a human, and thus they make one Whole around a human. A human by her living ought to enrich each of these Sub-Wholes.

Enrich My "Human Whole"

The Human Whole is a human's immediate Sub-Whole made of a human's Family, Society, Country, Humanity, and their Cumulative Achievements in all aspects of the human life. Each of these is a gradually increasing larger group of humans and has its own set of achievements in all walks of the human life. Taken altogether they form one vast pool of humanity with their Cumulative Achievements. A human is born in the Human Whole, lives in the Human Whole, and dies in the Human Whole. A human is affected by her Human Whole and she affects it too by her own actions. A human by her living and during her living ought to enrich each aspect of her Human Whole and the entire Human Whole.

Enrich My Family

A human's family is the first group of humans around her among whom she is born and lives. Family is a group of people related to a human by blood or by marriage. A human throughout her lifetime goes through two sets of families—"Family by Birth" and "Family by Marriage." A human is born and reared for the first twenty years of her life in her First Family—Family by Birth. A human's First Family is made of her parents, siblings, and other blood relatives. Sometime during adulthood a human marries and creates her Second Family—Family by Marriage. A human's Second Family is made of her spouse, In-Laws, and children. It is in the realm of her Second Family that a human spends the rest of her life. A human in her basic being is deeply attached to her both families and remains so till the end of her life. A human is affected by the type of family she has, and she affects it too by her own actions. A human by her actions ought to enrich her both families. Doing so helps her live a good life herself and enrich her whole too. **"Care, Communicate, and Support"** are three key ways to enrich your family. Caring for your family, talking to them regularly, meeting them once in a while, and helping them in need makes you happy from within and enriches your family too. Also, a human ought to play her each family role—relationship title well and fulfill its obligations—duties. For example, a woman ought to be a good "daughter," a good "sister," a good "wife," a good "mother," a good "daughter-in-law" etc. And a man ought to be a good "son," a good "brother," a good "husband," a good "Son-In-Law" etc. These are universal family roles with their universal set of Do's and Don'ts. A human ought to abide by them. Living so helps a human retain the unity and sanctity of her family.

Enrich My Society

A human and her family live among a bigger group of humans around them—a human society. A society is a group of people tied to one another by—living in close vicinity, and by personal and business relationships. A human is affected by the type of society she lives in, and she affects it too by her own actions. A human ought to have a concept of her society and its importance in her life. A human by her actions ought to enrich her society. Doing so widens her mental world, and makes her happy. Also, it strengthens and betters her society. A human by her living sets an example for others. A human ought to do her share in keeping her neighborhood clean and green. A human ought to enrich her society by giving her best to it. If you are rich you can help the poor in your neighborhood. If you are educated you can teach the less educated and illiterate ones around you. If you have some spare time on your hands you can visit your local orphanage or old people's communities and help them. Your first charity starts from your neighborhood. A human ought to be honest and moral in her dealings with others. This strengthens the fabric of human society. Also, work is the prime mode through which a human enriches her society. A human's work ought to be the contribution of her best to her Whole.

Enrich My Country

A human, her family, and her society live in and are parts of a bigger Whole—a country. *"A Country is a vast tract of land enclosed within certain geographical and political boundaries, having its own territory, resources, and its own people tied to one another by same country citizenship."* (my definition) A human is a part of her country by birth and by living. A human may leave her own country of birth and live in some other country, but she remains deeply attached to her country of birth. A human ought to enrich her country of birth by giving her best to it—by helping the poor, Illiterates or by contributing to some social reform et cetera. Doing so is deeply satisfying to a human. A human is a closer part of the country she lives in. She is affected by the type of country she lives in and she affects it too by her own actions. A human ought to have a concept of her country and its importance. A country, after all, is made of its citizens. A human ought to enrich her country by being a good citizen—have a good understanding of her country, its history and its politics, pay her taxes on time (her taxes after all go to build and strengthen her country), vote, do her jury duty etc.

Enrich My Humanity

A human, her family, and her country, in turn, live amid and are a close part of humanity. *"Humanity is a group of All—some 196 countries and their 7 billion humans tied to one another by sharing the same Earth home and its resources, by inter-country treaties and alliances, by various other relationships, and by their Cumulative Achievements."* (my definition)

The entire Human Whole is made of Humanity and its Cumulative—total Achievements in all aspects of the human life ranging from a needle to an Airplane, a thatch-roof hut to a sky-scraper, from one single number to Advanced Calculus, and from one single alphabet to the most complex philosophical treatise, its sprawling Cities, its Monuments, its Hospitals, its Museums, and its Libraries et cetera—in sum each and everything we humans have ever achieved and live by on the face of this Earth. This marvelous spread of humanity's achievements was not created in a day or two but is a product of humanity's thousands of years' consistent labor.

The Human Whole is like a Palace under Construction where each new generation of humans is born, works hard, adds on to its achievements, and departs, making it more beautiful than they found it. This Palace is made of humans and their varied achievements in different branches of human labor—ranging from basics like Farming, Housing, Textile, and Food to the highest endeavors of human mind like Science, the Arts, Law, Philosophy, and Religion et cetera. Every product and service in the Human Whole belongs to some branch of human labor or profession, created and preserved by the humans who worked hard and honest in their professions. Thus there are two major components of the Human Whole—"humans" and their "profession" or "work." And this fact makes "Child" and "Work" as two prime modes through which a human enriches the Human Whole.

A human is temporary, but the Human Whole is permanent. A human is born and dies, but the Human Whole goes on. Our

Human Whole of today—the world in which we live—is a product of millions of human generations' labor, each of whom came here, worked hard, added on its contributions, and departed. Similarly we humans of today work, add-on fruits of our labor to it, and will leave one day. By our "work" we make it more beautiful than we found it, and leave our **Human Whole—the Palace under Construction** to our children.

I as a human will die one day but will leave behind my "Work" and my "Child" to the Human Whole. My "Work" and my "Child" ought to be the contribution of my best to my Human Whole: my "Work"—the best of my talent, education, and skills—and my "Child"—the carrier of the best of my genes and the best of my moral and life Values.

A human ought to choose a profession that best matches her talent, work hard at it, be ever productive and thus add-on her contributions to her Human Whole. A human ought to produce a child with an equally matching spouse, rear her child well by giving her a good education, and instilling lifelong moral and human Values in her. Such a child will be a good human—a future member of our Human Whole.

Enrich "The Whole of Life"

The Human Whole nestles in the lap of the Whole of Life. This is the second Sub-Whole of a Human's Whole. A human is a deep and intrinsic part of The Whole of Life.

The Whole of Life is the Earth veiled inside its atmosphere, with its Flora—acres of greenery on its lands and inside its oceans; and its Fauna—trillions of flying beings in its airs, trillions of crawling and walking beings on its lands, and trillions of swimming beings in its oceans (where the entire humanity is just a thin streak of walking beings on its lands), All -interrelated and liv-ing in a way so that The Whole of Life flourishes and goes on. The Whole of Life is a close-knit web made of the Earth's Flora and Fauna, engulfed inside the Earth's atmosphere, where each and every being plays its part in maintaining The Whole of Life. The Flora blossoms and nourishes the Fauna. The Fauna by its living survives itself and helps Flora blossom. They all need one another. Every being—every plant and every animal in The Whole of Life—is there because it is required by The Whole of Life to be there. It has its own place and play in running The Whole of Life.

This Whole of Life breathes inside the Earth's veil of atmo-sphere. The Earth's atmosphere filters the sunshine and pro-tects the Earth from the Sun's direct heat. The atmosphere around the Earth is a thin layer containing a mixture of water vapors and various gases. It is a very fine balance of certain gases that makes life possible on the Earth. A slight disruption in this balance can finish the whole Life on the Earth. This balance is maintained by the Earth's gravity, its movement, and proper functioning of its Flora and Fauna.

Human activity is disrupting the balance of the Whole of Life. The greatly increasing human population is causing large-scale destruction of forests and with it the extinction of many animal species whose living is vital to the Whole of Life. Human's merciless killing and use of animals further contrib-utes to that. Air and water pollution are risking the lives of many a species. Further, constantly increasing air pollution is causing the depletion of the ozone layer—the most important layer of the Earth's atmosphere—that protects us from direct sun.

All of us humans are responsible for it. It is our own actions and the way of living that is causing the disruption of the Whole of Life. Every single human by her way of living can make a difference to this.

A human ought to have a concept of the Whole of Life, understand the humanity's and her place in it, and play her part in enriching The Whole of Life. *A human ought to cause less pollution, grow more plants, have fewer children, and be compassionate towards all living beings.* This is Human Dharma—The Right Way of Living.

A human ought to do her Dharma—cause less pollution by driving less and walking or cycling instead; using more of car pools, public transport like train, bus etc.; using less of gas operated equipments, less of Air conditioner and electricity. One can stop using plastic or at least reuse it. A human ought to keep her rivers and lakes clean, grow more plants in her neighborhood. A human ought to have fewer children—just one or maximum two and rear them well. A human ought to understand the Web of Life, see the importance of all living beings and their lives in it. A human ought not to kill mercilessly or for fun; and respect all living beings. Respect means to give them certain distance and let them live too. A human ought to view all other living beings, even a fly or a snake, with compassion—after all, it is a living being who is just trying to survive and if possible, enjoy life. "Live and let live" should be the maxim of living for every human.

Enrich "The Universe"

Our Earth housing The Whole of Life in its lap is a part of the bigger Whole—our Solar System. Our Earth together with seven other planets is moving around our Sun. Our Solar System, in turn, is a part of the bigger Whole—our Galaxy—the Milky Way. Our Sun is moving around the center of our Galaxy.

Our Galaxy— the Milky Way, in turn, is a part of the Cluster where the Center Sun of the Milky Way is moving around the Center Sun of the Cluster, with millions of other galaxies moving around the Center of the Cluster. Our Cluster is a part of the bigger whole—a Super Cluster, where the Center Sun of our cluster is moving around the Center Sun of the Super Cluster, with millions of other clusters moving around the Center of the Super Cluster. The Super Cluster is the largest known Collection containing many clusters, galaxies, and solar systems within it. This is the Universe—where All are moving around one Center, and this is how a human is a part of it.

All within the Universe are moving around one Center—The Power Point of the Universe, the invisible force creating and moving All.

The Universe is like a constantly moving Potter's Wheel creating new and new artifacts and throwing them in—the Sun, the Moon, the Earth, an ant, a human. A human ought to view herself as a special creation of the Universe, created with a deep, specific purpose to enrich The Whole. A human ought to understand her true nature—her talent—and make a "work" of it or seek a profession in that field. This is the supreme Dharma of a human—to enrich her Whole, her Human Whole by her true being, give it her very best in the form of her "work"—her profession.

This is "U" of Om—the world outside a human—a Human's Whole of which a human is an inseparable part. A human ought to enrich her Whole: first her 'Human Whole' by giving it her very best in the form of her "Work" and her "Child"; then her "Whole of Life" by causing less pollution, growing more plants, having fewer children, and viewing all other living beings with compassion; and finally the Universe by viewing herself as its special creation—created in a special way to enrich the Whole—find her true nature, her talent, and live and work as per them.

Thus Om is The Prime Principle of Living for a human. As per this—"Ahm"—I as a human, ought to live a good life myself, and "U"— enrich my Whole too.

This finishes my discussion on Om—the Central Truth of the Human Dharma and its each Sub-Truth: "Om—The Whole"; "Om—The Prime Energy Channel within which The Whole moves"; and "Om—The Prime Principle of living"; and the derivative Right Way of Living from each.

CHAPTER 12

The Human Dharma Way of Living

The Human Dharma Way of Living is a Value-oriented life with Short-term Goals, and Daily Objectives of a Rich, Healthy, Happy, and Meaningful life.

As the Truth of Om dawned upon me so too did the Human Dharma Way of Living. Both "Om" and "The Human Dharma Way of Living" are highly abstract, compact truths containing the gist of derivatives from my thorough analysis of "What is a human?" and "What is Human Life?" and certain core issues of human life, namely, "Death," "Soul," "God," and "Truth" (as discussed in Part One of this book).

"Death is the end of a human's one lifetime and a transition into another." My this definition of Death brings forth the importance of a human's life on this Earth—how she lives her life, her lifelong Karmas, and her Achievements in her life.

A human at her death leaves an Edifice behind. This Edifice is a Construct containing pearls of that human's lifetime's Achievements in certain realms of human life like, money in the form of her house(s), property(s), and bank balance etc; a loving

436

family of a lifelong spouse and well-raised children; and "Work"—some significant contribution in a certain field of human labor. This Edifice is a Construct that a human builds by her lifelong karmas—by working every day in all these fields. These pearls of Achievements exhibit a human's lifelong Values of Money, Family, Child, and Work, in which she invested years of labor.

A human creates this Edifice during her lifetime by her everyday's Karmas, lives in it, rejoices in her existence, and leaves this Edifice to the Whole at the time of her death.

A human creates and maintains this Edifice—The Construct of her lifetime's Achievements—by her everyday's karmas. Each new day is a brick that a human places in the construction of this Edifice in her life. It is by "working" every day that a human earns and saves money. It is by devoting certain parts of every day to her family that a human maintains her loving family of a lifelong spouse, well-raised children, and other family relations. And, it is again by "working" every day that a human builds some significant Achievement(s) in certain fields of labor—like a book; some great scientific discovery; a marvelous dam or a skyscraper; a series of some great symphonies, songs et cetera. Therein lies the importance of every day in a human's life—how she plans it, how she spends it, what karmas she does during the day.

The above brings up the importance of every day in a human's life as well as the importance of Five (5) Eternal Human Values of "Family," "Education," "Work," "Marriage," and "Child" through which a human not only lives a good life herself but also enriches her Whole.

In my earlier analysis of "What is Human Life?" there had emerged Five Eternal Human, Lifelong Values. These are **"Family," "Education," "Work," "Marriage,"** and **"Child."**

Therein we saw how a human needs them from her birth until her death. We saw how a human is born as the most helpless infant who needs constant love and care of her family in order to survive and live well. We saw how education strengthens and enriches a developing human's mind and distinguishes her from an ape. We saw how an adult human needs to work in order to earn money and to contribute the best of her talent, education, and skill to her society. We saw how a human needs to marry to fulfill her daily needs of SSCC—Support, Sex, Companionship, and Children. And we saw how marriage has to be a *sacred tie* between a woman and a man that brings forth their child; and how Marriage is a *Cradle* in which a child is born and reared; and how Marriage is the very *Founding Stone* of a Family. And we saw how a child is the genetic product of a married couple—a woman wife and a man husband—and how the child is a carrier of her parents' genes and the best of their moral and life Values.

In tracing the history of humanity we saw how these Five Values—"Family," "Education," "Work," "Marriage," and "Child" are Eternal Human Values. They originated with the inception of the human civilization, built the human civilization, and have remained with us till date; and, how these Five Values are closely interlinked to a human's survival and her needs. Till there is a human left on this Earth, these Values will prevail.

A human not only needs these Values, but it is these very Values that give direction, purpose, and meaning to a human's life on this Earth. A human's life is like a pathway enclosed between two doors of Birth and Death. A human is born, lives, and dies.

*** .... ***

Birth   **Living**   **Death**

A human is born and reared for first twenty years in her *First Family*—Family by Birth. She receives *education* up to the age of twenty years or so. Then she starts *working*, and works until old age. Sometime during adulthood she *marries*, has *children*, and creates her *Second Family*—Family by Marriage. Thus these Values emerge as basic human institutions that shape and support a human throughout her life.

These Five Values are the milestones that create the trail of a human's life. They are milestones—major events through which a human's life journey is assessed. They give flow and a certain direction to her life. They give a human a deep purpose in life—something to live for. And they give meaning to a human's life—again something to live for and something which a human leaves to the Whole at her death. A human is temporary. She dies one day, but she leaves behind her best in the form of her "Work" and her "Child(ren)" to the Human Whole.

These Values help a human live a good life herself and enrich her Whole too. Thus they help a human live the Right Way—the Dharma Way.

A human ought to view her life as a journey between the two doors of birth and death. A human is born, lives for some seventy to ninety years, and dies. A human ought to acquire these Five Values, and maintain them throughout her life. She ought to view these Values as Milestones on the trail of her life. Milestones mean major events that she chooses very carefully and lives throughout her life. She ought to view these Values as a solid wall against which she walks on the trail of life. They give her support throughout her life. They work as buttress against the flow and storms of life.

Based on the importance of these Five Values in a human's life, I have envisioned the Human Dharma as a Value-oriented life, where I view a human's life as a pathway enclosed between two doors of her birth and death. A Pathway shaped and shaded by Five lifelong Values of "Family," "Education," "Work," "Marriage," and "Child," where these Five Values altogether not only create the pathway but also build a hedge and a Canopy on the pathway of a human's life that give her shade and support throughout her lifetime.

Each of these Values has its own importance in a human's life. Each gives to a human what another does not. A human needs all Five of them.

A human ought to plan her life along these Five Values—Family, Education, Work, Marriage, and Child—and remember them every day, derive short-term goals from each, break down the goal into the day's tasks, and live them. This is how she builds the Edifice—the Canopy in her life that supports her, helps her live a good life and enrich her Whole too. And ultimately, this is the Edifice that she leaves to the Whole at the time of her death.

Every Day

The Human Dharma is a human's everyday Dharma. A human remembers it every day, plans her day as per it, and lives it as planned.

A human lives a long life of some seventy to ninety years but she lives it on an everyday basis. Every day is a new day in a human's life with a lot of scope and possibility—a day in which she can plan and achieve a lot. Also, every day is a new brick that a human places in constructing the Edifice of her life.

Every day is a new day in a human's life as well as a long day too. A human gets up in the morning, works throughout the day, handles the day's problems, and goes to sleep at night. (S)he lives a lot during a day. It is as if she lives the gist of her life in a day. Every day of a human's life ought to be a good day too. A human ought to live every day of her life with daily objectives of a Rich, Healthy, Happy, and Meaningful life. Doing so helps a human live a good day and in the long run live a good life too.

CHAPTER 13

THE DAILY PRAYER OF THE

HUMAN DHARMA

The Daily Prayer is the most important aspect of the Human Dharma. It is not enough to know and understand Dharma; what is most important is to practice it in our everyday lives. Then only we grasp its teachings, test them, and see the difference in our lives. The teachings of the human Dharma are to be remembered for the First Truth, the deep purpose of a human's life, and at critical moments of life like death et cetera. Still, it is an everyday Dharma too, that a human ought to remember and practice every day.

The Daily Prayer of The Human Dharma contains the gist of the Human Dharma—its Central truth, and its total way of living. This prayer is in the prose form that the human Dharma Practitioner says silently to herself. In this the Practitioner first remembers Om—the Prime Truth and the Central Truth of the Human Dharma: its three Sub-Truths—"Om is the Whole," "Om is the Prime Energy Channel within which the Whole moves," and "Om is the Prime Principle of living"; and their derivative Right Way of Living. Then she remembers the Human Dharma Way of Living—*"A Value-oriented life with short-term goals and daily Objectives of a Rich, Healthy, Happy, and Meaningful life"*; plans her day as per them; and lives the day as planned.

The Practitioner starts her day with the Daily Prayer of the Human Dharma. She remembers it the first thing in the morning, and plans her day as per it. It takes some 20 minutes to remember the Daily Prayer of The Human Dharma and plan your day as per it. One can do it while taking a morning walk out in the fresh air (which is an excellent health habit by itself) or while sitting alone quietly. One needs silence and solitude. The Practitioner needs to focus, recite the whole prayer, and plan her day's tasks as per it.

Remembering Om—the Central Truth of the Human Dharma

The Practitioner starting the Daily Prayer of the Human Dharma first remembers Om—the Prime Truth, and its three Sub-Truths. She says silently to herself, "Om is the Central Truth of the Human Dharma. Om is the Whole. Om is the Prime Energy Channel within which The Whole moves. And, Om is the Prime Principle of Living."

Then she remembers **the First Truth of Om—"Om is The Whole."** She says to herself, "Om is The Whole. Om is a word made of two letters— Ahm and U. Ahm means I, and U means everything other than I, or the world outside me." First she remembers her human make, "Who am I? I am Jane or Peter (says her/his name), a human woman (or a man—as applicable to the Practitioner): Evolved, Multidimensional, and a Part of The Whole." Then she remembers her soul make (says to herself), "I am a soul. My soul is my deepest Self located in the center of my body a little below my navel, containing my deepest memories, attachments, and desires of my all previous lives and this life too." Then she remembers "U"—everything other than I, or the world outside me. She says to herself, "U" means everything other than I, or the world outside me—my Whole. My Whole is neatly divided in three Sub-Wholes—my Human Whole, my Whole of Life, and my Universe. My human Whole is a network of my Family—my First Family and my Second Family; my society—people I live among and work with; my Country—USA (or the country where the practitioner lives); my Humanity—some 200 countries and their 7 billion humans; and our Cumulative Achievements in all aspects of the Human Life ranging from a needle to an airplane, a thatch-roof hut to a skyscraper, one single alphabet to the most complex Philosophical Treatise, and one single number to Advanced Calculus, our sprawling Cities, our Monuments, our Libraries etc.—in sum each and every thing we humans have ever achieved and live by on the face of this Earth. I'm affected by my Human Whole, and I affect it too by my own actions." While saying so the Practitioner mentally visualizes a quick picture of the Human Whole, starting with her "First Family"—a small group of people she is related to by blood, like her parents, siblings etc, and her "Second Family"— another small group of people she is related to by marriage like her spouse, children, and in-laws; her "society"—a bigger group of people around her she lives among and works with, like her neighbors, her friends and her work relationships etc; then her "Country"—its borders and a vast group of people she is related to by same country citizenship; and the "Humanity" as the biggest group of some 7 billion humans around her and their Cumulative Achievements spread among them in the form of a needle, an airplane, a thatched-roof hut, tall buildings, dazzling lights of cities, monuments, books, and millions of other small and big things we humans need and live by.

Then the Practitioner remembers the Second Sub-Whole— The Whole of Life. She says quietly to herself, "my Human

Whole nestles in the lap of the Whole of Life. The Whole of Life is the vast blue-green Earth, veiled inside its atmosphere; with its Flora—acres of greenery on its lands and beneath its oceans; and its Fauna—trillions of flying beings in its airs, trillions of crawling and walking beings on its lands, and trillions of swimming beings inside its oceans, where the entire Humanity is just a thin streak of walking beings on its lands amid multitudes of other crawling and walking beings. I'm affected by my Whole of Life, and I affect it too by my own actions." Saying so, she mentally visualizes the Whole of Life as the vast blue-green Earth with its greenery on its lands and beneath its oceans; and its living beings in its air, on lands, and inside its oceans; and all of humanity as a thin streak of walking beings on its lands amid multitudes of other crawling and walking beings.

Next, the Practitioner remembers the Universe—the biggest Whole around her. She says quietly to herself, "My Earth housing The Whole of Life in its lap is a part of the bigger Whole— our solar system. My Earth with seven other planets is moving around our Sun, taking its sunshine, life, and energy from it. Our Solar System, in turn, is a part of the bigger Whole—our Galaxy —the Milky Way. Our Sun is moving around the Center Sun of our Galaxy, with millions of other solar systems moving around it. Our Galaxy the Milky Way, is a part of the bigger Whole— our Cluster. The Center Sun of our Galaxy is moving around the Center Sun of our Cluster with millions of other galaxies moving around it. Our Cluster, in turn, is a part of the Super Cluster. The Center Sun of our Cluster is moving around the Center Sun of the Super Cluster with millions of other clusters moving around it. This is Universe—an organized Whole where all stars and planets are moving around one single Center. This Center is the PowerPoint of the universe creating and moving All. I am a special creation of the Universe created to enrich the Whole." Saying so, she mentally visualizes each Sub Group of the universe and her relationship to it—the Earth, the Solar system, the Galaxy, the Cluster, the Super Cluster, and finally the Universe as one vast pool of all suns and planets moving around one Center. Thus the practitioner completes the "U" of Om.

"When I combine these two letters of Ahm and U, the word *Om* is formed. Thus Om is The Whole. I meditate upon Om." So the practitioner says to herself and finishes reciting the First Truth of Om—"Om is the Whole." Then the Practitioner schedules time for her Om medication during the day—40 minutes in the morning after saying her Daily Prayer, and 40 minutes in the evening after the day's work. (As a reminder, Om meditation has to be done on an empty stomach or a minimum of four hours after eating anything).

Next, the practitioner remembers **The Second Truth of Om—"Om is the Prime Energy Channel within which The Whole Moves."** Thus she remembers and says quietly to herself, "The Whole is moving. All in the universe are moving around one single Center. This is the Center of The Whole as well as the Center of each and every entity in the Whole. This is your Center, and my Center too, located in the deepest depth of my Self— my soul—"Ahm." The Whole in its prime form exists and moves in the form of pure conscious energy within the conduit of Om—all arising from my Center—"Ahm," going out—(Ah)U..., and all coming back to the same Center M of "Ahm"—All bound and moving within one word Om. The Whole inside me moves in the form of my breath—pure conscious energy. I breathe by Om. Breathing by Om keeps me connected to my Center—the Center of the Whole, and to the Whole's pure conscious energy moving inside me the O..m.. way."

Then the practitioner remembers three ways to breathe by "Om": First— the "Breathe by Om exercise," Second—doing 300 *Japas* of Om thrice a day, and Third—live by asking myself constantly, "What am I doing? What am I feeling? What am I thinking? And, the rest of the times saying silent Om to myself. Then she schedules time for each of these. She says quietly to herself, "After meditation, I will do the "breathe by Om exercise" for 35 minutes. I will do 300 *Japas* of Om thrice a day at 10:00 in the morning, at 2:00 in the noon, and at 6:00 in the evening (each for 15 minutes after three hours of eating anything); and I will live the whole day by asking myself constantly, "What am I doing? What am I feeling? What am I thinking? and the rest of the time saying silent Om to myself."

Next, the practitioner remembers **the Third Truth of Om—"Om is the Prime Principle of Living."** She says silently to herself, "Om is the Prime Principle of Living. Every entity in the universe primarily exists for its own survival and happiness—Ahm; and somehow in the process it has to enrich its Whole too—its "U"— the world outside it. Following this Truth, I as a human live a good life myself and enrich my Whole too. A Good Life is a Rich, Healthy, Happy, and Meaningful life. And I enrich all three Sub-Wholes of my Whole. First I enrich my Human Whole by giving it my very best in the form of my "Work" and my "Child." I as a human will die one day but will leave behind my "work" and my "child" to my Human Whole. I enrich my Whole of Life by causing less pollution, growing more plants, and by having fewer children." Then she schedules at least one activity during the day to this. For example, "I will carpool today" or "I will not use any plastic today." And "I enrich my universe by living true to my nature and talent."

Remembering the Human Dharma Way of Living—"The Human Dharma Way of Living is to live a Value-oriented life with short-term Goals and Daily Objectives of a Rich, Healthy, Happy, and Meaningful life."

After finishing three Truths of Om, next the Practitioner remembers the Human Dharma Way of Living. Thus she says silently to herself, "The human Dharma way of living is to live a Value-oriented life with short-term Goals and daily objectives of a Rich, Healthy, Happy, and Meaningful life." Going further, she remembers thus: "There are Five eternal Human Values that give direction, purpose, and meaning to my life. These are: Family, Education, Work, Marriage, and Child. My family is a group of people related to me by blood or by marriage. They love me and care for me." Saying so she mentally visualizes members of her First Family—her Family by blood—Parents, siblings, etc; and members of her Second Family— Family by Marriage—spouse, children, and in-laws. "Care, Communicate, and Support are the three key do's for my family. I care for my family. I talk to them once in a while. And I help them in need." Saying so, the Practitioner then defines her day's goals for her Family. For example she says to herself, "I need to talk to my mother-in-law today. It has been a while since I talked to her. I will call her at one today." Or "I need to take my sister to the hospital at twelve o'clock today."

Then the Practitioner remembers her Second lifelong Value of Education. She says quietly to herself, "Education is the prime difference between a human and an ape. Education strengthens and enriches my mind, and also prepares me for my profession. Education is of two types—basic (graduation) and professional (for a specific profession)." Then she remembers her short-term goals for Education. For example, she says to herself, "I am a graduate. I have done my basic education. Now

I want to get my professional education. I want to get a degree in law and become a lawyer." Next the Practitioner breaks this Value oriented short-term goal into every day's objectives. "My educational objective for today is to do some Internet research on a few good law schools and their admission requirements." Then she schedules some 30 minutes for this task: "I will do this task at five today."

Another example of a short-term educational goal for a Practitioner who has finished both her basic and professional education will be thus: First the practitioner remembers her lifelong Value of Education. Then she says quietly to herself, "I have finished my basic and professional education. Currently I'm working as a Marketing Manager. My short-term educational goal is to finish my one-year Advanced course in Marketing. Today I will study for an hour and do my class assignment. Passing this course will boost my career." Then she schedules an hour during the day for her study. "I will study during my office lunch hour." (The same goes for every profession. Every profession requires continuous education—extra classes or private study to keep your professional knowledge updated.)

The keys is to remember the basic lifelong Value of Education and its Short-term goals of a few years, and then to break down the goal into everyday's tasks—devote part of each day toward the completion of the goal. Doing so helps the Practitioner retain her Lifelong Value of Education and achieve her educational goal.

Next, the Practitioner remembers her third lifelong Value of "Work"—profession. She says quietly to herself, "My Work is the contribution of my best to my Whole. I as a human will die one day but will leave behind my Work to my Human Whole. Also my work gives me money, and if Right, happiness and the prime meaning of my life." Remembering so she chooses the Right Profession—profession which best matches her talent, education, and skill. Having chosen the Right Profession, then she derives short-term goals from it. It may be that the Practitioner has two professions—one as a Lawyer and one as a Writer. She derives short-term goals from both professions. "In Law, I need to open my own law office. My today's objective is to decide on a good location for my office. I will spend half an hour after lunch today to do this task." Then she remembers her Second profession of writing. "I am writing a book. My today's objective is to finish the second chapter. I will write for an hour today morning from 7:00 to 8:00." Thus the Practitioner remembers her lifelong Value of Work, it short-term goals, and her Day's tasks toward completion of these goals.

Next the Practitioner remembers her Fourth lifelong Value of Marriage, its short-term goals, and its every day's tasks. Thus she says to herself, "Marriage is the foundation of my family, a sacred tie between my husband (or wife as applicable) and me, and a lifelong relationship of our mutual love and support. I love my husband (or wife as applicable for the Practitioner). I care for his well-being and happiness. My marriage gives me my spouse's SSCC: Support— both financial and personal—Sex, Companionship, and Child(ren). It is my Dharma to give my SSCC: Support—both financial and personal—Sex, Companionship, and Child(ren) to my spouse."

Then she defines the day's tasks for her SSCC of marriage. For example, she says to herself, "Regarding financial support, I already transferred my share of money toward our monthly household expenses (a certain monthly amount) to our common bank account. Regarding personal support, I will cook dinner this evening. Regarding sex, I plan to spend this Saturday evening with my spouse—a lovely evening together just for the two of us— wine, dine, listen to good music, and lure him (or her, as applicable for the Practitioner) to sex. For Companionship, I will watch a good movie tonight with my spouse. Regarding our children, I will talk to my spouse about our son's poor grades in his last exam, discuss, and decide together on some extra tuition for him. (Marriage requires consensus of both the spouses on every issue, which is very hard indeed, but the key is to avoid arguments and fights, and reach a common consent agreeable to both.)

Next, the human Dharma Practitioner remembers the last and the most important Value of "Child." First she mentally remembers the definition of the "Child"—"My Child is the contribution of my best to my Human Whole, the Carrier of my genes and the best of my moral, lifelong and other Values. I as a human will die one day but will leave behind my Child to my Human Whole." Then she defines her short-term goals from this Value. For example, she says silently to herself, "My short-term goal for my son is to get him admission in a good school. I will do some Internet research and ask a few friends about a good school nearby. I will do this search for half an hour today from 5:00 to 5:30 in the evening. Also I will make him sit and study for an hour in the evening, feed him a healthy dinner, read him a good story or some noble thoughts, and put him to bed on time."

Thus the practitioner remembers Five Eternal Lifelong Values of the Human Dharma, derives short-term goals from each of these Values, and then derives the day's tasks from each of these goals. In this way she acquires and nurtures the Five Lifelong Values that help her live a good life herself and enrich her Whole as well.

Remembering Daily Objectives of a Rich, Healthy, Happy, and Meaningful Life

Next, The Practitioner remembers her Daily Objectives of a Rich, Healthy, Happy, and Meaningful life. As said earlier, a human lives a long life of some 70 to 90 years, but she lives it on an everyday basis. Every day is a single unit of a human's life, a shackle in the long chain of her life, a brick toward the building of her life's Edifice in which she lives, and which she leaves to the Whole at her death. Thus every day of a human's life is very important. It is important that a human plans it well, and lives it well.

A day—every single day of a human's life not only goes toward building of a human's life's Edifice, but is important in and of itself too. Every day of a human's life is a long, long day of some 16+ wakeful hours in which she gets up in the morning, does her day's tasks, and goes to sleep at night. It is as if she lives the gist of her life in a day. At the end of the day, she ought to be able to say to herself that she lived a good day.

In order to live a good life, a human ought to make every day of her life good through daily conscious objectives of a Rich, Healthy, Happy, and Meaningful life, incorporate them in her day, and live them.

After defining and scheduling her day's tasks from short-term goals for her Five lifelong Values, the practitioner remembers her daily objectives of Rich, Healthy, Happy, and Meaningful life, derives her day's tasks from them, and completes them during the day. It is these tasks—Karmas of every day—that help her live a good day and a good life in the long run.

First, the Practitioner remembers "Rich"—the very first ingredient of a good human life. She says to herself, "'Rich' means having basic plus surplus money. My income target for being rich is $7000 a month." (Or whatever the ceiling amount for the Practitioner is.) (As said earlier, it is important that the Practitioner defines the ceiling in her income—the amount required to be rich. If she does not define the ceiling, her blind race for more and more money may usurp her Life Values and other important goals like health, happiness, and a meaningful life.) Having remembered her income target, then the Practitioner says, "Work and Money Management are two ways to become rich and remain rich." Then the Practitioner remembers her work: "I work as a carpenter/a lawyer/ a Business Person (or whatever the practitioner's work is). I earn an average monthly income of $.... (whatever the income of the practitioner is)." Now it may be that the Practitioner is already earning her "Rich" figure or she may be short by a certain amount. If she is short she may plan to take a second job or run a side business to earn some more money to meet her income target.

Next, the practitioner remembers "Money Management"—another important aspect of being Rich. Money Management is done by making a budget, following it every day, and checking bank accounts every day. She says quietly to herself, "Regarding money management, I will spend money today as per my budget. I have to fill gas (petrol) in my car for fifty dollars, and I have to buy lunch for ten dollars." Then she schedules some time of the day—some 15 minutes—for checking her all bank accounts. She says to herself, "Today 1 will check my bank accounts at 10:00 in the morning."

Remembering and living by the Daily Objective of being "Rich" and doing the required tasks for it—"Work" and "Money Management"—help a Practitioner to become "Rich" and remain "Rich."

Next, the Practitioner remembers her daily objective of being "Healthy." Thus she says to herself, "Being 'Healthy' means having a slim, supple, and energetic body. 'Right Diet' and 'Right Exercise' are two ways to become healthy, and remain healthy." Then, the Practitioner plans her "Right Diet" and "Right Exercise" for the day and schedules time for each. For example she says to herself, "My Right Diet today will be three to four healthy meals of Breakfast, Lunch, Supper, and Dinner. For breakfast I will have one toast, one apple, and a glass of fresh juice at 9:00. At 1:00 in the noon, I will have my lunch of one bowl of rice with lentils, some yoghurt, and some salad. At 5:00 in the evening, I will have my supper of some fresh bread with hot soup. Later, if I feel hungry, I will have a light, early dinner; otherwise I may skip dinner." The point is that the Practitioner has a concept of "Right Diet" —eating three to four small healthy meals a day—(after a gap of four hours between meals) which overall contain some milk, yoghurt, or juice; some lentils, bread, or rice; and a good amount of fresh fruits and vegetables. Planning a day's diet as per that and eating all meals as planned will ensure part of Practitioner's good health. "Eat healthy" should be the Maxim every day.

Next the Practitioner remembers the second aspect of being healthy—"Right Exercise"—and schedules time for that. For example, she says to herself, "I will do my 'Breathe by Om exercise' in the morning from 8:00 to 8:35; then I will do my organ-cum-stretching exercise for 10 minutes. In the evening I will go for a brisk walk or jog for half an hour from 7:00 to 7:30." (Here also the Practitioner ought to have a concept of "Right exercise," which includes a breathing exercise, an organs and stretching exercise, and 30 to 40 minutes of brisk walking or jogging every day—or at least five days a week.)

While taking a walk and remembering one's Daily Prayer of the Human Dharma and planning her day as per that, the Practitioner next remembers her daily objective of being "Happy." She says silently to herself, "Being happy means being calm and joyous from within. "Happy work" and "Happy relationships" are two prime ways to be happy. Happy work is work that best matches my talent, knowledge, and skills. I am a teacher. I love my job." Now it may be that the Practitioner is doing a job she dislikes. In that case she decides what her "Happy work" is and plans to seek some education or a job in that field. While planning her "Happy work" the Practitioner also ought to remember her hobby and schedule an hour for that during the day. For example, she tells herself, "I love painting. I will paint for an hour today from 7:00 to 8:00 in the evening." Practicing one's hobby for an hour a day makes a person calm and joyous from within.

Next the Practitioner remembers her "Happy relationships." She says to herself, "Happy relationships are those with family and friends whose company I enjoy. Also having happy exchanges with other people makes me happy." Then the Practitioner remembers her family and friends, and schedules a time slot during the day to talk to some of them or to meet with them. For example, she tells herself, "I will call my sister in the evening today and share nice things with her," or "I will have lunch with my best friend Susie today." Also she tells herself, "I will smile at every family member and my colleagues, and I will share happy exchanges with them."

The last and the most important everyday objective for the Practitioner to remember is to live a "Meaningful life." First, the Practitioner remembers the definition of the term "Meaningful life." She says to herself, "My life on the Earth has a deep purpose behind it. I am a special creation of the Whole, created to enrich the Whole with my special nature and talent. I live true to my nature and talent, and I practice a profession that best matches my inborn talent. Thus I play my part in enriching the Whole and fulfill its deep purpose behind my creation." It may be that the Practitioner does not do the "Right Work"—the Profession that best matches her nature and talent. In such a case, the Practitioner schedules a part of the day—a minimum of an hour to practice and develop her favorite hobby and eventually make a profession of that.

"Child" forms another deep meaning in a human's life. Thus the Practitioner remembers, "I am a human. I will die one day but will leave behind my "Work" and my "Child" to the Human Whole. She schedules sometime of the day for her child. For example she says to herself, "I will spend an hour in the evening with my child to play with her and teach her good things."

Also, the Practitioner remembers some deep relationship or a Cause which she loves dearly and schedules some time of the day for that.

Thus the Practitioner remembers Four Everyday Objectives of a "Rich, Healthy, Happy, and Meaningful life"; remembers ways to achieve each of them; schedules time for each; and lives her day as planned. These four ingredients of good life have to be remembered and lived as every day's conscious objectives in order to live a good day and a good life.

Practice *"Subhava," "Suvichara," and "Sukarma"*

"I will top my day by *Subhava, Suvichara, and Sukarma"*— thus the Human Dharma Practitioner remembers the last practice of the Human Dharma. She says quietly to herself, "During the day I will practice '*Subhava*'— feel positive feelings of love and happiness, and will view others with compassion and good-will. Also "I will practice 'Suvichara'— think noble and beauti-ful thoughts. I will think of others, think for All, think of 'The Human Whole,' 'The Whole of Life,' and 'The Universe.' I will read some noble thoughts, literature, or poetry before going to bed at night. Above all I will practice 'Sukarma.' A 'Sukarma' is a preconceived, pre-planned Karma with positive effects for all. My karmas affect me and others too. I will watch my every Karma, plan, and do those Karmas that shed positive effects for me and for others. Above all, I'll live by 'Svadharma'— do my Dharma—my Right thing to do, even if others don't." (Svadharma is such an important aspect of any Dharma—a part of Dharma itself that I have devoted one special chapter to the discussion of 'Svadharma.' Also it is the proper ending of the Human Dharma.)

Thus The Human Dharma Practitioner ends her Daily Prayer of the Human Dharma armed with its teachings, ready to live the day as planned, ready to face the world. She lives the whole day as planned—does her "Om meditation" in the morn-ing, does "Breathe by Om exercise"; completes each task as planned and scheduled toward "Value oriented living and Daily Objectives of a good life"; does 300 *Japas* of Om thrice a day—once in the morning, once in the noon, and once in the evening. She lives each moment of the day by asking herself constantly, "What am I doing? What am I feeling? What am I thinking? And the rest of the time she says a silent Om to herself, which keeps her connected to her Center, the Center of the Whole, and to the Whole's conscious energy inside her; and tops her day with *Subhava, Suvichara,* and *Sukarma.* Above all, she prac-tices "Svadharma."

Thus the Human Dharma Practitioner walks the trail of life the Dharma way. Thus she lives the Dharma way—lives a good life herself, and enriches her Whole too.

Night is as long as the day is. At night just before going to sleep, the human Dharma Practitioner closes her eyes, and remembers the Truth—the Basic Reality underlying All. She says to herself, "The entire Universe with all things in it is One vast pool of pure conscious energy all arising from my own Center—Ahm, going out Ou..., and all coming back to my own Center—M.. (of Ahm)—All bound and moving within one word O...m..." While saying so, she mentally visualizes the Universe with all things in it as One vast pool of golden energy, all bound and moving within one word "Om." Thus she remembers, says a silent Om to herself, and goes to sleep in Om consciousness— one with the Truth hidden deep inside her.

CHAPTER 14

SVADHARMA

(DOING MY DHARMA)

No Dharma is complete without *"Svadharma."* No Dharma will last unless we practice *"Svadharma."*

Svadharma is a Sanskrit term made of two words: *Sva* and *Dharma*. *Sva* means "my," and *Dharma* means "duty" or "the right thing to do." Thus *Svadharma* means doing my duty or my doing right thing. A Duty is a set of certain Right do's which emanate from the nature of a relationship. A Duty is an obligation, a debt I owe to the other person by the virtue of the relationship. For example, I as an employee, take payment from my boss. It is my duty to do my job well for which I get paid. Similarly, I as a parent, produced my child. It is my duty to rear my child well. I don't do any favor to my boss by doing my job well. I owe this to my boss. And I don't do any favor to my child by rearing her well. I owe this to her.

The term *Svadharma* can be best illustrated by an anecdote mentioned in old Hindu Scriptures. It is actually a classic example of this term. It goes like this: Once upon a time, there was a Sadhu (a Hindu monk who forsakes all worldly goods, wanders from place to place, and helps those in need. It is like a profession). This Sadhu was standing by a riverside, trying to save a drowning scorpion by pulling him out of the water. Every time he tried to pull the scorpion out of the water, the scorpion stung him. Still the Sadhu kept trying to pull him out of the water, and the scorpion kept stinging him at every pull. There was a man who was watching this for a long time. He asked the Sadhu, "Why are you trying to save him when he is stinging you? Let him drown." The Sadhu replied, "I am a Sadhu. It is **my Dharma** to save. I am doing my Dharma. He is a scorpion. It is his Dharma to sting. He is doing his Dharma." This is *Svadharma*— a person's doing her duty to the other despite the other's not responding by kindness but by hurting instead. Why did the Sadhu do this—save the scorpion? Saving others and doing good to others was the Sadhu's basic nature, and his occupational duty to All. The Sadhu was doing his job duty—his Dharma. Why did the Sadhu still try to save the scorpion despite the scorpion's hurting him? Because the Sadhu was a far more enlightened and knowing person than the scorpion. He knew that he could save the scorpion, and he knew that the scorpion did not know this. (So if you know better than another, you help him with that.) There is an element of truth in this, that you do your duty to the other even if the other does not respond. And, you do your duty even if the other does not respond positively—by praising you or by doing his duty to you. And, you go on doing your duty—your Dharma—even if the other hurts you. In the first instance, you do your duty because you get an inner satisfaction from it— you are doing the Right thing. In the second, you do your duty not because of some return or reward, but solely because it is your duty—the Right thing to do. And in the third instance, you keep doing your duty to the other even if he hurts you because you know better than the other. You know what the other does not know. You know that if you keep moving Right— doing your duty—your Dharma—the other will benefit by it and may eventually come around, realize his mistake, and start moving on the Right path too.

This is *Svadharma*—doing my duty—my doing Right thing. It means initiating my every action by *Svadharma*, responding to others by *Svadharma*, and sticking to my Dharma despite all opposition to it.

It is hard to adopt a Dharma—the Right thing—the Right Way of Living. But once you adopt it, then live by it every day and every moment of your life in all your actions and in all your behavior toward others.

The Human Dharma is a human's Right Way of Living. It helps a human live a good life herself and enrich her Whole. Once you test the Human Dharma, and adopt it; then practice it every day and every moment of your life in all your actions and behavior to others. Even if the other does not understand it, even if the other does not do his Dharma—the Right thing— and even if the other harms you or hurts you. You do your Dharma. As you practice so, you will see its effects. The Right Way always goes a long way. The Right Way always wins against all adversities and adverse people. It keeps you calm. You know exactly what to do and how to behave with others. It gives you immense peace of mind and stability of behavior in life. This is living like a Lotus amid dirty waters—untouched by it. This is living with your goodness and nobility in the world amid all sorts of people.

Once you adopt The Human Dharma, practice it in every realm of your life as *Svadharma*—your Dharma—your duty to yourself for your own well-being and happiness, and your Dharma—duty to the Creator and to the All, by which you enrich your Whole. Do your Daily Prayer of The Human Dharma first thing in the morning, schedule your day as per it, and live the day as planned even if others don't. Create a quiet place and proper time for your Om meditation. Do your "Breathe by Om exercise" out in the open amid nature. Do 300 *Japas* of Om thrice a day—once in the morning, once in the noon, and once in the evening. If possible, do this by counting on beads or—if among people—do it quietly by counting on your hand. Live the whole day by asking yourself constantly, "What am I doing? What am I feeling? What am I thinking?" and, the rest of the time, saying a silent Om to yourself. Focus on your each Karma, each feeling, and each thought. Monitor and control yourself all the time. This way you conserve your mental energy and channel it toward bigger goals. Top your day with *"Subhava," "Suvichara,"* and *"Sukarma."* Practice *Subhava* as *Svadharma*— my Dharma. View all others, even your enemy, with compassion and goodwill. Practice *Suvichara*— think beautiful and noble, think for others, think for All, think of Human Whole, The Whole of Life, and the Universe. Practice *Sukarma*— your each karma ought to be preconceived, preplanned, and with positive effects for All.

It is in dealing with others that we need to remember *Svadharma* always. The moment you deal with another person, she or he has a relationship title. The other may be a "stranger," a "neighbor," or one of the professional relationships like your "boss," your "colleague," your "client," or some "seller"; or one of the personal relationships like some "family member," or a "friend." Deal with the other as per the relationship title within its limits even if the other does not. Do you do's—duties of your own relationship title. Be honest in your business dealings. *"Care, Communicate,, and Support"* your family and friends, even if they don't. Be a good spouse—do your share of *"SSCC— Support, Sex, Communicate and Childcare,"* even if your spouse does not. Eventually (s)he will come around and do her/his share. Be a good parent—care for your child and teach her good things, even if she is not happy doing them. They will work for her. Be a good sister or brother— keep in touch with your siblings and help them in need, even if they don't. Doing so will make you happy from within. Love and support your parents even if Dad was not a very good dad and even if Mom was not a very good mom. You owe it to them. Doing so will make you happy.

Respect every being and every person—give her space and time to be herself. Be polite even if the other is rude. She will learn. Deal with others by *Svadharma*. Remember The Human Dharma: "If the other is angry, I will not get angry. The other has her own reason for being angry. I will give her space and time and try to understand her." The essence is not to behave by "tit for tat," but by doing what is Right.

Living by *Svadharma*—I do my Dharma—the Right thing even if others don't is hard. We live among people. They try to push and pull us all the time. But, if practiced, it keeps you supremely calm. You know what you have to do and when. You don't get pushed and pulled by people around you and by their ways. You stand calm and steadfast amid all the turbulence and turmoil of life. You walk the Right Way—the Dharma Way—and thus live a good life yourself and enrich your Whole too.

CHAPTER 15

CONCLUSION

This is **The Human Dharma—<u>a Code of Conduct to be adopted by a human.</u>** Till there is a human on this Earth, the Human Dharma will prevail; because **<u>"The Human Dharma is a Human's Way of Living; the Right Way of Living; and a Way of Living that helps a human (an individual) live a good life herself and enrich her Whole too."</u>**

The human Dharma is a human's way of living. A Human is the Center of the Human Dharma. The entire human Dharma starts from a human—one single individual human—a woman or a man; proceeds further, takes into account the entire human life with its four age spans, human life Values, and the end of life—death, and issues of eternal human curiosity—Soul, God, Truth; checks out the vast Whole around a human of which a human is an integral part, and its three Sub Wholes—the Human Whole, the Whole of Life, and the Universe; and comes back to the same individual human. In its wake, it brings up *Five Eternal Human, lifelong Values—the Values of Family, Education, Work, Marriage, and Child*—Values closely linked to human survival, human life, and human happiness. It defines death as the end of a human's one lifetime—not to be mixed up with living. It reveals the existence of a human soul as her deepest, eternal "Self," located in the Center of her body (a little below her navel). It remains silent about God. It defines Truth—the basic Reality of All as One vast pool of pure, conscious energy, which is All-bound and moving within one word "Om"—the Truth to be remembered and lived by a human. It observes the vast world around a human and divides it in three Sub-Wholes—the Human Whole, the Whole of Life, and the Universe; defines the individual human's relationship to each of the Sub-Wholes; and the relationship of each Sub-Whole to the its bigger Sub-Whole; and thus The Whole. For the very first time in Humanity's history, it traces the entire background of a human—and the humanity—up to its very origin point, and uncovers the Human Whole: our human-made world in which we humans live, where everything we humans use has been created and maintained by a human—*"the Palace under construction"*— to which each new generation of humans comes, makes its contribution, and departs—somehow making it more beautiful than they found it. And, it is from this fact—the Human Whole—that it derives the deep meaning of a human's life—to give her best to The human Whole in the form of her 'Work' (Profession), and her 'Child(ren).' *"I as a human will die one day, but I will leave behind my 'Work' and my 'Child' to The Human Whole."* It checks out the vast Whole of Life—the Earth with its flora and fauna within which the entire Human Whole nestles, and where the entire humanity is just a thin streak of walking beings on its lands among multitudes of other crawling and walking beings. It notes the individual human's relationship to it—how a human affects the Whole of Life by her actions; defines it; and derives the Right Way of Living for a human— **"Respect all living beings, live, and let them live too. Grow more plants, cause less pollution, and have fewer children."** From there it moves on and sees the Whole of Life— the Earth's—relationship to its bigger Whole, our Solar System, and then our Solar System's bigger Whole—our Galaxy—the Milky Way, our Galaxy's being part of the bigger Whole—our

Cluster, and our Cluster's being part of the biggest Whole—the Super Cluster—which envelops All within it, where all are moving around one Center. It defines The Whole. It likens The Whole to a moving Potter's Wheel, which is constantly moving and creating new and new artifacts; where every single individual human and every being is a creation of the Whole, created in a very special way to enrich the Whole. This fact gives deep meaning to a human's life on this Earth—to enrich her Whole. It sums up all this in the Prime Truth of "Om—The Whole," which starts from a human's "Ahm"—I—her human Self; takes into account her "U"—the world outside her—Ou..., and comes back to her "Ahm"—her Soul Self—"Ou..m.."

The human Dharma gives a human her/his basic identity of being a human—**_I am a human_**— a pure human without any tag of caste, creed, race, or religion, where every human hides an immense potential in herself and is basically the same—holding the same eternal Truth within her. It uncovers the basic equality of all humans where every human is Evolved, Multi-Dimensional, and a Part of the Whole—and where every human holds the same divine within her soul. It restores to a human her/his basic human dignity.

It restores **_Five Eternal Human Life Values—"Family," "Education," "Work," "Marriage," and "Child"_**—Values that create a wall in the stormy ocean of life against which a human walks, builds her life, and lives in. These Values not only give her support but provide the very material with which she builds the entire Edifice of her life, in which she lives and rejoices in her existence, and which she leaves to the Whole at her death.

It is only a human who can understand the human Dharma, its fine, all- encompassing Truths; its depth; understand the Whole and her own place and part in it; understand the divine, its deep purpose behind every creation, and its deep purpose in creating her as a human; and live to fulfill that purpose.

The Human Dharma is a Human's Right way of living. The Right Way of doing a task is to do it in a way which ensures an efficient and fruitful completion of that task. Where "efficient" means doing a task well and in a timely manner, and "fruitful" means you get out of that task what you wanted. In other words, you achieve the purpose of the task. The Human Dharma ensures an efficient and fruitful completion of the task of living. If you live as per the Human Dharma, you don't waste your time and energy into living aimlessly—you give your life a definite meaning and purpose and employ all your energies toward achieving that purpose. This way you don't waste your time, and you live a good life too.

The Human Dharma helps a human live a good life herself and enrich her Whole too. **A good human life is a "Rich, Healthy, Happy, and Meaningful life."** And, there are two prime ways through which a human enriches her Whole. These are her "Work" and her "Child." The Human Dharma's Value oriented living with Short-Term Goals; and daily objectives of a Rich, Healthy, Happy, and Meaningful life ensures that a human lives a good life herself and enriches her Whole too.

It is one thing to know and understand Dharma. It is another to practice it. It is only when we practice Dharma—the Right Way—that we truly test it in our everyday lives, see the positive differences it makes in our lives, and stick to its practices. The same goes for the Human Dharma. The Human Dharma needs to be read, understood, and practiced every day and every moment of life. Once the Practitioner practices it, she (or he) will see the difference it makes to her life—difference in her outlook toward herself, her life, and toward others; difference in her health, vitality, and love for life; the touch of sublimity in her inner being; her overflowing joy and calmness; and her total love for life. Once she sees the difference, she will continue to practice the Human Dharma.

The End

LIST OF FIGURES

List of Key Terms' Definitions

Term	Definition
Child	*A child is a genetic product of her both parents and their ancestors. (Chapter 2, Page 10)*
First Family	*A human's First Family is comprised of her/his Parents (Mother and Father), siblings (sisters and brothers), and other blood relatives, like grandmother, grandfather, aunt(s), uncle(s), and cousin(s). (Chapter 2, Page 54)*
Second Family	*A human's Second Family—Family by Marriage, consists of a human's spouse(a female wife or a male husband), In-Laws (Spouse's family), and Children—Sons and Daughters. (Chapter 2, Page 55)*
Family	*A human's family is a group of humans related to her by blood or by marriage. (Chapter 2, Page 57)*
Society	A society is a large group of humans living together and tied to one another by their common interests; personal relationships, business relationships; or by some common culture or goal. Some of the building blocks

of a society are a family; a group of friends, neighbors, colleagues; and a Sub-society or an organization. In sum, *A Society is a network of a human's personal and business relationships, and a vast reservoir of various products and services that a human needs for her survival, comfort, and happiness. (Chapter 2, Pages 64,65)*

Country | *A Country is a political entity located in a specific geographical area within fixed borders; having its own territory, resources, and people controlled and governed by its government; and recognized as an independent political power by other countries in the world. (Chapter 2, Page 72)*

Humanity | *Humanity is the largest group of All—seven billion humans, tied by their common human needs, dreams, and human compassion; living in 196 different countries, which are further tied by their mutual treaties, trade, and other relations, interflow of products and knowledge and thus All creating One of Humanity.* **Humanity is One.** *(Chapter 2, Page 82)*

The Human Whole | *Starting from a human (one single Human) as the Center, The Human Whole is the network of a human's Family, Society, Country, Humanity, and their Cumulative Achievements in all aspects of the human life—ranging from a needle to an airplane, a thatch-roof hut to a skyscraper, one single alphabet to the most complex Philosophical Treatise, and one single number to Advanced Calculus; our Cities, our Monuments, our Museums, our Libraries, our Universities—in sum, each and everything we humans have ever produced and live by on the face of this Earth. (Chapter 2, Page 106)*

The Whole
Of Life

The Whole of Life is our vast blue-green Earth, surrounded and protected by its fine veil of atmosphere, with vast expanses of green flora on its lands and beneath its oceans, and with a vast array of fauna— trillions of flying beings in its airs, trillions of crawling and walking beings on its lands, and trillions of swimming beings inside its oceans. (Chapter 2, Page 117)

The Universe

The Universe is a Whole: a very well-organized system containing All within it, made of infinite space, and an infinite number of bodies, like stars, planets, meteors, asteroids, and others—all gravitationally bound—each body moving around its own center and the center of the bigger Whole, each a part of the other, and all bodies organized in the forms of gradually increasing, bigger wholes of a solar system, a galaxy, a cluster, and a super-cluster. (Chapter 2, Page 124)

The Whole

The Whole consists of one single human (a woman or a man) in the center, her Human Whole, her Whole of Life, and The Universe (around her), where each is a part of the other. (Chapter 2, Page 126)

A Human	*A human is an Evolved, Multi-dimensional, and Part of The Whole living being. (Chapter 2, Page 127)*
Living	*A Continuous Process of Feeling, Thinking, Acting, Facing the Consequences of One's Actions; and Coping with The Whole. (Chapter 3, Page 145)*
Karma	*A karma is any single activity requiring physical and mental effort, discipline, and concentration; shedding its own effects in the form of specific feelings, thoughts, and practical consequences that shape one's being and one's life. (Chapter 3, Page 157)*
Human Life	*A human's life is a journey of certain number of years— average seventy years— starting at her birth; lived in four major age spans of Childhood, Youth, Middle age, and Old age; and ending at her death—Life lived as a Whole, as well as everyday and every moment, where living is a continuous Process of feeling, thinking, acting, facing the consequences of one's actions, and coping with The Whole; a Continuous struggle for survival and happiness, but overall a highly meaningful Process by which a human lives a good life herself and enriches her Whole too. (Chapter 3, Page 166)*
Five Eternal Human, Lifelong Values	*Family, Education, Work (profession), Marriage, Child (Chapter 4, Page 167)*

First Family (Value)

A human's First Family is her Family by Birth— her root in this world. It is a group of her parents, siblings, and other blood relatives. This is her first home, where all her survival needs are fulfilled, all her education and other expenses are paid, where she feels strong and happy amid the love and support of her parents, siblings, and other blood relatives, and where she learns her lifelong habits and Values. (Chapter 4, Page 173)

Second Family (Value)

A human's Second Family or Family by Marriage is a group of her/ his Spouse, In-Laws, and Children. It is created and maintained by marriage. A human spends a major part of her life—from youth until death—in the arena of her Second Family. It is in here that she has her own home and the love and support of her Spouse, Children, and In- Laws. (Chapter 4, Page 179)

Family (Value)

Family is a ship of love and warmth in the vast, hostile ocean of life—a group of your own people who love and care for you. (Chapter 4, Page 182)

Education

Education is a long and hard process of learning; gaining knowledge, and professional training in different disciplines of human knowledge and professions. Education is of two types —Formal and Informal. Formal education is gained in a school, college, and university, while informal education is gained at home in private. Formal education grants one with universally acknowledged certificates, diplomas, and degrees, which are required for entry into a profession. Informal education adds onto one's knowledge throughout one's lifetime. Education cultivates, strengthens, and enriches a human's mind. (Chapter 4, Pages 196,197)

Work

Work is a human's physical and mental labor in the form of a business, a profession, or a job, performed in a specific field throughout one's lifetime—from adulthood until old age, for eight plus hours every day, and thus a major realm of a human's life. Work is a human's prime survival mode (gives her money to live); if Right, it is a prime source of happiness and the prime mode through which she enriches her whole. Therefore it ought to be Right —work as per one's nature, talent, and aptitude— and it ought to be the contribution of her best to her Human Whole. (Chapter 4, Page 212)

Marriage

Marriage is a sacred and legal bond between a woman and a man, created and maintained by threads of sexual faithfulness of both the spouses and their mutual SSCC—Support, Sex, Companionship, and Children. These are the very threads the relationship of marriages is made of. They connect both spouses—wife and husband to each other. Also, SSCC are the four legs on which the Noble Institute of Marriage stands and functions. Marriage is a Cradle in which a child is born and reared, and is the Foundation of the human Family and human Society. (Chapter 4, Page 226)

Child (Value)	*A human child is a product of her both parents— mother and father—a product of their genes, and product of their love and rearing; part of their deep selves, reflecting their deepest life Values; a true extension of her parents in the world; and finally a contribution of their best and the purest to the Human Whole. (Chapter 4, Page 244)*
Death	*Death is the end of one lifetime and the transit phase into another (life). (Chapter 5, Page 265)*
Soul	*A soul is a human's (every living being's) deepest, eternal Self located in the center of one's body, a little below the navel containing one's deepest memories, attachments, and desires of her all previous lives and this life too. It enters a mother's womb at the point of conception, acquires a physical body, lives a certain lifetime, leaves the body at death, goes into a transit phase, and then takes a new birth. (Chapter 6, Pages 294,295)*
Subhava	*Subhava* is a Hindi word made of two separate words: *"Su"* and *"bhava."* *Su* means "beautiful," and *bhava* means "emotions." *Subhava* means beautiful and positive emotions. *(Chapter 6, Page 300)*
Suvichara	*Suvichara* is made of two words: *Su* and *Vichara. Su* means beautiful, and *Vichara* means thoughts. *Suvichara means beautiful thoughts.* (Chapter 6, Page 301)

Sukarma	*A Sukarma is a Preconceived, Preplanned Karma with Positive Effects. (Chapter 6, Page 305)*
God	*UNDEFINED. (Chapter 7, Page 321)*
Truth	*In Truth or in Basic Reality, All things in the world—the entire universe—exists as One vast pool of extremely fine, pure, conscious energy that is all One, is moving, originating from One Center point, going out, and coming back into it. This Center is the PowerPoint of the Whole, from whom the Whole originates and into whom the Whole comes back. This is the Center of the Whole as well as the inner center of each and every entity in the Whole. This is your center and my center too, residing in the deepest depth of yours and my soul. This Center—The Truth—can be accessed by genuine search for Truth, intense Self-searching, and by meditation. (Chapter 8, Page 339)*
Om	*Om is the Prime Truth, which has three Sub-Truths:*

- *First, Om is The Whole;*

- *Second, Om is The Prime Energy Channel within which The Whole moves; and*

- *Third, Om is The Prime Principle of Living. (Chapter 10, Page 349)*

The Human Dharma Way of Living	*The Human Dharma Way of Living is a Value-oriented life with Short-term Goals, and Daily Objectives of a Rich, Healthy, Happy, and Meaningful life. (Chapter 12, Page 436)*
Good Life	*A good human life is a Rich, Healthy, Happy, and Meaningful life. (Chapter 11, Page 417)*
Rich	*Being "rich" means having "basic" plus "surplus" money. (Chapter 11, Page 417)*
Healthy	*Being healthy means having a disease-free, slim, supple, and energetic body. (Chapter 11, Page 419)*
Happy	*Happiness is distinct from short-term pleasure. Happiness is a constant, lingering feeling of self-satisfaction accompanied by feeling calm and joyous from within. (Chapter 11, Page 423)*
Meaning of Human Life	*Every human is distinct and is a special creation of The Whole—created to enrich the Whole by her own special way. (Chapter 11, Page 425)*
Svadharma	*Svadharma means doing <u>my duty</u> or <u>my doing right thing</u>. (Chapter 14, Page 459)*

28369879R00276

Made in the USA
Charleston, SC
07 April 2014